Herb White, D.O.
St. Mary's Hosp.
1044 Kabel Ave.
Rhinelander, WI 54501

M000158938

THE DISORDERED COUPLE

In memory of
Candace Ward Howell

THE DISORDERED COUPLE

Edited by
Jon Carlson, Psy.D., Ed.D.
and
Len Sperry, M.D., Ph.D.

BRUNNER/MAZEL, *Publishers*
A member of the Taylor & Francis Group

Library of Congress Cataloging-in-Publication Data

The disordered couple / edited by Jon Carlson and Len Sperry.
    p.   cm.
    Includes bibliographical references and index.
    ISBN 0-87630-815-9
    1. Marital psychotherapy.   2. Mentally ill—Family relationships.
I. Carlson, Jon.   II. Sperry, Len.
RC488.5.D59   1997
616.89'156—dc21   97-24085
                                            CIP

Published by
BRUNNER/MAZEL, INC.
A member of the Taylor & Francis Group
1900 Frost Road, Suite 101
Bristol, Pennsylvania 19007-1598

Manufactured in the United States of America
1 2 3 4 5 6 7 8 9 0 B R B R 0 9 8 7

Contents

Contributors

Jack S. Brandes, M.D., Ph.D., is Head of the Family and Marital Therapy program at the Toronto Hospital and Assistant Professor of Psychiatry at the University of Toronto. He has been a teacher and supervisor in the Department of Psychiatry at the University of Toronto since 1974. In private practice, he sees individuals and couples who suffer with affective disorders, eating disorders, and personality disorders. He is a charter member of the American Family Therapy Academy and sits on its Ethics Committee.

Jon Carlson, Psy.D., Ed.D., is Professor of Psychology and Counseling at Governors State University (Illinois) and a psychologist at the Lake Geneva (Wisconsin) Wellness Clinic. He is Past President of the International Association of Marriage and Family Counselors and Editor of *The Family Journal: Counseling and Therapy for Couples and Families*. He holds a Diplomate in Family Psychology (ABPP) and Marital and Family Therapy (ABFamP). He has authored 25 books and 120 articles.

Charlene A. Carter, Ph.D., is Assistant Clinical Professor, Medical College of Wisconsin, Milwaukee. Dr. Carter has authored several journal articles.

Michele M. Carter, Ph.D., is an Assistant Professor of Psychology at American University, Washington, D.C. Dr. Carter's primary interest is in the anxiety and mood disorders. He has published several articles, contributed to a number of books, and has made numerous presentations on these topics.

Ross E. Carter, Ph.D., Diplomate, Family Psychology, is Associate Professor and Director, Division of Family Therapy, Medical College of Wisconsin, Milwaukee. Dr. Carter has authored several journal articles.

Michael Dimitroff, Ph.D., is Professor at Governors State University and Clinical Director of the Institute for Comprehensive Pain Management located in northwestern Indiana. He also supervises the Christian Counseling Center in Dyer, Indiana.

Arthur Freeman, Ph.D., is Professor and Chair, Department of Psychology at the Philadelphia College of Osteopathic Medicine and Director of the Doctoral Program in Clinical Psychology. He is a Past President of the Association for Advancement of Behavior Therapy and Northeast Regional Examination Coordinator for the American Board of Clinical Psychology. Dr. Freeman has earned diplomates in Clinical and Behavioral Psychology from the American Board of Professional Psychology. He has published 17 books and over 40 chapters and journal articles. His work has been translated into eight languages. He has lectured throughout the United States and in twenty countries around the world.

Marsha J. Harman, Ph.D., has a doctorate in counseling psychology and is licensed as a psychologist, professional counselor, and marriage and family therapist. She is Assistant Professor in the College of Education and Applied Science at Sam Houston State University. She is a member of the American Counseling Association and the American Psychological Association. She also provides therapy in private practice.

Steve Hoekstra, M.A., is a Christian Counselor and a graduate of Governors State University. He currently directs the Refuge Christian Counseling Center, South Holland, Illinois, and consults with various Christian schools in his area.

Gerald K. Hoffman, M.S., M.D., is a Diplomate of the American Board of Psychiatry and Neurology. He is also a member of the Self-Psychology Study Group (accredited by the Department of Psychiatry and Behavioral Medicine, Medical College of Wisconsin) and is in private practice in Rockford, Illinois.

Patricia Hoffman, B.A., M.F.A., is a member of the Self-Psychology Study Group (accredited by the Department of Psychiatry and Behavioral Medicine, Medical College of Wisconsin.

George R. Jacobson, Ph.D., is Associate Professor in the Department of Psychiatry and Behavioral Medicine, Medical College of Wisconsin. He is a member of the Self-Psychology Study Group (accredited by the Department of Psychiatry and Behavioral Medicine, Medical College of Wisconsin) and is in private practice in Wauwatosa, Wisconsin.

James A. Johnson, Ph.D., has a doctorate in counseling psychology and is licensed as a psychologist. He is Professor of Psychology at Sam Houston State University, where he teaches human sexuality and sex counseling courses.

Ikar J. Kalogjera, M.D., is Associate Clinical Professor in the Department of Psychiatry and Behavioral Medicine, Medical College of Wisconsin. Dr. Kalogjera is also Director and Founder of the Self-Psychology Study Group in Milwaukee, Wisconsin and in private practice in Wauwatosa, Wisconsin.

Joan Lachkar, Ph.D., psychotherapist, maintains a private practice in Pacific Palisades, California. She is the author of *Narcissistic/Borderline Couples: A Psychoanalytic Perspective on Marital Treatment* (Brunner/ Mazel, 1992), *The Many Faces of Abuse: Treatment of Emotional Abuse in High Functioning Women* (with the primary emphasis on women) (Jason Aronson, forthcoming), numerous articles, book reviews, and other publications. Dr. Lachkar is also a nationally known lecturer, teacher, supervisor, and guest instructor at conferences, workshops, clinics, and hospitals.

Jan B. Lackstrom, M.S.W., C.S.W., is the Coordinator of Family Services in the Eating Disorder Ambulatory Program at The Toronto Hospital. She is also a Sessional Instructor at the School of Social Work, York University, Toronto.

Ardis Leonard-White, B.S.N., M.A., is a member of the Self-Psychology Study Group (accredited by the Department of Psychiatry and Behavioral Medicine, Medical College of Wisconsin) and is in private practice in Wauwatosa, Wisconsin.

Michael P. Maniacci, Psy.D., is a clinical psychologist in private practice in Chicago, Illinois. He is a core faculty member and Clinical Supervisor at the Adler School of Professional Psychology in Chicago and Assistant Director of the Dreikurs Psychological Services Center. He has published extensively in the field of psychotherapy in professional journals and textbooks.

A. Rodney Nurse, Ph.D., holds a Diplomate in Clinical Psychology from the American Board of Professional Psychology. He practices family psychology and is Co-Director of Family Psychological Services and Balance Point, a multidisciplinary group seeking integrated interdisciplinary solutions to the divorce process, participating in reorganizing with the Judy Wallerstein Center for Families in Transition.

Carol Oster, Ph.D., is Associate Dean at the Adler School of Professional Psychology. She earned her doctorate at the Forest Institute of Professional Psychology in 1986. She is on the Gender Issues Committee of the National Council of Schools and Programs in Professional Psychology and maintains a private practice serving children and families.

Dorothy E. Peven, M.S.W., is a Licensed Clinical Social Worker in private practice in the Chicago metropolitan area and Professor at the Adler School of Professional Psychology, Chicago. She has served as Vice President of the North American Society of Adlerian Psychology and has consulted and lectured at the Alfred Adler Institutes in the United States, Canada, the Netherlands, and Japan. She is a Diplomate in Clinical Social Work, a member of the Academy of Certified Social Workers of the National Association of Social Workers, and a clinical member of the American Association of Marriage and Family Therapy.

Irving H. Raffe, M.S.S.W., is Clinical Professor and Associate Director in the Division of Child and Adolescent Psychiatry, Department of Psychiatry and Behavioral Medicine, Medical College of Wisconsin. He is a member of the Self-Psychology Study Group (accredited by the Department of Psychiatry and Behavioral Medicine, Medical College of Wisconsin).

Kathleen M. Schultz is currently a graduate student in the Department of Psychology at American University, Washington, D.C. Her areas of interest are decision making and cognitive processes as they relate to the anxiety and mood disorders. She is currently completing her thesis, which examines the effect of state anxiety on the interpretation of ambiguous stimuli among high-trait-anxious and low-trait-anxious subjects.

Lorie Shekter-Wolfson, M.S.W., C.S.W., is Director of Social Work and Multicultural Health at The Toronto Hospital, Adjunct Field Professor on the Faculty of Social Work, University of Toronto, and Lecturer, Department of Psychiatry, University of Toronto. She previously served as the Director of Family and Social Services, Eating Disorder Centre, at The Toronto Hospital.

Bernard H. Shulman, M.D., is a Life Fellow of the American Psychiatric Association and formerly Clinical Professor of Psychiatry at both the Northwestern University School of Medicine and the Stritch Medical School of Loyola University. He is Past President of the North American Society of Adlerian Psychology and of the International Association of Individual Psychology. He is author or coauthor of several books and many papers on Adlerian Psychology and other topics.

Steven Slavik, M.A., is a graduate of the Adler School of Professional Psychology. He is the author of a number of articles in *Individual Psychology* and in *The Canadian Journal of Adlerian Psychology.*

Marion F. Solomon, Ph.D., is an expert in the field of relationships. She has a private practice in West Los Angeles specializing in group therapy and conjoint therapy with couples. She is Director of Clinical Training, The Lifespan Learning Institute Continuing Education Seminars and Sciences, UCLA Extension. She is the author of *Narcissism and Intimacy: Love and Marriage in an Age of Confusion* (W. W. Norton, 1989), *Lean on Me: The Power of Positive Dependency in Intimate Relationships* (Simon & Schuster, 1994), and an upcoming book, *Crazy Love: When Love Spirals Out of Control.* She is also Coeditor of *The Borderline Patient* (The Analytic Press, 1985). She is a moving force in training mental health professionals in new approaches to treatment.

Len Sperry, M.D., Ph.D., is a Professor of Psychiatry and Behavioral Medicine and Preventive Medicine at the Medical College of Wisconsin. In addition, he is Director of its Division of Organizational Psychiatry and Corporate Health, and Executive Director of the Foley Center for Aging and Development. Dr. Sperry is board-certified in psychiatry, preventive medicine, and clinical psychology, and is a Fellow of the Division of Family Psychology of the American Psychological Association. He has published 25 professional books—including *Marital Therapy: Integrating Theory and Technique*—as well as more than 200 chapters and journal articles, and is Associate Editor for research for *The Family Journal.* He is a member of the American Family Therapy Academy and of the Coalition of Family Diagnosis.

Michael Waldo, Ph.D., is Professor and Department Head with the Department of Counseling and Educational Psychology at New Mexico State University. He is a member of the American Counseling Association and the American Psychological Association. He is certified as a Relationship Enhancement Marriage and Family Therapist and has more than 10 years' experience employing this approach.

Herbert C. White, D.O., is Director of Behavioral Medicine at St. Luke's Medical Center, South Shore, Medical Director, Chemical Dependency at Milwaukee Psychiatric Hospital, and Assistant Clinical Professor of Family Medicine, Medical College of Wisconsin. Dr. White is a member of the Self-Psychology Study Group (accredited by the Department of Psychiatry and Behavioral Medicine, Medical College of Wisconsin). He is also in private practice in Wauwatosa Wisconsin.

D. Blake Woodside, M.D., Msc, FRCPC, is Director, Eating Disorders Inpatient Program, The Toronto Hospital, and Associate Professor, Department of Psychiatry, University of Toronto. He is an Approved Supervisor of the American Association for Marriage and Family Therapy. His major research interests are in the area of family therapy for eating disorders and in genetic factors in eating disorders.

Preface

The importance of assessing and providing direct treatment for relational disorders is increasing. Until a few years ago clinicians were beginning to feel comfortable and confident using some of the newer, focused brief treatment methods for a variety of anxiety, depressive, and other Axis I disorders. Then along came a tidal wave of anxious and depressed individuals who were, for all practical purposes, nonresponsive to these methods, even when bolstered by medication, because of the presence of a concurrent Axis II personality disorder. Clinicians then began to understand the importance of effective treatment of the Axis II personality disorders. However, the approach did not seem to make a difference. *Now* clinicians are realizing that in addition to treating Axis I and Axis II pathology, it is important to address the relationships of their clients.

The literature in marital and couples counseling/therapy seems to focus heavily on techniques, strategies, and theoretical approaches. Authors have seemed to overlook psychopathology and characterological issues, and yet these are at the very root of unresolved relational conflict and tension. Although there have been many texts describing psychopathology and personality disorders, relatively little has been published on how to diagnose and treat these disorders within a relational context. The literature that has been published tends to consist of articles or book chapters on a single disorder. This book focuses on how to clearly assess psychopathology, personality disorders, and the couple relationship in order to develop effective treatment protocols. It brings together leading researchers and clinicians and shows how effective treatment stems from effective assessment. The chapters discuss couples with diagnoses of major psychopathology, personality disorders, and problems of social adjustment.

We are indebted to the contributors of this text, to colleagues at Governors State University and the Medical College of Wisconsin, and to Candace Ward Howell for her attention to the many details of manuscript preparation.

Jon Carlson, Psy.D., Ed.D.
Len Sperry, M.D., Ph.D.

Foreword

I am worried about the title of this excellent and important book. I am afraid that some might think that it is simply about "confused" or disorganized couples. It is, in fact, partly about couples in which one or both of the spouses have diagnosable "disorders" (we should not let the editors' pun go unacknowledged). But it is more than that: It is about couples who have serious difficulties in living, some of which cut to the heart of the human condition: psychosis, panic attacks, bipolar disorder, spiritual or religious issues, and what might be termed "unfortunate pairings" of serious neuroses. I also worry that some marriage and family therapists might initially mistake this volume as a return to a time when individual diagnoses defined who "the patient" was and how he or she was to be treated. Indeed, many MFTs rightly decry the pressures inherent in a "medicalized" world of managed care which coerce them to return to the individual definitions of illness within social systems. "It was this focus," we might complain, "that we worked so hard to overcome! Why would we want to reorient ourselves to an individual diagnostic apparatus in the treatment of couples?"

While it is not a perfect instrument, the DSM IV—whose diagnoses inform much of this book—is a distinct improvement over past versions. It orients the user to the individual's clinical symptoms, makes provisions for personality disorders, and includes medical conditions, psychosocial stressors, and prior levels of functioning. As Carlson and Sperry note, the DSM-IV forms an important basis for treatment planning throughout the world. Not only is it perhaps the most important component in reimbursement systems, but it forms the basis for many training programs and textbooks. Of special significance to marriage and family therapists, its inclusion of psychosocial stressors allows a bridge to social and interactional influences that impact the individual; of course as systems therapists, we also explore the reciprocal influence of the individual on the family system.

The need for this text has existed for some time. An important discussion among family therapists was initiated by Shields et al. in an article in the *Journal of Marital and Family Therapy* in 1994. In this article, the authors addressed what they termed the "marginalization" of marriage and family therapy, a phenomenon they traced to the field's progressive isolation from other mental health disciplines. According to the Rochester group, as marriage and family therapists began to separate from their multidisciplinary origins, they formed distinct and autonomous organizations and training programs. These systematically oriented programs tended to train therapists outside traditional mental health settings (their patients came from university counseling centers, for example), where they did not see seriously disturbed individuals in their caseloads. Furthermore, the Rochester group argued, MFTs began to see other disciplines—particularly psychology and psychiatry—antagonistically; rather than working with other disciplines, marriage and family therapists formed their own "marginalized" professional worlds. The Rochester group called for MFT students to become familiarized with the world of individual disorders and diagnoses, and to learn to work cooperatively with mental health practitioners from other fields. *The Disordered Couple* seems particularly suited to meet such a prescription.

In a very strong reply to the Rochester group, Ken Hardy maintained that rather than being a sign of marginalization, the separateness of marriage and family therapists was an indication of the field's developing maturity. Hardy asserted that family therapists need to be separate and to train their students in work with systems; MFTs see may clinical issues differently from the other professions. And as a field matures, he argued, it is inevitable that it would have "turf" battles with some other disciplines. Hardy insisted that MFT students often *do* work in traditional clinical settings, and that they are experienced with individual pathology. His argument implied that the call for more "traditional" training for MFTs was an invitation to return to the past.

While I concur with Hardy's assertion that marriage and family therapy is more revolutionary than we generally acknowledge, and that its separateness is a sign of its growth and maturity. I also agree with the Rochester group that most marriage and family therapists need more awareness of the significant individual pathologies that spouses bring them to conjoint sessions. It is not that we simply need to "rediscover" the individual within the family; we need to embrace the full complexity of the human condition: its biology, its social and interactional influences, and the entire vast and muddy realm between the social/interactional and the biological. Not only does this book reorient us to the importance of individual pathology within family systems; it holds "in tension" a number of polarities that, taken together, demand that we grapple with the full range of complexity of married life.

As they shift to include more of the full range of human complexity, the mental health fields like many areas of human endeavor—tend to overreact. In the early days of family therapy, several of our pioneers (Jackson, Haley, Weakland, and Watzlawick, among others) began to focus on the power of communication to shape and regulate relationships. While their work is now fundamental to all students of the family, this communications focus for a time denied the power of the human past. No more inquiries about childhood, no more hypothesizing about projection and transference. Look at the behavior happening between these people right now! The influence of the past in our thinking about relationships had to reappear eventually; but when it did, an important dimension had been added: Not only did we acknowledge the power of the historical family, but we realized that we could and should bring these players into the treatment process.

This book represents this kind of "return with an important difference." First, it acknowledges what every experienced clinician knows: In addition to having communications difficulties, problems in trust or intimacy, and systems stressors—problems which we tend to see as "symmetrically" organized, or as more or less equally shared by both individuals—the couples in our practices are made up of individuals who often have clearly diagnosable disorders. Sometimes we acknowledge this fact when we complain to a colleague, "I am seeing these two narcissistic personalities." Or we may lament, "I am working with an obsessive and a hysteric." In such conversations we may be counseling ourselves as well, as in "Don't expect yourself to work miracles with this couple when they bring these deeply entrenched difficulties into your office."

But just as this book encourages us to look carefully at the ways in which individual diagnosis can inform our understanding of couples dynamics, it also insists that we not forget what we have learned about relationships. We need to know how anorexia affects the individual, but we also need to understand and work with this woman's spouse, whose "helpful" attempts to urge her to eat not only make the problem worse but may recapitulate the origins of this dynamic between her and her mother. How do we work effectively with an individual's dilemma within the context of his/her most intimate relationship? Or, how do we work effectively with the dynamics of a relationship when its members have potent individual problems?

One of the many good things about this book is that it can be seen from these two different perspectives, or "lenses." It will be very useful to the individual therapist who realizes that successful treatment of the "patient" must include work with that individual's intimate partner. It will also be helpful to the systematically oriented therapist who needs to become more aware of and adept at working with couples where one or both partners have "diagnosable" difficulties: a physical illness, a psychiatric illness, a personality disorder, to name a few.

There are positive aspects to the current requirements for diagnostic and treatment specificity. We are being required to think clearly about the problems we are seeing, to design treatments that are tailored to these problems, and to make these treatments replicable and testable. This emphasis on accountability is healthy, and it may lead to advances in the treatment process, *particularly if we can avoid surrendering our hard-won understanding of systems dynamics and can remain loyal to our commitment to treating systems in distress.* The fact that we need to be able to see the details in the landscape more clearly, and the patterns that arise from them, does not excuse us from trying to comprehend and transform the family.

Like the DSM-IV, this book assembles a complex set of points of view, and it presents well-thought-out examples of theoretical, treatment, and research considerations. Virtually all these authors work with the tension between important polarities. The theme of the book, of course, is the omnipresent pull between the needs and predilections of the individuals and the needs and characteristics of their marriages. A number of highly developed theoretical and practical approaches appear here which were evolved in the treatment of individuals; and we witness skillful (but never "easy") transpositions of these approaches to a couples therapy context. Chapter 11's blending of self psychology and systems dynamics by Kalogjera et al. is an excellent example of this "conceptual marriage"; I also found Freeman and Oster's adaptation of behavioral and cognitive principles to the couple's arena to be especially successful. But a number of other significant polarities appear, and demand attention: In Chapter 4, for example, Maniacci's examination of the impact of psychosis on the marital system plunges us into the mind/body debate, one which we therapists should always be aware of. In Chapter 9, Carter and Carter focus on physical illness in couples as a prime area for both research and treatment. While they do not neglect treatment issues, their dedication to clearly delineated and carefully controlled research reminds us of the need for a dual focus on research and treatment—and of the pull we often feel in one direction or the other. The implicit pull between the religious issues of couples and the largely secular world of therapists is one of the subjects of Chapter 7, by Dimitroff and Hoekstra.

The authors of *The Disordered Couple* are not only expert and highly experienced in their area of interest, but the thoroughness of these presentations reveals how much they care about their subjects. The treatment considerations here will provide relief and guidance for many practitioners and students who are struggling daily with difficult couples. These are those memorable pairs which Phil Guerin and his associates have termed "Stage Three" marriages, or relationships in which there are serious interpersonal distortions, boundary violations, and failure to own a sense of self.

The basic tension that this book raises, however, is the pull *within marriage* between the potential for destructiveness, and the promise of healing. Couple by couple we must ask this question: Will these individuals' dilemmas, talents, and yearnings, intimately juxtaposed and sometimes amplified as they are by marriage, lead this couple toward agony and ruin; or will this pair find hope and solace and joy with each other? Most of us who work with couples believe in the possibilities for growth and for deep satisfaction in marriage. As we lend our effort and energy to these possibilities, this book can make us a solid and very useful fulcrum.

Augustus Y. Napier, Ph.D

CHAPTER 1

Assessment, Diagnosis, and Tailored Treatment

Jon Carlson
Len Sperry

Many marriage and family therapists tend to rely on systems thinking and, therefore, perform assessment and treatment using only its concepts. In many couples, however, one or both members have serious psychopathology. When this is the case, systems thinking alone does not provide the understanding needed to produce effective treatment. This book discusses the disordered couple and offers alternate methods of viewing, assessing, diagnosing, and tailoring treatment. Specifically, the five-axis system presented in the *Diagnostic and Statistical Manual of Mental Disorders*, fourth edition (DSM-IV), (American Psychiatric Association, 1994) and the relational diagnosis system are discussed in this chapter.

More and more, couples therapists are accepting classification systems that focus on both the individual and the relationship. In his foreword to *A Handbook of Relational Disorders* (Kaslow, 1996), Reiss (1996) talks about understanding relationships in four broad categories:

1. *Well-delineated disorders of relationships.* In addressing disorders in this category, the couples therapist focuses primarily on relational disorders (a manifestation of this might be physical battery). These are often called relationship disorders.
2. *Well-delineated relationship problems that are associated with individual disorders.* For disorders of this category, the relationship is still the primary focus of treatment. Part of the reason for treating the relational problem is that it is likely that this problem evokes or

1

influences a more serious problem in one of the individual couple members. This level of analysis is used when both relationship and individual disorders are detected.

3. *Disorders that require relational data for their validity.* In this category, an individual disorder is central in the presentation of the problem to the couples therapist.

4. *Individual disorders whose evaluation, course, and treatment are strongly influenced by relationship factors.* In this category, the individual disorder is the primary focus and the continuing focus of attention, but additional treatment is needed for the couple in order to promote a rapid and full recovery.

DIAGNOSIS IN COUPLES THERAPY

DSM-IV is a diagnostic system. Its multiaxial approach to diagnosis is helpful in distinguishing different aspects of a person and focusing the therapist's attention on them: clinical symptoms (Axis I), personality disorders (Axis II), medical conditions of significance (Axis III), psychosocial stressors (Axis IV), and prior levels of functioning (Axis V). This approach to diagnosis helps the therapist keep in mind the complexity of factors that potentially contribute to an individual's presenting symptoms. Interestingly, the authors of the DSM-IV noted the limitations of diagnostic criteria for treatment planning. They believe that a DSM-IV diagnosis is only the initial step in the comprehensive treatment planning process. They readily acknowledge that practitioners guided by their own theoretical preferences will need to gather additional information in order to plan and select relevant treatment, and this is especially true for couples therapists.

The DSM-IV forms an important basis for treatment planning throughout the world. It lies at the core of record keeping and of structures training programs and textbooks and is perhaps most important as the critical component in reimbursement systems and health care planning. Couples therapists need to be aware of the DSM-IV and the importance of diagnosis. It is time that therapists understood that the merits of diagnosis probably outweigh their concerns. Goldberg (1989) believed that diagnosis is particularly helpful in the recognition and assessment of a marital partner's potential for suicide, homicide, or other self-destructive behavior. Individuals with major depression, borderline personality disorder, or alcohol or substance dependence are at a particularly high risk for these self-destructive behaviors. Similarly, individuals in a manic state must be promptly and accurately identified, because they can do considerable damage to themselves and their partners with inappropriate, uncontrolled behaviors such as wild spending or promiscuity.

Hof and Treat (1989) believed that couples therapists should have a thorough knowledge of individual psychopathology and diagnosis. They contend that an individual's pathology greatly affects couple functioning. With a working knowledge of the DSM-IV criteria, therapists can preliminarily assess the nature and severity of individual issues—chronic anxiety and mood disorders, thought disorders, and personality disorders—as well as the influence of personality traits on marriage and family functioning. Such knowledge of diagnosis can also increase the likelihood that couples therapists will work within the limits of their training and experience and facilitate decisions about appropriate referral when necessary.

It is also our opinion that understanding the information provided by the DSM-IV can help the therapist to better understand just what is occurring in a couple system, rather than just in an individual. This knowledge can help in treatment planning.

Most people, including insurance companies, focus most on the Axis I clinical symptoms included in the DSM-IV, such as anxiety and depression. Axis I also includes a category titled "V Codes"—Conditions not attributable to a mental disorder—that appears to have some relevance for couples therapists. "Partner relational problems," one of its categories, refers to difficulties that do not stem from a mental disorder. This category is used when the focus of clinical attention is a pattern of interaction between spouses or partners characterized by negative communication, distorted communication, or noncommunication that is associated with clinically significant impairment in individual or family functioning or with the development of symptoms in one or both partners. This category includes other relational problems, such as relational problems related to a mental disorder or general medication condition, parent-child relational problems, sibling relational problems, and relational problems not otherwise specified.

An additional section has been added to include problems related to neglect or abuse, and categories include such problems for both children and adults. These problems are included because they are frequently a focus of clinical attention among individuals seen by health professionals. We find that these categories are not very useful in our clinical practice. Nevertheless, much of the rest of Axis I and the other four axes have considerable value in designing effective treatment for couples.

Axis I: Clinical Syndromes

Beavers (1985; Beavers & Hampson, 1990) indicated that unrecognized and undiagnosed Axis I conditions can wreak havoc in couples therapy. From a systems perspective, he believed that anxiety, mood, and thought disorders greatly influence couple functioning, and that couples influence the expression of these disorders. In his research on levels of family functioning and family styles, he has shown how certain family styles generate diagnosable disorders. For instance, couples and families functioning in the normal range typically "generate" adjustment disorders, whereas families functioning in the borderline centripetal range tend to generate obsessive-compulsive disorders. Families in the midrange are more likely to generate behavior or anxiety disorders. Not surprisingly, couples in the severely dysfunctional range tend to harbor individuals with psychotic or antisocial disorders.

Axis II: Personality Disorders

Axis II distinguishes personality disorders; information that can be very useful in understanding specifically how individuals will operate in a social setting, as well as how effectively they will respond to treatment. The following is a list of the 10 DSM-IV personality disorders and the interpersonal style associated with each (Millon, 1981):

Personality Disorder	Interpersonal Style
Paranoid	Provocative
Schizoid	Indifferent
Schizotypal	Detached
Antisocial	Vindictive
Histrionic	Attention-seeking, seductive
Borderline	Needy
Narcissistic	Exploitive
Avoidant	Reticent
Dependent	Submissive
Obsessive-compulsive	Respectful

Therapists can very quickly understand how an individual's responses to a partner will be very similar to that individual's response to treatment. Paranoid clients will be provocative, borderline clients will be needy, and so on. It is important to use this information to understand how individuals function in a marital or family system and how their functioning affects their partners. The complementarity of a narcissistic exploitive style with a dependent submissive style, or an avoidant reticent style with a histrionic attention-seeking style, must be considered in couple interactions. This information not only helps to explain the dynamics, but also helps to determine the types of treatment style therapists need to follow. Dependent clients have to learn assertiveness and independence skills. Histrionic clients have to learn control and how to specify issues. Avoidant clients have to learn how to connect more effectively within the couple or the family unit. Although personality-diagnostic information does not predict exact cause and effect, it does give a therapist important information that may assist in understanding the dynamics of the couple.

Axis III: Medical Conditions

Because couples therapy is usually associated with the social and psychological sciences, the notion of associating biological factors may at first appear odd. It is becoming readily apparent, however, that therapists practice in a variety of treatment settings with diverse age groups. Because the general population is getting older, health problems typically associated with aging are becoming more prominent in the lives of couples and families and do affect their functioning. To adequately understand their concerns and effectively treat them, therapists will have to consider biological, as well as psychological and social, factors (Sperry & Carlson, 1989). Couples therapists need to understand issues such as longevity and health status, medication side effects, biological rhythms, nutrition, psychosomatic illness, and common medical and surgical conditions. The relationships may be complementary, in that health and physical well-being affect couple functioning/dysfunctioning, and vice versa. Couple and family systems dealing with chronic illness such as cancer or heart failure undergo significant change, and several researchers have described the corollary whereby couple and family dysfunction not only weaken the immune system, but may also be at the root of such problems as heart failure (Sperry & Carlson, 1989; Williams, 1989). Axis III requires the therapist to look at medical conditions of significance. Systemic therapists need to assess how these conditions affect and are affected by the couple system.

Axis IV: Psychosocial Stressors

Axis IV provides useful information as to the client's presenting problems, as well as his or her motivation level and suitability for therapy. Ascertaining the degree of social stress is very useful for the couples therapist. Couples with less stress may be more reluctant to continue treatment. For couples experiencing too much stress, however, stress may have to be reduced before any insight or underlying dynamics are assessed. This information is very helpful in setting priorities for treatment issues, as well as understanding the level of support that is available for the couple.

Axis V: Current and Prior Levels of Functioning

The assessment of levels of functioning of each partner, as included in Axis V, can help to determine degrees of mutuality and dependency, as well as whether or not insight or approaches requiring a partner's higher intellectual capacity are even possible. This information can allow specific tailoring of an approach, with high-functioning couples probably needing less direction and support than lower-functioning couples.

Classification of Relational Disorders (CORD)

In an attempt to reconcile a relational diagnostic formulation with the DSM nomenclature, the Group for the Advancement of Psychiatry Committee on the Family has proposed a common language to describe and classify relational thinking and to formulate an additional Axis I diagnosis as part of a comprehensive multiaxial diagnostic assessment. The CORD (Classification of Relational Disorders) and the GARF (Global Assessment of Relational Functioning) are invaluable tools for a clinician in comprehensive treatment planning.

Classification of Relational Disorders (CORD)
Group for the Advancement of Psychiatry
Committee on the Family

I. **Relational Disorders Within One Generation**
   A. Severe Relational Disorders in Couples
      1. Conflictual Disorder with Physical Aggression
      2. Conflictual Disorder Without Physical Aggression
      3. Sexual Dysfunction
      4. Sexual Abuse
      5. Divorce Dysfunction
      6. Induced Psychotic Disorder (Folie à Deux)
   B. Severe Relational Disorders in Siblings
      1. Conflictual Disorder
      2. Physical Abuse
      3. Sexual Abuse
      4. Induced Psychotic Disorder (Folie à Deux)

II. **Intergenerational Relationship Disorders**
   A. Problems Relating to Infants, Children, Adolescents
      1. With Overt Physical Abuse
      2. With Overt Physical Neglect
      3. With Problems in Engagement
         a. Overinvolvement
            i. Intrusive Overinvolvement
            ii. Emotional Abuse

        iii. Family Separation Disorder
            (a) Preadolescent Type
            (b) Adolescent Type
        b. Underinvolvement
            i. Reactive Attachment Disorder
            ii. Failure to Thrive
    4. With Problems in Control
        a. Undercontrol
        b. Overcontrol
    5. With Problems in Communication
        a. Communication Deviance
        b. With Lack of Affective or Instrumental Communication
B. Problems Relating to Adult Offspring and Their Parents
    1. With Physical Abuse
    2. With Physical Neglect
    3. With Problems in Engagement
        a. With Burden
        b. With Overinvolvement
    4. With Problems in Communication
        a. With Cutoffs
        b. With Severe Verbal Conflict

The GARF scale can be broken into three component scales. These can be very valuable measures for rating a couple. They are meant to be a measure analogous to the GAF (Global Assessment of Functioning) scale used for individuals. Problem Solving (PS), Organization (O), Emotional Climate (EC), and Global Assessments can all be plotted, session to session, to show a therapeutic change of the relational unit.

In summary, certain problems are relational by their very nature and simply cannot be understood or described by assigning a diagnosis to only one of the individuals. To make meaningful and useful clinical assessments, one must examine the relationships in which people are on the most intimate terms. This practice of assessing relationships is already evident in such DSM categories as Shared Paranoid Disorder and Sexual Disorder, in which the relationship is a determinant in making the diagnosis.

Although diagnosing individual dysfunction is consistent with the medical model of diagnosis, it often leads to incomplete diagnosis and ineffective intervention. If we tend to diagnose each individual in a relationship without making a relational diagnosis, we often overlook the fact in many cases that the most significant aspect of the problem is relational. It is also noteworthy that different people will act differently in different relationships. Therefore, they would be diagnosed differently according to the context they are in, whether it be work, family, or out in public. In some cases an individual may be a burden on an employer, but may function very well in the marital relationship.

DIAGNOSIS AND SYSTEMS ANALYSIS

Shea (1988) provided a useful diagnostic system that involves systemic work building on Birk's (1988) proposal that an accurate diagnosis should include three components: (1) behavioral knowledge, (2) psychodynamics, and (3) social systems. The DSM system adequately presents behavioral knowledge, and the Shea system provides information as to psychodynamics and the social system.

In a systems analysis, individuals are conceptualized not as static entities with permanent characteristics, but rather as an intertwining series of processes. Each process or system offers a potential wedge for therapeutic intervention (Shea, 1988). In this approach, each person is viewed as representing the conjunction of seven progressively larger systems: (1) the physiological system, (2) the psychological system, (3) the dyadic system, (4) the family system, (5) the group system, (6) the societal system, and (7) the existential system (i.e., the client's framework for meaning). Each smaller system is subsumed by the system above it. Like the axes of DSM-IV, each of these systems can be used as a level at which to organize data and subsequently develop a list of potential treatment modalities, each system providing a clarifying lens through which to understand the client (Shea, 1988).

Employing this system, the counselor will hunt for evidence of medical illness, as well as for the presence of symptoms suggesting that somatic treatments are of value in the physiological system. In the psychological system, the counselor seeks to understand the clients, both in the phenomenological sense and in the psychodynamic sense, and as a product of past development, in an attempt to understand them in a human context. The dyadic system looks at the two-person interactions that fill each client's life. The family system assesses not only the presenting families, but also the multigenerational structure of each system. The group system investigates how people function within groups outside the family, especially their relationships at work and within networks of friends. The societal system considers the various social forces shaping an individual's functioning within the community. These forces include economic, political, institutional, and social class factors. Finally, the existential system seeks to understand each person's spiritual and philosophical beliefs and ethical standards. Symptoms are often directly related to unrest within these basic existential areas.

Shea (1988) went beyond these areas and suggested that it is imperative that counselors also understand the basic core pains that may be driving any individual family member. He identified the following seven core pains: (1) fear of being alone, (2) fear of worthlessness, (3) fear of impending rejection, (4) fear of failure, (5) fear of loss of external control, (6) fear of loss of internal control, and (7) fear of the unknown.

By using the DSM-IV with the two additional assessment perspectives of Shea (1988), the counselor can assess the presenting data and quickly generate a powerful list of treatment options. Utilizing these three systems, couples therapists can rapidly integrate the large data base often presented to them.

TAILORING TREATMENT AND DIFFERENTIAL THERAPEUTICS

The easiest way to practice couples therapy is to view all couples and their problems as essentially similar and to apply a standard therapy or standard mix of therapies to all couples. This strategy advocates the "one size fits all" approach to treatment. Many counselors continue to use this approach. In the past, when only a limited number of treatment strategies and little wisdom as to the selection and tailoring of treatment of couples were available, this strategy was defensible. But this view is no longer theoretically, economically, or even ethically tenable. Recently, a number of strategies for effectively selecting and "fitting" treatment interventions to couples' needs, expectations, and life-styles have been developed.

There are several ways of tailoring treatment. Sperry (1992) has described six such models. One of the most notable is called "differential therapeutics." In this approach, the counselor elicits relevant background information and formulates treatment based on a diagnosis, which includes biological, psychodynamic, cognitive/behavioral, and systems hypotheses that lead to effective treatment alternatives. Such treatment alternatives must be carefully planned; they include (1) the treatment setting (i.e., residential treatment, hospitalization, or outpatient setting), (2) format (individual, family, couple, heterogenous/homogenous group, or any combination of these), (3) time (frequency, duration of sessions, duration of meeting), (4) techniques (exploratory, directive, or experiential approaches), and (5) somatic therapies (consideration of medication, as well as use of other prescriptive modalities such as exercise and diet interventions).

By utilizing the differential therapeutic model, the counselor can effectively decide which couple receives what kind of treatment. Without such a model, counselors are overwhelmed by data and treatment possibilities.

INTRODUCTION TO THE DISORDERED COUPLE

This book brings together therapists from a wide variety of theoretical persuasions to address major disorders in couples. Each of the chapters offers insight into how to diagnose and treat the identified disorder. Peven and Shulman, in a carefully crafted chapter (2), describe how a partner with a diagnosis of bipolar disorder impacts the marital relationship. The diagnostic presentation and relational understanding are rooted in Adlerian psychology. The authors acknowledge the importance of pharmacological intervention, but also stress the significance of relational counseling.

In Chapter 3, Carter and Schultz clearly present anxiety as a major factor in couple dysfunction. The authors describe how people tend to avoid activities that are associated with anxiety; the first activities that go are usually couple activities. Therefore, when one partner experiences anxiety, the significant other is also affected at some level. The nature of the relationship is changed, and the roles must be adjusted. This situation is exemplified by the severely agoraphobic person who cannot leave the house and therefore becomes dependent on the partner to interact with the social world. These adaptive changes must be reversed if recovery is to occur.

Maniacci, in Chapter 4, provides an excellent guide on how to understand and treat couples in which one or both partners have a psychotic disorder. Maniacci believes that the relationships of such couples are of two dominant types: (1) psychotic/controlling and (2) psychotic/dependent. He describes the relationship dynamics, using a psychosocial model based on Adlerian psychology. The treatment follows a four-step protocol in which the psychotic episode is managed and the nonpsychotic partner is involved with the goal of decreasing stress and further psychotic incidents.

In Chapter 5, Harman, Waldo, and Johnson describe how a couple can be treated when one of the partners is experiencing sexual dysfunction. In their presentation, the problem is vaginismus and the modality of treatment is Relationship Enhancement therapy. This is a method that imparts attitudes and skills to the couple through psychoeducational interventions.

In Chapter 6, Freeman and Oster describe the challenges of working with couples who have relationship difficulties. The authors describe practical guidelines for treatment and explore the concept of intimacy.

Dimitroff and Hoekstra describe, in Chapter 7, how couples with religious problems create relationship dysfunction. The DSM-IV provides a V Code pertaining to spiritual or religious problems; however, most therapists tend to avoid value issues in their treatment protocols. These authors highlight the importance of direct treatment of spiritual and religious issues with couples.

Woodside, Brandes, Lackstrom, and Shekter-Wolfson, in Chapter 8, review the basic information about the eating disorders anorexia nervosa and bulimia nervosa. They then describe the impact of disordered eating on marriages and how treatment can occur. A case example clearly presents the treatment model they have developed at the University of Toronto.

Carter and Carter describe how physical illness impacts the marital relationship. In Chapter 9 they present an overview of the psychology of physical illness and their own object-relations approach to treatment.

Sperry and Maniacci, in Chapter 10, present the histrionic-obsessive couple. This combination, in which either partner can manifest the obsessive or histrionic style, is seen with regularity in clinical practice. The psychological dynamics and treatment strategies are presented.

Kalogjera, Jacobson, Hoffman, Hoffman, Raffe, White, and Leonard-White have developed a brilliant contribution that blends systemic and self-psychology in the understanding and treatment of narcissism. For most clinicians, this is often an untreatable disorder. The authors of Chapter 11 clearly show how the individual must sacrifice the marriage to protect the self. A case study describes the treatment process.

Solomon presents the narcissistic and borderline relationships. In Chapter 12 she describes how partners come together and develop collusive means of protecting themselves and each other. They stay together not to grow and mature, but rather to avoid having to face issues that they consider overwhelming.

Lachkar takes the discussion of the narcissistic/borderline couple further when she describes her psychodynamic approach in Chapter 13.

Waldo and Harman, in Chapter 14, describe the diagnosis and treatment of couples with borderline personality disorder. They utilize Relationship Enhancement marital therapy, with its emphasis on structure and skill-training.

In Chapter 15, Slavik, Carlson, and Sperry discuss the passive-aggressive couple. Although this disorder is not included in the DSM-IV, the dynamics are still present in many dysfunctional relationships. The authors believe that Adlerian therapy, with its emphasis on goal-directed behavior, is the ideal treatment modality.

Nurse describes the dependent female and the narcissistic male as "made for each other." In Chapter 16 he demonstrates how the pathologies support each other and may actually be tolerated in moderation. As disorders, they create myriad problems and treatment challenges.

REFERENCES

American Psychiatric Association. (1994). *Diagnostic and statistical manual of mental disorders* (4th ed.). Washington, DC: Author.

Beavers, W. R. (1985). *Successful marriages: A family systems approach to couples therapy.* New York: Norton.

Beavers, W. R., & Hampson, R. B. (1990). *Successful families: Assessment and treatment.* New York: Norton.

Birk, L. (1988). Behavioral/psychoanalytic psychotherapy within overlapping social systems: A natural matrix for diagnosis and therapeutic change. *Psychiatric Annals 18*, 296–308.

Goldberg, M. (1989). Individual psychopathology from the systems perspective. In G. R. Weeks (Ed.), *Treating couples: The intersystem model of the Marriage Council of Philadelphia* (pp. 70–84). New York: Brunner/Mazel.

Hof, L., & Treat, S. (1989). Marital assessment: Providing a framework for dyadic therapy. In G. R. Weeks (Ed.), *Treating couples: The intersystem model of the Marriage Council of Philadelphia* (pp. 3–21). New York: Brunner/Mazel.

Kaslow, F. (Ed.). (1996). *Handbook of relational diagnosis and dysfunctional family patterns.* New York: John Wiley & Sons.

Millon, T. H. (1981). *Disorders of personality: DSM-III, Axis II.* New York: John Wiley & Sons.

Reiss, D. (1996). Foreword. In F. Kaslow (Ed.) *Handbook of relational diagnosis and dysfunctional family patterns* (pp. ix–xv). New York: John Wiley & Sons.

Shea, S. C. (1988). *Psychiatric interviewing: The art of understanding.* Philadelphia: Harcourt Brace Jovanovich.

Sperry, L. (1992). Tailoring treatment with couples and families: Resistances, prospects, and perspectives. *Topics in Family Psychology and Counseling, 1*(3), 1–6.

Sperry, L., & Carlson, J. (1989). *Marital therapy: Integrating theory and technique.* Denver: Love Publishing.

Williams, R. (1989). *The trusting heart.* New York: Times Books.

CHAPTER 2

Bipolar Disorder and the Marriage Relationship

Dorothy E. Peven
Bernard H. Shulman

Good marital relationships are delicate creations, held together primarily by our ability to understand what is required in an intimate relationship and the ability to meet life's challenges with courage and determination. We bring to marriage that which we bring to life—a physical being with genetic propensities and a life-style we have created through our own experiences. It is thus reasonable to assume that if we bring into marriage poor health or a "neurotic" life-style, we handicap the marriage from the beginning. Any condition that interferes with our ability to cooperate or to use consensual thinking will interfere with marriage. Bipolar disorder is just such an illness.

THE CHARACTERISTICS OF BIPOLAR DISORDER

Bipolar (or manic-depressive) disorders are distinguished from other affective disorders by the circularity of the moods. Depression follows mania, which follows depression, in a fashion that colors the whole psychic life even though there may be euthymic periods when functioning is not disturbed.

Manic episodes are characterized by a period of abnormally and persistently elevated and/or irritable mood lasting at least one week. For a

13

Exhibit 2.1
DSM-IV CRITERIA FOR MANIC EPISODE
(American Psychiatric Association, 1994)

(1) Inflated self-esteem/grandiosity

(2) Decreased need to sleep (manic persons may go for days without sleep)

(3) Press of speech

(4) Flight of ideas

(5) Distractibility

(6) Psychomotor agitation

(7) Poor judgment: demonstrated by an inability to understand the consequences of behavior such as unrestrained buying sprees, promiscuous sexual behavior, and foolish business investments

---

diagnosis of Manic Episode to be made, at least three of the seven symptoms (Exhibit 2.1) must be present.

Occasionally during the manic state, paranoid delusions or hallucinations occur. The uncritical self-esteem and marked grandiosity are often of a delusional nature. There can be a flight of ideas and a nearly continuous flow of accelerated speech with abrupt changes from topic to topic. But the most common associated feature is lability of mood, with rapid shifts from laughter to anger to extreme irritability and depression. The depression may last moments, hours, or days and, not uncommonly, the depressive and manic symptoms intermingle and alternate rapidly.

A depressive episode is characterized by a change of mood, from a usual "normal" mood to a predominantly dysphoric mood, and/or a loss of interest or pleasure in usual activities. For a diagnosis of Depressive Episode, at least five symptoms (Exhibit 2.2) must be present for at least a two-week period.

It is not difficult to imagine how trying such emotional behavior must be on the efforts of spouses to establish a harmonious affiliation.

Exhibit 2.2
DSM-IV CRITERIA FOR DEPRESSIVE EPISODE
(American Psychiatric Association, 1994)

1. Depressed mood all day, every day, usually subjective

2. Little interest or pleasure in activities all day, every day

3. Sleep difficulty, either measurable insomnia or measurable hypersomnia

4. Psychomotor agitation or retardation

5. Decrease of energy, or chronic fatigue

6. Feelings of worthlessness, hopelessness, and helplessness

7. Diminished ability to think or concentrate

8. Suicidal ideation, thoughts of dying

MARRIAGE

Alfred Adler conceived of marriage as the solution to one of the life tasks—sex and love—and discussed marriage as a social institution designed to facilitate family processes, nurture the young, provide a set of rules for sexual relations, and create a socioeconomic unit suitable to the existing social structure. From this point of view, marriage is an institutional part of the social structure, influenced by the dominant mores of the culture and changing as the culture changes (Adler, 1992). Adler believed:

> Love, with its fulfillment, marriage, is the most intimate devotion toward a partner of the other sex, expressed in physical attraction, [and] in comradeship, . . . love and marriage are one side of co-operation—not a co-operation for the welfare of two persons only, but a co-operation also for the welfare of humanity (Ansbacher & Ansbacher, 1978, p. 122).

To make such an institution work, the personal desires of each mate has to take second place to cooperation, and essential to cooperation is love and social interest. Ideally, a marriage is an equal partnership and the husband and wife are devoted to each other and to the enterprise. Ideally, there exists love, physical attraction, a desire for each other's company, and a feeling of commitment to each other.

Dreikurs (1946) elaborated this theme, pointing out that marriage is "the most intimate association between two [adult] human beings" and thus requires a more intense cooperation in more areas of living than any other relationship. He believed that the lack of a "feeling of belonging" limited cooperation and that personal feelings of inadequacy and hesitation before the obligations of the contract can interfere with bonding (p. 102). Sometimes, one spouse begins to distrust the other, feels cheated or unsatisfied, and becomes unwilling to cooperate. Sometimes, the couple lack effective ways of cooperating, of resolving conflicts, and of adjusting to each other or helping each other. Sometimes, the personal agenda of each becomes more important than devotion to the relationship, for whatever reason. Any of these reasons can result in dissatisfaction with the marriage.

THE EFFECT OF BIPOLAR DISORDER ON THE MARRIAGE RELATIONSHIP

Bipolar, or manic-depressive, disorders are among the most crippling mental illnesses, and it is not surprising that they can have marked effects on marital relationships. But studies of these effects are scarce (Mayo, 1979; Hooley et al., 1987). Other studies have examined the effects on patients of their spouses' responses to the illness and participation in treatment (VanGent & Zwart, 1991; Marks et al., 1992; Goering et al., 1992; O'Connell et al., 1991).

Frank (1981) studied 16 bipolar-well spouse couples and concluded that their marital relationships did not differ significantly from those of nonpatient couples. Mayo (1979) studied 12 couples attending a marital therapy group in a lithium clinic and mentioned that spouses were very critical when the patients were either hypomanic or mildly depressed and more accepting when bipolar symptoms were severe enough to convince the well spouse that the patient was truly ill and not willfully misbehaving. Many spouses believe the odd behavior is directed against them personally in a hostile fashion.

> Linda was a 55-year-old woman with a long history of bipolar disorder, including many hospitalizations. She was compliant with medication, but would cycle at six-month intervals. She and her husband, Arthur, had always quarreled with each other. Arthur was fairly tolerant when Linda was depressed because she was then more passive, less argumentative, and did less to provoke Arthur. When Linda was manic or hypomanic, she did

not sleep, spent a lot of money, and made unreasonable demands; the two argued constantly. In a full-blown manic phase, Arthur recognized Linda's illness and would bring her to the hospital. When she was only mildly elated—shopping, traveling, and awake a good part of the night—he was critical, complaining and endlessly arguing with her. In his own way, he was a devoted husband and cared for her as well as he could. However, like the couples in the study, he was more accepting when the symptoms of the illness were severe.

Dreikurs (1946) pointed out that each couple establishes its own equilibrium and thought the marital relationship can tolerate a great deal of stress if the equilibrium is not upset.

Robert and Louise had a distant marital relationship in which they went their own way, talking little to each other and having little in common. Robert was a successful entrepreneur and provided well. Louise was obviously happy with her material benefits and required little intimacy with Robert. She appeared to pay little attention to Robert's manic episodes, which were usually of brief duration. During these episodes Robert would travel to another city, drink excessively, and end up in jail or in hospital. When he returned home, the manic behavior was resolved, his depression was mild, and he was able to resume his occupation. His episodes never disturbed the marital status quo.

The effects of bipolar illness on marital relations is easier to see in individual cases than in general. Each marital relationship has its own unique circumstances. In the aforementioned study by Frank (1981), the author tried to assess the influence of different aspects of the marriage, such as length of time married and degree of satisfaction with the marriage, but was unable to come to any conclusions. Our own experience with the marital adjustment of bipolar patients suggests that these couples are not very different from nonbipolar couples. The manner in which the couple respond to the mood swings of one spouse depends a great deal on the marriage relationship that has already been established and the personality traits and psychodynamics of the spouses.

HOW ASPECTS OF THE ILLNESS AFFECT THE MARRIAGE RELATIONSHIP

Mood swing episodes may be mild or severe, of short or long duration. The behavior of the patient during a mood swing is an important influence on the response of the spouse. Infrequent mood swings of short duration usually do not have significant marital effect. However, a crippling illness with a long hospitalization, economic losses, and inability to perform daily duties strongly affects the daily life of the family and certainly disturbs the established relationship. Under these circumstances, if a severe episode occurs early in a marriage, it is more likely to lead to a breakup of the marriage than in the case of a marriage that has lasted several years or when several children are present. Spouses often wait a long time before they break up a well-established marriage, if ever, and do so only after multiple episodes of hospitalization. Psychotherapists see cases in which a long-suffering spouse chooses to wait until all the children are grown before divorcing a mate who has become increasingly dysfunctional.

> Laura came from a family in which depression was prominent in her parents and siblings. One sibling had committed suicide, and another had been hospitalized for major depression. Laura had her first depression at age 20. At age 21 she married Steve, a dynamic and ambitious man, who was protective but quite critical. Laura tried hard to please him and usually succeeded.
>
> At age 35, Laura began to have excited episodes and would become very angry at Steve and his domineering manner. These excited episodes were interspersed with major depressions that would last for months. As time went by, one of the children and then another began to develop affective disorder. These stressors resulted in Laura's condition becoming more chronic and more severe. At this point, Steve became depressed and began to question the value of his life. When Laura and the ill daughter began to fight endlessly, Steve decided to move out of the house. He told Laura he would continue to provide for her, but needed more happiness in his life than his wife and children were providing him. He did continue to provide for the family, but refused to live with them any longer.

In most cases, partners stay together. Usually, the nonbipolar spouse learns to recognize the signs of developing episodes and quickly seeks help for the sick mate, who often does not recognize the need for intervention.

INTERPERSONAL DYNAMICS AND ASPECTS OF SPOUSAL PERSONALITY

People with bipolar disorder can be effervescent, enthusiastic, attractive, and expansive at times, but sad, anergic, and anhedonic at other times. In a hypomanic state, they are charming and witty and exciting to be with. In a depressed state, they can be frustrating, unattractive, and gloomy. They can be hardworking, productive, and creative in a euthymic state, and even productive in a depressed state, but chaotic, overtalkative, and annoying in a manic state. Obviously, such behavior has a much more direct effect on a spouse or child than on friends or work associates. The effects of bipolar parental illness on children has been studied by Laroche and colleagues (1985), and the effect on spouses, as mentioned earlier, was related to the severity and duration of the illness, the stability of the marriage, and the spouse's own personal issues. These factors, as well as individual personality traits, affect the interaction within the marital relationship, leading us to see each couple as different from every other couple—even if one spouse suffers from bipolar disorder.

The character of the well spouse also influences the marital adjustment. If the disturbance is clearly recognized by the spouse as an illness, then that spouse is usually more tolerant of both depression and mania. On the other hand, some mates find it much easier to live with a depressed spouse who is passive and nondemanding than with a bombastic manic partner. Spouses who prefer to remain loyal can be loving and nurturing, patiently accepting the mood swings of the mate. Others are less sympathetic, more critical and complaining. The question of how much a critical, sometimes punitive, spouse can affect a bipolar person's mood swings is still a matter of controversy. Sometimes it seems that an attack of mania or depression is precipitated by a severe marital argument or other family stress. At other times the mood cycle seems to follow its own course without any obvious precipitating factor, but there is little doubt that the behavior of the well spouse can precipitate a mood swing in the bipolar spouse.

> Martha had been married to Paul for 25 years and had begun to experience bipolar cycling early in the marriage. There was a family history of affective disorders, with a mother who spent a considerable amount of time in the hospital in uncontrollable manic states.
>
> Paul was a quiet, somewhat emotionally distant man who accepted Martha's illness with equanimity, when he saw her mood cycling (either up or down), he took it upon himself to get help for her. He did not get excited, he did not become critical, he took care of Martha and their child and picked up the slack whenever Martha was unable to function. Both Martha and he understood her illness and accepted it. For one period, Martha went for as long as 10 years without cycling either up or down.
>
> In his mid-forties Paul died, and five years later Martha remarried. Within a few months there was trouble. While he was courting her, Frank was kind, considerate, thoughtful, and flattering. Shortly after the wedding, however, Frank would go into rages late at night and scream at Martha for hours. Martha had

never before been treated like that, and she did not know what to make of such behavior. Within a few months Martha was hospitalized "high." Martha had told Frank about her disorder, but he did not understand and he did not change his behavior. Drinking and fighting continued and the hospitalizations became more and more frequent until there were only a few weeks of euthymia between breakdowns.

Martha's first husband, Paul, was a quiet, educated, unemotional, rational man, while her second husband, Frank, is loud, much more sexually intense, uneducated, coarse, and sometimes vulgar. She had gone from one extreme to another.

"Under continual stress Martha was unable to accommodate herself. As long as she lived a relatively placid, subdued life and continued maintenance medication, her moods did not cycle. With the stress of a continually troubled marriage, under pressure that wouldn't cease and over which she had no control, the circuits overloaded and it is not surprising that the built-in cycling system was activated" (Peven, 1996).

It seems clear now that Martha's partners had a profound effect on the severity and the frequency of cycling she experienced.

PSYCHODYNAMIC ISSUES

The psychodynamics of bipolar disorder have recently been reviewed by Peven (1992, 1996), and the material in this section is based primarily on the 1996 paper. She reviewed both the empiricists and the personality theorists and found that both

suggest that the premorbid personality of the bipolar is cyclothymic; that is, marked alternations of lively and depressed moods are common before a psychotic episode. Kraepelin (1902), Kretschmer (1936), and Turns (1978), as well as Akiskal and associates (1983) and Adler (Ansbacher & Ansbacher, 1956), believed that a certain type of person who has . . . a particular set of personality traits becomes ill with bipolar disorder (Peven, 1996).

The psychoanalysts believe manic patients are trying to ward off depressed feelings; otherwise, the superego would flood the ego and overwhelm it. Mania is the ego's insistence that the injury has been repaired and the superego conquered. Since ego has defeated superego, the need to inhibit impulses no longer exists and the manic has a triumphant feeling of omnipotence; thus, manics enjoy the release of their inhibitions. But superego fears persist in the mania. Mania is thus understood as an attempt to stave off and deny depression. At another time, Freud (1960) said that mania results from the release of energy that has been bound up by depression, thus reverting to an earlier hydrodynamic theory.

Shulman (1962) compared the manic-depressive person to the schizophrenic individual in regard to the meaning each gives to social relationships. The schizophrenic is discouraged about social relationships, does not find much satisfaction in them, and is not skilled at social interaction. The manic-depressive is a much more social creature, usually an extrovert, who seeks approval, attention, and admiration. The manic-depressive seeks contact when elated and bemoans the lack of it when depressed, but is almost never secretive or aloof like the schizophrenic.

Alfred Adler (1968) believed that bipolar persons are those who display, in the most extreme fashion, the "hesitating," "back and forth" movement that he saw in all neurotic behavior. He suggested that people who suffer from psychological disorders are those who are attempting to evade what is subjectively perceived as a challenge. Those who see a challenge as a situation to be dealt with move forward directly into problem-solving behavior. Those who see a challenge as a threat to a precarious self-esteem will either falter or move away from the perceived "danger."

> According to Adler, neurotics are distinguished from psychotics by their ability to retain their grasp on reality, i. e., they understand that there is a situation that has to be dealt with, but they don't like it, they feel frightened and behave in a timid way. Psychotics, on the other hand, try to deceive themselves as well as others by acting *as if* the threatening situation were not there at all (in which case they deal with other issues like "voices") or *as if* the problem had already been successfully solved. (Peven & Shulman, 1983, p. 5).

Adler understood mania as a "bluff to over-run others" (Ansbacher & Ansbacher, 1956, p. 323). In "Life-Lie and Responsibility," Adler (1968) said that mania occurs in ambitious people who do not believe in themselves to the extent of imagining that they would be able to gain their goal of superiority by direct methods. Mania is, therefore, according to Adler (1968), an "act" meant to deceive both the manic person and his or her social circle into believing the deed has already been done. But bipolar persons cannot continue their deception indefinitely, "so even though they begin every act enthusiastically . . . [they lose] interest soon after . . ." (p. 247) . . . [Excitement] rapidly wanes into depression . . . [and] brilliant beginnings and sudden anticlimaxes are repeated at intervals throughout [their] life histories" (Adler, 1964, p. 27).

Although at first he stressed the relationship between inherited constitutional factors and personality traits, Adler later made psychological processes and personality traits more important than inherited factors in determining final outcome. If his later theory is considered, then it becomes a question of which personality traits are most likely to be associated with bipolar disorder. Are these personality traits precursors of the disorder, merely associated with the disorder, or actual *forme fruste* symptoms of the disorder? Will the same stressor always precipitate a disorder, or only sometimes? If so, what other factors are involved?

THE WORK OF PEVEN AND SHULMAN

The present authors (Peven and Shulman, 1983) examined a series of 17 well-established cases of bipolar disorder to search for common personality traits. They found some evidence to support earlier findings about affiliative tendencies and ambitions, as well as other traits that fit into the cyclic behavior of the bipolar individual. First, bipolar persons showed a tendency to have strong emotions, both negative and positive, and to express them. They were sensitizers rather than repressors (Bell & Byrne, 1978), sharpeners of emotion rather than levelers, sensation seekers rather than stimulus avoiders (Zuckerman, 1979).

Second, bipolar people had a strong need for achievement. They tended to set high standards for themselves and to push themselves to be "successful," to impress and win admiration. Third, they harbored an inner, covert rebellion against the feeling of obligation to achieve. They felt oppressed by it, but not free to lay down the burden. Thus, they usually lived with a feeling of not being good enough, of not having accomplished enough.

This group of patients shared a particular cognitive style. They tended to *sharpen* (accentuate) sensations and emotions. Sharpeners (Holzman & Gardner, 1960) are more open to new experiences and more emotionally intense then *levelers* (people who play down their emotional reactions). Zuckerman (1979) described a similar style in what he called the *sensation-seeking motive*, which he associated with hypomania, impulsivity, and overactivity.

Kurt Adler (1961) suggested that bipolar persons show extremes of antithetical perceptions and emotional responses, an all-black or all-white style of experiencing the events of their lives. Both Kurt Adler and Alfred Adler believed that bipolar individuals have a strong need to impress other people because their ability to feel positive about themselves depends on the feedback they receive from those around them. They are dependent on others to reassure them of their worth by attention, appreciation, and admiration (Peven & Shulman, 1983). The strong need for achievement and the exaggerated goals of the bipolar patient fit in with this tendency to persuade others to give positive feedback.

A review of these traits suggests that bipolar persons have a specific set of cognitive and emotional schemata. Whether these schemata have their origin in genetic endowment or in developmental experiences is still a matter of controversy.

THE QUESTION OF MARRIAGE COUNSELING

What happens in the marital relationship when one partner experiences bipolar disorder differs from case to case. The important factors seem to include severity of symptoms, duration of illness, and whether or not the illness behavior of the patient interferes with the spouse's own personal agenda and thus prevents an equilibrium that suits both partners.

In bipolar disorders, both severe depression and mania interfere with insight and make the usual psychotherapeutic interventions useless. When the patient is in the euthymic state, he or she can certainly develop insight, understand what is happening, and try to cooperate. However, the benefits of such insight do not seem to help when the next mood swing occurs. What seems more helpful than marriage counseling is an educative approach. Teaching spouses about the illness is probably the most helpful single thing a therapist can do. Showing a spouse how to recognize the signs of a mood swing and teaching specific response behaviors (what to say and what to do) makes it easier for the spouse to cope with the mate's illness. The therapist thus becomes a support to the spouse as well as to the bipolar patient.

A relationship of trust between patient and therapist is a helpful tool in the management of the bipolar patient. If the patient trusts either spouse or therapist enough to comply with *direct* advice (e.g., you must take more medicine, you must get more sleep, you must not make phone calls at midnight, you must go into the hospital, etc.), the case management becomes easier and necessary treatment can be started earlier. The spouse becomes an accessory to the treatment and can learn to calm down the mate's excitement and support the mate during times of despondency. Therefore, the therapist should endeavor to empower the spouse as an effective therapeutic influence.

This is not the usual form of marriage counseling, nor is it what most marriage counselors are accustomed to doing. This is a situation in which the sick partner cannot cooperate/participate in the customary manner, and in which the well mate is the only responsible party. Marriage counseling during an episode of illness is best devoted to assisting, guiding, and maintaining the well spouse. Traditional marriage counseling can be done only during euthymic periods.

CASE EXAMPLE: TONY AND MARA

This last hospitalization was the rude awakening. I began to realize things were never going to get better, and I saw a lifetime of no change, of going through the same issues over and over again. She no longer appeals to me, and I just don't want to be with her any more. The only things we have in common are problems and kids.

This last time, when she really whacked out, I started to think that whether I stay with her or not, she's going to be the same. I can't take it any more . . . I don't want to take it any more.

This was Tony's response when he was asked why he had decided on divorce, now, after 19 years of marriage. After all, Mara had been "sick" on and off all the years of their marriage, her first hospitalization occurring after the birth of their first son.

Tony and Mara met while both were at state college in their third year. He was greatly attracted to her and pursued her actively. She was pretty and much sought-after by the young men on campus, and Tony felt he had scored a coup when Mara returned his interest. However, his family objected to Mara. A year later they were graduated and started planning a wedding. This led to a serious family disruption.

Tony is the younger of two siblings, the only boy, who grew up in a family atmosphere of sadness. His mother was diagnosed with cancer when Tony was seven years old, and the family cared for her lovingly until she died seven years later. His father was a warm and loving man, who kept the household together.

Mara was the oldest of three siblings and the only girl. The brother following her was never a competitor nor a rival inasmuch as he early on displayed the social awkwardness of the burgeoning schizophrenic. Although he was a very successful scholar (he was graduated from a highly rated law school), he became nonfunctional in his middle twenties. The youngest brother was a successful doctor.

Mara's mother was ineffectual and demanding and made no secret of the fact that she preferred her two sons over her only daughter. Mara's father ran a successful luggage shop and was considered a smart businessman, but cold and impersonal. Tony describes Mara's parents:

They were aloof, insulting, arrogant, and paranoid. They assumed others were out to get them, so they did it first. They didn't get along with anybody . . . they had no friends. Father was abusive to the kids, and, although he made a lot of money, he spent nothing. Mother was totally dependent on others, always sickly. She thought life was a disaster and her sick son a burden. I remember her best sitting on the couch, wringing her hands, saying, "What am I going to do?" At one time, they wrote John (the youngest son) out of their will, but Mara turned them back again. When they died, nobody came to their funerals.

Mara grew up emulating mother's histrionic, demanding, hypochondriacal ways. As the oldest child and only girl, she was expected to take care of the household whenever her mother took to her bed. As time went on, she would complain bitterly that she was "tired of all the responsibility." Actually, she exaggerated her accomplishments; although she tried hard, she seldom accomplished much, as she spent hours each day in bed, or going to various doctors' appointments. She thought Tony and the children should be more grateful for whatever she did, and she began to see herself as the plucky, unappreciated heroine who gives her all to save others. In states of excitement she showed grandiose trends, seeing herself as much more important and successful than she actually was.

As her feelings of frustration grew, so did her feelings of entitlement. She never did have the insight that her behavior provoked and alienated others. Like many bipolar individuals, she had little social intelligence.*

A particular incident provides an example of her grandiosity. When Tony bought her a diamond engagement ring, Mara (and her father) returned the ring, demanding a larger stone because, they said, the proffered diamond did not demonstrate enough "respect." Tony's father was furious and spoke out against the marriage, which led to an angry confrontation between the two fathers. Tony's father died a few years later, and Tony never forgave himself for taking Mara's side against his own father.

After the birth of their first son, Mara suffered postpartum depression and had to be hospitalized. Tony began to take on more and more household responsibilities. He worried about the future and about Mara's indiscriminate spending habits. In addition, Mara's elderly parents and psychotic brother were being cared for by Mara and Tony.

Three more hospitalizations for depression and panic followed during the next 10 years. The following is an excerpt from medical records of one of the hospitalizations:

> Patient has been in outpatient treatment since last fall and has not responded to medications. She has become agoraphobic, unable to pursue her work, unable to function at home without tremendous anxiety and symptoms of panic, including an impending sense of doom, tremulousness, diaphoresis, excessive anxiety, occasional shortness of breath and palpitations. But this is a depressive equivalent we are seeing now. As her anxiety has increased, she has become more irritable, unable to sleep, unable to enjoy usual pleasurable activities and feels helpless . . . She is

---

*It is difficul or people with bipolar disorder to develop insight since much of their thinking is concrete, and between episodes they seldom agree that they are in need of help. During the high and low cycles it is not possible to conduct analytic psychotherapy.

becoming more and more desperate for relief from the anxiety, and suicide is a major concern at this time.

Although this note emphasizes anxiety, the depressive symptoms are noticeable. In between hospitalizations, Mara had multiple somatic concerns and was preoccupied with her health. There were periods when she was euthymic, as well as periods when she was "high," although never clinically manic until the summer three years later when she was put on a new antidepressant. The following are notes from that hospitalization:

For the last three to four weeks, the patient has been extremely intrusive, not sleeping, spends all night cleaning, and her grandiose behavior has alienated friends and family. The situation progressed to the point where her family was about to break apart: both husband and children leaving the home in order to get away from her intrusive behavior and grandiose manner. The patient herself is extremely angry, labile, irritable, and dysphoric in her manic state. She is not sleeping, her appetite is poor, her energy is greatly increased, her belief in her productivity is also increased although it is clear she has not completed any projects. She has been spending a great amount of money on nonessentials such as jewelry and continues to have absolutely no insight into her behavior. She projects her problems upon members of her family. In addition, she is noncompliant with the treatment regimen.

Mara left the hospital at 2:00 A.M. one morning after leaving 14 phone messages for the psychiatrist. In her manic state she had decided she would feel better at home, taking whatever medications she decided were right. After 10 days of nonstop talking, no sleep, desperate children, and phone calls at work every hour, Tony decided to leave Mara. He felt he could no longer tolerate her behavior. He had endured years of Mara's illness, and perhaps he was too proud to admit that his father had been right. They had children, and the equilibrium they had established was one in which Tony took care of everything, including Mara. Her mood swings were primarily depressive, with just a few highs through the years, and it was only when she became openly manic in her behavior, and when both children left the house, that Tony felt he could no longer tolerate the marriage and left. He reported feelings of relief, "as if a giant burden has been lifted off my shoulders."

He did not want marriage counseling, nor mediation; he just wanted to end the marriage. He moved out of the house, even though Mara continued to call him night and day, whenever the mood struck her or a thought about him entered her head. Many months later she continues to ask when he is going to come back to her and to their marriage.

Mara is no longer manic. In fact, at the present moment she is hospital-ized for depression. Her major complaints remain somatic ones. She experiences a great deal of anxiety and worries about what is going to happen to her. The youngest child has started college (one of the reasons Tony felt free to leave at this time). Mara has never held a full-time job, and Tony believes he may very well have to pay lifetime alimony. Mara continues to hold out hope that Tony will return to her, for she sees no future for herself without a close support system.

SUMMARY AND CONCLUSION

The effect of bipolar disorder on marriage is not always drastic. However, this illness creates a great strain on any marriage relationship, and the importance of marriage counseling cannot be overestimated. When a diagnosis of bipolar illness has been made in a married person, early edu-cation for both patient and spouse about the vagaries of the illness is urgent. Spouses are most helpful when they recognize early signs of the illness and intervene quickly with treatment.

In the case cited in this chapter, we found that by the time we became involved in the case the husband, Tony, had lost all patience with his wife and her illness was out of control. Unfortunately, Mara had no interest in learning anything about her illness and wanted only relief from her dis-tress. There was, therefore, no happy ending to our story. But there is a lesson to be learned: when a diagnosis of bipolar disorder is made, a wise counselor will involve the spouse as early as possible, before anger and bitterness at all the disruptions become intolerable. Support, education, and guidance are the directions for successful marriage counseling.

REFERENCES

Adler, A. (1964). *Problems of neurosis*. New York: Harper & Row.

Adler, A. (1968). Life-lie and responsibility in neurosis and psychosis. In *practice and theory of individual psychology*, pp. 235–245. Totowa, NJ: Littlefield, Adams.

Adler, A. (1978). *Cooperation between the sexes*. In H. Ansbacher & R. Ansbacher (Eds). Garden City, NY: Anchor Books.

Adler, A. (1992). *What life could mean to you*. Oxford, England. Oneworld.

Adler, K. (1961). Depression in the light of individual psychology. *Journal of Individual Psychology*, 17, 56–67.

Akiskal, H., Hirschfield, R., & Yerevanian, B. (1983). The relationship of personality to affective disorders. *Archives of General Psychiatry*, 40, 47–60.

American Psychiatric Association. (1994). *Diagnostic and statistical manual of mental disorders* (4th ed.). Washington, DC: Author.

Ansbacher, H.L. and Ansbacher, R.R. (Eds.) 1956. *The individual psychology of Alfred Adler*. New York: Basic Books.

28 *The Disordered Couple*

Bell, P., & Byrne, D. (1978). Repression-sensitization. In H. London & J. Exner (Eds.), *Dimensions of personality* (pp. 449–486). New York: John Wiley & Sons.

Dreikurs, R. (1946). *The challenge of marriage.* New York: Hawthorn.

Frank, E. (1981). A comparison of nonpatient and bipolar patient-well spouse couples. *American Journal of Psychiatry, 138* (6), 764–768.

Freud, S. (1960). Mourning and melancholia. In *Collected Papers,* Vol. 4. (pp. 152–170). New York: Basic Books.

Goering, P., Lancee, W., & Freeman, S., (1992). Marital support and recovery from depression. *British Journal of Psychiatry, 160,* 76–82.

Holzman, P., & Gardner, R. (1960). Leveling and sharpening and memory organization. *Journal of Abnormal and Social Psychology, 61,* 176–180.

Hooley, J., Richters, J., Weintraub, S., & Neale, J. (1987) Psychopathology and marital distress: The positive side of positive symptoms. *Journal of Abnormal Psychology, 96* (1), 27–33.

Kraepelin, E. (1902). *Dementia praecox and the manic-depressive disease.* In T. Millon (Ed.) Theories of personality and psychopathology (3rd ed.) New York: Holt, Rinehart and Winston.

Kretschmer, E. (1936). *Physique and temperament.* London: Routledge and Kegan Paul.

LaRoche, C., Cheifetz, P., Lester, E., Schibuk, I., DeTomaso, E., & Engelsmann, F. (1985). Psychopathology in the offspring of parents with bipolar affective disorder. *Canadian Journal of Psychiatry, 30,* 337–343.

Marks, M., Wieck, A., Seymour, A., Checkley, S., & Kumaz, R. (1992). Women whose mental illnesses recur after childbirth and partners' level of expressed emotion during late pregnancy. *British Journal of Psychiatry,* 211–216.

Mayo, J. (1979). Marital therapy with manic-depressive patients treated with lithium. *Comprehensive Psychiatry, 20* (5), 419–426.

O'Connell, R., Mayo, J., Flatow, L., Culbertson, B., & O'Brien, B. (1991). Outcome of bipolar disorder on long-term treatment with lithium. *British Journal of Psychiatry, 159,* 123–129.

Peven, D. (1992) Individual psychology and bipolar mood disorder. L. Sperry & J. Carlson (Eds.), In *Psychopathology and psychotherapy.* (pp. 81–120). Muncie; IN: Accelerated Development Inc.

Peven, D. (1996). Individual psychology and bipolar mood disorder. In L. Sperry & J. Carlson (Eds.), *Psychopathology and psychotherapy: From DSM-IV diagnosis to treatment,* 2nd ed. Washington, DC: Accelerated Development.

Peven, D., & Shulman, B. (1983). The psychodynamics of bipolar affective disorder: Some empirical findings and their implication for cognitive theory. *Journal of Individual Psychology, 39,* 2–16.

Shulman, B. (1962). The meaning of people to the schizophrenic and the manic-depressive. *Journal of Individual Psychology, 18,* 151–156.

Turns, D. (1978). The epidemiology of major affective disorders. *American Journal of Psychotherapy, 32,* 5–19.

VanGent, E., & Zwart, F. (1991). Psychoeducation of partners of bipolar-manic patients. *Journal of Affective Disorders, 21,* 15–18.

Zuckerman, M. (1979) *Sensation seeking: Beyond the optimum level of arousal.* Hillsdale, NJ: Lawrence Erlbaum.

CHAPTER 3

Panic Disorder with Agoraphobia: Its Impact on Patients and Their Significant Others

Michele M. Carter
Kathleen M. Schultz

Anxiety has been described as one of the most common of human emotions (Barlow, 1988). In addition, it is considered to be a natural response to a real or perceived threat. In the presence of threatening stimuli, this innate emotional response is often considered to be adaptive, resulting in self-preservation of the organism (Barlow, 1988). However, it is not unusual to feel anxious even when a real threat is not present (Snaith, 1986). It is not, for example, out of the ordinary to become anxious while watching a horror movie. Although the observer is in no true danger, he or she may experience sensations such as a racing heart or sweating palms or a general feeling of nervousness or agitation—in other words, anxiety. When the experience of anxiety becomes too intense, occurs too frequently, or happens in situations where anxiety is uncommon, then this natural, self-preserving response may approach clinical severity and warrant treatment.

Not surprisingly, intense, dysfunctional levels of anxiety may also have a profound impact on the significant others in an individual's life. In this chapter, we first discuss the diagnostic criteria for a specific anxiety disorder thought particularly to have implications for the couple: panic disorder and agoraphobia. Then we present some of the major theories concerning the etiology of panic. We follow with an examination of the empirical literature addressing relationship difficulties among this population, and the impact these difficulties have on the treatment of the panic-disordered couple. Finally, we end with an example of how to manage panic within a cognitive-behavioral couple's treatment framework.

PANIC DISORDER WITH AGORAPHOBIA

One of the more commonly experienced and most debilitating of the anxiety disorders is panic disorder with agoraphobia. The hallmark of this disorder is, of course, the experience of unexpected rushes of anxiety or intense fear, or what is labeled a panic attack. According to the *Diagnostic and Statistical Manual of Mental Disorders*, fourth edition (American Psychiatric Association, 1994), a panic attack is a period of intense fear or distress that usually reaches maximum intensity in a very short amount of time (usually less than 10 minutes). The attack is characterized by at least four physical and/or cognitive symptoms (see Exhibit 3.1). In addition, panic attacks can be categorized as one of three types: unexpected or uncued, situationally bound, or situationally predisposed. **Unexpected panic** attacks are not associated with a specifiable trigger and seem to occur spontaneously or "out of the blue." **Situationally bound** panic attacks *invariably occur upon exposure to*, or in anticipation of, a particular cue or trigger. For example, one may panic whenever one sees a crowd or an elevator. In contrast, **situationally predisposed** panic attacks are *likely to occur* upon exposure to certain cues or situations, *but do not always occur*. To illustrate: a person may panic most times upon attempting to enter an elevator, but there are occasions when the person does not experience a panic attack in that situation. The diagnosis of Panic Disorder is assigned to patients who have experienced at least two unexpected panics, one of which must be followed by one of the following: (1) at least a month of persistent concern about having another attack, (2) persistent worry about the consequences of having an attack, or (3) significant behavioral change (American Psychiatric Association, 1994).

A substantial percentage of panic disorder patients also display symptoms of agoraphobia, defined as avoidance of activities, situations, or events from which escape might be difficult in the event of a panic attack (American Psychiatric Association, 1994; see Exhibit 3.2). Consider, for example, a patient of one of the present authors, a 30-year-old healthy male, who noticed that during sexual intercourse his heart began to pound as though it were going to "burst out of my chest." In addition, he became nauseated, dizzy, breathless, and felt a pain in his left arm. He had experienced his first severe panic attack. The patient became distressed

---

Exhibit 3.1
DSM-IV CRITERIA FOR
PANIC DISORDER WITHOUT AGORAPHOBIA
(American Psychiatric Association, 1994)

(1) Recurrent unexpected Panic Attacks (a discrete period of intense fear or discomfort, in which 4 or more of the following 13 symptoms developed abruptly and reached a peak within 10 minutes: palpitations, pounding heart, or accelerated heart rate; sweating; trembling or shaking; shortness of breath or smothering; choking feelings; chest pain or discomfort; nausea or abdominal distress; feeling dizzy, unsteady, light-headed, or faint; feelings of unreality or of being detached from oneself; fear of losing control or going crazy; fear of dying; paresthesia; chills or hot flushes).

(2) At least one of the panic attacks has been followed by 1 month or more of at least one of the following:
     (a) persistent concern about having additional attacks
     (b) worry about the implications of the attack or its consequences
     (c) a significant change in behavior related to the attacks

(3) Absence of Agoraphobia

(4) The Panic Attacks are not due to the direct physiological effects of a substance or to a general medical condition.

(5) The Panic Attacks are not better accounted for by another mental disorder.

---

because he believed his symptoms fit the description of a heart attack. Upon visiting an emergency room, he was correctly informed that he had experienced a panic attack and that he was otherwise in good physical condition. However, he found that future attempts at intercourse produced similar sensations, which, despite the insistence of his physician to the contrary, continued to lead him to the conclusion that he was having a heart attack and that his death was imminent. As a result of these experiences, this particular patient began to avoid all sexual contact and had also begun to avoid other situations, like exercising, that produced similar

---

Exhibit 3.2
DSM-IV CRITERIA FOR
PANIC DISORDER WITH AGORAPHOBIA
(American Psychiatric Association, 1994)

(1)   Recurrent unexpected Panic Attacks.

(2)   At least one of the panic attacks has been followed by
      1 month or more of at least one of the following:
      (a)   persistent concern about having additional attacks
      (b)   worry about the implications of the attack or its conse-
            quences
      (c)   a significant change in behavior related to the attacks

(3)   The presence of Agoraphobia
      (a)   Anxiety about being in places or situations from which
            escape might be difficult (or embarrassing) or in which
            help may not be available in the event of having an un-
            expected or situationally predisposed panic attack or
            panic symptoms.
      (b)   The situations are avoided (e.g., travel is restricted) or
            else endured with marked distress or with anxiety
            about having a Panic Attack or panic-like symptoms, or
            require the presence of a companion.
      (c)   The anxiety or avoidance is not better accounted for by
            another mental disorder, such as Social Phobia, Specific
            Phobia, Obsessive-Compulsive Disorder, Posttraumatic
            Stress Disorder, or Separation Anxiety Disorder.

(4)   The Panic Attacks are not due to the direct physiological ef-
      fects of a substance or to a general medical condition.

(5)   The Panic Attacks are not better accounted for by another
      mental disorder.

---

sensations. Over the course of a year, his circle of activities greatly
decreased and he became increasingly more avoidant.

This brief case description serves to illuminate two significant issues
regarding this disorder. First, the subject initially avoided a specific activity associated with his panic attacks. As the attacks became more frequent
and his concern about the possibility of having a heart attack increased, he

began to avoid additional situations. While his avoidant behavior is generally considered to be of moderate severity, the degree to which people avoid can at times become so severe that they become virtually housebound.

Second, because the patient mentioned is in a relationship, his avoidance of sex became a problem that extended beyond him and reached into his relationship with his significant other. As is common among individuals suffering with panic disorder with agoraphobia, the impact of this condition is often experienced, on some level, by significant others in their lives. Regardless of whether the severity of avoidant behavior is mild (and the person avoids only a few specific situations) or severe (when the person is housebound), this disorder has the capacity to change the nature of a relationship. In fact, clinical lore suggests that the level of avoidance characteristic of panic disorder with agoraphobia places a heavy burden on the significant others in the patient's life. They typically need to adjust their roles in the relationship so that they may be available for emotional and physical support during the conduct of tasks previously handled by the agoraphobic patient alone (e.g., shopping). The increased dependency has been hypothesized to change the nature of the relationship, or at least to produce distress (Goldstein & Chambless, 1978). The conflict generated from a dependent relationship is, in essence, a vicious cycle that places more stress on the individual with the disorder, in turn serves to increase his/her pathology and, consequently, dependence (Hafner, 1977, 1984).

Although, clearly, this is a disorder that significantly affects a relationship, it may seem that successful treatment would produce a positive change in the relationship. However, this is often not the case (Carter, Turovsky, & Barlow, 1994). There is some evidence in the literature that successful treatment of this disorder can have a deleterious effect on a relationship (Barlow, Mavissakalian, & Hay, 1981). In fact, it has long been suggested that the nature of the agoraphobic person's significant relationships may actually contribute to the development and/or maintenance of the disorder (Webster, 1953). To better understand how this complex disorder occurs, we turn to an examination of relevant theories in this area.

ETIOLOGICAL THEORIES OF PANIC DISORDER WITH AGORAPHOBIA

Cognitive-Behavioral Model

Although there are a variety of theories to account for the development of panic disorder with agoraphobia, few have received as much empirical attention as cognitive-behavioral models. Barlow (1988), for example, describes anxiety as a cognitive-affective structure characterized by high negative affect with a principal component of fear, he distinguishes between true and false alarms in the genesis of panic. A true alarm, commonly referred to as fear, occurs when one is directly threatened with a dangerous situation or event. A true alarm is beneficial to the organism because it prepares it to deal with a threat (Barlow, 1988; Carter & Barlow, 1995). Conversely, false alarms, or panic, occur in the absence of an obvious external cue. These alarms feel like real fear to the individual, except that nothing appears to be responsible for the alarm. According to Meadows and Barlow (1994), 8 to 10 percent of the general population in a given year experiences a false alarm or unexpected panic.

False alarms can become learned alarms if the individual begins to associate physiological changes with the fear feelings (a process known as interoceptive conditioning). For example, if one has learned to fear heart palpitations, a change in one's heart rate may precipitate an alarm reaction. Consequently, the individual may become apprehensive about future alarms (or panic) and become hypervigilant for the occurrence of internal sensations (Carter & Barlow, 1993). Ironically, the resulting attentional shift may increase the probability of noticing somatic sensations.

Associated with learned alarms are catastrophic cognitions (e.g., "I will have a heart attack and die"). These thoughts typically increase the intensity of individual attacks and serve to exacerbate avoidance behavior. As such, they are considered central to the symptom profile of the panic patient. The stage is then set for learned alarms to recur from negative thoughts, physiological sensations, or both (Barlow, 1988; Carter & Barlow, 1995). Although this theory explains many of the facets of this complicated condition, it does not directly address the relationship issues thought by many to constitute a key factor in this disorder.

The earliest suggestion that the interpersonal system of the agoraphobic person is a dysfunctional one came from Webster (1953), who compared the cases of 25 agoraphobic females with two additional control groups, one of patients with conversion hysteria, the other of patients with anxiety neurosis. Webster concluded that the husbands of the agoraphobic group evidenced a tendency to be "unstable" and "inadequate." He further concluded that because other factors involved in the etiology of agoraphobia are irreversible (e.g., lack of an adequate father figure), the husband "is the only means of entrance into a closed self-sustaining system" (Webster, 1953, p. 12). This early investigation, of course, is far from comparable to the controlled clinical trials of today, as it was based largely on clinical ratings from the case notes of psychotherapists (Kleiner & Marshall, 1985). Nevertheless, it serves to highlight the long-standing belief in the importance of interpersonal relationships for this population.

Interpersonal Model

Goldstein and Chambless's (1978) conceptualization of panic disorder with agoraphobia has implications for understanding the role of interpersonal relationships in the development of agoraphobia. They proposed two types of agoraphobic syndromes—simple and complex. The term "simple agoraphobia" is used to describe patients whose symptoms are precipitated by the occurrence of panic attacks brought on by physical disorders or drug experiences. These patients do not necessarily present the same personality characteristics as those in the more common "complex" type.

The term "complex agoraphobia" is used to describe pervasively fearful individuals who view themselves as incapable of independent functioning (Goldstein & Chambless, 1978). In addition, persons with complex agoraphobia are unable to assign causal responsibility of emotional responses to precipitating events. These factors, in combination, produce marked social anxiety and generate a conflict between the desire to become autonomous and the "need" to remain in a familiar and secure environment (Goldstein & Chambless, 1978). When the conflict persists or is worsened, the individual may experience panic attacks that precipitate the agoraphobic syndrome. These authors note that, interpersonally, the agoraphobic syndrome may be associated with secondary gains, such as attention from significant others. These theorists postulate that attempts at autonomy, in addition to reinforcing dependency, may be met with punishment and/or negative reinforcement.

Consider, for example, the agoraphobic patient (part of a couple) who spends most of his time at home owing to excessive fear of experiencing panic attacks. Over time he may become a good homemaker, assuming responsibility for the majority of the cleaning, cooking, paying bills, and so forth. He one day decides to enter treatment for his problem. As part of treatment, he begins to confront his fears via exposure and becomes considerably more independent, consequently spending less time at home managing day-to-day issues and completing household tasks. While he has become more independent, the nature of the couple's relationship has changed. Now his partner must assume a greater share of household management tasks. As a result, his partner may become dissatisfied with the change and conflict may ensue. In this manner, both the agoraphobic person and his significant other may become dependent on disordered behavior (Fry, 1962; Goldstein & Chambless, 1978; Hafner, 1986; Jacobson, Holtzworth-Munroe, & Schmaling, 1989).

Psychodynamic Model

An alternative perspective concerning the etiology of panic and agoraphobia is provided by the psychodynamic model and its emphasis on the
importance of the infant-mother relationship (Ballenger, 1989; Roth, 1987).
According to this theory, healthy emotional and psychological development hinges on the ability of the mother to form a bond of trust with the
infant. Specifically, the mother must be able to successfully calm and reassure the infant during times of emotional and/or physiological arousal,
thereby helping the child develop a personal sense of control over its affect
in times of stress. It is the quality of parenting a child receives that can deter
the development of the disorder, or can serve as a catalyst for the expression
of panic. A mother who is unable to appropriately reassure a normal infant
in stressful situations may actually facilitate the emergence of panic. On the
other hand, the disorder may be deterred by effective mothering skills in a
child who is biologically prone to experiencing autonomic hyperarousal.
(Ballenger, 1989).

Psychodynamic theory further postulates that normal child development
involves the creation of an internalized object representation of the mother
(Ballenger, 1989). This internal representation serves as a calming agent in
times of stress when the mother is absent. Later in life, there may be a stage
when the child transfers this representation to another object, which then
assumes the mother role and exerts a calming influence. Ballenger (1989)
notes that for adult panickers there is almost always a safe person (a trusted
individual, usually a significant other or parent) who can accompany the
patient during stressful situations and, thus, allow the patient to avoid or
decrease the severity of a panic attack. This observation has been supported
in recent empirical investigations (Carter, Hollon, Carson, & Shelton, 1995;
Rapee, Telfer, & Barlow, 1991).

Psychodynamic theory explains the development of panic disorder in
relation to the anxiety experienced in the early child-parent relationship
that the child has pushed into the unconscious (Roth, 1987). When the individual encounters stimuli that symbolically represent real fears (e.g., concern about separation issues), the anxiety tends to enter conscious
awareness. As it pushes into awareness, uncomfortable, fearlike feelings are
brought with it, resulting in a panic attack (Roth, 1987). The ego defends
itself by displacing the fear onto objects and situations that do not appear to
have any connection with the real sources of anxiety, but that represent
them symbolically. Because the anxiety is displaced onto a tangible object or
situation, the person learns to avoid or escape those things connected with
the panic in order to end the anxiety. Each time the anxiety-provoking
stimuli are escaped, the avoidance pattern of dealing with the feeling is
reinforced and the real problem remains unresolved (Roth, 1987).

EMPIRICAL EVIDENCE OF
RELATIONSHIP DIFFICULTIES

As suggested in the theories presented thus far, the belief in the importance of the interpersonal system in agoraphobia has led researchers to
postulate two major tenets. First, successful treatment of the disorder will
result in a positive change in the relationship. A corollary to this assumption is that agoraphobic persons in "bad" or "poor" relationships will fair
less well in treatment (Milton & Hafner, 1979). Second, given the impact of
the disorder on the interpersonal system, inclusion of the partner will
result in greater treatment efficacy than treatment of the client alone
(Barlow, Mavissakalian, & Hay, 1981). We turn first to an examination of
the relationships of agoraphobic patients.

Despite the suggestion that the significant relationships of patients with
panic disorder with agoraphobia are often dysfunctional, the evidence for
such relationships among this population is inconsistent. For example, in
early investigations, uncontrolled studies (e.g., Webster, 1953) reported
evidence of relationship difficulties. Torpy and Measey (1974) examined
the marital interactions of agoraphobic women and their husbands. On
ratings of marital satisfaction, these authors found that 43 percent of their
sample reported some degree of marital dissatisfaction, indicating that the
problem may be quite common among agoraphobics patients. Based on
the ratings of marital satisfaction, subjects were then divided into those in
"good" and "poor" marriages. Partners in the poor marriage groups displayed a tendency to misperceive each other, whereas those in the good
marriages were accurate in their perceptions of each other (Torpy &
Measey, 1974). This study, however, is limited by the absence of an adequate control group and the apparent artificial division of subjects into
"good" and "poor" marriages.

Contradictory results were provided by Buglass and colleagues (1977)
in their comparison of agoraphobic females and their spouses to matched
control subjects and their spouses. On most measures of marital interaction and domestic organization, it was reported that the agoraphobic
couples were very similar to the control couples. Both husbands and
wives of the two groups described their marriages in a similar fashion
before the onset of the disorder. Afterward, however, the agoraphobic
subjects reported that their husbands were "less well disposed toward
them," suggesting that marital or interpersonal difficulties may not be a
causal antecedent but simply a consequential manifestation of the disorder (Buglass, Clarke, Henderson, & Kreitman 1977).

In a more recent controlled investigation, Arrindell and Emmelkamp
(1986) compared the responses of agoraphobic females and their partners
with those of three groups: (1) nonphobic female psychiatric patients

and their husbands, (2) maritally distressed couples, and (3) maritally nondistressed couples. On measures of marital maladjustment, the agoraphobic patients were found to be significantly more maladjusted than nondistressed couples, but significantly less maladjusted than maritally distressed or nonphobic psychiatric controls (Arrindell & Emmelkamp, 1986). Furthermore, on measures of marital dissatisfaction, no significant differences between the agoraphobic subjects and the maritally nondistressed subjects were noted (Arrindell & Emmelkamp, 1986). The investigators noted that the generalizability of these findings is limited because of the restricted sample (agoraphobic females only).

In the most recent investigation to date, McLeod (1994) examined the perceived marital quality of panic-disordered patients where neither, one, or both members were disordered. The author noted that husbands of disordered wives reported no detrimental impact on the marital relationship. But when husbands were the disordered members of the dyad, wives reported significant levels of marital distress. McLeod (1994) further noted that both members' suffering from the same disorder did not increase marital dissatisfaction.

At best, there appears to be mixed evidence regarding the relationship difficulties theorized to be characteristic of the agoraphobic patient's interpersonal system. The studies finding support for this position have been based largely on uncontrolled investigations, or those conducted retrospectively, and inherently lack the methodological sophistication necessary to allow strong conclusions to be drawn (Kleiner & Marshall, 1985). In one controlled study, the results were suggestive of differential marital maladjustment.

The results from these studies have been criticized owing to the utilization of questionably validated measures of interpersonal relationships for agoraphobic persons and the use of samples that are less representative of the agoraphobic sample at large (Carter et al., 1994). It seems that until very recently, the composition of the agoraphobic samples investigated has been primarily Caucasian, married, and female. Recent epidemiological investigations indicate that a truly representative sample would include multiple races and at least some males (Regier, Narrow, & Rae, 1990). More important, these studies have traditionally excluded subjects involved in committed nonmarital relationships. There is no theoretical, let alone empirical, indication that the presupposed interpersonal difficulties would not be present in nonmarried couples, perhaps even transcending the primary interpersonal relationship and being more reflective of how the agoraphobic person relates to the world in general. If, as Goldstein and Chambless (1978) propose, agoraphobic patients are pervasively fearful and dependent people, it seems that they would exhibit similar interpersonal deficits in relationships other than with their identified significant others. This interesting possibility has not been considered theoretically or empirically.

Given that there is some evidence, albeit inconsistent, of relationship difficulties among persons with agoraphobia, the next issue is to provide effective treatment that not only alleviates symptomatology stemming from the identified disorder, but also addresses relationship concerns, as they may have maintained and/or exacerbated the problems facing the identified patient and the partner. To date, several investigations examining the interaction of treatment outcome and marital relationships have been conducted and have yielded some interesting findings. We turn now to an examination of that literature.

COUPLES TREATMENT OUTCOME LITERATURE

The hypothesized importance of relationship issues among agoraphobic patients has led several investigators to examine the impact of treatment on the relationship and vice versa. In general, however, the results are mixed. Several studies found evidence that the client's pretreatment level of marital satisfaction, in part, predicts treatment outcome. Although significant improvement over the course of treatment was noted for all patients involved, those rated as "better" adjusted maritally improved most (Hafner, 1976, 1984; Milton & Hafner, 1979; Monteiro, Marks, & Ramm, 1985). In each of these studies, treatment largely consisted of in vivo exposure conducted over a short period of time (usually 2 weeks). There have also been a few investigations disconfirming an association between marital satisfaction and treatment outcome (Arrindell, Emmelkamp, & Sanderman, 1986; Craske, Burton, & Barlow 1989; Emmelkamp, 1980). Treatment in these studies, again, consisted of in vivo exposure, except in one case (Craske, Burton, & Barlow, 1989), which was cognitive-behavioral. It seems that despite a person's current level of marital satisfaction, behavioral and cognitive-behavioral treatments are effective in alleviating agoraphobic symptomatology.

Researchers have also attempted to incorporate the patient's spouse directly in treatment. Only seven such investigations have been conducted in this manner, thereby making firm conclusions difficult. Although spousal involvement clearly does not detract from treatment, available studies offer contradictory results as to its effectiveness. More cognitively focused studies have generally found an advantage to incorporating the spouse in treatment. For example, Barlow, Mavissakalian, and Hay (1981) treated six agoraphobic women and their husbands in a group therapy program consisting of exposure and cognitive restructuring. The spouses acted as cotherapists and were instructed to elaborate on techniques learned in sessions and to assist their wives with between-session exposure exercises.

Two patterns of results were observed in the couples. For four couples, a parallel relationship was observed between severity of agoraphobia and marital satisfaction. As the former improved, so did the latter. For two couples, however, improvements in agoraphobia were correlated with a decline in marital satisfaction. At posttreatment, all patients showed at least moderate improvement (Barlow, Mavissakalian, & Hay, 1981). Interestingly, at least three earlier studies (Hafner, 1976, 1984; Milton & Hafner, 1979) also noted that the relationships of some agoraphobic patients were adversely affected by treatment success, at least initially. Such results, therefore, provide some support for the notion that agoraphobic persons and their partners may both be dependent on disordered behavior (Goldstein & Chambless, 1978).

Two more recent controlled trials also found greater efficacy for including the spouse directly in treatment (Barlow, O'Brien, & Last, 1984; Himadi, Cerny, Barlow, Cohen, & O'Brien, 1986). In these investigations the treatment was similar to the cognitive behavioral treatment of Barlow and colleagues (1981). It has also been noted that the superiority of the spouse-involved group was maintained over a two-year follow-up period (Cerny, Barlow, Craske, & Himadi, 1987).

Empirical studies utilizing exposure techniques, however, have not found evidence favoring spousal involvement in treatment (Cobb, Mathews, Childs-Clarke, & Blowers, 1984; Emmelkamp, et al., 1992). In these studies, both groups of subjects improved significantly and maintained their gains throughout follow-up periods. It is possible that the mixed results achieved in comparing cognitive with behavioral treatment studies may simply reflect differences in the treatments employed.

An additional study involving the spouse in treatment was conducted by Arnow, Taylor, Agras, and Telch (1985). Arnow and colleagues examined the effects of enhancing agoraphobia treatment outcome by adding intensive communication skills training (CST) following behavioral treatment. Unlike the studies mentioned thus far, the addition of communication training to treatment directly addressed the problem of marital issues that may interfere with treatment gains and spouse behaviors that may inadvertently contribute to patients' agoraphobia. At posttreatment, subjects in the CST condition performed significantly better than the relaxation training group on behavioral measures, and reported lower levels of avoidance. The advantage in favor of the CST group was maintained at 8-month follow-up (Arnow et al., 1985), suggesting that directly targeting marital issues enhances treatment outcome.

It would be interesting to incorporate nonspousal significant relationships in treatment. We know little about the utility of involving friends, wives, and cohabitants in the treatment process. Certainly, there are many other relationships in the agoraphobic person's world that may prove important in treatment and/or recovery. Thus far, only one study has attempted to investigate the utility of including alternative significant others in treatment. Oatley and Hodgson (1987) contrasted the effects of including a female friend as a cotherapist with the effects of including a husband cotherapist in treating 30 agoraphobic married women. Overall, there were no differences between patients assisted by their husbands and those assisted by their friends. Both groups evidenced significant improvement on behavioral measures and anxiety scores and maintained improvement during follow-up. Because all the measures used were self-reports and the treatment program relied heavily on the subjects' use of manuals, with only sporadically held treatment sessions, it is difficult to ascertain the actual level of involvement of the cotherapist, and their contribution to treatment. Nevertheless, this study addressed an interesting question that is worthy of further investigation. If we are to fully examine the interpersonal context of the agoraphobic patient, the subjects selected must reflect the full variety of possible relationships and not focus exclusively on couples in which the wife is the patient and the husband is the partner.

Thus far the literature has yielded interesting information in the area of couples treatment for panic disorder and, as such, has raised additional questions for researchers in this area. For example, is the efficacy of couples treatment dependent on the type of treatment delivered? If couples treatment is effective, what is the mechanism of action? Is there a fundamental change in the nature of the relationship, or does it simply increase the amount of practice in which the patient engages? What is the effect of the patient's or spouse's personality on treatment? These are among the many questions yet to be addressed in the literature on couples treatment for agoraphobia.

In conclusion, there is at least some evidence that involving the spouse of the disordered patient may produce incremental benefits. Part of the discrepancy may lie in the fact that most studies have relied on different methods for incorporating the spouse in treatment. Although this is a complicated issue to manage, there is at least one treatment modality (Panic Control Treatment; see Barlow & Cerny, 1988) that has consistently demonstrated its effectiveness in providing treatment of this kind. In the following sections, we present a case that exemplifies both the problems inherent in assessing and treating such a couple and the techniques used from a cognitive-behavioral perspective. We have chosen to present the case within a cognitive framework for two reasons. First, it is the perspective with which the authors have the most familiarity, theoretically and practically. Second, and more important, although psychodynamic and interpersonal models may appear more applicable to this issue, orthodox psychoanalytic therapy has generally not been considered successful in the treatment of agoraphobia (Milrod & Shear, 1991; Roth, 1987), but the efficacy of an interpersonal approach has yet to be tested. It is our hope that providing such a case description will facilitate the reader's understanding of how to effectively manage issues related to the couple within the context of treating the primary disorder of the identified patient.

CASE DESCRIPTION

Michael is a 42-year-old Caucasian male. Upon presentation to the clinic, he was administered a structured clinical interview to determine his primary diagnosis. The diagnostic evaluator assigned him a primary diagnosis of panic disorder with agoraphobia, with a clinical severity rating of 6 (indicating that the patient was experiencing several severe panic attacks weekly and that he had greatly restricted his life-style as a result of experiencing such intense panic attacks). As well, Michael was assigned a secondary diagnosis of major depressive disorder, recurrent (see Exhibit 3.3 for a Five-Axis diagnosis).

Michael reported that he experienced his first panic attack at 18 years of age while smoking marijuana with friends. It was the middle of his second semester in college, and he was under considerable stress. Not only was he on academic probation at the university he attended, but his parents had recently decided to separate. Michael had never considered the possibility of his parents' separation and had previously assumed that their family was very close. In fact, he had actually chosen to attend college close to home so he would be able to continue to live with his parents. At the time of his first panic Michael was uncertain as to what his future would be, inasmuch as college was not working out as he had planned and his family life was taking a turn for the worse.

Following the initial panic attack, Michael stopped smoking marijuana, as he assumed it was responsible for the occurrence of the attack. For several months he did not experience another attack; then his parents decided to divorce. At that time he experienced one of the most severe attacks he could recall. He recalled sitting in his room listening to music when his mother came home. Upon her arrival he sensed a tightening in his chest, and noticed he felt very warm. As his body temperature continued to rise, he noticed that his heart was racing and his vision was a little blurred. He tried to force himself to relax, but continued to note the symptoms as they escalated. At that point he was convinced that something terrible was wrong and that he was about to die. He rushed downstairs and insisted his mother take him to the emergency room, because he was convinced he was having a heart attack. At the emergency room he was given a clean bill of health and sent home.

Exhibit 3.3
FIVE-AXIS DIAGNOSIS FOR MICHAEL

Pretreatment

Axis I—Panic Disorder with Agoraphobia (300.21)

—Major Depressive Disorder, Moderate, Recurrent (296.32)

Axis II—No diagnosis on Axis II; Dependent and Avoidant Personality Features

Axis III—None

Axis IV—None current. History of Problems with Primary Support Group (parental divorce)

Axis V—GAF = 52

Posttreatment

Axis I—Panic Disorder with Agoraphobia, in partial remission (300.21)

Axis II—No disorder on Axis II; Dependent Personality Features

Axis III—None

Axis IV—None

Axis V—GAF = 80

Six-Month Follow-Up

Axis I—No disorder on Axis I

Axis II—No disorder on Axis II

Axis III—None

Axis IV—None

Axis V—GAF = 89

For several months after that incident the attacks became more severe, but then suddenly stopped at about the time he met the woman who would eventually become his wife. For the next several years Michael did not experience a panic attack. He got married and held an enjoyable position. Then one day in the midst of an argument with his wife, Janice, he experienced another very severe panic attack and had to be taken to the hospital. Once again, no physical abnormalities were found. However, this time Michael became concerned that whatever he had had several years earlier was returning and that it might get worse. He began to look for any signs (e.g., his heart racing) that an attack was about to happen, and the attacks became more frequent. He noticed that the majority of them happened when he was at the gym, so he decided that it was probably best for him not to exercise.

Michael then noticed that the attacks were beginning to happen in other situations, most notably at the grocery store and while he was driving on the highway. As a result, he started to avoid these situations as well. Within one year of the attack that resulted in his visit to the emergency room, Michael had become virtually housebound. He had stopped working, socializing, taking hot showers, going to stores, and driving. This pattern continued for a full year, until his wife insisted he get help for his problem because they were going into financial ruin. Only at her insistence and her threats to terminate the relationship did Michael agree to attempt treatment. He initially tried medication, but he could not tolerate the side effects and was subsequently referred for psychological intervention.

When we spoke with Janice, it seemed that Michael's panic was impacting her as well. At first, she had driven him to work daily. When he stopped working, she continued to do most of the driving. She had also assumed virtually all of the family-oriented tasks, such as taking the kids to school events, shopping, tending to car repairs, and so on. In addition, she reported that their previously active social life and their many friends had ebbed away because Michael refused to go very far from home. When they did attempt to be involved socially, Michael often interrupted their activities by insisting on leaving early because of his concern about experiencing a panic attack. Consequently, they were communicating less, and she reported that her enjoyment of being married to him had diminished as well.

TREATMENT PROCESS

Following the initial interview, Michael and his wife agreed to enter couples Panic Control Treatment for his problem. The basic aim of this treatment approach has been described in detail elsewhere (see Barlow & Cerny, 1988; Craske & Barlow, 1993). In general, the goal of this treatment is to influence the cognitive aspects of panic and anxiety by providing accurate information regarding the nature of panic and to teach specific cognitive restructuring techniques that allow the patient to correct or modify the catastrophic cognitions underlying the experience of panic attacks. In addition, the couple is taught to use diaphragmatic breathing to alleviate some of the physical sensations resulting from panic and hyperventilation. Finally, the patient is given specific in vivo exposure instructions and exercises to combat the avoidance behavior. In this fashion, each of the major components of panic and anxiety (cognitive, physiological, behavioral) is addressed in a systematic fashion.

Session 1

The first meeting is a data-gathering session, during which the patient is asked to provide information concerning his experience with panic in terms of frequency, types of symptoms, and situations in which the attacks occur. More important, during this session the stage is set for the patient and spouse to work collaboratively as a couple. The following interchange occurs between Michael (P), Janice (W), and their therapist (T).

> **T:** Why don't we begin with you telling me the kinds of situations that are problematic for you in terms of experiencing or managing the panic attacks? In what types of places do you have the panics?
> **P:** Well, they can happen almost anywhere, but I guess I have the most problem with driving or going to the store. But even when I have an attack in those places, it doesn't bother me that much, because I'm used to them a little. What's harder for me to deal with is when they just come out of the blue. Like the other day when I was watching a football game [on TV], it just came over me like a wave and scared me to death. I thought I was going to have to go to the hospital.

After discussing several of the most problematic situations, the therapist attempts to involve Janice in the discussion.

> **T:** Janice, Michael mentioned that he is concerned that people will know he's having an attack. Can you tell when Michael is having an attack?
> **W:** Yes. He gets very pale and starts to shake just a little. Then he gets quiet and goes off by himself. At that time, I think he doesn't want anyone around, especially me.

T: That sounds like an important issue, and we will come back to it in just a few minutes. Let me ask, first, if there are there any situations that Michael couldn't think of that you think might be important?
W: Not really. Well, sometimes I think that we are having less sex than we used to because of this. I mean it just seems that way to me.

Here the therapist is attempting to get both the patient and his significant other to present their views about the specifics of the panics and avoidance behavior. The goal is to encourage both the patient and the significant other to view the specifics of the disorder in an objective, collaborative manner. Next, the therapist addresses the rationale for including the spouse in the treatment.

T: Now that we have discussed some of the situations in which panics occur. I think it's a good time to discuss why I've decided to include you [*speaking to W*] in this treatment. There are three basic reasons. As we can see from our conversation so far, there will be times that Janice can help with some of the information gathering. In addition, a lot of what we'll be doing will involve learning specific techniques. And in order for you to derive the most benefit from treatment, I will ask that you practice at home as well. Is there a way that Janice can be helpful in this regard?
P: I guess she could remind me when to do them. Sometimes I forget those things.
W: Well, I don't think he'd want me to, since whenever I even ask him a question when he's anxious, he snaps at me and he doesn't want me involved.
P: It's not that, it's just that I don't think you can do anything to help me.
T: It sounds as if you both think she may be able to be involved in some of the aspects of homework, but we really need to work on exactly how Janice would be involved so that it doesn't provoke those same reactions. That's the second reason for Janice's involvement in treatment. When that does happen, Janice, how does it make you feel?
W: As though I might as well not exist. Or that I'm not a part of his life or something.
T: That raises the third issue. Let me ask if you two have noticed that the relationship has changed as a result of the panics that Michael experiences?
P: Not really.
W: A lot. Now I have to do a lot of the things that he used to do, like shop, or take the kids out. We don't go out anymore, and if we do I

have to do the driving, and we have to leave when he says it's time because he might have an attack. Sometimes we even drive separately.
T: It sounds as if you think the relationship has been affected to some degree. You don't feel that way, Michael?
P: Well, I guess a little, but it doesn't seem as bad as she makes it seem.

The rest of this session is used to discuss the impact the disorder has had on the relationship, not just in terms of the patient's spouse assuming more responsibility, but also in terms of the resentment she feels for having to adjust her life dramatically. An additional issue is also discussed in this session.

T: I'd like to let you know that what you are talking about isn't unusual when one member of the couple has severe panic. Let me ask, how will the relationship change when we see some progress in Michael's panic?
P: I guess we'll be a lot better off, because she won't have to do all of the stuff that she has to do now.
W: Yeah, we could have our life back.
T: It sounds as though you are both looking forward to some positive changes in the relationship as a result of treatment. Although I expect that your relationship will benefit from treatment, I guess what I am wondering is, do you think the relationship might change in a direction that might produce some problems?
P: What do you mean? Will we like each other less because I don't have problems with anxiety anymore?
T: Well, kind of like that. Sometimes, when a couple has become used to things being a certain way, when a change occurs, it can come with a period of adjustment. Is there anything that you think either of you will have to adjust to that might not be as positive?
P: Like I won't be able to stay at home as much, or like my wife won't be around as much?
T: Yes. How do you think you will feel about those kinds of issues?
P: I think I'll be OK; what about you?
W: I can't wait. I don't think there will be anything negative at all. We'll be back to what we used to be like.
T: How will you feel to have to assume some of the responsibility around the house again?
P: I'll get used to it, I guess.

At this point the therapist accomplishes two important goals. One is to normalize the couple's experience that the relationship has changed as a result of treatment. The second is to mention the fact that there are occasions when relationships worsen as a result of treatment. Although this couple is currently unable to imagine any negative effects from treatment, open discussion of the issue will make it considerably easier to manage should it arise in later sessions.

Session 3

By Session 3, the couple have gained knowledge about the disorder and have spent a considerable amount of time discussing the relationship issues that have arisen as a result of the disorder. The therapist begins to teach some of the specific skills that will be central to this treatment approach. Early in this session the patient was taught diaphragmatic breathing. Now the therapist discusses how to incorporate the spouse into the upcoming homework assignment.

> T: Well, it seems that you are not having much problem with the breathing technique. It'll get a little easier once you have practiced it several times. Janice, how do you think you can be helpful to Michael during these practices?
> W: I'm not sure. But I guess I could remind him when he has forgotten.
> T: How would you feel if she reminded you to do the breathing practices?
> P: Well, as long as she does it without being demanding, I guess it would be OK.
> T: What happens when you feel that she is demanding?
> P: I usually just tune her out.
> T: Does that mean you would not do the exercises?
> P: Maybe. But probably not. I'd do them anyway.
> W: No he wouldn't. That's why I've stopped trying to help him. He just shuts me out completely.
> T: It sounds as if there are some important feelings around this topic. What I'd like to do is to talk a little about those feelings and about some ways that we can think of to allow Janice to remind you about your practice without your feeling as though she is being demanding. . . . In addition to just reminding you to do the exercises at home, she may also be helpful in helping you concentrate on the exercises at times when you are feeling very anxious and panicky. What do you think?
> P: I guess so. It is kind of hard for me to really focus when I get that way.

The discussion turns toward solving this issue. What is important here is that this is often the first point at which the patient will begin to acknowledge that his or her partner may not always be welcome in treatment. It is important to allow the couple to experience any emotions they may be having and to discuss them openly. It is likely that they may not have expressed these feelings to each other directly. The primary responsibility of the therapist, then, is to help the couple find solutions to obstacles that may prevent the partner from becoming an active participant in the treatment process. This was difficult in this case because Michael was feeling ashamed and embarrassed that his wife knew of his panic, an issue that comes to the fore in Session Five.

Session 5

In the fifth session the couple are introduced to cognitive restructuring. There are two goals here. One is to help them understand that panic is generated from the experience of catastrophic cognitions. The second is to teach them to effectively manage anxiety by identifying negative thoughts and challenging them. A third issue is to have the couple realize that the techniques are not just for dealing with anxiety, but can also be useful on any occasion when negative thoughts are involved. In this session both Michael and Janice demonstrate that they are reasonably effective at identifying the underlying beliefs as well as countering them with appropriate restructuring. While discussing the next week's homework, they are able to identify important relationship cognitions and to challenge those as well.

> **T:** Let's take another example from last week. You noted that while you were in the grocery store with Janice, you became very anxious. Walk me back through that situation and see whether you can identify the kinds of negative thoughts that occurred and then challenge them. Janice, it will be OK for you to help if you can.
> **W:** OK.
> **P:** Well, I was standing in line with Janice, and it was pretty crowded. Just about the time we got to the place that we couldn't leave if I had to because there were too many people behind me, Janice takes off to go and get some bread or something and just leaves me there. By myself!
> **T:** When did the anxiety start to increase for you?
> **P:** As soon as she said, "I'll be right back." Then I thought, "She can't leave me here by myself. She knows I'll panic." Then my anxiety shot through the roof.
> **T:** We've talked some about how to identify the core thoughts that may be associated with periods of anxiety or panic. Do you think you could identify the negative thoughts that were associated with that anxiety episode and then challenge them?

P: I can try. The first thought was, "I'll panic. Then everything will get terrible and I'll have to run out of the store." That's it.

T: It sounds as though you can identify some of the important thoughts about that period, but I'm wondering if there are any additional thoughts that may be underlying those, which might be making your anxiety worse. Janice, can you think of any ways that Michael can get those thoughts?

W: I think we talked about asking yourself first, "What am I concerned will happen if I do actually experience a panic attack at this time?"

T: Thinking back to that situation, Michael, what would your answer to that question be?

P: I guess I am concerned that I will have to leave the store.

T: What is it about the panic that makes you feel that you have to leave? What are you concerned will happen if you stayed there during the attack?

P: I guess that the anxiety will get worse and won't stop, and then maybe I'll die or something. Maybe I still believe that a little.

T: Remember, we want to be as specific as possible. When you say "or something," what else do you imagine could happen in that situation?

P: That somebody might see me and think that I'm crazy.

T: It sounds as if you'd feel embarrassed.

P: Yeah, I would. A lot.

W: I even think he gets embarrassed when he knows that I'm around during one of his attacks.

T: Michael?

P: Well, I guess a little, but who wants their wife to see them act like an idiot?

T: Well, there are two issues here. One is the likelihood that someone can tell when you actually have an attack. It sounds that at least your wife can at times. So when you experience a panic attack around her, she is likely to know. The second issue is, What about that bothers you?

P: I just don't want her to see me that way.

T: What way?

P: Panicky.

T: What do you imagine she'll think if she does see you in the middle of a panic attack?

P: It's not a pleasant sight. I guess she'll think that I'm just having another panic attack.

T: It's possible that she'll think that. But what is the worse that you imagine she'll think of you as result of experiencing a panic?

P: I know it sounds stupid, but I think that she'll think that I'm weird or something.

T: Weird in what way?

P: Like I'm some kind of nut who needs to be locked up.

T: If she does think that, what do you imagine will happen?

P: I guess the worse would be that she'd think I'm a lousy father and husband, and that I'm weak.

T: Remember, we want you to get to some of the implications of the core thoughts. What if she does feel that way?

P: She'll leave me, and I'd be miserable.

T: Hmm. Now that we've uncovered some of the core thoughts associated with feeling anxious, let's work on how to manage them. First, Janice, what impact do you think such thoughts have on your husband's anxiety?

W: If it were me, I think they would make me very nervous.

T: That's a good point. Most people who have those kinds of thoughts and believe them would become very nervous and frightened. So, in that situation, Michael, your anxiety is understandable. How do you think you would feel if you didn't believe those thoughts to be completely true at the time you had them?

P: I probably wouldn't get as anxious.

T: The key, then, is to find a way of managing those thoughts in a manner that will make them less powerful and have less impact on your anxiety. How can we challenge those thoughts, keeping in mind that we don't want you to simply think positively, but we want your thoughts to be as accurate as possible.

P: Well, first, I guess I can start by asking myself how realistic it is that my wife will think badly of me because of the panic.

At that point, the therapist first confirms with Janice that she will not think badly of Michael because of the panic and then helps Michael realize that his worst fears are not likely to happen. They then move on to decatastrophize the negative thoughts about embarrassment. The key during cognitive restructuring is to pursue the anxious episode until the patient's worst fears are expressed and then to counter those thoughts by examining the realistic probability of the event's happening and/or whether the thought is truly as catastrophic as it first seems (for examples of cognitive restructuring, see Barlow & Cerny, 1988; Craske & Barlow, 1993).

Michael's case, as is common for this disorder, suggests that there are two important levels of negative thoughts. One is related to issues of panic and the possible consequences of panic. Michael has a strong concern about possibly dying or of being overwhelmingly embarrassed. The second set of thoughts and feelings are related to his wife and the possible deterioration of their relationship as a result of his panic disorder. As such, it is important that therapists uncover and manage the negative thoughts on both levels.

During the next several sessions the couple became more comfortable discussing relationship issues and more adept at applying the cognitive restructuring techniques. They were encouraged to apply similar strategies to relationship issues and relationship changes that might occur as a result of a decrease in panic symptoms. By the end of treatment, Michael's panic attacks had stopped and he was engaging in several activities he had avoided as a result of the panic. Moreover, the couple reported that they were communicating better and had a much clearer understanding of each other as a result of treatment. These gains were maintained at 6- and 12-month follow-up assessment periods. Of course, not all cases proceed as smoothly as this one, but it serves to illustrate the utilization of cognitive techniques in the management of panic disorder with agoraphobia within a couple framework. The treatment goal of this approach is threefold. The primary goal is to alleviate the suffering of the identified patient. The secondary goal is help the partner understand the nature of the disorder and to help the couple find effective ways that both of them can be involved in the treatment process. The tertiary goal is to help the couple manage relationship issues that might have developed as a result of the patient's panic disorder. In this fashion, *all* aspects of this often debilitating condition can be effectively managed.

It should be noted that although the case discussed here is typical, there are cases in which the spouse or partner will serve as an impediment to treatment. In other words, as suggested by Goldstein and Chambless (1978), the spouse may not want the relationship to change and may present various roadblocks on the patient's road to recovery. In a particular case of one of the present authors, each instance of improvement was met by blatant attempts at sabotage. Specifically, the husband would find reasons to become angry with the patient during her in vivo exposure exercises, which included her being a passenger in an automobile or entering fearful situations (e.g., the grocery store). When angry while driving, the husband would simply stop the car and walk away. When angered while in the grocery store, the husband would leave, go home and lie on the bed motionless for hours, refusing to utter a single word to the patient. Either occurrence would catapult the patient into a devastating panic and decrease the chances that she would attempt the next exposure assignment. While atypical, this particular case illustrates that sabotage is a possibility, because the partner of the patient is sometimes unwilling or unable to tolerate the perceived change in the relationship.

FUTURE DIRECTIONS

The nature of agoraphobic persons' interpersonal relationships is theoretically and clinically interesting, however future research and clinical efforts must strive to improve upon previous studies. Of primary concern is the provision of a clear definition of the nature of the interpersonal relationship difficulties hypothesized to impact, or be impacted by, treatment. Such interpersonal difficulties may, for example, center on conflict, issues of separation, dependency, some combination of each, or none of these. Considering the importance assigned to "faulty" interpersonal relationships, it is surprising that none of the studies to date has clearly explicated a specific dysfunctional interpersonal pattern, its relationship to agoraphobia, or its impact on the syndrome.

In terms of treatment, there is much that is currently unknown. For example, we have little information regarding the inclusion of nonspousal relationships in treatment. It is our experience that the impact of this disorder extends beyond the primary significant relationship. It is not uncommon, for example, for panic-disordered patients to rely heavily on their children as "safe-persons" (i.e. people with whom the patient feels comfortable and believes that their presence will make it less likely for a panic attack to occur). Consequently, a child's activities may be greatly limited so that he or she can remain in close proximity to the disordered individual. It would be interesting to examine the impact of treatment on that relationship. In addition, there is a paucity of research from different theoretical perspectives. The use of different approaches (e.g., interpersonal) may prove to be quite effective in managing some of the issues raised in this chapter.

Finally, we have no information about the utility of treatment for this condition when both members of the dyad share the same pathology, or when the partner of the identified patient suffers from a different disorder. It seems that treatment would become more complicated if both members are experiencing psychological problems, perhaps excessively so if they suffer from diagnostically distinct conditions, although the results from the McLeod (1994) study suggest otherwise. Along these lines, it would be interesting for future efforts to examine the impact of personality (disorders and style) on the treatment of this syndrome in the couple. There has been only one investigation in this area. Chernen and Friedman (1993) conducted Behavioral Marital Therapy with four panic-disordered patients with personality disorders and reported substantial improvement in marital satisfaction and panic symptoms in the two maritally troubled subjects. The two subjects who were not maritally maladjusted, however, showed no improvement following treatment.

The empirical examination of these types of issues will expand the knowledge of the field concerning the specific mechanisms responsible for the maintenance and exacerbation of couple issues in this population. We feel this process will eventually have a tremendous positive impact on the panic-disordered couple.

REFERENCES

American Psychiatric Association. (1994). *Diagnostic and statistical manual of mental disorders* (4th ed.). Washington, DC: Author.

Antony, M. A., & Barlow, D. H. (1996). Emotion theory as a framework for explaining panic attacks and panic disorder. In R. M. Rapee (Ed.), *Current controversies in th.² anxiety disorders*. New York: Guilford Press.

Arnow, B. A., Taylor, C. B., Agras, W. S., & Telch, M. J. (1985). Enhancing agoraphobia treatment outcome by changing couple communication patterns. *Behavior Therapy, 16,* 452–467.

Arrindell, W. A., & Emmelkamp, P. M. G. (1986). Marital adjustment, intimacy and needs in female agoraphobics and their partners: A controlled study. *British Journal of Psychiatry, 149,* 592–602.

Arrindell, W. A., Emmelkamp, P. M. G., & Sanderman, R. (1986). Marital quality and general life adjustment in relation to treatment outcome in agoraphobia. *Advances in Behavior Research and Therapy, 8,* 139–185.

Ballenger, J. C. (1989). Toward an integrated model of panic disorder. *American Journal of Orthopsychiatry, 59,* 284–293.

Barlow, D. H. (1988). *Anxiety and its disorders: The nature and treatment of anxiety and panic.* New York: Guilford Press.

Barlow, D. H. (1991). Disorders of emotion. *Psychological Inquiry, 2,* 58–71.

Barlow, D. H., & Cerny, J. A. (1988). *Psychological treatment of Panic: Treatment manual for practitioners.* New York: Guilford Press.

Barlow, D. H., O'Brien, G. T., & Last, C. G. (1984). Couples treatment of agoraphobia. *Behavior Therapy, 15,* 41–58.

Barlow, D. H., Mavissakalian, M., & Hay, L. R. (1981). Couples treatment of agoraphobia: Changes in marital satisfaction. *Behavior Research and Therapy, 19,* 245–255.

Buglass, D., Clarke, J., Henderson, A. S., & Kreitman, N. (1977). A study of agoraphobic housewives. *Psychological Medicine, 7,* 73–86.

Carter, M. M., & Barlow, D. H. (1993). Interoceptive exposure in the treatment of panic disorder. In L. VandeCreek (Ed.), *Innovations in clinical practice: A source book.* Sarasota FL: Professional Resource Press.

Carter, M. M., & Barlow, D. H. (1995). Learned alarms: The origins of panic. In W. O'Donohue & L. Krasner (Eds.), *Theories in behavior therapy.* Washington, DC: American Psychological Association.

Carter, M. M., Turvosky, J., & Barlow, D. H. (1994). Interpersonal relationships in panic disorder with agoraphobia: A review of empirical evidence. *Clinical Psychology: Science and Practice, 1,* 25–34.

Carter, M. M., Hollon, S. D., Carson R., & Shelton, R. C. (1995). Effects of a safe-person on induced distress following a biological challenge in panic disorder with agoraphobia. *Journal of Abnormal Psychology, 104*, 156–163.

Cerny, J. A., Barlow, D. H., Craske, M. G., & Himadi, W. G. (1987). Couples treatment of agoraphobia: A two-year follow-up. *Behavior Therapy, 18*, 401–415.

Chernen, L., & Friedman, S. (1993). Treating the personality disordered agoraphobic patient with individual and marital therapy. *Journal of Anxiety Disorders, 7*, 163–177.

Cobb, J. P., Mathews, A. M., Childs-Clarke, A., & Blowers, C. M. (1984). The spouse as co-therapist in the treatment of agoraphobia. *British Journal of Psychiatry, 144*, 282–287.

Craske, M. G. & Barlow, D. H. (1993). Panic disorder and agoraphobia. In D. H. Barlow (Ed.), *Clinical handbook of psychological disorders* (2d ed.) (pp. 1–47). New York: Guilford Press.

Craske, M. G., Burton T., & Barlow, D. H. (1989). Relationships among measures of communication, marital satisfaction and exposure during couples treatment of agoraphobia. *Behavior Research and Therapy, 27*, 131–140.

Emmelkamp, P. M. G. (1980). Agoraphobics' interpersonal problems: Their role in the effects of exposure in vivo therapy. *Archives of General Psychiatry, 37*, 1303–1306.

Emmelkamp, P. M. G., Van Dyck, R., Bitter, M., Heins, R., Onstein, E. J., & Eisen, B. (1992). Spouse-aided therapy with agoraphobics. *British Journal of Psychiatry, 160*, 51–56.

Fry, W. (1962). The marital context of an anxiety syndrome. *Family Process, 1*, 245–252.

Goldstein, A. J., & Chambless, D. L. (1978). A reanalysis of agoraphobia. *Behavior Therapy, 9*, 47–59.

Gray, J. A. (1982). *The neuropsychology of anxiety.* New York: Oxford University Press.

Gray, J. A. (1987). *The psychology of fear and stress,* (2d. ed.). Cambridge, England: Cambridge University Press.

Gray, J. A. (1991). Fear, panic, and anxiety: What's in a name? *Psychological Inquiry, 2*, 77–78.

Hafner, R. J. (1976). Fresh symptom emergence after intensive behaviour therapy. *British Journal of Psychiatry, 129*, 378–383.

Hafner, R. J. (1977). The husbands of agoraphobic women and their influence on treatment outcome. *British Journal of Psychiatry, 131*, 289–294.

Hafner, R. J. (1984). The marital repercussions of behavior therapy for agoraphobia. *Psychotherapy, 21*, 530–542.

Hafner, R. J. (1986). *Marriage and mental illness.* New York: Guilford Press.

Himadi, W. G., Cerny, J. A., Barlow, D. H., Cohen, S., & O'Brien, G. T. (1986). The relationship of marital adjustment to agoraphobia treatment outcome. *Behavior Research and Therapy, 24*, 107–115.

Jacobson, N. S., Holtzworth-Munroe, A., & Schmaling, K. B. (1989). Marital therapy and spouse involvement in the treatment of depression, agoraphobia, and alcoholism. *Journal of Consulting and Clinical Psychology, 57*, 5–10.

Kleiner, L., & Marshall, W. L. (1985). Relationship difficulties and agoraphobia. *Clinical Psychology Review, 5,* 581–595.

Meadows, E. A., & Barlow, D. H. (1994). Anxiety disorders. *Encyclopedia of Human Behavior, 1,* 165–173.

McLeod, J. D. (1994). Anxiety disorders and marital quality. *Journal of Abnormal Psychology, 103,* 767–776.

Milrod, B., & Shear, M. K. (1991). Dynamic treatment of panic disorder: A review. *The Journal of Nervous and Mental Disease, 179,* 741–743.

Milton, F., & Hafner, J. (1979). The outcome of behavior therapy for agoraphobia in relation to marital adjustment. *Archives of General Psychiatry, 36,* 807–811.

Monteiro, W., Marks, I. M., & Ramm, E. (1985). Marital adjustment and treatment outcome in agoraphobia. *British Journal of Psychiatry, 146,* 393–390.

Oatley, K., & Hodgson, D. (1987). Influence of husbands on the outcome of their agoraphobic wives' therapy. *British Journal of Psychiatry, 150,* 380–386.

Rapee, R., Telfer, L. A., & Barlow, D. H. (1991). The role of safety cues in mediating the response to inhalations of CO_2 in agoraphobics. *Behaviour Research and Therapy, 29,* 353–355.

Regier, D. A., Narrow, W. E., & Rae, D. S. (1990). The epidemiology of anxiety disorders: The epidemiological catchment area (ECA) experience. *Journal of Psychiatric Research, 24,* 3–14.

Roth, M. (1987). Some recent developments in relation to agoraphobia and related disorders and their bearing upon theories of their causation. *Psychiatric Journal of the University of Ottawa, 12,* 150–154.

Snaith, P. (1986). Assessment and treatment of pervasive anxiety. *Psychotherapy and Psychosomatics, 46,* 23–34.

Torpy, D. M., & Measey, L. G. (1974). Marital interaction in agoraphobia. *Journal of Clinical Psychology, 30,* 351–354.

Webster, A. S. (1953). The development of phobias in married women. *Psychological Monographs, 67,* 1–18.

CHAPTER 4

The Psychotic Couple

Michael P. Maniacci

If I had to give a single reason why life with Jon became unbearable, I would say it was my growing feeling of guilt. I already had a tendency to feel guilty well before meeting my husband. But after I married, this tendency prevailed. I felt guilty because I could neither ease his suffering nor give him the confidence he lacked so dramatically. But most of all I felt guilty because I began to resent the endless struggle of dealing with Jon's strange world and the endless daily complications it brought about. The strain of being the only link between him and the outside world, of having to translate his behavior to our daughters, of not being able to talk to them without being accused of collusion, of having to adapt to his unpredictable moods and having to live with ghosts, all those wore me down. . . . I felt like fleeing from this situation, but how could I abandon him? . . . I became increasingly snappy and irritable. And the nastier I became, the guiltier I felt. We were caught in a vicious circle. (*Schizophrenia Bulletin*, 1994, p. 229)

The preceding quotation is from the wife of a psychotic husband whose disorder caused moderate impairment in his overall functioning, but severe disruption in the marriage. She was willing to offer her insights about what it was like to be married to a man who frequently believed "they were out to get him." She articulates her self-doubt, guilt, and feelings of isolation more clearly than many clinicians have stated it in more "professional" or "clinical" terms.

Psychosis is a disruptive, difficult disorder for those who experience it, yet the quite frequently overlooked partner/spouse/significant other of the psychotic individual very often experiences considerable subjective distress and pain as well. Because of the glaring dysfunction typically evident in the psychotic patient, the spouse's needs and issues are very frequently "put on hold" while the more obviously impaired partner is intensively (though often insufficiently) treated. As authors have detailed, the spouse of the psychotic individual is typically very important in the treatment (Hafner, 1986; Winefield & Harvey, 1994). Thus, recent research has articulated,

> . . . this sample of long-term caregivers has much to tell us about changes in mental health services. . . . Change cannot occur unilaterally, and the challenge for researchers and policymakers is to ensure that caregivers' needs are acknowledged and that responses to these needs are integrated with the professional mental health care system (Winefield & Harvey, 1994, p. 565).

The researchers cited here noted that the most popular recommendation for possible improvement of services in the treatment of psychotic individuals was "earlier professional help at signs of imminent relapse" (p. 565). They noted that caregivers felt they could predict when an acute psychotic episode was about to emerge, but that these caregivers were frustrated in their attempts to receive the kind of professional interventions they believed were needed to prevent the disorder from deteriorating into a major psychotic episode. In short, the caregivers felt left out of the loop not only when it came to their own needs being met, but in providing input regarding their partners.

DSM-IV AND THE CONCEPT OF PSYCHOSIS

The concept of *psychosis* has undergone considerable debate throughout the history of psychotherapy. Various explanations for it have emerged, with everything from demonic possession to vitamin deficiency being labeled as the "cause" of the aberrant behavior. Even the term itself has had numerous definitions, as the *Diagnostic and Statistical Manual of Mental Disorders* (4th ed.) (DSM-IV) has recently detailed:

> The term has historically received a number of different definitions, none of which has achieved universal acceptance. . . . Based on their characteristic features, the different disorders in DSM-IV emphasize different aspects of the various definitions of *psychotic* (American Psychiatric Association, 1994, p. 770).

In the current edition of the DSM, the psychotic disorders are categorized under the heading "Schizophrenia and Other Psychotic Disorders" (pp. 273–315) and include the following diagnoses:

Schizophrenia
Schizophreniform Disorder
Schizoaffective Disorder
Delusional Disorder
Brief Psychotic Disorder
Shared Psychotic Disorder
Psychotic Disorder Due to a General Medical Condition (including substance abuse)
Psychotic Disorder NOS (not otherwise specified)

All of these disorders are associated with psychotic behavior. Individuals with these disorders tend to hallucinate, exhibit delusional thinking, have periods of gross impairment in daily functioning, and, in general, demonstrate episodes of severe impairment in reality testing. The course, prognosis, and presentation of a particular type of psychosis varies from disorder to disorder, as does the overall severity of symptoms.

For the purposes of this chapter, *psychosis* is used as a generic concept applying to any and all of the previously listed disorders, especially to those conditions that are more acute and cyclical in presentation, with relatively less overall gross impairment, but not to these seen in the case of schizophrenia, chronic undifferentiated subtype.

THE PROCESS OF MATE SELECTION

As the works of clinicians such as Hafner (1986) and Pittman (1987) have detailed, psychotic individuals do marry. Early theoreticians, such as Sullivan (1953), felt that psychotic manifestations in general, and schizophrenia in specific, were not likely to occur in individuals who were able to successfully integrate their sexuality into their personalities in such a way as to be able to form long-term, steady interpersonal relationships. Hence, according to Sullivan, being able to reach such a psychosocial stage of development precluded the type of personality disturbance likely to lead to the manifestation of psychotic behavior. As research by Brekke, Levin, Wolkon, Sobel, and Slade (1993) points out, the level of psychosocial functioning, including work and interpersonal relationships, varies greatly, even among those with a diagnosis of schizophrenia. When the other psychotic diagnostic categories are included in the spectrum, the range of an individual's overall functioning is even broader, varying from being barely able to care for self to performing relatively self-sufficiently. Psychotic individuals are not uniformly impaired in their functioning, presentation, or prognosis.

The marriage of an individual to someone who experiences psychotic episodes does seem to have some distinct patterns that can be discernible. The "typical" pattern appears to begin with this scenario:

> I was 18 and Jon was 23 when we met at the university. He was brilliantly intelligent, sociable, and eccentric. Five years later we married.
>
> Jon did behave a bit strangely sometimes, but then so did many other people I knew. His relationship with his parents struck me as rather odd, but since we came from very different backgrounds, this didn't really worry me. Besides, Jon's explanations were so beautifully rational and convincing (Anonymous. *Schizophrenia Bulletin*, 1994, p. 227).

Because of the broad definition of *psychotic* being used in this chapter, the particular dynamics of the psychotic couple must be painted in broad strokes. The histories of these individuals vary greatly in their particulars, but discounting the more chronic cases, a general pattern can be conceptualized according to a biopsychosocial formulation.

A biopsychosocial approach to conceptualizing psychopathology is a useful perspective that has recently gained strong support in the literature. Such an approach has its roots in the early psychoanalytic literature, particularly in the writings of Adler (1912/1983a) and Erikson (1950/1963) and more recently in the works of Beck (1985), Carpenter (1987), Pittman (1987), and Sperry and Carlson (1993). As Gabbard (1994) so eloquently states:

> The complexity of the mind-brain problem may become obscured by the vicissitudes of the marketplace in day-to-day practice, but we must never lose track of the need to address both the person and the illness. We continue to walk the tightrope between the twin pitfalls of biological and psychological reductionism. The balancing act requires unswerving attention and concentration, but the satisfactions derived from practicing on the cutting edge of the mind-brain interface more than make up for the occasional loss of one's footing and the struggle to regain a safe and sensible position on the high wire (p. 443).

Biologically, the affected individuals tend to have a vulnerability, a predisposition, to developing psychotic disorders. The sites and specifications of the particular vulnerabilities have been widely investigated, though the research has been directed mostly toward schizophrenia and schizophrenic spectrum disorders, and has been most clearly articulated by Anderson, Reiss, and Hogarty (1986), Andreasen (1984), and Garza-Trevino, Volkow, Cancro, and Contreras (1990). Interested readers are encouraged to review the literature themselves. Briefly summarized, the diathesis-stress model states that the biologically vulnerable individual interacts with stressful circumstances, overloads his or her compromised biological systems, and fails to receive adequate support from his or her social network. As tension increases, stress increases, and the individual becomes more and more symptomatic.

Psychosocially, as these people grew up, their preferred style of relating to their families was to detach. Even when they were social, it was in a nontraditional manner, often described as "eccentric," as the woman married to the psychotic man articulated earlier. For some reason, they felt they did not belong, or that they were different (perhaps an outgrowth of subtle neurologic dysfunction, which contributed to their being neuro-developmentally "behind" others), and they were sometimes clearly reinforced in such thinking. Their thinking began to develop along two distinct paths, one consensually validated, and the second not so, being kept idiosyncratic and personal (Adler, 1912/1983a; Sullivan, 1953). Consensually, they understood life's demands, rules, and obligations, but personally, privately, they tended to eschew such demands, preferring instead to follow their own inner fantasies, daydreams, and conceptualizations, which often bore little resemblance to the conventionally articulated rules with which they were surrounded. As long as they kept life's stressors at a minimum and were able to withdraw into their private worlds without fear of humiliation and rejection, they coped relatively well. They knew what life demanded of them and were typically satisfied with meeting the minimum consensual requirements and maintaining a polite, but detached, interpersonal style.

Typically, the rigidity of their cognitive style was fairly well known to those around them, even from childhood. They set high, yet idiosyncratic, goals, they tended to be ambitious, and they were rather inflexible in the pursuit of their personally meaningful goals. Upon failure to achieve those goals in a consensually validated manner, they set their goals even higher, thereby increasing the stress in their lives. As goal attainment became increasingly less likely, they became self-critical, withdrew into their fantasies, and attempted to seek satisfaction through their imagination. As this process escalated and stress levels increased, their biological vulnerability "kicked in" and their imagination began to expand to psychotic proportions. Any overindulgence in mind-altering substances only added fuel to the neurochemical fire.

The nonpsychotic partners are typically one of two types. In the first case, they are relatively high-functioning and successful people; they strongly value control, organization, and efficiency. They enjoy the role of leadership, handle it well, and take on a sense of dominance in the relationship, which well suits the psychotic partner. In the second case, the nonpsychotic partners are rather shy, withdrawn, and dependent. Their previous contact with suitable partners was typically rather limited, and upon meeting the psychotic partners, they found these individuals to be inoffensive, driven in a way they themselves were not; they found themselves oddly comfortable with the detached, laid back interpersonal dynamics. Not all partners of psychotic individuals fit these descriptions, but in this author's clinical experience, many of the couples that stay together throughout recurring psychotic episodes fit these patterns.

The nonpsychotic partners, in what will hereafter be termed the *controlling* or the *dependent* style, can exhibit either a relatively normal or dysfunctional pattern. In the normal pattern, these partners are flexible enough to lend support and strength to their partners and still maintain some flexibility in their problem-solving approach. Their styles are preferences, albeit strong ones. In the more dysfunctional pattern, the controlling partner takes on pathological significance and frequently presents with Axis II diagnoses such as obsessive-compulsive personality disorders, narcissistic personality disorders, paranoid personality disorders, and Axis I diagnoses such as panic disorders, obsessive-compulsive disorders, and somatoform disorders. The dependent patterns, in their more dysfunctional presentations, frequently have Axis II diagnoses of dependent personality dis-orders, avoidant personality disorders, and histrionic personality disorders, with Axis I conditions such as alcohol abuse/dependence, depressive spectrum disorders, and agoraphobia/social phobia. An examination of each combination (i.e., psychotic/controlling pairing, psychotic/dependent pairing) reveals slightly different relational histories and attractions.

The Psychotic/Controlling Pairing

In psychotic/controlling couples, the controlling partners were typically parentified children who ran their families of origin. Very frequently, they had a dysfunctional parent or sibling who required extra effort, time, and attention, and these controlling partners/children were more than up to the task. In fact, they thrived on it. Their sense of significance became predicated upon caretaking and leading, and they carried out their role well. Yet, on some level, they were tired and felt unappreciated. They secretly longed to have the caretaking returned, but they barely articulated such desires, hardly even to themselves. Instead, they wished to be rewarded for their efforts and they hoped that by demonstrating such attitudes they would (somehow) communicate to others that they themselves needed such caring and attention. Seldom did they get it. When these controlling individuals meet their partners, it is typically (though not exclusively) *after* their partners have begun to show signs of "wear and tear," as the controlling partners phrase it. If there has not yet been a frankly psychotic episode, there have been signs of dysfunction, extreme mood lability, and "eccentricity." The controlling partners feel a chemistry, an attraction, to these people. They have been prepared for just such people since childhood, and they know their scripts so very well. They become the guides, the organizers, even the mentors of their partners, and they develop the fiction that through patience, perseverance, and "pushing" they can improve their partners' lives. Frequently, they do just that, but at a price: psychotic decompensation in their partners.

The psychotic partners with controlling mates live life under a great deal of stress, guilt, and pressure. They are subtly told they are not "quite enough," and this feeds into their already long-standing trend to be over-ambitious. However, they are usually lacking in the social skills to fully actualize their goals and, somehow, they never seem to be able to go the final distance, to follow through, to "close the deal," so to speak. They are attracted to these controlling partners in a sincere, loyal way, for many reasons, including the fact that they believe that with these partners, they may be able to "stick to their guns," "follow through," and be "all that they can be." But there persists a nagging sense—sometimes rather clearly communicated, and sometimes not so clearly communicated but *felt* nonetheless—that as they are, they simply are not good enough.

The Psychotic/Dependent Pairing

The dependent individuals in the psychotic/dependent pairing usually came from rather isolated families. Somehow these families were never at home in their communities. The children, in school, at the playground, in the parks, "stuck out"—they did not quite fit in. Some of these children developed the attitude that interpersonal relations could be painful, and that it is better to play it safe than be sorry. Hence, the only way to be assured of interpersonal success was to have others come to them, rather than venture out and risk being rejected. Unfortunately, not many ventured to them, and this increased their sense of isolation while simultaneously increasing their reliance on a "special someone" who could reach out and touch them.

These dependent individuals developed a notoriously poor ability to differentiate substance from posture, and if they were in a position to form early romantic attachments to peers, they frequently failed miserably (at worst) or left the relationship disappointed (at best). Somehow, they never became totally discouraged, but instead became almost stubbornly but quietly optimistic that their true love was "out there." When they met their psychotic partners, it was typically early in the life span cycle and almost always before their partners had begun to show signs of dysfunction. From their dependent pattern perspective, they believed in the psychotic partners' ambitions, believed they had a "kindred spirit" who knew of life's isolation, and felt grateful to be attached—so grateful that they tended to overlook the "eccentricities" that had caught the attention of others. These tendencies to not provoke, to not question, led the pair to difficulties in which the burden of navigating through life's hardships fell to the psychotic partners. It was a task that they managed, but at a cost that periodically caught up to them.

RELATIONAL CONFLICTS IN PSYCHOTIC COUPLES

The conflicts that arise in psychotic couples generally fall into two categories, prepsychotic and postpsychotic. *Prepsychotic* refers to certain conflicts that are likely to occur to the couple as a result of their interactional styles, as an outgrowth of their personality patterns which, if unchecked, increase the stress and strains on the psychotic partner to such an extent that a psychotic episode emerges as a way of *coping with* the conflict. The psychosis is a solution to the demands of the situation, brought about by biological vulnerability, early psychosocial training, current interpersonal transactions, and *choice* on the part of the psychotic individual (Shulman, 1984).

Postpsychotic refers to particular conflicts that arise as a result of a psychotic episode or the threat of an impending psychotic episode. In many cases, the *threat/possibility* of a psychotic episode takes on the experiential quality of an *actual* psychotic episode, especially for the nonpsychotic partner. Many clinicians and researchers, in working with such couples, fail to take into account these "near misses" the couples experience. These microstresses and strains take their toll and can often be as disruptive to the relationship as an actual psychotic decompensation. Both prepsychotic and postpsychotic conflicts should be examined in greater detail.

Relational Conflict in the Psychotic/Controlling Pair

In the psychotic/controlling pair, prepsychotic conflicts typically center on themes of power, perfection, and achievement. The controlling partners communicate standards that the psychotic partners feel compelled to attain. Responsibility, or lack thereof, for a failure to achieve becomes the rock upon which the relationship begins to crack.

The psychotic partners attempt to meet the challenges that have been laid out before them. Bosses communicate expectations that are dutifully communicated back to the controlling partners. Parents and in-laws set up requirements that the psychotic partners apparently agree to meet. Children ask for things that may cost more (either financially or emotionally) than the psychotic partners can afford. Whatever its genesis, the pressure begins to build. Either directly, through clear communication, or relatively indirectly, through expectations, the issue of *having* to meet the challenge is transferred onto the shoulders of the controlling partners. They may not, in all sincerity, be aware of having become symbolically linked to the challenge. For example, Ted, a gentleman with a history of delusional disorder, grandiose type, feels inadequate to scale the mountain he has established as signifying his having "arrived" in life. Joan, his controlling partner, expects to be able to live at a certain level of comfort, move in the "right" circle, and provide for the children in a manner she deems appropriate.

Ted continues to push himself, and at the first sign of potential failure, his delusions of greatness "kick in" to bolster his flagging self-esteem. Gradually, he begins to see Joan's attitude toward him as indicative of the respect he fails to get from life as a whole. He symbolically places on their relationship the weight of approval he desires to receive from the world— and her glances at him, her demeanor around him, even her lack of attention to him (possibly even for understandable reasons) become the bone of contention from which she learns to extract leverage. *Their relationship begins to represent a microcosm of his posture toward the world as a whole. As goes his attitude toward the world, so goes their relationship, and vice versa.* Joan symbolically represents the forces in the world he struggles to overcome, to win over.

Blame is typically shuttled back and forth between this pair, as each attempts to play out his or her script. At this point, the psychotic individuals begin to withdraw and either attain their goals in fantasy or, more commonly, create opponents who are responsible for their not being able to achieve their goals. As they begin to become frankly psychotic, the battleground shifts. The real psychosocial stressors fade into the background, and the controlling partners become disgruntled, then worried, and eventually passive. They are seldom up to dealing with the twists and turns of logic their psychotic partners throw at them. They yield, the psychotic partner is attended to, the pressure is relieved, and the controlling spouse feels oddly sullen, lost, and generally "sick and tired." As the psychosis "lifts," the controlling partners assume more and more responsibility for putting things back on track, and the cycle begins anew.

Relational Conflicts in the Psychotic/Dependent Pair

In the psychotic/dependent couple prepsychotic conflicts tend to be of a different sort. Whereas the psychotic/controlling pair have conflicts about achievement, perfection, and power, the conflicts for this pair tend to center on intimacy, loyalty, and dependability. The dependent partners tend to develop great expectations around their seemingly much more outgoing partners. The weight of carrying the relationship falls to the psychotic partner in a subtle manner. While the dependent partner is usually perceived as the "heart and soul" of this couple, the expectations to nurture, protect, and assure the dependent partner fall on the psychotic one.

> Rachel is a woman with a history of schizophrenia, paranoid subtype, who has periods of relatively symptom-free functioning. She is married to Bill, a soft-spoken, shy gentleman who is employed as a factory worker. Rachel has always wanted more in life, for herself and Bill, but he is a modest man of simple tastes who had not dated much. He experienced a mixture of pleasant surprise and fearful hesitancy when Rachel boldly began to "court" him. She seemed a bit wild to him, but well meaning and fiercely protective of their relationship. He had always wanted someone like her, and their marriage seemed the perfect opportunity to feel the connectedness he longed for.
>
> Rachel, after years of being with Bill, feels drained by his lack of assertiveness, his passivity, and his acceptance of the status quo. She cannot seem to get much of a reaction from him, and he has a hard time dealing with her emotional extremes. She feels ever so gently smothered by him, for she has become his sole support. She feels responsible for him and often is torn by having to devote so much time to him while nurturing her own ambition to achieve all she wants to achieve in life. When she "stresses out," as they call it, he begins to rally, to become more active and, at times, even a bit more vigorous in his fights with her, but just a bit. As her tension increases, because she feels torn "between two masters" (i.e., her ambitions and her marriage), she overworks, overindulges, and, before long, becomes psychotic. Bill rallies and through great effort takes over, while Rachel requires "rest." As she becomes increasingly more stable, he backs off, and she assumes a more dominant role again.

Postpsychotic Conflicts

In either type of pairing, the postpsychotic conflicts are draining for all involved. They may not happen very often, but when they do, they can be quite disruptive. In each type of pairing, they serve a different purpose. In the psychotic/controlling pair, the psychosis serves to relieve the tension to achieve, to be perfect, through either attaining those ambitions in fantasy or creating enemies to blame for the lack of progress. In the psychotic/dependent pair, the psychosis serves to rally the dependent partner into action, to share some of the weight of the achievement, and to create some active intimacy. The psychotic partner does not feel up to carrying all the weight, but is typically too proud to admit it. Psychosis allows a vacation from the dominant role.

In any case, the psychosis takes its toll. With each ensuing episode, it becomes harder and harder to return to the "old ways." In the more chronic psychotic patterns, the prepsychotic dynamics become less and less pronounced as the personalities of the psychotic partners become more and more impoverished. In the cases discussed in this chapter, the psychotic episodes do not necessarily deteriorate the personalities so much as they serve to crystallize the conflicts and raise the issues to a draining, extremely serious level. Although in these cases the psychotic episodes may not occur more than once every two to three years (if that often), their impending emergence serves to drive the couple into increasingly intractable postures. The psychotic/controlling pair become more rigid in their conflicts of achievement, power, and control; in the psychotic/dependent pair, their conflicts become even more pronounced around the issues of passivity, intimacy, and support.

THE TREATMENT PROCESS

The treatment process in working with psychotic couples is complicated. As noted earlier in this chapter, most of the treatment attention is typically directed to the more floridly dysfunctional partner. The aforementioned anonymous woman who was married to "Jon" has courageously and sincerely shared her experience so as to enlighten and teach others, including professionals:

> I am convinced that if someone had helped me understand my husband's illness without my having to go through the long, painful process of learning step by step, and *if I had been made aware of my own weaknesses before being drawn into inescapable vicious circles, much pain could have been avoided.* But during those 22 years, none of the psychiatrists I met attempted to give me this help. When I showed undue anxiety or stress, they only offered me pills to calm me down [italics added] (Anonymous. *Schizophrenia Bulletin*, 1994, p. 229).

Treatment usually involves four phases. The phases are not set in stone, but tend to be the following: (1) managing the psychosis and attaining some sort of stability in the psychotic partner; (2) engaging the non-psychotic partner to address his or her needs and lend support and under-standing, (3) upon stabilization, exploring the relational dynamics that may have added to the stressors that precipitated the psychotic episode; and (4) modifying individual psychodynamics through clarification, artic-ulation, skill building, and rehearsal.

Managing the Psychosis

There was a time when the debate about the "functional versus organic" etiology of a psychotic episode occupied more time and debate than the actual treatment of the episode itself. When viewed from a holistic, biopsychosocial perspective, such distinction loses its relevance. Both biology and psychology play a part, and clinicians must address both.

> To say to a patient that his or her condition is a "chemical imbal-ance" or a "psychological disturbance" is likely to be a partial explanation at best. The fact that biochemical processes are altered does not automatically mean that they are the causal agents. . . . An event in the environment, and particularly the subjective meaning of the event, may be the direct cause of a neurochemical change that then becomes the mediating mecha-nism (or pathogenesis) of the illness. . . . This formulation allows the patient to have a greater sense of mastery and understand-ing than the construct of a "chemical imbalance" (Gabbard, 1994, p. 432).

Medication helps. For nonmedically trained clinicians, consultation or cotherapy with a physician is beneficial, especially for the patient. Along with using medication, psychiatrists such as Carpenter (1987), Gabbard (1994), and Pittman (1987) recommend dealing with the subjective mean-ings that psychotic episodes have for their patients and family members. Adler (1920/1983b), Mosak and Fletcher (1973), Mosak and Maniacci (1989), and Shulman (1984) have all written about the process of helping psychotic patients understand the meanings and purposes of their hallu-cinations and delusions. Clarifying such issues can go a long way to abat-ing a psychotic episode, sometimes to the point of even stopping it before therapeutic blood levels have been attained for psychotropic medications. As Pittman (1987) notes, handling the psychotic episode may require hos-pitalization, but if at all feasible, keeping the patient out of the "sick role" and therefore as functional as possible will make the transition back to the consensual world all the more easy for everyone concerned.

One technique is to attempt to translate the hallucination or delusion into commonsense, consensual language. The goal for the clinician is to differentiate the psychotic verbalizations along three dimensions: *meaning, purpose,* and *response.* Once the first two have been clarified, the last can be formulated.

First, the meaning of the hallucination must be grasped. What does it mean to the patient? Given this individual's life history and cognitive style, what could it signify? There is no blanket rule; every clinician must understand the particular patient's life history, cultural idioms, current psychosocial network, and personal lexicon. Once the meaning has been clarified, the second phase entails deciphering the purpose of the hallucination or delusion. Whereas the meaning tells the clinician *what* is happening, its purpose tells the clinician *why* it is needed. It is to that final, purposeful dynamic that the clinician must respond. For example:

> Jenny believed the cups in her apartment were moving all by themselves. This hallucination had proven persistent, intractable, and unresponsive to medication. Using the triad approach of *meaning, purpose,* and *response,* the following approach was worked out. Jenny had recently moved into her own apartment. Everyone was "very proud" of her, especially her parents. She had attempted to manage for several weeks, but her psychotic symptoms had increased to the point of impending hospitalization. The author was called in as a consultant and first determined, with Jenny's help, the meaning of her symptom—that life was moving without human intervention. She was feeling out of control. The purpose was next examined—to alert others that she needed someone to help her regain control. The therapeutic response, both in session during the consultation and from then on with concerned family: "It's OK to be frightened. I'd be frightened too if I thought so much was going on I couldn't control. What can we do to help?"
>
> Within the session and thereafter at home, the hallucination stopped. Jenny was taught to communicate her concern in a consensually validated manner and told that whenever she believed the "cups were moving" she was probably feeling out of control and this was her way of asking for help without having to appear weak.

Engaging the Nonpsychotic Partner

Be it through medication, phenomenological understanding, hospitalization, or any combination of these, the psychotic episode is managed. The next stage entails working with the nonpsychotic partner. Support, education (e.g., about the particular disorder the partner has manifested and the effects and potential side effects of the medications used to manage it), comfort, and empathy during this phase go a long way in lessening confusion and easing the burden. As noted earlier, the meaning of the psychotic episode for the nonpsychotic partner must be explored as well, for in many cases the psychosis has personal meaning for both halves of the pairing. This can serve as a bridge to the couple's work as the partners calm down, stabilize, and begin the process of returning to functioning. Referral to support groups and networking can be of great assistance in the process as well (Maniacci, 1991).

Exploring the Relational Dynamics

Conjoint sessions begin as soon as possible. Clinicians must be sensitive to the danger of overstimulating the newly stabilized partner, a fact that Anderson, Reiss, and Hogarty (1986) review. Research into negative expressed emotion and relapse rates of discharged schizophrenic patients provides guidelines for therapists. Too much "heavy" confrontation, interpretation, and intensity usually do more harm than good, particularly during the early stages of treatment (Pittman, 1987). No one is blamed, no one is told that he or she "caused" the psychosis; rather, the couple is to understand that somehow, some way, the psychosis emerged in order for the patient to deal with an untenable situation. It was his or her way of saying, "Time out! I can't handle this." If we are going to prevent this from happening again, the therapist says, we all need to find out just exactly what "this" was and how it got so far. The patient was trying to communicate something, and it is time we all listen and see whether there is anything we can learn from what happened. An additional statement is made by this clinician, which can be something like this:

> I'm an expert in psychology and psychotherapy, but you [the couple] are experts on each other. What I know about the brain, personality, and interpersonal relations has to be combined with what you know about yourselves. If we combine our knowledge, we'll probably get somewhere; but if you look solely to me to "figure this damn thing out," it may take a very long time and we'll probably hit a lot of blind alleys before we get to where we're going. Therefore, I need your help . . .

Most people find this approach agreeable. The therapeutic stance establishes the clinician as an expert, a needed guide during this disruptive, tumultuous disorder, but it models collaboration, cooperation, and mutual respect, a process many couples must introduce into their transactions with each other.

In the case of the psychotic/controlling pair, the potentially stressful pressure that the nonpsychotic partner places on the psychotic partner has to be explored. *Rarely, if ever, does the nonpsychotic partner deliberately intend to "stress out" his or her partner. More often than not, the stress is an unintended consequence based on misguided attempts to "help" improve life for the couple.* Similarly, in the case of the psychotic/dependent pair, it is important to explore the stress of the failed attempts at finding a fulfilling sense of intimacy and the burden the psychotic partner feels in regard to his or her partner.

Many of the traditional techniques, including family-of-origin work, analysis of transactions and communication patterns, and exploration of central themes in the couple's relationship, will be used but in a less intensive, less provocative manner. For psychotic individuals, the issue is not what level of functioning can be attained in between episodes, but what level can be maintained throughout the life span. Too much in-session intensity all too often translates into too much intensity at home, and unless the therapist keeps a careful eye on the proceedings, such intensity usually serves to exacerbate the dynamics, not change them.

Modifying Individual Dynamics

As each partner feels more confident and the crisis passes, the therapeutic contract can be renegotiated to explore how the selection of this particular partner could have been an attempt to work out/improve/perpetuate an ongoing, long-standing issue for each of the pair. As Dreikurs (1946) has noted, the dynamics that drew a couple together are generally the dynamics that pull them apart, should they separate. Psychotic partners who are drawn to their controlling counterparts initially find those partners to be well organized, methodical, responsible, and even a bit inspiring. After years of living with such a style, it is not uncommon to find those same individuals complaining that their partners are rigid, tyrannical, lacking in spontaneity, and demanding. The behavior in and of itself has not radically changed, but the meaning, the value ascribed to it, has changed. What was once cherished (at best) or tolerated (at worst) is now difficult (at best) or impossible (at worst).

The psychotic partners must explore their tendencies to communicate indirectly, metaphorically, and irregularly. Their private worlds have to be articulated in consensual terms. The duality of their cognitive style must be addressed. On the one hand, they accept the common, consensual goals the rest of their social network accepts. On the other hand, they have a private, personal agenda that they barely express, even to themselves. This private sense of what is important and how it cannot be shared has to be explored, both in individual sessions and later in couples' sessions. Withdrawing as a problem-solving enterprise and speaking in symbolic, metaphoric terms as an acceptable alternative to communicating directly must be explored.

As practice is gained in communicating more realistically, in-session behavioral training and skill building can be utilized. The skills learned and rehearsed in session can be applied at home, as can such frequently helpful but often overlooked skill-building exercises such as leisure training, progressive relaxation, and assertiveness training (Maniacci, 1991).

A Final Step

A final phase of treatment entails returning to one of the earlier phases, that is, the management of the psychotic episode. Its previous usefulness in attaining a certain goal, the warning signs of its being used yet again, and how to manage such a "relapse" should it emerge are discussed. "Emergency procedures," such as the freedom and knowledge of how and when to take extra doses of medications, the judicious use of "time out" methods, systematic desensitization, and how to set up and best utilize emergency sessions, if taught to the couple, can give them a greater sense of responsibility and mastery over their future.

CASE STUDY

Dan and Vicky were referred for help after Dan's third psychiatric admission, his second in the last three years. He was in an acute psychotic state, unresponsive to medication, and nearing discharge from the hospital. The couple were referred by their married adult daughter, Sharon, who had seen the clinician some years earlier for a mild but increasingly chronic depressive condition that responded well to couple therapy. Sharon had found the conjoint sessions with her husband to be so helpful that she referred two of her sisters for similar issues over the course of a two-year period.

Dan was in his early 60s, retired from a local union trade job, and married to Vicky for well over 30 years. They had seven children, all but the youngest grown and married (she was away at college, finishing her last year), and had been adjusting to life in retirement. Vicky continued to work, though at reduced hours, as an independent real estate agent. Some three weeks prior to admission, Dan had been in his second car accident in three years. The damage to the cars was extensive, but in both cases no one was seriously injured. Just as with the first accident, Dan's "upset" over this accident did not seem to abate with time. Over a period of weeks, his ruminations became uncontrollable and his mood labile, and he began speaking of plots against him, his family colluding to "ruin" him, and the police being out to "destroy" him. Neuroleptic medication was prescribed again by the psychiatrist who had treated him after the first accident. However, as with the earlier experience, although the medication appeared to calm his agitation, his ideation was unaffected and he was hospitalized. No psychotherapy was recommended during either hospitalization because, as the attending psychiatrist told the family (and later, this clinician), "This is a chemical imbalance—therapy with these things never works."

Dan's first hospitalization, some 10 years or so prior to his current one, had been occasioned by similar symptoms that occurred after an incident at work, reported to be a serious error that resulted in much lost time and money to the company, for which he almost lost his job. He signed himself out of the hospital at that time, refused medication, and simply "got on with life," as his family put it. It worked, and he had no recurrence of psychotic symptoms until his first car accident.

At this time, Dan wanted to get out of the hospital, his benefits were running out, and his family's patience with the current course of treatment was wearing thin. He and Vicky agreed, reluctantly, to try psychotherapy. He was accepted for treatment with two stipulations: first, given the severity of his psychotic symptomology, the medication was to be continued under the care of a psychiatrist, preferably one who was somewhat more amenable to psychotherapeutic approaches; and, second, Dan *and* Vicky would agree to come to sessions, with Vicky initially serving as cotherapist to learn how to help manage her husband during his psychotic episodes. They agreed, and he signed himself out of the hospital after consulting with and then switching to another psychiatrist within the same group practice. They were seen for a course of 15 sessions over a four-and-a-half-month period. The new psychiatrist prescribed Navane, 1 mg twice a day, and Doxipin, 25 mg twice a day.

Stage One: Managing the Psychosis (Sessions 1–4)

During the first crucial sessions, Dan reported sporadic medication compliance. He was delusional, believing that people were breaking into his house and "burying" his medication, sometimes replacing it with "poison." He thought that these people were his former employers. Vicky was noticeably upset by this talk, but she persisted. The triad approach—meaning, purpose, and response—was tried with his delusions.

> **Delusion:** "My former employers are breaking into my house, burying my medication, and occasionally substituting poison in its place."

Meaning: We explored what such a delusion might mean to him and finally hit on the following. "My employers are tired of having to be responsible for my screw-ups! They can't wait to get rid of me!" (They still paid his benefits.)

Purpose: He felt his work issues were intruding ("breaking") into his home life. He was seeking reassurance that he was not a burden to his wife and family.

Response: "It must be hard to feel like such a burden after all those years of useful contribution. Tell me, what can we do to help you feel as though you're a contributing member again?"

This worked. After two sessions, Vicky and Dan reported that with this approach the delusion ended, despite his still being inconsistent with his medication. Another delusion, one he hadn't even reported to his new psychiatrist, was presented.

Delusion: "The police officers and judge [adjudicating the accident] are out to destroy me!"

Meaning: "Making mistakes is horrible. Those who commit them are in for a lot of trouble, and I should not make mistakes. If I do, I deserve to be severely punished."

Response: "You really do have high standards for yourself. You value perfection and should not allow yourself to have anything less than that. I/we admire your determination to be so good."

Once again, this response seemed to calm him down. Vicky started using it and even began to get smiles and some occasional grins from Dan when she used the phrases. This, along with the aforementioned response and several others, helped stabilize Dan's condition.

Stage Two: Calling in the Nonpsychotic Partner (Sessions 1–4)

Vicky was seen once without Dan; for the rest of the time during this phase she was in session with him. She was frustrated, guilty, and quite worried. She loved her husband very much, and seeing him "like this" was wearing on her. We explored how she could take care of herself, something she admitted she had never been any good at. The oldest born in a family of nine, she had taken care of other people her whole life.

Dan was the youngest of two children in his family, having a very powerful older sister who sometimes "babied" him. Vicky felt it was her responsibility to look after him; after all, he did need some looking after, always did, probably always would. A "vacation" was prescribed for her. Every week, she was to take one evening; after making sure that Dan was all right, she was to go and do something for herself, no matter how trivial or inconsequential it might be. Though she was initially resistant to this suggestion, it was pointed out that Dan's therapy might be a long, trying affair, and her strength and assistance throughout would not only be needed but was crucial to its success. If she did not "pace herself" now, she might not have the energy for the long haul. This helped, and she did take some time for herself.

Stage Three: Modifying the Relational Dynamics (Sessions 4–11)

This was a challenging stage. The couple had been together for a long time, produced and launched a robust family, managed their lives relatively well, and were, by and large, happy with things the way they were. For the most part, they were right to express a measure of satisfaction. This couple had many strengths that should be acknowledged and appreciated not only during sessions, but as "homework assignments" in between sessions as well. They were instructed to "count their blessings" and focus on how secure they had helped make the lives of their children, their grandchildren, and each other. This was hard for Dan, who was beginning to understand the meaning of his symptoms: he felt he had "ruined" his image as the patriarch of the family. Being raised in a strict Catholic household, he believed in the power of confession and atonement of sins. His symptoms were placed in that context—he was busy confessing his sins and seeking atonement, which seemed to comfort him.

This relationship was a variant on the psychotic/controlling pairing discussed earlier. Vicky had high standards, not only for her husband and children, but for herself. She was a dominant, tough-minded individual who pushed herself hard and expected her husband to do the same. Dan was less driven. He was a very ambitious man but relatively quiet, unintrusive, and a bit of a loner. He characterized himself as a "big dreamer with little drive, but lots of great ideas." Vicky was generally regarded as the steam that powered his engine. The issue of the balance of power in the relationship was gently raised.

Dan, after much gentle nudging, admitted he was intimidated by his wife—not as much by her yelling (which she seldom did) as by her "goddamn perfection!" She was always on the go, constantly giving, giving, and giving some more. Now that "they" were retired—though it bothered him that she did not retire with him—she was still busy taking care of the kids, the grandkids, and the neighbors. Dan felt pressure, for money was going to be tight for a while until he hit a certain age when the rest of his benefit package would begin. As of now, he was receiving only part of it, and that had to do until the "whole thing kicked in."

Vicky said that while, yes, money was tighter than usual, she could still afford to do for the children and grandchildren. She said that Dan was worrying over nothing. Dan vehemently protested, in what was one of the more emotionally charged sessions of the treatment. Sure enough, that night, his psychotic symptoms "returned," but he had the ability to take an extra dose of medication (which was still being taken sporadically—he had discontinued the Doxipin but was willing to use the Navane on an as-needed basis) and some knowledge of how his mind worked, as he put it. He and Vicky scheduled an emergency session, and we explored what had kept him up all night worrying and thinking "crazy thoughts."

He saw himself as a failure. Money was tight and would be tight for some time, and he had had not one, but two accidents. That kind of stuff was not supposed to happen to him. How could he have been so careless? This led the couple to the insight that that was precisely what he had thought about his "accident" at work, some 10 years earlier. He was struggling with whether he could take care of himself, as against needing someone to "always" look over his shoulder. His belief, after three "accidents," was that he had never really "grown up" and, therefore, he was a failure. He still needed someone to look after him.

Vicky was surprised—and a bit angry. She thought he was "pushing it now" with his self-pity. So what if she needed to be so assertive? *He needed it!* Dan was stunned. We explored the implications of such a statement over the course of the next several sessions.

Through the use of role playing, role reversal, and mapping, the couple were shown their typical interactional style. Vicky was the patient, strong one who completed Dan's sentences, organized his schedule, and "ran things" in general. Dan, while outwardly protesting, "set her up" for such behavior. His tendency to hesitate, to be indecisive, often "invited" Vicky to jump in, take over, and quietly assume he couldn't do it, not that he didn't want to.

For her part, Vicky began to understand how she encouraged Dan to be slow, to hesitate, in order for her to have reason to "jump in." She was experiencing a belated empty-nest syndrome. The last of her children did not need her anymore (or so she felt), and her purpose in life was slipping away. Through her job, she could still assure that she had a place in life by helping others to feel at home, find a home, create a home. She was continuing in her role as a "homemaker."

Dan, while admittedly glad that she was working and bringing in some income, had ascribed a completely different meaning to her decision to continue working. He had assumed it was a signal that his skill as a provider was lacking. It had not occurred to him that she was simply finding a way to maintain her role as homemaker.

They were instructed to notice when she treated him like one of her children. He was instructed to periodically act like one of the children. This was to be his "gift" to Vicky, his way of "taking care of her" and giving her something to do. She, for her part, was to encourage him to act "helpless" or "childlike" every now and then. They genuinely seemed to enjoy this phase of the treatment. Both appeared to soften their overall demeanor.

These changes helped to reduce the tension in the home considerably. Dan was taking little, if any, medication, except to help him sleep, and his psychotic symptoms were gone. What was left was rumination about money. Though far from delusional in proportion, it caused him a great deal of stress, and Vicky reported that both she and the children were growing tired of hearing him talk about finances. Dan, while reporting that the sessions had seemed to help him considerably, was feeling that he was spending too much time in therapy and that the time to stop was nearing. Vicky and the children all felt that ending therapy would be a mistake, that not only Dan, but the couple, seemed to be doing well. Dan revealed that he was concerned about using up his benefit package. He would give therapy just a little while longer, then he would stop. We agreed and then set out to explore some individual dynamics in greater detail.

Stage Four: Modifying Individual Dynamics (Sessions 6–15)

Dan reported the following set of early recollections:

> **Age 6 years:** I remember being locked in a closet, at home. My [female] cousins wouldn't let me out. I had to punch the glass window on the door to break out. They were all surprised.
> **Most vivid moment:** Being locked in the closet.
> **Feeling:** Good, it was fun.

> **Age 4 years:** I set fire to the curtains. Mom came running out of the bedroom, naked, and put out the fire.
> **Most vivid moment:** Holding the match to the curtains.
> **Feeling:** I did something wrong.

> **Age 4 years:** I had an appendicitis attack. There were people all around me while I was on the floor.

Most vivid moment: Being on the floor.
Feeling: Scared, something was really wrong with me, and all
these people were around.

Age 2 years. George, my cousin, was coming over to baby-sit
me. I'm at the top of the stairs watching him come up.
Most vivid moment: He's coming up the stairs.
Feeling: Excited.

The use of early recollections as a projective technique has received considerable support and attention in the clinical literature (Adler, 1956;
Bruhn, 1990; Mosak, 1958). These four memories reveal Dan's basic attitude toward himself, life, and others. With Vicky's and Dan's help, we
began to search for themes in each of the memories.

From the first one, of being in the closet at age six, we pulled the
following issues. It's sometimes not so bad to be isolated, especially
from women. After all, it's the women who cause him to be isolated. He
can break through the isolation by creating a little excitement and
mischief.

From the second memory, the one about the fire, we culled these
issues. Dan can create some excitement, and when he does, a woman will
come running to his aid, especially if it involves dealing with a crisis he
"starts."

The third memory, about the appendicitis, led us to this conclusion: when
Dan's feeling low and hurting, it's nice to have people rally around him.
Sometimes he hurts a great deal for reasons of which he is not always
aware.

The final memory, involving his cousin coming to baby-sit, reinforced
many of the preceding issues. Dan likes having people come to him. It ele-
vates him and makes him feel excited.

From all of the memories, we composed this summary:

Dan is a man who, under the right conditions, values people and excitement. He looks forward to their coming to him, but he realizes that too
much attention, especially from women, can lead him to seek isolation.
People should take care of him and help him control what he starts,
especially when it looks as if what he starts may get out of his control.
Sometimes he hurts inside and feels really low, though he will not necessarily communicate that to others; yet somehow they should know and
come running.

He and Vicky found the assessment to be fascinating. The connections
to his current situation were strikingly clear to him. A new, heretofore
untouched issue emerged. Dan was feeling isolated. He had retired, and
his contacts with friends had decreased dramatically. His children didn't

come by as much as they used to, and he was lonely. With Vicky working and Dan not being as busy as he was in the past, he had trouble structuring his own time and found himself drinking more than he thought he should. His first automobile accident happened while he was intoxicated. The second, fortunately, had not, but the guilt and the knowing looks from his children and friends gave him the feeling that they suspected more than they said. Vicky admitted that, yes, the children were concerned. She had assured them that their father was *not* drinking at the time of the accident. Nonetheless, this constituted a stress. Dan had controlled his drinking on his own.

The ruminations about money were reframed as his attempt to achieve two purposes. First, he was trying to communicate indirectly to Vicky and the children that he was concerned about *their* spending too much of his money. He could never imagine himself saying something like that to them, but he was concerned, and by creating the ruminations about whether he had enough money to live on he very subtly communicated his desire that they curtail their requests. It worked, and the kids had stopped asking for things as much as they had in the past. Vicky, however, was still spending on them, and Dan was trying to communicate to her to "cool it." He could not express his concern verbally to her, but still she responded by curtailing her spending.

The second purpose was less obvious but more emotionally significant to Dan. He was asking for attention from his children and from Vicky. He wanted her to spend more time with him and less at work. She was stunned. She had felt that he saw her as in his way, that he would be glad to get her out of his hair. One of the more tender moments of the treatment involved his admitting how much she still meant to him, even after more than 30 years of marriage.

A "visitation" schedule with the children was set up. He would no longer simply rely on them to visit him; he would have to go and seek them out. In addition, a similar schedule was established for use with his friends, whom he had let "slip" out of sight since his retirement. Next, Dan would spend part of his time going back to work. He took on a part-time, small, easy-paced job in town that helped ease his financial worries; more important, it structured his time. Finally, a paradoxical prescription was established. Dan did not like it as much as the other ideas, but Vicky absolutely loved it.

In one of the final sessions a letter was drafted by the clinician, addressed to the children and given to Vicky to send should certain preconditions be met. If Dan continued to vocally communicate his ruminations about money the way he did, he would drive everybody away. If he did not tone down his ruminations, Vicky was instructed to send the letter, which stated the following:

To The _____ Children:

As you know, your father has had some considerable pressures placed on him in the last several months. He is a proud man who takes his obligations seriously. Should you hear him speaking too much about his concern over money, acknowledge his fears and gently change the topic. Should he continue, please reach into your wallet and give him a dollar for every time he complains.

Thank you for your time,

Vicky, who had been frustrated and somewhat embarrassed by her husband's constant references to money, thought this was wonderful. Even Dan had to laugh, though he found the thought of his children giving him money extremely distasteful. By his own admission, he found this letter rather bothersome, was none too fond of the therapist for writing it ("Gee, Doc, I thought you were on my side. How could you do a thing like that to me?"), and proceeded to decrease his comments about money—at least within earshot of others. (A footnote: Vicky thought she would make a copy of the letter for several of her girlfriends, whose husbands had similar complaints.) The letter never had to be sent.

Vicky's individual dynamics were addressed as well, though with much less specificity. Her role as a caretaker, leader, and at times too much of a controller was addressed. She knew she had to walk a fine line between maintaining the role that had worked so well for so long and overdoing it to the point of recreating the very dynamics that helped give rise to some of her husband's symptoms.

The final three sessions were spaced appropriately as we began to taper off the therapy. Follow-up phone calls were scheduled at one month, three months, six months, and one year. As of one year, Dan remains symptom free, off medication, and working part-time. Vicky reports good progress toward "backing off," but still shows some tendencies to overregulate Dan's life. The couple have recently referred one of their daughter's best friends for therapy, Dan sending along this caveat about "that therapist": Don't let him write any letters.

REFERENCES

Adler, A. (1956). *The individual psychology of Alfred Adler*. H. L. Ansbacher & R. R. Ansbacher, Eds. New York: Harper Torchbooks.

Adler, A. (1983a). *The neurotic constitution*. B. Glueck & J. E. Lind, Trans. Salem, NH: Ayer Company. (Original work published 1912.)

Adler, A. (1983b). *The practice and theory of Individual Psychology*. P. Radin, Trans. Totowa, NJ: Rowman & Allanheld. (Original work published 1920.)

American Psychiatric Association. (1994). *Diagnostic and statistical manual of mental disorders* (4th ed.). Washington, DC: Author.

Anderson, C. M., Reiss, D. J., & Hogarty, G. E. (1986). *Schizophrenia and the family: A practitioner's guide to psychoeducation and management.* New York: Guilford.

Andreasen, N. C. (1984). *The broken brain: The biological revolution in psychiatry.* New York: Harper & Row.

Anonymous. (1994). First-person account: Life with a mentally ill spouse. *Schizophrenia Bulletin, 1,* 227–229.

Beck, A. T. (1985). Cognitive therapy, behavior therapy, psychoanalysis, and pharmacotherapy: A cognitive continuum. In M. J. Mahoney & A. Freeman (Eds.), *Cognition and psychotherapy* (pp. 325–347). New York: Plenum.

Brekke, J. S., Levin, S., Wolkon, G. H., Sobel, E., & Slade, E. (1993). Psychosocial functioning and subjective experience in schizophrenia. *Schizophrenia Bulletin, 3,* 599–608.

Bruhn, A. R. (1990). Cognitive-perceptual theory and the projective use of autobiographical memory. *Journal of Personality Assessment, 55*(1 & 2), 95–114.

Carpenter, W. T., Jr. (1987). Approaches to knowledge and understanding of schizophrenia. *Schizophrenia Bulletin, 13,* 1–8.

Dreikurs, R. (1946). *The challenge of marriage.* New York: Duell, Sloan & Pearce.

Erikson, E. H. (1963). *Childhood and society* (2d ed.). New York: W. W. Norton. (Original work published 1950.)

Gabbard, G. O. (1994). Mind and brain in psychiatric treatment. *Bulletin of the Menninger Clinic, 58,* 427–446.

Garza-Trevino, E. S., Volkow, N. D., Cancro, R., & Contreras, S. (1990). Neurobiology of schizophrenic syndromes. *Hospital and Community Psychiatry, 41,* 971–980.

Hafner, R. J. (1986). *Marriage and mental illness: A sex-roles perspective.* New York: Guilford.

Maniacci, M. P. (1991). Guidelines for developing social interest with clients in psychiatric day hospitals. *Individual Psychology: The Journal of Adlerian Theory, Research & Practice, 47,* 177–188.

Mosak, H. H., (1958). Early recollections as a projective technique. *Journal of Projective Techniques, 22,* 302–311.

Mosak, H. H., & Fletcher, S. J. (1973). Purposes of delusions and hallucinations. *Journal of Individual Psychology, 29,* 176–181.

Mosak, H. H., & Maniacci, M. P. (1989). An approach to the understanding of "schizophrenese." *Individual Psychology: The Journal of Adlerian Theory, Research & Practice, 45,* 465–472.

Pittman, F. S., III. (1987). *Turning points: Treating families in transitions and crisis.* New York: W. W. Norton.

Shulman, B. H. (1984). *Essays in schizophrenia* (2d ed.). Chicago: Alfred Adler Institute.

Sperry, L., & Carlson, J. (Eds.). (1993). *Psychopathology and psychotherapy: From diagnosis to treatment.* Muncie, IN: Accelerated Development.

Sullivan, H. S. (1953). *The interpersonal theory of psychiatry.* New York: W. W. Norton.

Winefield, H. R., & Harvey, E. J. (1994). Needs of family caregivers in chronic schizophrenia. *Schizophrenia Bulletin, 3,* 557–566.

CHAPTER 5

The Sexually Dysfunctional Couple: Vaginismus and Relationship Enhancement Therapy

Marsha J. Harman
Michael Waldo
James A. Johnson

When a couple come for therapy because their sexual relationship is unsatisfactory due to reported sexual dysfunction on the part of one or both spouses, a therapist may find a systemic approach helpful in concep-tualizing and treating the difficulty. One systemic approach the authors have found beneficial is Relationship Enhancement Marriage and Family Therapy. The following sections briefly describe the sexual dysfunction known as vaginismus, then describe Relationship Enhancement Marriage and Family Therapy and how it can be a useful approach in treating vaginismus. A case study provides an example of how Relationship Enhancement (RE) therapy was utilized with a couple in which the woman was diagnosed with vaginismus.

Note: This chapter draws heavily from research previously published as "Relationship Enhancement Therapy: A Case Study for Treatment of Vaginismus" in *The Family Journal: Counseling and Therapy for Couples and Families, 2,* 122–128.

DSM-IV AND VAGINISMUS

Sexual dysfunction is described by the DSM-IV (American Psychiatric Association, 1994) as an inhibition in sexual desire or in the psychophysiologic changes that characterize the sexual response cycle, including excitement, orgasm, and/or resolution. The dysfunction may be described as lifelong or acquired and as generalized or situational. Its etiology may include psychological factors or a combination of psychological and medical factors. Vaginismus is characterized as a recurrent or persistent involuntary spasm of the musculature (pubococcygeus) of the outer third of the vagina, which interferes with coitus. Masters, Johnson, and Kolodny (1988) estimated that 2 to 3 percent of all postadolescent women have vaginismus. Reid (1989) suggested that in some cases vaginismus is at least in part a physiological manifestation of emotional conflict. Women who experience these spasms of the pubococcygeus and related muscles have difficulty engaging in intercourse but may be quite capable of becoming sexually aroused, lubricating, and experiencing multiple orgasms (Leiblum, Pervin, & Campbell, 1989). The DSM-IV indicates that vaginismus may be diagnosed when the disturbance causes marked distress not caused solely by a physical disorder and is not attributed to another Axis I disorder. In addition, the disturbance may contribute to interpersonal problems between the couple.

THEORETICAL PERSPECTIVES

Religious orthodoxy, psychosexual trauma, psychological conflict, marital conflict, and social factors in the family of origin have been reported as contributing to vaginismus (Leiblum, Pervin, & Campbell, 1989; Rathus, 1983). In their treatment of many cases of vaginismus, Masters and Johnson (1970) found religious orthodoxy to frequently be a contributing factor. In addition, they found that in several cases the husband had developed erectile dysfunction as a result of repeated failure to achieve intromission.

Anxiety is a potentially important component of vaginismus, resulting in a tightening of the vaginal muscles and exacerbating the problem (Barbach, 1984). Rathus (1983) suggested that vaginismus most frequently stems from fear or other negative emotions concerning intercourse. Anxiety in a marital relationship, especially concerning sexuality, can then be seen as contributing to vaginismus. Indeed, Kaplan (1974) maintained that alleviation of the patient's anxiety is the initial objective of treatment.

Drenth (1988) explored vaginismus from a psychoanalytic orientation and suggested that it might be a conversion reaction. Kaplan (1974), on the other hand, viewed vaginismus as multicausal, resulting in a conditioned response. Meanwhile, learning theorists have viewed vaginismus as a phobia (Leiblum, Pervin, & Campbell, 1989). Masters and Johnson (1970) utilized a behavioral approach with couples, including demonstrations of the automaticity of the vaginal spasm and the insertion of a series of dilators of graduated size, eventually with the wife guiding the husband's insertion efforts. Rathus (1983) maintained that the behavioral treatment of vaginismus was appropriate, but added that sex therapy does not take place in an emotional and intellectual vacuum and that women patients often benefit from exploring the origins and meaning of the problem.

IMPLICATIONS FOR COUPLES

The experience of vaginismus contributes extraordinary stress to a marital relationship. The barrier to intimacy and fulfillment imposed by vaginismus generates distance and frustration in marriages. The stress is exacerbated when no physiological reason for the disorder can be isolated. The wife may question her identity as a woman, while the husband questions his identity as a man and his wife's desire for him. Both partners may fear the loss of opportunity to procreate. They may suspect each other's motivation and commitment. Communication may collapse. Such stress and lack of communication can lead to increased anxiety, which may heighten the vaginismus symptoms. Moreover, anxiety and poor communication can impede the couple's ability to take cooperative action to overcome the disorder.

TREATMENT APPROACHES

Recent treatment has focused on resolving sexual trauma using cognitive-behavioral models (McCarthy, 1992) and extensive sexual histories (McCarthy, 1990). Russell (1990) has described a model that utilizes a combined treatment approach to enhance physical and emotional intimacy.

Comprehensive treatment of vaginismus includes reading and participating in exercises that address communication skills, problem solving, and sexual dysfunction (Bornstein et al., 1984). Exercises for sexual dysfunction often include physical deconditioning of the vaginal musculature by graduated dilation of the vaginal opening accompanied by psychotherapeutic involvement. Psychotherapy concentrates on communication skills and the cognitive and affective domains. It is recommended that control of the sexual act be given to the client suffering from vaginismus (Barbach, 1984; Reid, 1989). It is also highly recommended that exercises be described in detail and provided in writing by the clinician. The dilation exercises and sexual activity should be carried out in privacy by the client (Masters & Johnson, 1970; Reid, 1989). Furthermore, therapists usually prefer that the husband be involved in the developmental process and progress maintenance in the treatment of vaginismus (Leiblum, Pervin, & Campbell, 1989; Masters, Johnson, & Kolodny, 1988).

RELATIONSHIP ENHANCEMENT THERAPY

The goal of Relationship Enhancement (RE) therapy (Guerney, 1977) is to impart attitudes and skills that will enable the participants to relate to significant others in ways that will maximize satisfaction of emotional and functional needs. RE therapy trains clients to express themselves fully and honestly in a manner that is least likely to provoke anxiety and defensiveness on the part of the spouses. It also trains clients to offer acceptance and understanding to their spouses when they are expressing themselves, resulting in the speaker's feeling respected and trustful in the relationship.

Use of these skills has been shown to increase trust and intimacy in marital couples (Guerney, 1987), which can facilitate the couple's supporting each other as they engage in treatment activities to overcome vaginismus. In addition, previous studies (Barrow, 1984; Bartol, 1983; Berkowitz, 1982; La Monica, Wolf, Madea, & Oberst, 1987; Mutchler, Hunt, Koopman, & Mutchler, 1991) have suggested that a person's receiving empathy is associated with reductions in anxiety. A general reduction of anxiety in their marital relationships may benefit clients suffering from vaginismus. If RE skills were used by a couple specifically to discuss their sexuality, it seems likely that anxiety about sexuality could be reduced, which would assist the couple in overcoming vaginismus.

Of the nine skills taught in RE therapy, the three fundamental skills are Expressive, Empathic, and Discussion/Negotiation. Detailed specific guidelines that participants follow in using these skills are described elsewhere (Guerney, 1977, 1987). Essentially, the purposes of these skills are discussed in the following paragraphs (Guerney, 1987):

Expresser

As Expressers, individuals are coached to express emotions, thoughts, and desires clearly and honestly, without generating unnecessary hostility and defensiveness in the recipient of the communication. They are taught to (1) state things in a way that acknowledges the subjectivity of perceptions and judgments, such as "I believe," "It seems to me," "By my standards . . ."; (2) associate the issue with the specific feelings; (3) identify the underlying positive feelings they have toward their partners; (4) be specific; and (5) offer a suggestion as to how the situation could be improved (stated subjectively, linked to feelings, and specific).

Empathic Responder

As Empathic Responders, individuals are coached to convey acceptance of others' communication and to show understanding of their perceptions, thoughts, and feelings, as follows: (1) temporarily put aside their own beliefs and judgments about what's being said; (2) imagine themselves in the others' place to determine how the others think and feel about the issue; (3) convey understanding and acceptance by tone, posture, and facial expression, as well as by stating the others' most important thoughts, conflicts, desires, and feelings.

Discussion/Negotiation

The third skill, Discussion/Negotiation, is the method of switching back and forth between Expresser and Empathic Responder as a dialogue progresses. Important aspects of this skill include making switches in a manner that allows for thorough expression and understanding and facilitates interpersonal and intrapersonal knowledge as well as solving problems or conflicts.

CASE STUDY

The use of RE therapy has been reported with abusive couples (Guerney, Waldo, & Firestone, 1987; Waldo, 1988), an alcoholic couple (Waldo & Guerney, 1983), and premarital couples (Ridley, Jorgensen, Morgan, & Avery, 1982). In addition, RE has been used with college roommates (Waldo, 1989), students and their teachers (Rocks, Baker, & Guerney, 1985), parents and adolescents (Guerney, Coufal, & Vogelsong, 1981), and single females (Overton & Avery, 1984). RE has been demonstrated to be beneficial in reducing tension and increasing trust and intimacy in marital relations (Brock & Joanning, 1983; Granvold, 1983; Jessee & Guerney, 1981; Waldo & Harman, 1993), and research has shown it to be a highly effective form of therapy for a variety of personal and interpersonal concerns (Giblin, Sprenkle, & Sheehan, 1985; Ross, Baker, & Guerney, 1985). To our knowledge, this is the first report of a case study in which RE was used to treat sexual dysfunction in a couple.

This study includes a brief description of the clients' background as a couple; the therapy process; a transcript of the couple's interaction, using RE skills, during a therapy session; and outcome data.

Clients

Tim and Dawn entered couples therapy after Dawn had attended approx-imately 12 sessions of individual psychotherapy and her physician had diagnosed her as having vaginismus. The physician and the individual therapist recommended marital therapy. Both Tim and Dawn were 21 years of age and had been married one year. They had met approximately two years earlier and had decided to marry because Dawn became preg-nant. Prior to the marriage, Dawn miscarried during the first trimester shortly after Tim had returned to college. Following the miscarriage, Dawn relocated to the city in which Tim resided and moved in with him. They were married several months later. Dawn reported that sexual inter-course was always painful, that Tim was concerned about his orgasm only and not hers, and that she was distracted by thinking about household chores while engaged in coitus. Tim reported that it did not matter what he did, that he simply could not please Dawn in any area of their marriage, including sexual intercourse.

Therapy Process

A male therapist and a female therapist worked with this couple. First, the rationale for using RE skills was offered to begin the process of attitude change. Then the skills were demonstrated, and, finally, the couple were coached as they practiced the skills. When the couple had become compe-tent in their use of RE skills, they employed the skills during the therapy sessions to discuss their sexual relationship. Educational information was provided for Dawn regarding masturbation and dilation of the vaginal musculature, followed by instruction regarding how to teach Tim what was comfortable for her. Two of Barbach's books (Barbach & Levine, 1981; Barbach, 1984) were provided, and the vaginismus exercises were reviewed with the couple.

Both Dawn and Tim expressed negative attitudes toward self-stimulation. Dawn initially expressed reluctance to attempt the exercises and criticized the readings. The therapists retreated from expecting compliance with the exercises and allowed Dawn the freedom to reject this aspect of treatment. Dawn concentrated on working with Tim regarding issues that impacted their sexual relationship. However, several weeks later Dawn reported hav-ing been successful in self-stimulation and other exercises that increased her knowledge of her individual and unique sexual responses.

Tim struggled with values instilled by family and church regarding sexual practices. He also struggled with Dawn's response to him and his resignation to his perception that it was impossible to please her.

An important aspect of helping a couple through RE is to assist participants to share fully their emotions and desires with their partners. The therapists reasoned from clinical experience that a couple with sexual dysfunction could use the assistance of RE to fully express their emotions and desires concerning sexuality with each other. Coaching clients in the Expresser role contributes to the process, because this skill requires that the clients be specific, fully express their emotions, talk about their desires, and make specific requests. Coaching clients in the Empathic role helps them offer understanding and respect to the thoughts and feelings the Expresser is trying to convey. This allows the Expresser to feel accepted, reducing his or her anxiety. The following transcripts from early therapy sessions demonstrate how the couple were coached to offer each other empathy and to be fully expressive.

Coaching Empathy

Tim: I sometimes get disturbed when you don't want to have sex, and I guess I feel sometimes that you're rejecting me. I sometimes feel that you do it a lot.

Dawn: You're disturbed when I don't want to have sex, and you feel like I'm rejecting you. Is that as a person or as a sexual person?

Male Therapist (MT): Just show understanding to what he is saying.

Dawn: Well, I'm unclear on what he's saying. I don't understand.

MT: You've got what he's said so far; that was beautiful. Now if you could just stop, and (*to Tim*) you could go on.

Tim: That's how I feel sometimes. Sometimes I feel real confused. I think: Why don't you want to have sex, why don't you want to have sex more often? Sometimes I don't understand why I get excited a lot and you don't get as excited as I do.

MT: (*To Tim*) That's great. Could you add any emotion that causes in you?

Tim: I'm not sure I know. I think confusion. Is that an emotion?

MT: Could there be some hurt?

Tim: Uh . . . no, not always. Well, yeah, sometimes.

Dawn: Well, what does the word *rejection* mean?

MT: Dawn, this isn't the time to question.

Dawn: Well, you're asking him about feelings. When he said *rejection*, you said *hurt*, and he said no. So what does he feel when he feels rejected—just nothing?

Tim: Well, it's not that I'm rejected right now. It's that sometimes I'm really confused when you don't want to have sex as often as I do, why you're not as sexual as I am.

Dawn: So, you don't understand why I don't want to have sex as much as you. (*Dawn's tone strongly suggested impatience.*)

Female Therapist (FT): On the cue card here, it says *understanding and acceptance.*

Dawn: I don't understand.

FT: You're not able to do that?

Dawn: No, I don't understand. I keep looking at that and I don't understand how he feels, I guess.

FT: You mean when he tells you he feels hurt, you don't understand?

Dawn: Right, in the sexual sense. How can I understand that? I mean he repeats back what I say. I repeat back what he says.

FT: Well, I think it has to do with . . . in the other handout we gave you, it talks about (*reading*) "convey[ing] understanding and acceptance by tone, posture, facial expression." What I'm concerned about is the tone. It's almost disinterest.

MT: I know it's hard, it's new.

Dawn: Well, maybe I . . . it's hard to act like this is fresh material. I mean he tells me this all the time. So what am I supposed to say? So, you feel rejected as a person? I mean that's a bunch of crap. But I hear this from him all the time, and how can I express that I understand when we've gone through the same thing? And I feel like he's not the problem, I'm the problem. And so I don't get it.

MT: OK, let me talk about that for a second. We can show you how to do it. The question, I think, is more—do you want to do it? What we're hoping to do is get you to a place where you have an effect on him where he's going to feel accepted and understood and he's going to want to talk about his feelings, which will make him more open to think about what's going on for him, which I think has been a problem. Plus, it will make him more likely to listen to you and try to understand you. If those are things that you'd like to try and achieve, I think we can give you a way to do that. As a matter of fact, I bet you know how, actually.

Dawn: Well, yeah . . .

MT: So, to have that effect on him, the trick would be to say—So it hurts you when I don't want to have sex with you and you don't understand—and to say that in a sensitive way.

Dawn: I'll try (*silence*).

MT: Could you please—just go ahead.

Dawn: (*Clears throat*) So it hurts you when I don't want to have sex with you.

Tim: Uh-huh.

MT: That was great, Dawn.

FT: Really good.

Coaching Expression

Dawn: Well, I guess the first thing is that I never thought we were ever romantic, that we have yet to be romantic. I know that may be hurtful, but I thought that we've practically never been romantic. I never thought you've been romantic toward me.

MT: You'd better stop and let him show understanding.

Tim: You think that we've, that we've never been romantic, that romance is not in our relationship or hasn't been.

Dawn: No.

Tim: You think that I'm never, you think that I, that we have not been romantic in the past.

Dawn: 'Cause I remember when we first had sex, it was like let's just get it over with. And after that, we just had sex, there was no relationship.

FT: And the feeling with that?

Dawn: And I felt used, rejected. I kind of felt like a slut.

Tim: So, you felt that when we first met, that we really didn't get to know each other, that we were immediately having sex, that I made you feel used and cheap that we were only having sex and nothing else.

MT: That's really good, you're staying with her. Now if you could cut it down to a few words that will catch her meaning like—*you felt used.*

Tim: OK.

MT: (*To Dawn*) Could I ask you to come up with an emotion? Used is kind of an emotion.

Dawn: I guess I felt lonely.

MT: Right.

Dawn: Anyway, I just felt like it wasn't very special because I'd never had sex before. And it still hurt. My girlfriends kept telling me—oh, it hurts the first couple of times but then it feels better. And I just feel like everyone's lied to me about sex.

Coaching Discussion/Negotiation

The therapists initially coached the skill of discussion/negotiation by asking whether the Expresser felt understood and whether both individuals were ready to switch Expressive and Empathic roles. Eventually, the couple was able to assume this skill and naturally invite role change.

Progress of Therapy

RE therapy provided Tim and Dawn with an arena to express emotions, thoughts, and desires as well as to express understanding and acceptance. Many areas were discussed, including previous sexual experience, respective family attitudes toward sex, religious beliefs, the pregnancy and miscarriage, and fantasies about marriage. Using the skills eventually allowed Dawn to tell Tim, in a nonthreatening manner, what pleased and displeased her in the sexual relationship. Tim was able to share with Dawn, in the same nonthreatening manner, how he felt he could never please her.

Communication resulted in an increase of intimacy and a reduction of anxiety regarding the discussion of sexual matters in general. This reduction in anxiety carried over into the sexual relationship, in that both Tim and Dawn were willing to experiment with their personal sexuality (self-stimulation) as well as their marital sexuality. Dawn, particularly, became less rigid in her beliefs regarding experimenting with her own sexual satisfaction, so that she began to differentiate her sexuality from Tim's and also began to take responsibility for her sexual pleasure in the relationship. Indeed, she even began to initiate sexual encounters with him. Tim began to be less demanding of Dawn in the sexual arena, to be open to self-stimulation rather than relying on her for all his satisfaction. He too read the materials provided for Dawn and began to take more time in the arousal process to facilitate Dawn's pleasure.

They reported that after a particularly unsatisfying sexual encounter, they went out for pizza and decided to use the RE skills to discuss the encounter. Thus, the RE skills were generalized to their personal relationship outside the therapists' office. Six weeks after therapy ended, the couple reported that their relationship was progressing in a positive manner and that both individuals were now maintaining a more effective level of functioning than when therapy had commenced.

SUMMARY AND CONCLUSIONS

The use of RE therapy as a component in the treatment of vaginismus with the couple in the case study appeared successful. They learned to subjectively express themselves and empathize with each other; their communication was less threatening and more focused on discussion and negotiation of problem areas that impacted their sexual relationship both directly and indirectly. Anxiety and guilt diminished while arousability and sexual satisfaction increased. The couple began to trust each other enough to attempt recommended exercises and experiment with their sexual relationship. The transcript excerpts illustrate the need for therapists to coach and train couples in effective communication skills, because the established systemic interaction may prove extremely difficult for even a willing couple to change.

Obviously, this is *one* case study of *one* couple who learned to manage their anxiety, communicate more effectively, and enjoy a more satisfying sexual relationship. Certainly, generalization to all couples from a study of one lone couple is impossible, but the results do encourage further research employing the critical factors of this case, including RE and sexuality education with experimental and control groups. Studies might investigate the effectiveness of a variety of communication therapies in the treatment of vaginismus, the effects of the therapist, the use of cotherapists, the number of sessions needed for effective treatment, and what components and structure constitute comprehensive treatment of vaginismus.

REFERENCES

American Psychiatric Association. (1994). *Diagnostic and statistical manual of mental disorders* (4th ed.). Washington, DC: Author.

Barbach, L. (1984). *For each other: Sharing sexual intimacy.* New York: Signet.

Barbach, L., & Levine, L. (1981). *Shared intimacies: Women's sexual experiences.* New York: Doubleday.

Barrow, R. (1984). Use of personal journals to reduce mathematics anxiety. *Journal of College Student Personnel, 25,* 170–171.

Bartol, M. A. (1983). Reaching the patient. *Geriatric Nursing, 4,* 234–236.

Berkowitz, D. A. (1982). Implications of the self object for the therapeutic alliance. *Hillside Journal of Clinical Psychiatry, 4,* 15–24.

Bornstein, P. H., Wilson, G. L., Balleweg, B. J., Weisser, C. E., Bornstein, M. T., Andre, J. C., Woody, D. J., Smith M. M., Laughna, S. M., McLellarn, R. W., Kirby, K. L., & Hocker, J. (1984). Behavioral marital bibliotherapy: An initial investigation of therapeutic efficacy. *American Journal of Family Therapy, 12,* 21–28.

Brock, G. W., & Joanning, H. (1983). A comparison of the Relationship Enhancement Program and the Minnesota Couple Communication Program. *Journal of Marital and Family Therapy, 9,* 413–421.

Drenth, J. J. (1988). Vaginismus and the desire for a child. *Journal of Psychosomatic Obstetrics and Gynecology, 9,* 125–138.

Giblin, P., Sprenkle, D. H., & Sheehan, R. (1985). Enrichment outcome research: A meta-analysis of premarital, marital, and family interventions. *Journal of Marital and Family Therapy, 11,* 257–271.

Granvold, D. K. (1983). Structured separation for marital treatment and decision making. *Journal of Marital and Family Therapy, 9,* 403–412.

Guerney, B., Jr. (1987). *Relationship Enhancement: Marital/family therapist's manual*, (2d ed.). State College, PA: Ideals.

Guerney, B. G., Jr. (1977). *Relationship Enhancement: Skill-training programs for therapy, problem prevention, and enrichment*. San Francisco: Jossey-Bass.

Guerney, B. G., Jr., Coufal, J., & Vogelsong, E. (1981). Relationship Enhancement versus a traditional approach to therapeutic/preventative/enrichment parent-adolescent programs. *Journal of Consulting and Clinical Psychology, 49*, 927–929.

Guerney, B. G., Jr., Waldo, M., & Firestone, L. (1987). Wife-battering: A theoretical construct and case report. *American Journal of Family Therapy, 15*, 34–43.

Jessee, R. E., & Guerney, B. G., Jr. (1981). A comparison of gestalt and Relationship Enhancement treatments with married couples. *American Journal of Family Therapy, 9*, 31–41.

Kaplan, H. S. (1974). *The new sex therapy: Active treatment of sexual dysfunctions*. New York: Brunner/Mazel.

La Monica, E. L., Wolf, R. M., Madea, A. R., & Oberst, M. T. (1987). Empathy and nursing care outcomes. *Scholarly Inquiry for Nursing Practice, 1*, 197–213.

Leiblum, S. R., Pervin, L. A., & Campbell, E. H. (1989). The treatment of vaginismus: Success and failure. In S. R. Leiblum & R. C. Rosèn (Eds.), *Principles and practice of sex therapy* (2d ed.) (pp. 113–138). New York: Guilford Press.

McCarthy, B. W. (1990). Treating sexual dysfunction associated with prior sexual trauma. *Journal of Sex and Marital Therapy, 16(3)*, 142–146.

McCarthy, B. W. (1992). Sexual trauma: The pendulum has swung too far. *Journal of Sex Education and Therapy, 18(1)*, 1–10.

Masters, W. H., & Johnson, V. E. (1970). *Human sexual inadequacy*. Boston: Little, Brown.

Masters, W. H., Johnson, V. E., & Kolodny, R. C. (1988). *Human sexuality* (3d ed.). Glenview, IL: Scott Foresman.

Mutchler, T. E., Hunt, E. J., Koopman, E. J., & Mutchler, R. D. (1991). Single-parent mother/daughter empathy, relationship adjustment, and functioning of the adolescent child of divorce. *Journal of Divorce and Remarriage, 17*, 115–129.

Overton, D. H. & Avery, A. W. (1984). Relationship Enhancement for single females: Inter-personal network intervention. *Psychology of Women Quarterly, 8*, 376–388.

Rathus, S. A. (1983). *Human sexuality*. New York: Holt, Rinehart, & Winston.

Reid, W. H. (1989). *The treatment of psychiatric disorders: Revised for the DSM-III-R.* New York: Brunner/Mazel.

Ridley, C. A., Jorgensen, S. R., Morgan, A. C., & Avery, A. W. (1982). Relationship enhancement with premarital couples: An enhancement of effects on relationship quality. *American Journal of Family Therapy, 10*, 41–48.

Rocks, T. G., Baker, S. B., & Guerney, B. G., Jr. (1985). Effects of counselor-directed Relationship Enhancement training on underachieving, poorly communicating students and their teachers. *The School Counselor, 32*, 231–238.

Ross, E. R., Baker, S. B., & Guerney, B. G., Jr. (1985). Effectiveness of Relationship Enhancement therapy versus therapist's preferred therapy. *The American Journal of Family Therapy, 13*, 11–21.

Russell, L. (1990). Sex and couples therapy: A method of treatment to enhance physical and emotional intimacy. *Journal of Sex and Marital Therapy, 16(2)*, 111–120.

Waldo, M. (1988). Relationship Enhancement counseling groups for wife abusers. *Journal of Mental Health Counseling, 10,* 37–45.

Waldo, M. (1989). Primary prevention in university residence halls: Paraprofessional-led Relationship Enhancement groups for college room-mates. *Journal of Counseling and Development, 67,* 465–471.

Waldo, M., & Guerney, B. G., Jr. (1983). Marital Relationship Enhancement therapy in the treatment of alcoholism. *Journal of Marital and Family Therapy, 9,* 321–323.

Waldo, M., & Harman, M. J. (1993). Relationship Enhancement therapy with borderline personality. *The Family Journal, 1,* 25–30.

CHAPTER 6

Treatment of Couples with Relationship Difficulty: A Cognitive-Behavioral Perspective

Arthur Freeman
Carol Oster

... There is nothing either good or bad, but thinking makes it so.

Hamlet (Act II, Scene 2)
William Shakespeare

WHERE THERAPY BEGINS

Couples may very well be the most difficult patient population for any therapist. This is interesting, because the individuals comprising the couple may, independently, be quite amenable to treatment and treatable for the range of psychological disorders. However, when these individuals are combined as a couple there appears to be a synergistic effect of difficulty and resistance. This comes about, in large part, because of the context for therapy, the emotional valence of the problem, and the reason for referral.

Individuals often seek therapy after a brief bout of depression or after their first panic attack. They come wanting rapid change and surcease of the problem(s) causing discomfort or dysfunction. Couples, on the other hand, do not generally seek therapy when the relationship begins to be a concern, nor do they seek help when they have begun to draw away from each other. The disagreements and spats can move quickly to open warfare. They often seek a therapeutic consultation at the behest or requirement of their respective attorneys or the courts. It is more toward the end of the difficulty, when the relationship is at risk or in significant danger, that they seek referrals for relationship/marital work. For many couples, therapy is seen as the court of last resort, albeit a court they would rather not visit.

One distinction we would make is between couples who are distressed and those who are conflictual. The distressed couple come to therapy with the relationship under attack. They come with an idea and/or complaint: "We are having trouble. We love and care for each other and would like help to overcome our difficulty."

The conflictual couple come to therapy with each partner under attack. They come with this idea: "I would like to rip the heart out of this son of a bitch while he (she) sleeps. Can or will therapy change my mind?"

THE COMPLEXITY OF COUPLES WORK

In individual therapy we can map a bidirectional interaction with the therapist. Couples therapy work is immediately more complex, because there are now six possible interactions that are operative (see Exhibit 6.1).

In working with couples, the therapist must attend to four broad areas of difficulty: situational, behavioral, affective, and cognitive. No one of these elements is superordinate; the comprehensive treatment plan must include all four. Depending on the couple (and the presenting problem), the time, effort, and focus on these elements will differ, as may the specific interventions to be used. For one couple the entry point may be situational, but the

Exhibit 6.1
POSSIBLE THERAPEUTIC
INTERACTIONS

Therapist

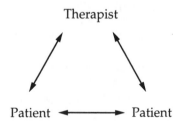

Patient ⟷ Patient

susequent points of intervention are behavioral, cognitive, and affective. For another couple the sequence may be situational, affective, behavioral, and cognitive (see Exhibit 6.2).

In treating most couples, the situational element is generally the entry point into the system, in that that is the reason for referral. The complaints may be direct, for example, "We are fighting all the time" or "We can't resolve even the tiniest disagreement." Or the complaints may be more general and vague, for instance, "The relationship is over" or "Things are going badly for us." This, then, becomes the starting point for therapy.

For many couples, the major area of behavioral concern (and the major source of their difficulty) is their lack of relationship/communication skills. It is of interest that these individuals may often have well-developed work-related or academically related communication skills. It is in the area of intimate one-to-one relationship/communication skills that they are deficient. Talmadge and Babbs (1990) found that the usual methods of improving communication between conflictual couples may be the means to a goal, but not the end. Typical communication training involves teaching partners to listen all the way through, to avoid interruptions, and to check meaning rather than completing each other's sentences or "mind reading."

Talmadge and Babbs (1990) found that more intimate couples had communication patterns that, in fact, broke social mores. For example, more intimate couples interrupted each other more, a finding in disagreement with Baucom and Epstein (1990). They were more likely to be affectively dissimilar, that is, both positive and negative, than conflictual couples, who were more uniformly negative. In addition, these authors' research echoed the common finding that conflictual couples reciprocated more negative affect than did relatively intimate couples. The partner who felt more intimate did more of the talking, as if there were some well-working

---

Exhibit 6.2
AREAS OF COMPLAINT

Situational—Stress at work

Affective—Anger, sadness

Behavioral—Crying
              Behavioral avoidance

Cognitive—Thoughts of suicide

agreement between the pair about who talks more and who interrupts more. However, in general, conversation between more intimate couples was less one-sided than between conflictual couples.

Another finding in their research was that younger couples reported themselves as more intimate than couples with longer histories together. Talmadge and Babbs attributed this perception to idealization processes early in relationships.

The affective element must be attended to, inasmuch it is the heat of the emotions that press heavily on the relationship and strain the bonds between the couple. Whether they involve anger, sadness, or anxiety, the therapist must identify the emotions and help the couple to cope with them. The key focus here is on the manner in which the emotions are generated, which is a cognitive function. For example, Mary discovered that Mel had had an affair ten years previously; he no longer had any contact with the woman. When asked what was most upsetting to her, Mary replied, "Every time I picture Mel with that woman, I get furious." It was not simply that Mel had had an affair and had broken the bond of trust, but Mary's ongoing visualization of what that behavior might have looked like that generated her upset.

The cognitive elements of relationship dysfunction take several forms. First are the relationship myths that interfere with intimacy, the dysfunctional prior beliefs about marriage, interpersonal connections, and romantic relationships (Ellis, 1982, 1986a, 1986b). These can be phrased as either "must" and "should" statements, as absolutistic statements, or as "or else" statements, such as,

> "We absolutely must be completely intimate or else our marriage is doomed."
> "You must give me the intimacy/closeness/love/sex I want, in the way I want it, or else you don't really love me."

The unspoken and parenthetic statements that follow these imperatives are usually, "You will be made to pay," or "I will suffer greatly and it will be your fault."

Other thoughts include (but are not limited to):

1. My partner must love and approve of everything about me.
2. Things should go the way I want them to go.
3. Our relationship should be perfect in every way.
4. Any problems or lack of perfection is intolerable.
5. When something goes wrong, it's my partner's fault; I am innocent and blameless.

Again, the imperative, dichotomous, perfectionistic, and demanding nature of the statements allow little room for negotiation and compromise. This bodes ill for the therapeutic work.

Kayser and Himle (1994) have identified specific intimacy-related beliefs that may interfere with relationships. Beliefs were considered dysfuntional when they "hindered the development of a desired level of intimacy" (Eidelson & Epstein, 1982), and irrational when they were unverifiable, self-defeating, and based on cognitive errors such as overgeneralization (taking one event and applying that experience to all experiences) and arbitrary inference (drawing conclusions based on no data, or even contrary data). (A more complete discussion of the various cognitive distortions can be found in Beck, Rush, Shaw, & Emery, 1979; Burns, 1980; and Freeman & Zaken-Greenburg, 1987) A summary of the beliefs and the accompanying themes identified by Kayser and Himle (1994) include the following:

1. If I become close to someone, he (she) will leave me (abandonment).
2. If there is any conflict in the relationship, I cannot be intimate (all-or-nothing thinking).
3. I will lose all personal control and power in a relationship if I am intimate (risk taking).
4. I am solely responsible for the lack of intimacy in my relationships (critical self-view).
5. In order to be intimate, I must do everything my partner wants (yielding of power).
6. If I am a good husband and father (support the family) or a good wife and mother (put my family's needs before my own), I will get intimacy in return (paying a price for intimacy).
7. Before I can be intimate, I must have strong loving feelings toward my partner (predisposing conditions).
8. I cannot be intimate without having sex in the relationship (more common in men); or, if I am intimate, I will be obligated to have sex in the relationship (more common in women) (equates intimacy with sexuality or the sex act).

To these generic beliefs about relationships we would add:

Relationship success comes from absolute compromise.
Change is never possible.
Opposites attract.
I should be able to read his (her) mind.
One partner is always to blame.
Thought insertion is the best method of communication.

Spontaneity is essential—planning is to be avoided.
Absolute honesty is the best policy.
Couples must always have the same sexual drive.
The therapist is the arbiter of rightness.
People are just born with relationship enhancement skills.
If something is "felt," it must be true.
A couple must spend no time apart.
Masturbation is unnecessary for couples.
Relationships just seem to happen, as in *Snow White*.

Kayser and Himle (1994) recommend assessing or detecting intimate beliefs through asking about patterns and themes related to intimacy evident in persons' prior relationships, including the nuclear family (social learning, modeling, vicarious learning, etc.). In addition, persons can be directly asked about their expectations of self and partner in the relationship. They emphasize that persons often have faulty beliefs about how intimacy works, about the "musts" and "shoulds," and about how intimacy should function.

What is manifested as relationship problems, is, in large part, the result of faulty knowledge (e.g., about the other gender, about the range of ways to express intimacy, about what intimacy is, about the normal range of emotional experience in relationships, etc.), faulty skills (in communication, problem solving, consensus reaching, affect identification and expression, and self-control of negative expression), and faulty attitudes or beliefs (the usual list of "shoulds" and "musts," the expectations learned through the usual family, societal, gender-related, ethnic schema).

Yovetich and Rusbult (1994) point out that intimacy diminishes when subjects in dysfunctional dyads tend to "respond in kind" to negative statements and behaviors of partners. They identify the ability to inhibit the impulse to respond in kind to provocation as requiring a "transformation of motivation"—that is, a tendency to pause and consider the long-term ramifications of one's actions on the relationship before acting, and then to act in accord with longer-term goals, taking into account broader considerations than the immediate provocation. They note that limited reaction time increases the tendency to "respond in kind" and that transformation of motivation requires delay or a longer reaction time. (Levenson and Gottman (1983) refer to this tendency as "high reciprocity of negative affect.")

Fletcher, Rosanowski, and Fitness (1994) suggest that prior beliefs about intimacy affect behavior within a relationship. That is, persons with a strong belief in the value of intimacy in a relationship are more likely to engage in intimacy-related behavior. On the other hand, those with a strong belief in the value of passion in a relationship are more likely to respond in accord with this belief. Some differences are noted between those holding one of these ideas as more dominant than the other. Those with a strong belief in intimacy tend to be more reflective about the nature of the relationship, as evident in longer response latencies to relationship-related statements. Those with a stronger belief in the importance of passion tend to respond more quickly. In addition, those who score as having weak beliefs in the centrality of intimacy also tend to respond quickly. If this finding is combined with observations that reciprocity of negative emotion is higher among conflictual couples (Levenson & Gottman, 1983; Talmadge & Babbs, 1990; Yovetich & Rusbult, 1994), a possible causal connection between speed of responding and negative experiences that diminish felt intimacy may be hypothesized (i.e., intimacy may be enhanced when persons are encouraged to "count to 10" before responding.)

Defining Intimacy

Before continuing, we believe that it is necessary to define *intimacy*. It is a term that is used by many authors, but which is often not defined or is defined in broad, abstruse constructions. One of the most comprehensive definitions with which we concur is offered by Prager (1995). She proposes five functions of a working definition of *intimacy*. First, the definition should be integrative and illuminate the linkages between extant theoretical perspectives.

Second, the definition should "specify whether intimacy is an individual capacity, a property of interactions, or a characteristic of a relationship" (p. 13).

Third, the definition should delineate between intimacy and the closely related concepts of love, sexuality, closeness, and support.

Fourth, the ultimate definition must be focused rather than fuzzy, and broadly attainable rather than esoteric.

Fifth, the therapeutic/professional definition should be "reconcilable with (if not identical to) lay definitions (p. 14).

Assessing Beliefs

The assessment of beliefs can be done in both unstructured and structured ways. Typically, one has to listen to patients' escalating complaints to see the shadows of the beliefs. The Relationship Belief Inventory (RBI) (Eidelson & Epstein, 1982) is an excellent scale that measures dysfunctional beliefs in five broad areas:

1. Disagreements are inherently destructive of relationships.
2. Spouses should "just know" what each other feels, thinks, and wants.

3. Relationships cannot be changed once patterns are established.
4. A marriage should be perfectly sexually satisfying.
5. Conflicts arise between husbands and wives because men and women are basically and profoundly different.

Although these are generic beliefs about relationships in general and have some degree of truth to them, it is their absolutistic nature that casts them as contributory to relationship dysfunction.

Another useful technique is the critical incident technique, in which the therapist asks both members of the dyad to describe a "critical incident" they have experienced. The question is asked to both simultaneously. They are asked for a single experience, event, or circumstance that in their view *best* describes or capsules the particular difficulty they are presently experiencing. This moves them away from the laundry list of complaints and offers a more projective approach. Each member may choose a different experience. The therapist asks that each be allowed to offer his or her "incident" without comment or editorializing by the partner.

For example, for one couple the critical incident was one that the husband and wife agreed on. The wife started by describing a situation in which, she reported, her husband said things that were very hurtful to her and she began crying.

As this interaction became more emotional for both of them, the husband asked "What would you like me to do?" and to this she replied, "Apologize."

His response was, "Is an apology what would make you feel better?" and she said, "Yes." He then said, "I'm really sorry that you're upset." The couple agreed that this was essentially what had happened. The meaning to each was the grist for the therapeutic mill.

The wife pointed out that in this critical incident her husband never apologized for what *he did*, or for what *he said*. Rather, he expressed sorrow that she was upset but saw no responsibility for contributing to, adding to, or stimulating her upset. She wanted an apology for what he did, that is, upset her.

The husband pointed to the incident as evidence of his wife's constant and unmeetable demands on him. "Even when I do exactly what she says, it is never good enough."

GUIDELINES FOR THERAPY

At the onset of treatment, the therapist must clearly, directly, and explicitly set out guidelines and rules for the therapy. These guidelines are general rules that will make the therapy more effective—for example, using "I" statements when expressing ideas, keeping a problem-solving attitude, limiting negative statements, maintaining a data-seeking stance, and withholding judgment. The rules once set, however, must remain inviolate until there is a renegotiation.

In addition, there must be rules about in-session conduct. These are essential in that they are required for safety; for instance, there can be no verbal or physical threats and no physical actions toward a partner (nor toward the therapist).

The therapy room must remain neutral territory—this point cannot be made too often. In effect, the therapy rule is, "This place is run under my (the therapist's) rules, and the prime requisite is that each of you be safe here." At times this may mean that the therapist calls "time out" during the session when there are insults, threats, or escalation of potentially dangerous negative emotion. Any intimidation or threat must be stopped immediately. The unbridled expression of negative thoughts and emotions is what the couple do on their own. To allow it to continue in therapy without helping them to effectively and constructively deal with such emotion is, in fact, no therapy at all.

If we believed that the expression of anger would lessen the pressure, both inter- and intrapersonally, we would support a cathartic model. However, anger and its expressions—verbal insults, physical threats or actions do not abate with airing. There may be a momentary experience of relief ("It was good to get that out)." Yet, given that the well of anger is fed, like most wells, from an underlying source, the draining of the well is temporary and the well will refill quickly. The underlying "aquifer" is the schema and automatic thoughts that surround relationships and the partners. They reflect schema developed early in life. We recommend a tight rein on any hostile expressions or activities, as they are antitherapeutic.

When the negative emotions and verbalizations arise, as they likely will, they must be identified and labeled in a neutral manner. The therapeutic question, "What is happening right now?" has several purposes.

1. It brings the conflict into the room so that it is "here-and-now" rather than the report of what happened at some point in the past,
2. It calls attention to the process so that both partners can become aware of it,
3. It demonstrates that escalation can be stopped, and
4. It shows that violence can be curbed.

The therapist can then ask the partners whether they can express their feelings and ideas in more adaptive and less relationship-threatening ways. If there is motivation to do so, communications training can result.

If, however, one partner has discovered the value of intimidation, then it will be more difficult to restrain (and retrain) hostile outbursts.

For example, Eric readily admitted that when Ellen "gets me pissed off," what works best is physical intimidation. Although both partners agreed that he has never hit her, she is always mindful of his strength, his short fuse, his threats, and the *possibility* of his finally hitting her. At several points in the first two sessions, Eric looked toward the therapist, made and held eye contact, and flexed his fists. After several of what the therapist experienced as clear but silent threats, the therapist asked Eric whether there was meaning to the fist flexing. (It is important *not* to interpret the anger or threat, but to pose the question as data seeking.) At first, Eric appeared puzzled. "What do you mean?" he asked. He said that he was not aware of doing it, and if he was flexing his fists, it was because his hands were stiff.

The therapist can accept such an explanation until there is evidence to the contrary. In this case it was quick in coming. Ellen began to tell of an incident in their lives, whereupon Eric raised his fist, shook it at her, and said, "I told you not to bring that up." It was clear that stiffness was not the problem here.

Related to the safety issue is the process of "equalizing" or "leveling" in therapy. This requires that the therapist model fairness and allow equal time to both partners. In addition, the therapist must contain the tendency to support the partner that he or she believes to be "right." There are several useful leveling techniques.

Heitler (1994) makes use of an imaginary wall. She poses to an individual that there is a wall between that person and the partner. What the person says will be heard but not responded to.

Another technique is to have the partners speak through the therapist until they have developed better communication skills.

A third possibility is to point out something to both partners. We have found that it is useful to make sure that whenever the therapist makes a point with one partner, that there is some approximately equal statement made to the other partner; this reduces the blaming issue. For example, the therapist might say,

"Eric—when you flex or wave your fist that way it has the effect of going beyond placing emphasis on what you say and moves toward possibly intimidating others, even when you aren't aware of it."

"Ellen—when Eric does that fist thing, you turn away and don't tell him how you feel when he does that. Maybe Eric isn't aware of what he is doing, and it would be helpful to know your reaction."

By keeping the statements balanced and about the same length, the therapist can remain neutral. Whenever there is overt violence, either within or between sessions, the therapist's neutrality must instantly disappear. There must be a clear statement that any violence is unacceptable.

If need be, the therapist must be willing to intercede with legal limitations, which may mean the end of therapy. To continue therapy with couples in the presence of ongoing violence within or without the session may even give it sanction. A referral should be made to a battered spouse resource, and therapy may continue as supportive with one partner.

COUNTERTRANSFERENCE

As possibly a partner in a relationship, as a man or woman, as a member of society, the therapist will have developed a number of personal biases and attendant reactions, which comprise the countertransference. The therapist must be exquisitely attuned to his or her own thoughts and feelings. Couples work has the potential to excite personal issues, which may even take the therapist by surprise. For example, in working with a couple of whom one partner was far more verbal and aggressive, the therapist needed to make many leveling statements. At one point the more verbal partner (the man) accused his wife of saying something, blaming him for some aspect of the relationship difficulty. The therapist, having heard something different, stated, "That's not what she said," to which the woman said, "Yes it is. He heard me just right. It is his fault." Was this a matter of the partners joining against the therapist (another good technique), or was the therapist being overprotective of the woman? The therapist determined after introspection that the latter was true. At this point it was important to acknowledge the error so as to maintain credibility and model the ability to make mistakes and recover from them.

PROBLEM-SOLVING TRAINING

Having looked at the cognitive issues, the therapist must work with the partners to build interpersonal skills, which includes the following steps:

1. *Give a clear, specific statement of the problem.* The therapist instructs each member of the couple to offer a statement, of no more than three sentences, about what he or she sees the problem to be. Such limitation avoids the long, repetitive, and laborious telling of a tale that usually begins, with apology to Dickens, "It was the worst of times and the worst of times." By asking each partner for a statement, the therapist begins the leveling process. In many cases the partners having been preparing mental legal briefs, just waiting for an opportunity to share them. The goal of each is

often to lay out the course of the difficulty in a manner that will immediately win over the therapist, and have the therapist proclaim the guilt of the partner and exonerate the teller of the tale from any contribution to the problem(s).

2. _Minimize blaming_. It is important to assume, from the beginning, a data-supported and problem-solving attitude. This implies that blaming must be limited. At times this is difficult, especially when it appears on the surface as if the problem really is the fault of one partner. The couple has collaborated (albeit in differing degrees) to develop the problem.

3. *Break down problems into their smallest parts*. Couples often see dealing with problems in therapy as tantamount to solving the problems of famine, pestilence, and plague. Indeed, the therapist cannot diminish the weight of the problems with a word of interpretation. The overwhelming nature of a couple's relationship problems must be broken down into the smallest possible parts. The couple can be helped to develop the ability to reduce problems to their component parts. This is not the same as seeking the lowest common denominator.

   The former involves taking major issues and disassembling them. The latter strategy involves seeking the single underlying theme that, once discovered, will cause the problem to implode. We recommend the former as a more reasonable strategy.

4. *Individually consider alternative explanations*. Part of the psychoeducational work of therapy is structured practice at developing alternative explanations for life events. This involves asking each partner to generate a list of *possible* alternatives without regard to probability. Each partner is asked to take as many perspectives as he or she can to build an alternative list. The goal, even to a point of silliness, is to start to put a wedge into the idea that the first explanation is the "right" one.

   Another point to consider in this regard is the individual's explanatory style (e.g., does he or she explain events as global versus specific, internal versus external, or stable versus changeable, Abramson, Tensdale, & Seligman, 1978).

5. *Have the couple brainstorm alternative explanations*. This is an extension of the exercise in step 4, done in a lighthearted manner with a very serious impact. Can the couple cooperate in looking at other possibilities for their behavior? The therapist can be a resource, consultant, and prompter for the couple's creativity.

   Any additional possibilities they can raise are all to the good in breaking through the rigid notions held by the individuals or by the couple about why things happen.

6. *Have individuals withhold judgment.* This may very well be the most difficult skill for the individuals to develop. They often hold well-developed and severe judgments that have been an ongoing part of their interaction.

    The therapeutic strategy of members of the couple witholding judgment can be accomplished by having both combine the perspective and alternative-taking position in combination with experimenting with the scientific process of withholding conclusions until more data are collected.

7. *Help the couple to anticipate roadblocks to solutions.* Surprise, whether real or feigned, is the enemy of problem solving. Couples often report that they feel that a partner has surprised them by word or deed. When this is pleasant, for example, giving flowers, doing a personal favor, offering a pleasant word, there is little complaint. However, when the surprise is a word or action that is less pleasant, it can serve to create a negative mindset.

    The therapist must assist the couple in anticipating any potential resistance or roadblocks to effective problem solving. This involves having the couple make joint lists of potential roadblocks: personal roadblocks or blocks expected from the partner, social system, family, or friends. Having made a list of possible roadblocks, the couple can then develop a plan for more adaptive coping.

8. *Select a trial period to implement the solution.* The use of open-ended therapy models has the effect of disheartening couples. They would like all to be resolved immediately. By setting small, sequential, time-limited, and proximal goals, the therapist models an effective (and required) problem-solving approach.

    Setting small goals to be accomplished within a trial period allows the couple to increase the potential for a growing number of successes. Using a focused intervention within a one-week time period allows the couple to report any success at the next therapy session.

9. *Make sure the necessary skills are in place.* The therapist must model, teach, and evaluate whether the individuals have the requisite skills for effectively coping with the range of stressors they must face. It is unconscionable to expect that individuals try to cope with long-standing problems when they have never developed the requisite skills.

    Social skills training, assertiveness training, communication training, listening skills, and skills at sexual interaction are all necessary parts of the couples work. The assessment and treatment planning must be collaborative and agreed to by both partners.

If one or the other maintains that they already have the skills they need, simple behavioral experiments can help them to see that their skills are good but have to be better.

10. *Jointly assess and modify as necessary.* There must be an ongoing evaluation protocol. The partners and the therapist must be constantly willing and able to assess progress toward agreed-upon goals, and to modify the therapy, as needed.

HOMEWORK

Therapy, of necessity, must continue beyond the confines of the consulting room. It is important for the couple to understand that the extension of the work of therapy to nontherapy hours allows for a greater therapeutic focus. The homework, which is the "laboratory" of the therapy, can be either predominantly cognitive or predominantly behavioral. It may involve having the couple complete a relationship activity schedule, an excellent homework assignment following the first session. This is an activity schedule that details their interaction from the time the couple wakes to the time they go to sleep. A common finding is that there is usually little contact.

They might also complete several Dysfunctional Thought Records (DTRs) relative to the relationship, or try new behaviors. The homework should flow from the session material, rather than being tacked onto the end of the session simply because the therapy should include homework. The more relevant and collaborative the homework, the greater the likelihood of compliance with the therapeutic regimen.

For example, Sean and Andrea debated the role of her parents in their difficulty. Andrea maintained that her parents were supportive of the relationship; they had said so on numerous occasions. Sean maintained that Andrea's parents were subtly sabotaging the relationship. The homework "experiment" involved Andrea's calling her parents with her usual tales of woe—"Work is going poorly; I may get fired. Sean and I fight all the time. Money is really tight and we can't pay our bills," and so forth. She was to assess her parents' response.

Her next call, two days later, was to be more positive—"I was wrong about work; I may get a raise. Sean and I are really doing well. He bought me a wonderful gift. We made an error in our bank account, and we have more money than we thought." She was then to assess her parents' response to her more positive and upbeat call.

Her conclusion was that when she was depressed and complaining, they were willing to speak with her at great length. When she was more upbeat, the call was terminated rather quickly. In therapy we were able to identify an interaction pattern. When her message was, "I am helpless and needy and must be supported or I will collapse," her parents responded by being available and helpful. When she was not helpless and needy and her relationship was going well, her parents seemed to have no need to play a role in her life. This homework was the beginning of a renegotiation of Andrea's role with her parents and an accommodation with Sean.

Another simple homework assignment involves having a couple assess a baseline of affectionate exchange. This exchange can be verbal ("I love you." "You look nice.") or physical (a touch without sexual follow-up). Once a baseline has been established, the couple can work toward increasing the affectionate exchange by some amount (e.g., 50 percent). The couple can then assess their reactions after the increase.

The homework should be reviewed at the next session. If it is not part of the session agenda, the couple will quickly stop doing the homework.

TECHNIQUES USEFUL IN COUPLES WORK

We can arbitrarily divide couples treatment interventions into cognitive and behavioral. It will be clear to the experienced therapist that this is a false dichotomy and used for description only.

Cognitive Techniques

1. *Clarifying idiosyncratic meaning.* The therapist cannot assume that a term or statement used by an individual, or as part of the private language of the couple, is completely understood. The therapist must ask for meaning and clarification. It is essential to question the partners directly on the meanings of their verbalizations. Although this practice may appear to be intrusive, it can be structured by the therapist as a way of making sure that he or she is not merely in the right ballpark in understanding but is right on target. This technique also models for the partners the need for active listening skills, increased communication, and a means for checking out assumptions.

2. *Questioning the evidence.* Individuals use certain evidence to maintain ideas and beliefs. It is essential to teach both partners to question the evidence they are using to maintain and strengthen ideas and beliefs. Questioning the evidence also requires examining the source of data. Many patients have the ability to ignore major pieces of information and focus on the few pieces that

support their dysfunctional views. By having a patient question the evidence with family members or significant others, a fuller accounting can be had. If the evidence is strong, the therapist can help to structure alternative ways of perceiving the data or of changing behaviors so that the evidence is either modified or no longer exists.

3. *Reattribution.* A common statement made by individuals in dysfunctional relationships is, "It's all my fault" or "It's all his (her) fault." When depression is a part of the picture, we can expect the depressed patient to take responsibility for events and situations that are only minimally attributable to that person. The therapist can help the patient distribute responsibility among all relevant parties. If the therapist takes a position of total support— "It wasn't your fault"; "She (he) isn't worth it"; "You're better off without him (her)"; or "There are other fish in the ocean"—the therapist risks sounding like friends and family whom the individual has already dismissed as being a cheering squad, not understanding his or her position. By taking the neutral middle ground, the therapist can help the patient to reattribute responsibility so as not to take all the blame nor unrealistically shift all blame to others.

4. *Examining options and alternatives.* Many individuals see themselves as having lost all options. Perhaps the prime example of this view appears in the suicidal patient. This cognitive strategy, a primary one in working with couples who see no way out, involves working with the partners to generate additional options.

5. *Decatastrophizing.* This is also called the "What if?" technique. It involves helping the couple to evaluate whether they are overestimating the catastrophic nature of their life situation. Questions that might be asked include "What is the worst thing that can happen?" "And if it does occur, what would be so terrible?" This technique has the therapist working against what might be termed a "Chicken Little" style of thinking, whereby the couple (or the individuals) see an experience (or life itself) as a series of catastrophes and problems. The therapist can work toward data collection and reality testing.

Patients can be helped to see that the consequences of their life actions are not "all or nothing" and, thereby, less catastrophic. It is important that this technique be used with great gentleness and care so that the individuals or the couple do not feel ridiculed or made fun of by the therapist.

6. *Fantasizing consequences.* In this technique the individuals are asked to fantasize a situation and to describe their images and the concerns. Often, as they verbalize their concerns, they can see

the irrationality of their ideas. If the fantasized consequences are realistic, the therapist can work to assess the danger realistically and focus on and develop coping strategies.

This technique allows the patients to bring imaged events, situations, or interactions that have happened previously into the consulting room. The explication and investigation of the style, format, and content of a fantasy can yield very good material for the therapy work, especially in involving feedback from the partner.

7. *Assessing advantages and disadvantages.* Assessing both the advantages and the disadvantages of maintaining a particular belief or behavior can help couples to gain a balance and perspective. Typically, distressed couples have dichotomized life events and may see only one side of an issue. This technique can be used to examine the advantages and disadvantages of acting a certain way (i.e., dressing a certain way), thinking a certain way (i.e., thinking of what others will think of them), and feeling a particular way (i.e., sad). Although individuals often claim that they cannot control their feelings, actions, and thoughts, it is precisely the development of this control that is the strength of a cognitive-behavioral approach.

8. *Turning adversity to advantage.* There are times that a seeming disaster can be used to advantage. The very distress that brings a couple into therapy can be reframed as positive, in that it has called a time out in their lives and forced them to take notice and attend to their relationship.

There is, once again in this strategy, a balancing that puts a couple's experience into perspective. They may simply not see the positive. However, individuals sometimes respond to the therapist's pointing out any positive aspects with greater negativity. They may accuse the therapist of being unrealistic, a Pollyanna or Mary Poppins. The therapist can point out that the view that he or she offers is no less real than the patient's unrealistically negative view.

9. *Guided association/discovery.* In a collaborative technique, through asking simple questions such as "Then what?" "What would that mean?" "What would happen then?" the therapist can help the couple to explore the significance they see in certain events.

The use of what we call the *chained* or *guided association* technique involves the therapist working with the patient to connect ideas, thoughts, and images. The therapist provides the conjunctions to the patients verbalizations, which then allows the therapist to guide the patients along various therapeutic paths, depending on the conceptualization and therapeutic goals.

10. *Use of exaggeration or paradox.* By taking an idea to its extreme, the therapist can often help to move the couple to a more central position vis à vis a particular belief, as there seems to be room at the extreme for only one person.

    Care must be taken to not insult, ridicule, or embarrass the patient. Given a hypersensitivity to criticism and ridicule, some individuals may experience the therapist who uses paradoxical strategies as making light of their problems.

    There is a risk, however, that a patient may take the therapist's statement as reinforcement of his or her position of abject hopelessness. The therapist who chooses to use paradox or exaggeration techniques must have (a) a strong working relationship with the patient, (b) good timing, and (c) the good sense to know when to back away from the technique.

11. *Scaling.* For those patients who see things as "all or nothing," the technique of scaling, or seeing things as existing on a continuum, can be very helpful. The scaling of a feeling can force patients to utilize the strategy of gaining distance and perspective. For those patients who are at a point of extreme thoughts and extreme behaviors, any movement toward a midpoint is helpful.

12. *Self-instruction.* We all talk to ourselves. We give ourselves orders, directions, instructions, and information necessary to solve problems. Each partner can start with direct verbalization which, with practice, will become part of the behavioral repertoire. Patients can be taught to offer direct self-instructions or, in some cases, counterinstructions. With this technique, the therapist is not introducing anything new. Rather, the patients are being helped to use and strengthen a technique that we all use at various times.

13. *Thought stopping.* Dysfunctional thoughts often have a snowball effect in the individual. What may start as a small and insignificant problem can, if left to roll along, gather weight, speed, and momentum. Once on the roll, the thoughts have a force of their own and are very hard to stop. Thought stopping is best used when the thoughts start, not in the middle of the process. The patient can be trained to picture a stop sign, "hear" a bell, picture a wall. Any of these can be used to stop the progression and growth of harmful thoughts. The therapist's hitting a desk sharply or ringing a small bell during a session can serve to help a patient stop the thoughts. The memory of that intervention can be used by the patient to assist his or her thought stopping. There is both a distractive and an aversive quality to the technique.

14. *Labeling of distortions.* The fear of the unknown is a frequent issue for patients with anxiety. The more the therapist can do to identify the nature and content of the dysfunctional thinking and to help label the types of distortions that patients use, the less frightening the entire process becomes.

15. *Developing replacement imagery.* If a couple is constantly generating images of failure or recalling defeat or embarrassment, the therapist can practice with the patients new, effective, coping images. Once well practiced, patients can perform image substitution.

Behavioral Techniques

The goals of using behavioral techniques within the context of cognitive therapy are manifold. The first goal is to use direct behavioral strategies and techniques to test dysfunctional thoughts and behaviors. By having a couple *try* feared or avoided behaviors, old ideas can be directly challenged. A second use of behavioral techniques is to practice new behaviors as homework. Certain behaviors can be practiced first during the session, then practiced at home.

1. *Activity scheduling.* The activity schedule is, perhaps, the most ubiquitous form in the therapist's armamentarium. For individuals who are feeling overwhelmed, an activity schedule can be used to plan the more effective use of time. For example, when the homework for the couple requires a specific amount of time, the activity schedule can offer the opportunity to better plan how they will spend the between-session time. For instance, time can be set aside for conversations, problem solving, or sex.

2. *Mastery and pleasure ratings.* Rating the sense of efficacy (mastery, 1–10), and pleasure (1–10): The greater the mastery and pleasure, the lower the stress on the relationship. Through discovering the low and high relationship–stress activities, plans can be made to increase the former and decrease the latter.

3. *Social skills training.* It is incumbent upon the therapist to help the couple gain the requisite social, conversational, active listening, and interaction skills as part of therapy. Social skills acquisition, which can include direct instruction during the session and homework between sessions, may involve anything from modeling how to properly shake hands to modeling conversational skills.

4. *Assertiveness training.* Like social skills training, assertiveness training may be an essential part of therapy. Patients who are

socially anxious can be helped to develop responsible assertive skills.

5. *Bibliotherapy.* Several excellent books can be assigned as readings for a couple's homework. These books can be used to socialize or educate patients to effective functioning and to the basic cognitive-behavioral therapy model. Readings, as appropriate, can emphasize specific points made during a session or can introduce new ideas for discussion at future sessions. Some helpful couples' resources include *Love Is Never Enough* (Beck, 1988), *The Ten Dumbest Mistakes Smart People Make* (Freeman & DeWolf, 1990), and *Men Are from Mars, Women from Venus* (Gray, 1992).

6. *Graded tasks assignments* (GTAs). GTAs involve a shaping procedure consisting of small sequential steps that lead to a desired (and proximal) goal. By setting out a task and then arranging the necessary steps in a hierarchy, couples can be helped to make reasonable progress with a minimum of stress. As the individuals (or the couple) attempt each step, the therapist can be available as a resource for support and guidance. At each step, the therapist has each patient rate the likelihood of success, as well as the emotional and cognitive issues in the behaviors.

7. *Behavioral rehearsal/role-playing.* The therapy session is the ideal setting to practice many behaviors. The therapist serves as teacher and guide, offering direct feedback on performance. The therapist can monitor the couple's performance, offer suggestions for improvement, and model new behaviors. In addition, anticipated and actual roadblocks can be identified and worked on in the session. There can be extensive rehearsal before the couple attempts a behavior in vivo.

8. *Relaxation training.* When anxiety is a component of the problem, the couple can profit from relaxation training, inasmuch as the anxiety response and the quieting relaxation response are mutually exclusive. When relaxed, the individuals are more likely to be open to change. Relaxation training can be taught during a session and then practiced for homework. Ready-made relaxation tapes can be purchased, or the therapist may easily tailor a tape for the couple. The therapist-made tape can include the patient's name, and can focus on particular symptoms, and can be modified as needed.

DEALING WITH NONCOMPLIANCE

How does a therapist deal with noncompliance? Noncompliance, sometimes called resistance, often carries the implication that the patient does not want to change or "get well," for either conscious or unconscious reasons.

Resistance may be manifested directly (e.g., through tardiness or missing appointments) or more subtly through omissions in the material reported in the sessions. The resistances of the individual partners are not merely additive, but synergistic.

Clinically, we can identify several reasons for noncompliance. They can appear in any combination or permutation, and the relative strength of any noncompliant action may change with the patient's life circumstance, progress in therapy, relationship with the therapist, changing relationship with a partner, and so forth. Among the many reasons for noncompliance, or resistance, are the following:

1. Lack of patient skill to change his or her behavior
2. Lack of therapist skill to help the patient change
3. Environmental stressors that preclude changing
4. Patient cognitions regarding the possibility of failure showed he or she try to change
5. Patient cognitions regarding the consequences for others (partner, family, friends) of his or her changing
6. Congruency of the partners' distortions
7. Poor socialization to the goals and strategies of therapy
8. The availability of a secondary gain from maintaining the dysfunctional behavior and interactions
9. Lack of collaboration or therapeutic alliance between the therapist and either or both partners
10. Good strategies and interventions used, but poorly timed
11. Lack of patient motivation to change
12. Compliance foiled by patient rigidity

In every case, it is important for any noncompliance to be overtly noted, labeled, and put on the agenda for discussion. At this point, depending on the reason(s) for noncompliance, the therapist can structure the therapy to accommodate for the resistant behavior.

SUMMARY

Couples may very well be the most difficult patient population for any therapist. Individuals often seek therapy after a brief bout of depression, wanting rapid change and surcease of the problem(s) causing discomfort or dysfunction. Couples, on the other hand, do not generally seek therapy when the relationship begins to be a concern, nor do they seek help when they have begun to draw away from each other. Couples seek help when the disagreements and spats generally moved to open warfare or at the request of a third party, often an attorney.

We make a distinction between couples who are distressed and those who are conflictual. The distressed couple come to therapy with the relationship under attack; the conflictual couple are actually attacking each other.

For many couples, the major area of behavioral concern (and the major source of their difficulty) is their lack of relationship/communication skills. While they may often have well-developed work-related or academically related communication skills, it is in the area of intimate one-to-one relationship/communication skills that they are deficient.

The assessment of beliefs can be done in both unstructured ways, using techniques such as the critical incident technique, and structured ways, using standardized scales and behavioral checklists.

The therapist must clearly, directly, and explicitly set out guidelines and rules for the therapy, which are designed to make the therapy more effectiv —for example, using "I" statements when expressing ideas, keeping a problem-solving attitude, limiting negative statements, maintaining a data-seeking stance, and withholding judgment.

In addition, there must be rules about in-session conduct, which are required for safety. The therapy room must remain neutral territory.

Having looked at the cognitive issues, the therapist must work with the partners to build interpersonal skills, which include a clear, specific statement of the problem by each partner, minimization of blaming, breaking down problems into their smallest parts, and individually considering alternative explanations. The therapist can have the couple brainstorm alternative explanations, have individuals withhold judgment, help the couple to anticipate roadblocks to solutions, select a trial period to implement the solution, make sure the necessary skills are in place, and jointly assess and modify the skills as necessary.

It is important for the patient to understand that the extension of the therapy work to the nontherapy hours allows for a greater therapeutic focus. Homework can be either cognitive or behavioral. It may involve having the patient complete an activity schedule (an excellent homework assignment following the first session), complete several DTRs, or try new behaviors. Interventions can be cognitive or behavioral.

Resistance in therapy may be manifested directly, (e.g., through tardiness or missing appointments) or more subtly through omissions in the material reported in the sessions.

REFERENCES

Abramson, L., Tensdale, J., Seligman, M. E. P. (1978). Learned helplessness in humans: Critique and reformulation. *Journal of Abnormal Psychology*, Vol. 87, pp 49–59.

Baucom, D., & Epstein, N. (1990). Cognitive behavioral marital therapy. New York: Brunner/Mazel.

Beck, A. T. (1988). *Love is never enough*. New York: HarperCollins.

Beck, A. T., Rush, A. J., Shaw, B. F., & Emery, G. (1979). *Cognitive therapy of depression*. New York: Guilford Press.

Burns, D. D. (1980). *Feeling good: The new mood therapy*. New York: The New American Library.

Chelune, G. J., Robinson, J. T., & Kommer, M. J. (1984). A cognitive instructional model of intimate relationships. In V.G. Derlega (Ed.), *Communication, intimacy and close relationships* (pp. 11–40). Orlando, FL: Academic Press.

Eidelson, R. J., & Epstein, N. (1982). Cognition and relationship maladjustment: Development of a measure of dysfunctional relationship beliefs. *Journal of Consulting and Clinical Psychology, 50*, 715–720.

Ellis, A. (1982). Intimacy in rational-emotive therapy. In M. Fisher & G. Striker (Eds.), *Handbook of rational-emotive therapy* (pp. 170–176). New York: Springer Publishing.

Ellis, A. (1986a). *Application of rational-emotive therapy to love problems*. In A. Ellis & R. Grieger (Eds.), *Handbook of rational-emotive therapy*, Vol. 2 (pp. 162–182). New York: Springer Publishing.

Ellis, A. (1986b). Rational-emotive therapy applied to relationship therapy. *Journal of Rational-Emotive Therapy, 4*, 4–21.

Fletcher, G. J. O., Rosanowski, J., & Fitness, J. (1994). Automatic processing in intimate contexts: The role of close-relationship beliefs. *Journal of Personality and Social Psychology, 67* (5), 888–897.

Freeman, A., & DeWolf, R. (1990). *The ten dumbest mistakes smart people make*. New York: HarperCollins.

Freeman, A., & Zaken-Greenburg, F. (1987). Cognitive therapy of families. New York: Brunner/Mazel.

Gray, J. (1992). *Men are from Mars, women from Venus*. New York: HarperCollins.

Kayser, K., & Himle, D. P. (1994). Dysfunctional beliefs about intimacy. *Journal of Cognitive Psychotherapy, 8* (2), 127–140.

Levenson, R. W., & Gottman, J. M. (1983). Marital interaction: Physiological linkage and affective exchange. *Journal of Personality and Social Psychology, 45*, 587–597.

Levinger, G., & Snoek, J. D. (1972). *Attraction in relationship: A new look at interpersonal attraction*. Morristown, NJ: General Learning Press.

McClellan, T. A., & Stieper, D. R. (1977). A structured approach to group marriage counseling. In A. Ellis & R. Grieger (Eds.), *Handbook of rational-emotive therapy* (pp. 281–291). New York: Springer Publishing.

Prager, K. (1995). *Psychology of intimacy*. New York: Guilford Press.

Talmadge, L. D., & Babbs, J. M. (1990). Intimacy, conversational patterns and concomitant cognitive/emotional processes in couples. *Journal of Social and Clinical Psychology, 9* (4), 473–488.

Walster, E., Walster, G. W., & Berscheid, E. (1978). *Equity theory and research*. Boston: Allyn & Bacon.

Yovetich, N. A., & Rusbult, C. E. (1994). Accommodative behavior in close relationships: Exploring transformation of motivation. *Journal of Experimental Social Psychology, 30*, 138–164.

CHAPTER 7

The Spiritually or Religiously Disordered Couple

Michael Dimitroff
Steve Hoekstra

The American Psychiatric Association's 1994 publication of the *Diagnostic and Statistical Manual of Mental Disorders*, fourth edition (DSM-IV) includes a new V Code entitled "Religious or spiritual problem." The DSM-IV lists the following information: "V62.89 Religious or spiritual problem. This category can be used when the focus of clinical intention is of a religious or spiritual nature. Examples include distressing experiences that involve loss or questioning of faith, problems associated with conversion to a new faith, problem or questioning of spiritual values that may not necessarily be related to an organized church or religious institution."

What is important about this particular new V Code is the recognition that spiritual values may somehow be involved, to a significant degree, within the context of a human being's overall mental health. Because many marriages and families are predicated on values of some sort, it is not unusual for a therapist to be faced with issues that may have strong roots within the religious beliefs of their clients. In fact, this V Code may even be a focal point, as opposed to a secondary concern.

This chapter is somewhat different from others in this book that examine the relationship between dysfunctional dyads resulting from personality disorders. In Chapter 10, dealing with the "love sick wife and cold sick husband" (histrionic-obsessive couple), the authors provide an excellent presentation of treatment by rebalancing the couple relationship. Here, we deal with an apparently sadistic husband and a dependent, self-defeating wife. Their defective coping styles are identified through psychological testing and interview. But in this couple's case, religious values are paramount because they are distorted and fuel the fires of discontent. Yet these problems have also allowed the therapist to rebalance the couple's relationship through examination and clarification of their serious distortion of religious values and matters of faith. Previous therapists had missed the religious and spiritual aspects of this case, as addressed by the V Code. As a result, although effectively dealing with the couple interpersonally, they were unable to resolve some serious hurts and issues. Thus, the personality disorders, although quite important, take a "back seat," so to speak, in the understanding and rebalancing of this couple's serious religious problems.

Finally, after the initial therapeutic alliance is established, dynamics are explored and treatment goals are recommended. Throughout the process, the reader, it is hoped, will realize that religious teachings can be distorted or misused. Such misunderstanding and misapplication can quickly develop into religious or value crisis, leading individuals to a serious questioning of faith. The view held by Jung (1963), that religion and values have an important function in analysis and treatment of interpersonal difficulties, becomes paramount.

THERAPIST ISSUES IN DEALING WITH RELIGIOUSLY DISORDERED COUPLES

Therapists are understandably uncomfortable, given background and training in most instances, in entering the realm of the client's spiritual values, beliefs, and views. In fact, it is not unusual for many counseling and therapy programs to state somewhat automatically, "Do not impose your values on another individual." However, reality dictates that therapists and the couples they deal with do indeed have deep values that can be diametrically opposed or in significant conflict (Rotz, 1993; Szasz, 1974; Menninger, 1973; Meltzoff, 1970). Thus, the therapist must be knowledgeable of and sensitive to the views presented by the people whom she or he sees in practice. A majority of the American population claims to be Christian. Within this so-called Christian community are diverse views as to what this means and the nature of the values connected to living the "Christian life" (Guernsey, 1994). It would not be uncommon for a counselor to be dealing with individuals who belong to sects or cults loosely connected with, or not even related to, Christianity. Although some counseling practices limit themselves to dealing with Christian belief systems, many others are comfortable within the context and values of Buddhism, Hinduism, Judaism, and Islam, as well as the cults related to these varied religious groups.

As noted earlier, the DSM-IV presents a V Code pertaining to spiritual or religious problems. Although *spiritual* and *religious* will be used interchangeably here, the reader should keep in mind the fact that the term *religion* used in this chapter refers to some sort of organized doctrinal and written pattern of beliefs relating to the relationship between God and the created, atonement, and salvation, as opposed to only spiritual aspects, which focus more on the experiental side of relationship between the Creator and the created one.

Along with these written doctrines often come values related to family life, marriage, and relationships, which are presented as rules and recommendations. Couples can be impacted by religious values. A husband who views himself as "the man of the house" can become an overbearing dictator or even abuser. Couples can have severe disagreements about child rearing, religious service participation, or discipline. A death of a child can lead to a severe upset in faith and a questioning of God's existence. Serious illness following some secret "shameful" act can be construed as divine punishment. One member of a couple may wish to change religious affiliation, which might lead to an emotionally charged family situation, especially if religion is highly culture-bound as well. A woman abused by her earthly father may have a distorted view of her heavenly Father. Thus, the V Code here offers a most appropriate Axis I symptom pattern, which requires assessment and treatment.

Christianity as an established religion has certainly impacted American society—more than other faiths, as far as history and values are concerned. Thus, even in this post-Christian era, familiarity with the general principles of Christianity can be helpful inasmuch as so many people seen in therapy incorporate basic Christian values. Christianity can be summed up within the various creeds and doctrines of the church (e.g., the Nicene Creed, the Apostles' Creed, the Canons of Dort, the Heidelberg Catechism, and the Westminster Confession of Faith) that have existed during the last 1,600 years. For instance, all Christian denominations believe in a triune God, a virgin birth, the deity of Jesus the messiah, and his death, resurrection, and atonement for sins of the world. All other doctrines flow from these basic beliefs.

The New Testament Gospels and, later, the Epistles of the various followers of Christianity crystallize specifically the religious values between men and women within the context of marriage. Over the many hundreds of years since these documents were written, there has been great controversy as to their interpretation and validity. It is beyond the scope of this chapter to explore those controversies. The importance of the Old and New Testaments—and the New Testament specifically—as to marriage and values is undeniable, however, even though their perceived relevance has been changing within the United States within the past 30 years. The approach taken here focuses primarily on the couple discussed later in this chapter. A review of their particular values, the context of their values, and how diagnosis and therapy were applied to help order an otherwise very disordered situation are presented at that point.

Current research supports the importance of considering religious values in therapy (Prest, 1993; Hinterkopf, 1994). It is our opinion that therapists need to make a transition into these sometimes diverse, complex, and uncomfortable areas by becoming familiar with the different attitudes, doctrines, and dogmas of the various religious groups of people with whom they might be actively doing couples therapy. It may be to the therapist's advantage to refer to a person credentialed in religious studies or to confer with that more knowledgeable consultant. For example, one might ascribe very different values to the roles of a husband and wife, depending on whether one comes from a Wisconsin Synod Lutheran, Orthodox Jewish, or Fundamental Islamic position. Lutherans are taught (but do not necessarily practice) that husbands and wives should submit to one another; wives are to submit to husbands, and husbands are to love their wives and give their lives for them as Christ did for his church. In Orthodox Judaism, women and men sit separately in religious ceremonies and have distinct rules and roles, as defined in the Talmud. Muslims also have distinct rules and roles, which include even dress and deportment in public, based on the Koran and the Hadith (traditional extra-Koranic teachings). These values can be deep—and very different from those of the secularly trained therapist.

Although counseling, psychology, and religion have experienced conflict in areas of human study and experience, they also join paths. For instance, M. Scott Peck (1985) in his best-selling book introduced lay people to an integration of psychology and religion by discussing good, evil, and the spiritual path. Since Peck's book, therapists are now inviting the investigation of spiritual issues and values within the entire therapeutic process. In his book, *Working with Religious Issues in Therapy*, Lovinger (1984) argued that people's religious beliefs, and even religious experiences, can provide important data as to their relationship with others. In fact it can be very helpful if some of these issues emerge in therapy, not only in establishing rapport, but also in understanding the person's views, beliefs, and coping mechanisms when subjected to the stressors of life. This does not require any therapists to change their own religion or their world and life view. Lovinger adds that the only notion or view a therapist would have to relinquish, if actually held, is "that religion is silly or meaningless." King (1978) researched concerns of Evangelical Christians about being misunderstood or ridiculed for beliefs by secular therapists. He found that 89 percent of respondents in his survey had such concerns.

Genia (1994) notes that current psychotherapies most likely have failed to meet the needs of individuals with strong religious beliefs. She recommends that secular humanistic psychotherapists be much more competent in treating people with strong and even different religious beliefs. It is her contention that professional training programs should actually teach, to some extent, various types of religious beliefs. In an article by Shafranske and Maloney (1990), their data suggested that a therapist's healthy understanding of his or her own religious orientation contributes more to a sense of competence in assisting clients in their spiritual development than does all sorts of other training in psychotherapy and religion. Basically, what they are proposing is that therapists should be familiar with their own religious beliefs, as well as with others, to provide not only good rapport, but overall change in coping and functioning.

In a recent article, "Infusing Religion into Counseling," Morrissey (1995), speaking to the training of therapists, noted, "The issue of spirituality makes most therapists very uncomfortable and is seen as more controversial than other cultural issues." However, this article was also very quick to point out the counseling and related educational program standards (CACREP) that address specifically the understanding of issues and trends in a multicultural society, "including but not limited to: Attitudes and behaviors based on such factors as age, race or religious preference."

In the context of this article, Robert H. Pate Jr., a professor at the University of Virginia, Charlottesville, suggested that course content include infusing clients' spiritual and religious aspects into the curriculum of training therapists and providing various experiences for therapists-in-training to enhance not only their own personal growth, but also their awareness of their attitudes and feelings about how their own religious values would be affecting their counseling. Pate asserts that secular therapists should be cultivating relationships with religiously oriented therapists, while cautioning about some of the ethical and professional limits of working with religious therapists who may or may not be trained in therapy.

In this same article, Eugene Kelly, a professor at George Washington University, also makes an interesting point in noting that it would be impossible for anybody to know everything about religion, and certainly not about all the various religious groups and sects within the United States. But he did say that if a therapist is talking to a client and religious issues come up that could be related to the DSM-IV V Code, the therapist may want to consult with someone from the religious community to better understand that client's value base and avoid confusing or upsetting the client by attempting to impose his or her own personal beliefs.

Kelly also provided the Quote of the Month: "A client's spiritual and religious beliefs and values, like any other set of personal beliefs and values, are potentially legitimate considerations in the counseling process." Thus, a DSM-IV V Code dealing with religious problems is a legitimate concern. Along these same lines, Goolishian (1992) noted that he had to really learn to listen to and comprehend what clients were saying relative to their own values, as opposed to his own views and theories. In other words, he realized that he needed to listen to the language of his clients, as opposed to his own worldview, so that he could become understanding and be aware of clients' understanding and assumptions within their value structures.

This is not to say that the attempt to integrate religious views into therapy has occurred entirely within the last few years. In fact, Griffith (1986) discussed the importance and practicality of utilizing a family's relationship to God, in family therapy with individuals holding those particular deep beliefs. It was his contention that God actually exists as a member of the family and serves as a stabilizing force in interpersonal relationships, as well as engaging in day-to-day family interactions. Griffith went on to note that he centered on God and the family's interactions with God as the therapeutic focus. He did not necessarily utilize specific religious beliefs in these interactions, but thought that the focus on family interaction was what was important.

DiBlasio (1991) examined the concept of forgiveness among marital and family therapists. In general, he was interested in the utility of forgiveness, specific techniques for assisting clients in forgiveness issues, individual perceptions about the role of forgiveness in resolving depression, and the openness of the client's religious issues as part of therapies. Findings indicated very small differences in the theoretical factors produced by the religiosity of the subjects. His conclusions seemed to indicate that practitioners with strong religious identification are probably more likely than less religious clinicians to actually extend forgiveness, as well as to use religious principles as part of their particular therapies. They are about equally inclined to develop forgiveness approaches into the belief that forgiveness is essential to relieving anger or depression.

Thus, some therapists now see the importance of considering religious or spiritual aspects in providing comprehensive help to individuals who may be suffering from a values-related crisis within the context of a dysfunctional marriage or relationship. The V Code can serve as a useful basis for identifying, assessing, and treating these difficulties.

CASE STUDY

This case study can help the reader understand some of the more subtle features and problems in counseling marriage partners who have similar religious convictions, but who have distorted the application of the religious teachings because of faulty and ineffective personality structures. This would earn them a DSM-IV V Code for Religious Problem. This case study will give depth to some of the evaluation and treatment issues. The particular case was selected not only because of the problems identified, but also because of its completeness, the assessment, and the successful outcome of the treatment; it is presented in clinical form for the reader's convenience. Though this is an actual case, some of the details, and certainly the names, have been changed for confidentiality purposes. The contention here is that distortion of religious values is a paramount factor in the understanding of a couple's dysfunction and in the treatment of their problems. Religious values offer a backdrop to roles, issues, and resolution of life's problems.

Reason for Referral

This couple was referred to the office by their pastor. Mr. and Mrs. S had separated for six weeks previous to the initial visit because of severe marital discord. Previous counseling had proven unsuccessful; it had not focused clearly on the religious issues and values clash of the couple. Rather, counseling had focused on communication and interpersonal relations. Thus, the pastor was hoping for another opinion, a fresh analysis, and a treatment plan that would successfully reconcile these two parishioners whom he loved. Mrs. S was living out of state at this time and was questioning whether reconciliation was really possible. Mr. S was quite reluctant to resume a counseling relationship. Because of their trust in their pastor, however, they were willing to have one more visit.

Background Information

Mr. S was a 48-year-old tradesman. He was raised as a foster child in a boys' home and had suffered abuse at the hands of various workers there. A few years prior to this particular contact, he had been hospitalized because of severe family problems. At that time, his wife left him for the first time. An 18-year-old son had left home prior to this incident because Mr. S had been abusive and threatening to all members of the family. Mr. S had previously been hospitalized at another psychiatric unit because of outbursts toward his family. He was threatening to kill himself and his wife. It is important to know that Mr. S's father had committed suicide when Mr. S was only 11 years of age. He had ended his life with a gun. As a child of 7, Mr. S had witnessed his father trying to gas himself in an oven. Tragically, seven months following the death of his father, his mother was killed in an auto accident when she drove beneath a semi-trailer. This circumstance led to his foster placement. In addition, when Mrs. S separated from him the first time, a child protection agency was brought in because he had paddled his daughter. Charges were eventually dismissed. Apparently, there was a lack of evidence of abuse.

Other information provided was that Mr. S's first wife had died of cancer. He is a Vietnam veteran. He is one of six children, with four older brothers and one younger brother. Mr. S also has a history of high blood pressure, high cholesterol, and asthma. His DSM-IV diagnostic impressions while hospitalized were 312.39 Impulse Control Disorder, rule out 296.66 Bipolar Disorder, Mixed, In Remission. Other practitioners who dealt with him assigned an Axis II of "Diagnosis Deferred."

As an adult in his 30s, he experienced a religious conversion. Although he had not been raised in any particular religious environment, at the time of assessment he professed a conservative Protestant value base. He was a regular church attendee and held high regard for the doctrines and precepts of his faith. In short, he readily accepted the validity of Scripture and the teachings of his church and was willing to acknowledge that source of authority.

Mrs. S was 44 years of age and entered the therapeutic situation with issues of Adult Children of Alcoholics. At the time of counseling she was working as an office temporary. She had had a hysterectomy and was taking estrogen. This was her third marriage. There was no psychiatric history in her family except for the fact that her father was an alcoholic. She has three siblings, two brothers and one sister. She had no children by her previous marriages. Both of the previous marriages involved spouses who engaged in substance and spousal abuse. Mrs. S did report a short bout with alcohol abuse herself. Upon entering the relationship and subsequent marriage with Mr. S, she was transformed quickly into a stepmother with three children, a son 16, a daughter 13, and another son 8. The relationship had been stormy from the beginning.

Mrs. S was raised within a conservative Protestant value structure. Mrs. S's mother took responsibility for her religious upbringing since her father was antagonistic to her church attendance and affiliation. However, Mrs. S, like her husband, was willing to accept Bible teaching as a source of authority.

Psychological Testing

Prior to the initial counseling session, Mr. and Mrs. S were administered the Millon Clinical Multiaxial Inventory–III. Both profiles rendered were valid, Mr. S's DSM-IV Axis I clinical syndrome was 300.40 Dysthymia, characterized by agitation and erratic qualities. The Millon indicated that his various provocations appeared to provide a vehicle for discharging tension and reasserting confidence, as well as leading to the buildup of resentments and anger. His personality pattern revealed "a moderate level of pathology typified by variable and unpredictable moods, irritability and a pessimistic outlook. He would behave obstructively, appeared to be deeply untrusting, fearful of domination and suspiciously alert to any efforts that would undermine his autonomy. He appeared to have an irascible demeanor and low tolerance for frustration. He viewed others as devious and hostile, and desires for retribution for past mistreatment would underlie his characteristic hostility, envy and suspiciousness." An Axis II diagnosis of 301.90 Personality Disorder, NOS, or Sadistic Personality Disorder was generated by the computer, based on DSM-IV criteria.

In a consideration of Mrs. S's Millon–III, Axis I syndromes emerged that indicated both anxiety and dysthymia, but primarily a 300.40 Dysthymic Disorder. She appeared to be the type of person "who would restrain her emotions because of a dread of rebuke and rejection. Rather than chance total abandonment, she would turn her anger inward, leading to self-generated feelings of unworthiness and guilt." Thus, her manifestation of depression, which was inwardly directed, was different from that of her husband, who was overt and hostile toward others. Given this circumstance, one might expect Mrs. S to be possibly more self-destructive than her husband, who had ended up in the hospital at least two times.

When one looked at her personality traits and patterns, Mrs. S's DSM-IV personality diagnosis of 301.6 Dependent Personality Disorder would be hallmarked by a "marked dependency, depressive self-pity, an anxious seeking of reassurance from others and an intense fear of separation from those who would provide support. She would be typically submissive and cooperative and she would also be self-denying, self-debasing, and pessimistic. But she would exhibit helplessness in experiencing anxious periods of prolonged depressive moods." It is remarkable that this woman who seemed so fearful of abandonment and rejection, and was so dependent, would muster up enough gumption to separate from her husband, indicating possibly how severe the situation between her and her husband had become.

Thus, testing revealed a sadistic personality and dependent personality marriage union with serious consequences resulting from the dysfunction.

Initial Interview

During the first session Mr. S focused on his "prophetic" prediction that his wife would desert him by leaving (as mentioned earlier, she had moved a great distance (at least 700 miles) away from him prior to this particular counseling session but was willing to return for therapy). She had left him before, which seemed to reinforce his general mistrust and feeling that she would do it again. He appeared overtly depressed and angry. Initially, he was reluctant to give any sort of commitment to an ongoing therapeutic relationship and reconciliation of the marriage. He was quite defensive about any possibility of his having contributed in any way to the marriage breakdown. This defensiveness was generated partly by his frustration with being identified as the hospitalized patient and "bad guy." One could quickly summarize his values as those of a "black-and-white" thinker, who interpreted life in terms of "right or wrong," "good or bad," "should or shouldn't." As a result of this sort of absolutist thinking, there was little room in his repertoire of interpersonal dynamics that would allow for differences, expressions of preference, and diverse methods of relating. This stance could be related to his underlying suspicion and mistrust of other people's motives, as well as to his possible distortion of Bible-based values.

One can see how an individual so conflicted and so defensive could interpret a therapeutic encounter as provocative and threatening. This attitude could expand even into other interpersonal areas, so that individuals expressing either a difference of opinion or taking a different stance might be interpreted by him as being very personally critical and against him. Given this man's anger, hostility, and rigid black-and-white thinking, it is not surprising that his view of religion, and even of God, was one that would focus on rules, regulations, critical judgment, wrathful thinking, and perfectionistic moral standards. Religion thus became an extension or projection of his own inner tensions and thinking that could then be utilized as a way of either controlling other people or relating to them in a mean-spirited, hostile manner. It became an excuse in a pattern of justifying his hostility toward others, thus preserving himself from any type of criticism and providing impetus to his sadistic coping style.

Mr. S's history of childhood abuse and the resultant reinforcement of his own hostile schemes and low self-esteem had given him, through religion, a method whereby he could attempt to earn his value through performance. In other words, he was the type of individual who might keep score on his good deeds and good behaviors to justify how perfect and wonderful he is, not only in the eyes of God, but before others. Therefore, any type of situation that would subject him to any kind of criticism would result in his provocation of others. One can readily see how fragile this man's inner value structure had become. Fortunately, in spite of his distortions, he did believe that Holy Scripture was true, and he was certainly willing to listen to what It said. This view is, to some extent, related to his predilection for rules and regulations and the fact that the Bible does set forth certain parameters for human behaviors. Therefore, he was more than willing to buy into this aspect of biblical teaching.

During the interview Mrs. S had a very weepy, depressed, tearful sort of reaction to her husband's many pronouncements, proclamations, and restrictions. She literally seemed to be frustrated, burned out, and fed up with the relationship. Dependency was expressed to some extent in her indecisiveness, her searching for someone to depend on and to make decisions for her. Although she had recently reacted somewhat out of character by making an assertive move to separate from her husband, she presented in the interview as an individual who lacked direction, who was emotionally fragile and overwhelmed. It was clear in interviewing her that in the past she had depended on other people to help her make major decisions in her life. She confirmed an overt fear of abandonment and rejection that had emerged during the interview and was noted on her Millon scales as well.

Mrs. S's self-confidence was viewed as poor at this time. It was interesting to note that she put herself into a psychological bind by depending on and requiring decisions to be made for her by individuals who had actually mistreated her. Not only was this going on in the situation with her current husband, but it had happened before. Fortunately for Mrs. S, she had already developed, prior to this appointment, some insight into her dependency problems and had shown some assertiveness by getting away from one of her tormentors. It is small wonder then that she would view her church, and religion in general, as an area where she could freely go and obtain nurturance and succor to help feed a great deal of her dependency needs and issues, as well as to bolster somewhat her greatly sagging self-esteem.

As a result of growing up in alcoholic system, her view of God was that of a father figure who would provide more acceptance and love, in contrast to her earthly father who had abandoned and rejected her. Ironically, this woman approached her faith in a way very similar to her husband's, in the sense that she had developed a relationship with her God within a performance-based acceptance model. Thus, Mrs. S's dependent coping style, which was quite dysfunctional, was also woven into her view of God and church.

In this case, we encountered two individuals, one with low self-esteem functioning in a hostile, sadistic relational mode, and the other clingingly dependent and self-defeating. Yet both had placed themselves on a performance-based, do-good-earn-points, gain-acceptance treadmill in their approach to "the Almighty." The danger of this treadmill might be that if one or both did not earn enough good points, did not do enough good things, were not perfect, then they would be rejected, damned, or somehow viewed as less than perfect by their Creator. No wonder couples who have placed themselves in a situation like this fold and succumb to their lack of perfection and good deeds (or performance), then downgrade themselves because they are "no good." Or they may become very hostile and rigid, refusing to accept any amount of imperfection in themselves. They fear being viewed by their God as less than adequate or, simply put, spiritual failures.

Although this couple approached relationships, including their relationships with God and with each other, in somewhat different ways (one hostile; the other self-defeating), these two personality types are actually similar, because they both have defective coping skills owing to their fear of rejection and abandonment by other people and by God himself. Fear of rejection and abandonment, lack of self-esteem, a faulty belief system about themselves and their Creator, as well as a history of emotional damage caused by parents and other abusive people, with resultant feelings of hopelessness, worthlessness, and powerlessness, had culminated in a very volatile relational style and situation. Clinically, the difference between their dysfunctional coping styles can be viewed as dramatic, but the similarities of their faulty belief systems are striking.

Treatment Process

Although the spiritual and religious content of their thinking has been distorted and misperceived by the couple, it is important, as contended earlier in this chapter, that sanctifying statements and validating points made by the couple be treated with respect and understanding. That they have distorted and misunderstood their religious framework does not disqualify that particular framework from being validating. Their distortions have not worked well but contribute significantly to dysfunction. At this point, the therapist must realize that if a couple's religious views become distorted, then they will in turn distort the religion upon which those views are based. Their perceptions of God and of themselves, and of humans in general, will carry their own misconceptions and their misinterpretations of Scripture. In other words, if an ordered religious doctrine ascribed to by many people is embraced or integrated within a distorted person, the result is a misuse or misunderstanding of the teachings of that particular religion. Therefore, their distortion of Bible teachings could be quite damaging and actually lead to the disorder identified in the DSM-IV code discussed earlier. This does not minimize the importance of the couple's antagonistic coping styles (hostile versus self-defeating), but it gives the therapist a chance to clarify distortions from a biblical standpoint and allow the couple to focus on a separate source of authority.

Often, when one discusses religion among a number of people, an individual will comment on how many people have been killed in the name of religion, merely highlighting the fact that many disordered people have used religion and distorted God's teachings to satisfy their own whims and self-centered needs for manipulation and control of others. In fact, such distortion of religious values to commit atrocities, although extreme, is not dissimilar to the acts of dysfunctional marriage partners who use Scripture to hurt, undermine, and manipulate their mates or to avoid significant responsibility within the matrimonial bond. The therapist's primary goal, as related to the discussion in this chapter, is to understand the precepts and principles of a couple's religion in a less disordered and more accurate manner. Initial treatment goals in dealing with the disorder described in the aforementioned V Code include the following:

1. Establishing the therapeutic alliance by beginning to access religious values, seen as fundamental to reconciling the relationship. In this case, the therapist shared the couple's spiritual values.
2. Modifying individual partner dynamics through reorienting the couple to their personal responsibility to the relationship, by drawing on their own religious views and dealing with distortions as they emerge.
3. Rebalancing the couple by establishing commitment to the relationships involved and commitment to the treatment process, based on their religious views.
4. Reconciliation
5. Establishing the therapeutic goals of applying grace, forgiveness, and reconciliation as ongoing processes through the life of the marriage.

THE THERAPEUTIC ALLIANCE

The first goal was the most germane, because it involved the religious values specific to this couple's personality and coping strategies. Within this framework, the therapist attempted to point out Bible-based concepts of marriage, personal responsibility, aspects of sin, and relationship to God.

This involved Scripture review and discussion. In this particular case, the couple's religious values and views were the most accessible, immediate, and mutual in understanding how they relate to each other. Their overall belief in the authority of the Bible was one they could easily accept from each other, consider valid, and use to provide unity. In fact, this was one of the very few areas in which these individuals could relate comfortably without lapsing into their usual dysfunctional relational style. Initially, the therapist focused on the roles and responsibility of the marriage relationship. This task was established, first, by the couples' being "quite accountable before God" and, second, toward each other. This particular strategy, focusing on their relationship with God first, helped to release the strain and stress of enmeshment, or their overinvolvement in monitoring the attitudes, behaviors, and especially the performance, of each other.

MODIFYING INDIVIDUAL PARTNER DYNAMICS

After moving this couple's focus toward God and their personal relationship and responsibility to him, the therapist then invited each member of the marriage to assess his or her personal contributions to the relationship and the possible destructive relational methods or strategies used. Central to this assessment was allowing them to open up more in regard to the condition of their own "hearts" whereby they could share their deep, innermost feelings about fear of judgment, shame, or humiliation. The result of this strategy, therapeutically, was that the couple began to profess a personal accountability and willingness to discuss their own painful life experiences and their effect on the marriage, rather than becoming entangled in evaluating and judging the other person's "disorder," which had led to their usual failure at meaningful communication.

Thus, the therapist initially helped the couple to focus on their values, beliefs, attitudes, and responsibilities toward God, which helped them to stop pointing the finger and evaluating each other. They were invited to report their own self-discoveries. As a result of this self-discovery and self-confession, the couple began to see that both had significant pain and issues to be resolved.

REBALANCING THE COUPLE RELATIONSHIP

The therapist moved the couple into comparing their problems, issues, and dysfunctions within the context of their agreed-upon religious values. In such cases, the religious structure begins transition, rather than being used only as a weapon to manipulate and hurt the other individual in the dyad, it becomes in and of itself a standard by which the two people decide to submit to God as a source of authority. The clarified religious structure takes on a rebalancing or reordering quality, bringing function into the dysfunction that a couple is exhibiting, whereas previously the couple's dysfunction disorders the religious structure and causes discontent, depression, anxiety, hostility, and a host of other pathological responses. Such a focus attenuates the dysfunction of the personality and targets the value structure as the source of goal realization. Hostility and dependency can be considered ineffective coping mechanisms that prevent a couple from achieving shared religious views and goals.

As the therapist moved into Goal 4 (Reconciliation), some periodic reconnoitering was made of other issues that would be affected to emerge relative to the other three goals. It was discovered very quickly that the main problem within this relationship, the core to all of the dysfunction, was a basic self-centeredness. This is similar to Sanford and Sandford's (1992) discovery: "The problem of becoming one in marriage is self-centered selfishness. Behind all the troubles every therapist, teacher and pastor has spoken and written about is one malady common to all mankind—simple, self-centered selfishness." Rainey (1993) also points out, "Although couples are so naturally close during dating, one of the main reasons for marital discord and breakup is basic self-centeredness." He identifies this self-centeredness as primarily destructive to intimacy. Inasmuch as the couple ascribed to a scriptually based worldview, it was not very difficult, through examination of Scripture, to convict them of their own particular selfishness and their need to control each other. Sadistic and self-defeating or dependent styles can be exposed as being selfish behaviors designed to control and manipulate so as to "get something out" of a relationship.

Once this realization had crystallized and their self-centeredness had been admitted to, both Mr. and Mrs. S then transformed themselves into a more submissive relationship to God and then, quite naturally, to each other. As a result, each partner's own defenses relaxed markedly. They were able to focus on each other rather than on just themselves, and, of course, the result was to focus on enhancing their relationship. They also admitted at a deeper level what they had been contributing to the relationship that had turned out to be so destructive. Because of this new insight, the couple not only were privy to their own personality dysfunction, but also appeared to accept more responsibility for what had happened within their relationship. They were willing now to reconcile.

APPLYING GRACE AND FORGIVENESS
(THERAPEUTIC GOALS FOR BOTH)

Both Mr. and Mrs. S acknowledged the centrality of ongoing forgiveness and its relationship to oneness or corporateness in the marriage. It has been said that marriage is a 24-hour-a-day practice in the art of forgiveness. Allender (1992) wrote, "Forgiving love does not merely get one through tough times or give purpose to the daily grind of life, [forgiving love] is the inconceivable, unexplainable pursuit of the offender by the offended for the sake of restored relationship with God, self, and others." In fact, the premise of his book was, "I will not live with purpose and joy unless I love; I will not be able to love unless I forgive; and I will not forgive unless my hatred is continually melted by the searing truth and grace of the Gospel." It is important to understand that when we discuss forgiveness, we are speaking here about true biblical forgiveness and that it is to be viewed as a glorious gift for both the offender and the offended. Many people who have ascribed to a Christian value structure have never really understood what Scripture means when it speaks of forgiveness. This is a harder concept than one might perceive on the surface, but it is infinitely more life giving.

Mr. and Mrs. S were able to acknowledge and clarify their concept of grace as related to their own common religious views. According to psychiatrist Verle Bell (1993), "Grace is a free, undeserved gift from God to me which provides three basic things to deal with my bent to sin—value, power, and hope." Within the context of this couple's religious values, the most destructive aspect to the relationship (sin) was most prominently each one's selfishness and desire to control the other.

Had this couple not discovered the concept of grace, which has always been a basic tenet of their values, order would not have been possible. There was the acknowledgment that, as in Bell's view of value, power, and hope, grace did not reside within them based on their own performance, but was a gift to them undeserved from God, expressed by God to them in the person of his Son Jesus the Messiah, whose life, death, and resurrection establishes for them infinite value and power through the Holy Spirit, imparting an internal hope and stability in spite of their circumstance. They realized an assurance of an intimate relationship with God not only in this life, but in the life after.

The reader realizing these particular convictions is hopefully aware of (even though not necessarily believing) how life changing these deep beliefs can be in the reconciliation and continued success within a marriage relationship. Grace becomes central to the intimate marriage relationship. So, the therapist's understanding and the clients' understanding of grace led to balance in their relationship, involving their emotional, social, intellectual, and sexual intimacy, as well as recreational and spiritual intimacy, which, of course, was instrumental in treating and ameliorating the symptoms of their religious disorderedness.

Thus, this couple's disordered coping styles were exposed and re-ordered through their anchor of trust and belief in their religious views. Ongoing accessing of grace, forgiveness, and reconciliation were recommended as goals for their lives.

REFERENCES

Allender, D. B., & Longman, T. (1992). *Bold love*. Colorado Springs: NavPress.

American Psychiatric Association. (1994). *Diagnostic and statistical manual of mental disorders* (4th ed.). Washington, DC: Author.

Bell, V. (1993). *True freedom*. Ann Arbor, MI: Servant Publications.

DiBlasio, F. A. (1991). *Journal of Psychology and Christianity, 10*, 166–172.

Genia, V. (1994). Secular psychotherapists and religious clients: Professional considerations and recommendations. *Journal of Counseling and Development, 72*, 395–398.

Goolishian, H. A., & Anderson, H. (1992). Strategy and intervention versus non-intervention: A matter of theory? *Journal of Marital and Family Therapy, 18*, 5–15.

Griffith, J. L. (1986). Employing the God-family relationship in therapy with religious families. *Family Process, 25*, 609–618.

Guernsey, D. (1994). Christian marriage counseling. *Journal of Psychology and Christianity, 13*, 117–124.

Hinterkopf, E. (1994). *Counseling and values, 38*, 165–175.

Jung, C. G. (1963). *Memories, dreams, reflections*. New York: Pantheon.

King, R. (1978). Evangelical Christians and professional counseling: A conflict of values. *Journal of Psychology and Theology, 6*, 276–281.

Lovinger, R. J. (1984). *Working with religious issues in therapy*. New York: Jason Aronson.

Meltzoff (1970). *Research in psychotherapy*. New York: Atherton Press.

Menninger, K. (1973). *Whatever became of sin?* New York: Hawthorne Books.

Morrissey, M. (1995). Infusing religion and spirituality into "secular" counseling. *Counseling Today, 37*, 1–2.

Pate, R. H., & High, J. H. (1995). The importance of client religious beliefs in practices in the education of therapists in the CACRAB-accredited programs. *Counseling Today*, 42–45.

Peck, M. S. (1983) *People of the lie*. New York: Simon & Schuster.

Prest, L. (1993). Spirituality in family therapy: Spiritual beliefs, myths, metaphors. *Journal of Marital and Family Therapy, 19*, 137–148.

Rainey, D. (1993). *Building your marriage*. Ventura, CA: Gospel Light.

Rotz (1993). The therapist who is perceived as spiritually correct: Strategies for avoiding collusion with a "spiritually one up" spouse. *Journal of Marital and Family Therapy, 19*, 369–375.

Sandford, J., & Sandford, P. (1982). *The transformation of the inner man.* Tulsa, OK: Victory House.

Shafranske, E., & Maloney, H. (1990). Clinical psychologists' religious and spiritual orientations in their practice of psychotherapy. *Psychotherapy, 27,* 72–78.

Szasz, T. (1974). *The myth of mental illness.* New York: Harper & Row.

CHAPTER 8

The Eating Disordered Couple

D. Blake Woodside
Jack S. Brandes
Jan B. Lackstrom
Lorie Shekter-Wolfson

Couples in whom one member has an eating disorder have been of interest for many years. In the case of anorexia nervosa, this interest initially arose because of the belief that anorexia was generally associated with an avoidance of sexuality and, therefore, that such marriages were dysfunctional in some way. The more recent interest in bulimia nervosa, which has perhaps more to do with the explosion in the incidence of this disorder, has included a recognition that bulimia is a very serious problem among women in their adult years, the years when more intimate relationships are most often formed.*

Theories about the nature of the relationships of couples with such disorders have been plentiful, but not usually supported by very much in the way of empirical evidence. Most of the theories have been generated by attempts to apply information gleaned from clinical experiences with young patients, directly to marital relationships. Two of the more exciting advances in this area have been the gradual development of a theoretical

---

*Given that the overwhelming majority of those suffering from eating disorders are female, we will use the female pronoun in this article. This is not meant in any way to ignore the occurrence of these illnesses in men.

base that is more directly derived from clinical experience with such couples, and the appearance of an empirical literature that has begun to test the theories about these couples.

DEFINITION OF THE ILLNESSES:
ANOREXIA NERVOSA AND BULIMIA NERVOSA

The definitions of anorexia nervosa and bulemia nervosa have undergone some modification in recent years. Exhibit 8.1 presents the diagnostic criteria for anorexia nervosa according to DSM-IV (American Psychiatric Association, 1994). The core requirement for a weight loss of 15 percent is maintained, along with a distortion in the way the body is viewed and a drive for thinness. The amenorrhea criterion is also retained, despite some evidence questioning its usefulness (Garfinkel et al., 1996).

It should be noted that the weight criterion is somewhat arbitrary. Diagnosis in adolescents requires the use of specialized tables that cross-reference weight, height, and age, and a failure to reach 85 percent of the expected weight counts as meeting the diagnostic requirement. Although most patients with anorexia nervosa admit to continuing to feel fat even at a very low weight, an occasional patient denies this or even claims to wish to gain weight. If it can be established that such a patient had a body image distortion at a very low weight, or that she would continue to feel fat at a higher, but still subnormal, weight, the existence of body image distortion is usually thought to be demonstrated. A similar assessment can be applied regarding the drive for thinness.

The criterion of a period of amenorrhea remains controversial. At the present time, it remains primarily as a marker for a sufficient level of star-vation, and earlier formulations that emphasized the psychological importance of lack of menstruation have been largely discarded; at least it has been recognized that such formulations are important for only a minority of patients. If an underweight patient is taking oral contracep-tives, it is not necessary to demonstrate a period of amenorrhea.

Anorexia nervosa is now classified into two subtypes, the restricting and binge/purge subtypes. In the former, patients lose weight solely by fasting or exercise. In the latter, purging by vomiting or use of laxatives or diuretics is a part of the clinical picture; some patients may have full-syndrome bulimia as well. Patients who have previously had anorexia nervosa and presently have bulimia nervosa should probably be diagnosed as "bulimic with a past history of anorexia nervosa, binge/purge subtype."

The diagnostic criteria for bulimia nervosa (Exhibit 8.2) are essentially unchanged from DSM-III-R. Binge-eating remains the hallmark symptom of bulimia, and the characterization of this behavior and the frequency

Exhibit 8.1
DIAGNOSTIC CRITERIA FOR ANOREXIA NERVOSA
(American Psychiatric Association, 1994)

A. Refusal to maintain body weight at or above a minimally normal weight for age and height (e.g., weight loss leading to maintenance of body weight less than 85% of that expected; or failure to make expected weight gain during period of growth, leading to body weight less than 85% of that expected).

B. Intense fear of gaining weight or becoming fat, even though underweight.

C. Disturbance in the way in which one's body weight or shape is experienced; undue influence of body weight or shape on self-evaluation, or denial of the seriousness of the current body weight.

D. In post-menarchal females, amenorrhea, i.e., the absence of at least three consecutive menstrual cycles. (A woman is considered to have amenorrhea if her periods occur only following hormone, e.g., estrogen, administration.)

Types of Anorexia Nervosa

Restricting Type: During the episode of anorexia nervosa, the person does not regularly engage in binge-eating or purging behavior (i.e., self-induced vomiting or the misuse of laxatives or diuretics).

Binge-Eating/Purging Type: During the episode of anorexia nervosa, the person regularly engages in binge-eating or purging behavior (i.e., self-induced vomiting or the misuse of laxatives or diuretics.)

Exhibit 8.2
DIAGNOSTIC CRITERIA FOR BULIMIA NERVOSA
(American Psychiatric Association, 1994)

A. Recurrent episodes of binge eating. An episode of binge eating
    is characterized by both of the following:
    1. Eating, in a discrete period of time (e.g., within any two-
        hour period), an amount of food that is definitely larger
        than most people would eat during a similar period of
        time and under similar circumstances, and,
    2. A sense of lack of control over eating during the episode
        (e.g., a feeling that one cannot stop eating or control what
        or how much one is eating).

B. Recurrent inappropriate compensatory behavior in order to
    prevent weight gain, such as self-induced vomiting, misuse of
    laxatives, diuretics, or other medications; fasting; or excessive
    exercise.

C. The binge-eating and inappropriate compensatory behavior
    both occur, on average, at least twice a week for three months.

D. Self-evaluation is unduly influenced by body shape and
    weight.

E. The disturbance does not occur exclusively during episodes of
    anorexia nervosa.

Types of Bulimia Nervosa

Purging Type: The person regularly engages in self-induced vomiting or the misuse of laxatives or diuretics.

Non-purging Type: The person uses other inappropriate compensatory behaviors, such as fasting or excessive exercise, but does
not regularly engage in self-induced vomiting or the misuse of laxatives or diuretics.

criterion remain the same, again despite evidence suggesting that the two-times-per-week criterion is somewhat arbitrary (Garfinkel et al., 1995). Of note is that the requirement for weight and shape preoccupation is slightly softened, and bulimia is now classified as a purging or a non-purging type, whereby "nonpurging" is defined as including only the compensatory behaviors of fasting and exercise. Some recent studies suggest that this latter type of bulimia is the more common in the community, as opposed to its incidence in the clinic (Garfinkel et al., 1995).

Binge-eating disorder is not formally included in DSM-IV, but some draft criteria are presented in an appendix to assist researchers in the further delineation of this condition. This chapter does not comment on this proposed diagnosis.

UNDERSTANDING THE NATURE OF EATING DISORDERS

Most authorities continue to support a multidetermined formulation of the eating disorders (Garfinkel & Garner, 1982). Exhibit 8.3 presents such a formulation, which is used in the Toronto Hospital program. It is thought that a variety of factors predispose an individual to the development of eating problems. These include as diverse items as one's genetic heritage; social, vocational, and cultural pressures for thinness; adverse events such as sexual or physical abuse or psychiatric comorbidity; and family or marital distress. At present, it is generally recognized that each individual will come to the eating problem via his or her own unique path and that no single description of causes will cover all possibilities.

The various factors described here are thought to begin a psychological process whereby an individual begins to feel less worthwhile or less effective. A common method used by young women in North America to deal with such feelings is to engage in calorie-reduced dieting, an activity that is presented culturally in a very positive light. In fact, dieting behaviors, which usually result in weight loss in the short run, do act as temporary methods of increasing self-esteem and enhancing a sense of effectiveness. Unfortunately, because dieting addresses only the symptoms of other, more complex problems, it becomes tempting to continue to diet in an effort to continue to feel good about oneself. The individual thus becomes dependent on either the maintenance of a low body weight or constant weight loss to modulate her self-esteem and sense of effectiveness. The allure of this course of action and the extent to which the previously described sequence has established itself in our culture can be seen in community surveys, which reveal that 50 percent of teenagers at a normal weight feel too fat (McCreary Centre Society, 1993) and 65 percent of 6- to 12-year-old

Exhibit 8.3
FORMULATION OF EATING DISORDERS

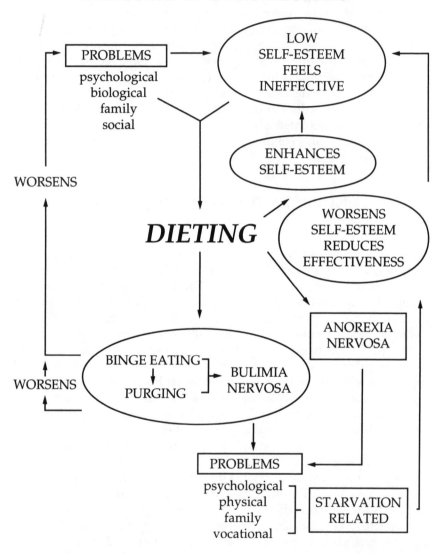

girls think that they need to lose weight (Maloney et al., 1989). Others have written extensively about the damaging nature of our society's "addiction" to the pursuit of thinness (Wolf, 1992).

In individuals who diet but do not develop an eating disorder, there is some evidence to suggest that the usual long-term consequence of this activity is weight gain rather than weight loss (for a review, see Ciliska,

1990). For a fairly small percentage of individuals, weight loss continues almost indefinitely and they develop full-blown anorexia nervosa. Patients do not usually come to treatment in the early stage of the illness— the symptoms are ego-syntonic. Eventually, the physical and psychological effects of starvation begin to affect the person adversely, and if she is able to make a connection between these adverse events and her weight loss, she may eventually decide to seek treatment. In the meantime, these adverse events—the physical changes and gradual diminution of her ability to carry out her usual activities and maintain her relationships— further reduce her sense of effectiveness and self-esteem and leave her even more vulnerable to engaging in further dieting behavior in an effort to feel better about herself.

The path to bulimia nervosa is somewhat different beyond that first critical decision to diet. Those who go on to develop bulimia nervosa, a larger group than those who develop anorexia, respond to chronic dieting by developing binge-eating. There is now a fairly strong body of empirical evidence to support the important causal relationship between dietary restraint and bingeing (various). In our formulation, the onset of binge-eating is greeted with horror by the weight-preoccupied dieter, who then intensifies her dieting behaviors in an attempt to reverse the effects of the binge-eating, which has left her feeling out of control and terrible about herself. This intensified dieting simply leads to more binge-eating and, in a percentage of cases, to purging behaviors. Although these may produce a temporary sense of relief, the shame associated with purging is fairly intense and serves to send the person's self-esteem spiraling downward, leading to further dieting in an attempt to restore self-esteem and effectiveness. The bulimic person becomes further embroiled in this cycle by virtue of experiencing many of the effects of starvation that occur in anorexia nervosa, although often in an attenuated form. The chaos that tends to occur in the life of the bulimic individual further intensifies the cycle, and difficulty is heaped upon difficulty.

Although food addiction models are popular to explain bulimia, it should be noted that, in our formulation, pursuing a strategy of food avoidance will simply lead to more bingeing—and formulations such as ours have been identified as controversial by the American Psychiatric Association in their practice guidelines for eating disorders (American Psychiatric Association, 1993).

EFFECTS OF EATING DISORDERS ON COUPLES

There is a limited theoretical and empirical literature describing the relationships of couples with eating disorders. The theoretical literature has generally focused on five themes, presented in Exhibit 8.4. The empirical

---

Exhibit 8.4
COMMON THEMES PRESENTED IN THE THEORETICAL
LITERATURE ON EATING-DISORDERED COUPLES

Distraction from other problems

Unresolved family-of-origin issues

Power and control

Avoidance of intimacy and sexuality

Pregnancy and childbirth

---

literature has attempted to investigate the extent to which eating-disordered (ED) couples report marital dysfunction and whether eating disorder theories related to families can be applied to couples with eating disorders.

Conflict Avoidance

The use of eating symptoms as a method of conflict avoidance is referred to by numerous theoretical authors (Root, Falon, & Friedrich, 1986; Schwartz, Barrett, & Saba, 1985; Fishman, 1979). This method is postulated by some authors to be direct distraction (Levine, 1988) and by others (Schwartz, Barrett, & Saba 1984) as self-soothing in response to ongoing marital distress. There is only a limited empirical literature examining these theories, with observations by Van Buren and Williamson (1988) supporting increased withdrawal from conflict as a methods used by bulimic wives. Van den Broucke and colleagues (1995a, b, c) studied this issue intensively and found that ED couples have fewer conflict resolution skills than normal couples, but have more such skills than a general pool of maritally distressed couples. They concluded that it is important to respect the heterogeneity in these couples and to avoid automatically assuming the existence of pathology.

A variant of this line of thinking focuses on the issue of the timing of the onset of the eating problem, with most authors thinking that the development of an eating disorder after a marriage is indicative of unresolved struggles concerning autonomy and separation (Andersen, 1985; Dally 1984; Van den Broucke & Vandereycken, 1989a,b). Heavy and colleagues

(1989), however, reporting on a sample of approximately 50 married women with anorexia nervosa, suggests that the exact timing of the onset of the disorder tends to be a reflection of the nature of the patient's family of origin, in that families who distance more are able to allow the ill child to leave home, whereas children of relatively disorganized families develop the illness at a time that relates more closely to their personal situations. These observations are supported by those of Dally (1984), who also reported on a fairly large sample of married anorexic women.

Family-of-Origin Issues

In the area of unresolved family-of-origin issues, boundary diffusion/pattern replication has received the most attention. Some authors (Kwee & Duivenvoorden, 1985; Brandes, 1991) have suggested that the apparent drive to replicate paternal relationships in the marriage is indicative of an underlying anxious attachment style. Other authors (Schwartz, Barrett, & Saba, 1985; Fishman, 1979) describe eating disorder symptoms as a way for the eating-disordered woman to remain closely connected to her family of origin and thus avoid dealing with family dynamics that impede appropriate separation and individuation. The cost of this strategy, unfortunately, is marital distress, inasmuch as the couple is unable to form a discrete and independent marital unit.

Dally (1984) and Schwartz and colleagues (1985) have suggested that another variant on this process is the development of complementarity in bulimic couples—one member of whom is defined as "overresponsible" and the other as "underresponsible"—as another method of putting off the completion of the individuation task.

Finally, an occasional author has commented on individual situations in which the choice of a bulimic partner has appeared to be driven by a multigenerational focus on appearance and/or physical activity (Root, Fallon, & Friedrich, 1986; Schwartz, Barrett, & Saba, 1984; Levine, 1988; Van den Broucke & Vandereycken, 1989b). There is no empirical literature to suggest how prevalent such a pattern might be in these couples.

Power and Control

Many authors have suggested that issues of power and control may be relevant in ED couples (Madanes, 1981; Schwartz, Barrett, & Saba, 1985; Root, Fallon, & Friedrich, 1986; Levine, 1988; Vandereycken et al., 1989a,b). In some cases these observations relate to the reports of complementarity in these couples—Van den Broucke & Vandereycken (1989a,b) suggest that couples with an anorexic member may be inherently more stable than couples with a bulimic member. Other authors have focused more on the apparent disempowerment of the ill member of the couple, whose unwell stance actually develops fairly rapidly into the more powerful position (Madanes, 1981; Schwartz, Barrett, & Saba, 1984). This view can be understood as an extension of observations of adolescent eating-disordered patients made by family therapists of the structural school.

Root and colleagues (1986) have carried this line of thought one step further by suggesting that the initial superiority of the husband in these marriages is more apparent than real, and that the development of the eating disorder symptoms in the wife is an attempt to distract attention from a weak or dysfunctional spouse. Obviously, such a relationship would be put under very significant strain were the wife to recover from her eating symptoms.

Sexuality, Pregnancy, and Parenting

The area of sexuality and intimacy has been brought into sharper focus in recent years as multiple reports have supported the observation that patients with anorexia nervosa and those with bulimia nervosa experience fairly high rates of sexual abuse. Although the rates quoted do not appear to be higher than those in most serious psychiatric illness (Pope & Hudson, 1992), such abuse is certainly relevant for the individuals involved and is likely to be a significant problem for some married eating-disordered patients, given its base prevalence.

These more recent findings do make it more difficult to know what to make of earlier theories that focused on conflicts about psychosexual maturity (Crisp et al., 1977; Crisp et al., 1980) and more recent findings that have linked observations about decreased physical or emotional intimacy to these earlier formulations (Barrett & Schwartz, 1987; Van den Broucke & Vandereycken, 1989a, b; Root Fallon, & Friedrich, 1986). It is likely most prudent to conclude that any observation of sexual dysfunction in a couple in whom an eating disorder is present should be very thoroughly assessed and not assumed to be due to a psychological deficiency on the part of the bulimic or anorexic member.

Pregnancy and childbirth in these couples have been the focus of a limited empirical literature (Lacey & Smith, 1987; Stewart et al., 1987; Brinch, Isager, & Tolstrup, 1988). Most of these reports have suggested some reductions in fertility in these patients, but there is not enough information available to discern whether this is the case with both anorexia nervosa and bulimia nervosa. There has been no systematic inquiry into such women's attitudes toward conception or as to whether these attitudes are different in actively ill versus recovered women.

Finally, the subject of parenting by women with eating disorders has also received very little attention. Several reports (Lacey & Smith, 1987; Woodside & Shekter-Wolfson, 1990; Evans & LeGrange, 1995), have indicated that women with eating disorders have difficulties in carrying out the role of parent, but there is no information as to whether this difficulty persists beyond recovery or about the extent to which possible illness-related problems might be buffered by the presence of a well partner.

In summary, the presence of an eating disorder in at least one member clearly affects multiple areas of functioning of a couple. It remains an open area of discussion as to how much of the observed problems are artifacts of the illnesses and how much is related to their onset or perpetuation.

APPROACHES AND INTERVENTIONS

Although the approach to eating-disordered couples has much in common with the treatment of other couples of whom one member is seriously ill, there are several areas in which specific differences are encountered.

Assessment

Exhibit 8.5 presents the components of the history of a couple of whom one member has an eating disorder. The general structure of this assessment should be familiar to most marital therapists; only areas that are specific to this patient population are discussed in the following sections.

Context.   Because patients with eating disorders are physically ill, the context of the referral for marital assessment is an important issue. Is the eating-disordered person in treatment elsewhere? Is her medical status being monitored? For the marital therapist who is not a physician, these are important issues, and it is advisable for such a therapist to develop an ongoing relationship with a physician so that unattached patients can be monitored regularly, as appropriate.

If the identified patient is in treatment, the marital therapist must clarify how the assessment will integrate with that treatment. If the marital therapist is part of the treatment team or works in the same setting where other treatment is being provided, this may be a simple task; if the additional treatment is given elsewhere, coordination may require some negotiation and education on both sides.

Exhibit 8.5
STAGES OF THE MARITAL ASSESSMENT

Reason for the assessment

Understanding of the eating disorder

History of the couple

Sexual history

Inc.ividual histories

Family life-cycle issues and family of origin

Role of food, exercise, and appearance in the marriage

Problem-solving abilities

Reason for the Assessment. The reason for an assessment of an eating-disordered person also relates to "context" (the subject of the preceding section), which offers an opportunity to assess issues of power and control in the relationship by examining the process by which the decision was made. Again, if a referral has been made in the context of a treatment program for the identified patient, they may not have a clear understanding of why they are meeting as a couple. Occasionally, couples are referred at the insistence of an anxious spouse whose stated agenda is to "fix up" the ill member of the couple, or perhaps at the urging of an individual therapist who is not familiar with eating disorders and is feeling overwhelmed.

Couple's Understanding of the Eating Disorder. As discussed later, the provision of accurate information to a couple about the illness is a critical intervention. It is thus imperative to identify where the couple is starting from. As in any clinical situation, couples vary wildly in the amount and accuracy of information they have available.

There are two special situations that frequently arise early in an assessment. In the first, the spouse of an emaciated anorexic patient may express considerable frustration at his inability to help his sick wife and may exhibit significant irritation at any element of the assessment that does not appear to be directly relevant to the immediate resolution of her physical problems. In the second, the ill person may have had a secret bulimia for some time, possibly years, and the spouse may be in a state of shock at this discovery. Often, in the latter case, it has been important for things to "look good" within the marriage relationship; the revealing of a major secret such as bulimia can be very destabilizing for these people. In both cases, gentle reassurance and the provision of basic information about the nature of the illness usually suffice as an immediate intervention.

Couple's History. The next part of the assessment, the couple's history, is performed in the therapist's usual style. It is worth evaluating the extent to which physical appearance, shared exercise, or dieting behaviors were an important aspect of the initial attraction. It may happen, but rarely, that behavioral changes required as part of treatment end up adversely affecting the relationship, such as when both members of the couple diet, but during treatment the eating-disordered member is encouraged to give up all diet products.

Assessing the timing of the onset of the illness is critical here. If the couple met after the onset of the illness, it is essential to assess the extent to which the spouse is invested in the perpetuation of the illness. What will it be like for him when the patient is well? It must be remembered that it is the rare spouse who acknowledges that he is anxious in this area, and evidence to support such a view is usually indirect.

Eating disorders that arise during the marriage are thought by most authors to be a response to marital stress; thus, a very active inquiry should be made about this situation. Sometimes the stress is more internal to the patient rather than structural in the marriage; this may be the case when the onset of the illness actually represents a relapse from a previous, remitted episode of an eating problem.

Sexual History. The sexual area of an eating-disordered couple's history has the same importance as in any marital assessment. There are, however, two specific areas that are most relevant to eating disorders. First, it is often assumed that sexual difficulties are related only to body image problems or fear of aging, and that when these go away the sexual problems will be resolved. This is, unfortunately, not the case; many of these patients have been victimized and the process of treatment for their eating disorder tends to activate concerns about sexuality. This may lead to a marked exacerbating of the couple's sexual relationship, to a much worse extent than experienced by couples in whom body image is the only issue to be dealt with.

Second, the spouse's expectations about the future sexual functioning of his wife should be assessed. Does he expect rapid improvements? Marked changes in sexual drive? The transient worsening of sexual function that often accompanies treatment may be intolerable to the already frustrated spouse, who may have married his wife primarily because of sexual attraction related to her physical appearance in the first place.

Individual Histories. Issues more important to the assessment of the eating-disordered couple are those related to boundaries—both interpersonal and intergenerational—and these require careful attention. It is important, although difficult at times, to distinguish between the normal concern of a family for an ill member and pathologic enmeshment. Both lead to a similar picture of over-rich relational bonds between the patient, her spouse, and her family of origin. It is wise to avoid making the assumption of pathology in these situations, but rather to search for evidence of boundary violations in other areas of the marriage or family of origin.

The presence of some comorbid illness, either psychological or physical, is often a factor in these marriages. Comorbid illnesses put an additional strain on the marriage, and the couple's pattern of adaptation to them must be fully understood.

Role of Food, Exercise, and Importance of Appearance. The eating patterns of the couple—including who shops for and prepares the food—should be carefully assessed. This usually includes a brief assessment of the eating habits of the two families of origin to determine whether the couple are replicating patterns learned in those settings. Furthermore, there should be an assessment of the degree to which the couple's eating habits are healthy adaptations to the presence of a chronic illness or perpetuators of it. For example, a decision by the husband of a severely anorexic woman to do all the shopping because he fears for her physical safety is a reasonable response. Yet a decision by a husband in a similar situation to buy only diet foods because "it's all she will even try to eat" might be a factor contributing to the ongoing illness in the anorexic spouse. If the husband has particular eating habits—say he is vegetarian—what will it be like for the couple if his wife's treatment program does not allow vegetarianism?

We have alluded earlier to the critical role that appearance may play in these relationships. It is very important to assess thoroughly what each partner thinks about the weight and shape of the other and to explore their fears about what would constitute unacceptable weights and shapes. It is actually fairly rare for a spouse to have an immovable idea in this area. It is more common for the spouse to inadvertently collude with the patient to "help her to be comfortable"—for example, by positively connoting less than normal weights for anorexic wives or by normalizing food avoidances or dieting behaviors in bulimic wives. When specific, unalterable ideas about weight and appearance are present, these are often related to long-standing patterns in one or both families of origin and may be very difficult to change.

Exercise patterns also require careful attention, especially if the patient has been using exercise as a purging technique. Occasionally, exercise either has been of critical importance in the initiation of the relationship or may be the sole remaining connection between the couple.

Problem-Solving Abilities.   Although a standard part of any marital assessment, their problem-solving abilities have special relevance to the eating-disordered couple. Most couples will readily frame an eating problem as a significant challenge to the marriage, and an inquiry into the ways in which the couple have tried to deal with this issue usually illustrates clearly the couple's problem-solving styles. In addition, many issues will be identified that can be helped by the psychoeducational component of the treatment.

Special Issues.   Patients who are parents require a thorough assessment of parenting skills. The children should likely be interviewed as well if they are old enough to participate meaningfully. There is sufficient evidence available about the very difficult challenges that eating-disordered women face as parents to make inclusion of the children mandatory. It is very important to frame this part of the assessment as being in support of the woman's ability to parent and not allow it to be seen as punitive or blaming.

We use the same assessment format for same-sex couples routinely, and find it useful and relevant.

Elements of Treatment

We identify two phases in the treatment of eating-disordered couples beyond the assessment. The first, brief treatment, is most typically provided in association with the ill person's receiving concurrent treatment for her eating disorder. Longer-term treatment tends to occur outside the institutional/agency setting and may often not require a sustained focus on eating symptoms.

Brief Treatment (Up to 10 Sessions).   The most critical intervention in a brief treatment is the establishment of a treatment contract acceptable to both the couple and the therapist. The nature of this contract, usually determined by the context of the referral, can vary from an agreement for the therapist to provide a few sessions of psychoeducation to the identification of specific, usually eating-related, issues that the couple wish to address.

We cannot emphasize sufficiently the importance of providing accurate information as a strategy in the treatment of these couples. Many intuitively obvious ideas or behaviors about eating disorders actually worsen the situation and impair recovery. For example, the spouse of a bulimic woman may decide either to lock up specific binge foods or to empty the house of food in a desperate (and fruitless) attempt to help or police her. The husband of an anorexic patient may position himself as the "food police," carefully observing every minute portion of food she is consuming, weighing her daily, and totally infantilizing her. Therapists who are engaged in the treatment of such couples must become knowledgeable about the nature of the illnesses. It is always a mistake to assume that the intervention into the marital problems of an eating-disordered couple can proceed somehow divorced from the course and treatment of the eating disorder.

Three issues are most often prominent in the first 10 sessions with these couples. The issue of inclusion and boundaries is always critical. For bulimic patients, the chaos produced by the bingeing and purging may serve as a way to modulate emotional distance—either by drawing people in as helpers or by distancing others through secrecy. Dieting behaviors by such individuals may represent an effort to differentiate and become autonomous, although at very high cost. For anorexic women, thinness may be highly valued by family members, with the anorexic patient's beliefs being viewed as basically congruent with the family's, although perhaps taken a bit far.

In either case, the decision to marry may have brought to the fore unresolved issues about independence and autonomy that very often become prominent again as the ill person begins to recover and her spouse begins to demand a more separate relationship.

These issues are manifest in treatment in regard to decisions such as, Who should be involved in the treatment—just the spouse, or also the family of origin? Who will be responsible for the patient's eating? Will she? Or will she be presented as helpless and requiring continuous monitoring? Although we feel that, with adult patients, the patient must always be identified as responsible for her own eating, there are many times when involvement of family of origin may be critical in resolving specific impasses, especially in families where connections between the patient and family of origin are adversely affecting the marriage. At times, this factor will seem more relevant to the therapist than to the family, and the therapist must walk the line between prematurely forcing a couple to focus on an issue they are not prepared to address and ignoring a serious problem for fear of discomforting the couple.

Issues of control are most conveniently addressed in these couples by interventions that focus on food-related issues. The insistence of the therapist that the patient be responsible for her eating is the basic such intervention and will always elicit a response from the spouse. Spouses who have difficulty in permitting their wives to move in this direction can be helped by the technique of symptom separation, whereby discussion of a particular topic (say, bingeing) is forbidden for a period of time, or when a specific behavior (such as locking the refrigerator) is directly identified as unhelpful.

The purpose of this intervention is to reinforce the patient's shaky sense of effectiveness and autonomy. Spouses who are unable to comply with symptom separation (or patients who cannot comply!) are usually able to engage in a dialogue about the origins and meaning of the difficulties, and as a result of this discussion can often begin to make useful changes. The negotiation that may accompany this approach can allow the therapist much opportunity to illustrate appropriate behaviors concerning the sharing of power in the relationship, and the successful negotiation of this phase of treatment usually heralds a significant shift away from the position "I'm well (and powerful)—and you're sick (and powerless)."

Couples who are successful to this stage usually find that the patient's eating is quite improved, and they generally begin to examine issues of emotional and physical intimacy at this point. Old patterns of modulating intimacy, suitable for a situation in which one member of the couple is well and the other ill, become less useful, and the recovering patient will begin to demand changes. This is usually the point at which the couple must make a decision as to whether they need further treatment or feel able to progress satisfactorily on their own.

Common Issues in Longer-Term Treatment.   Issues related to intimacy dominate longer-term treatment. These may include issues of sexual intimacy, emotional intimacy, shame, and trust. The lack of balance in the relationship—one well, one sick—must be reordered. Issues of abuse and trauma, if present, are gradually worked through at this time.

Sometimes the period just after recovery is marked by the reemergence of family-of-origin issues that had lain dormant during the period of illness and acute treatment. Although these can relate to any number of matters, unresolved separation and autonomy issues very commonly arise. The couple may become quite distracted by this turn of events, but a careful and ongoing clarification of boundaries by the therapist can usually see the couple through such a stage. The process of labeling the ex-patient as competent to deal with an intrusive family mimics the earlier symptom separation interventions and can serve to reinforce healthier patterns that developed during the earlier stages of treatment.

Impasses that develop during longer-term treatment may relate to several factors. Some couples appear to make good progress, moving quickly to non-eating-related issues. Sometimes this rapid movement masks a couple's failure in resolving basic conflicts in the areas of inclusion or control. Usually, this failure will be made evident by a recurrence of eating symptoms in the patient. At times a patient will remain symptomatic at a lower level of severity as a method of retaining some sense of psychological stability; this is often the case when she is dealing with difficult material in concurrent individual therapy. Although worrisome, this situation may not require other active intervention if there is adequate evidence that the individual therapy is proceeding well and there is no evidence of deterioration in the couple.

In some cases the couple appear to have satisfactorily adjusted to the new balance of power but will then find that the formerly well member of the couple has become dependent, as a way of salvaging past relational patterns by reversing the roles. This phenomenon is most common when the spouse has his own preexisting area of illness, whether physical or psychological.

Most couples will make a reasonable adaptation to the recovery of the ill person. At times, the process of recovery involves one member of the couple becoming more aware that the foundation of the marriage is simply not compatible with continuing the relationship. Reactions to such a realization vary; a symptomatic relapse is fairly common. Another development maybe a therapeutic impasse characterized by ongoing tension in the relationship, but with an inability to directly confront the causes in sessions. In our experience, it is usually the previously ill person who makes the decision to end the relationship in such cases. Although there is no definite empirical evidence, it is our clinical opinion that these marriages are more likely to survive if the eating symptoms developed within the context of the marriage; thus, the couple have had some experience of having been together without one having been ill. This is not to say that all such marriages that occurred in the setting of an active eating disorder are doomed to failure. Rather, we seem to have observed a higher rate of failure in these marriages as compared with the former type.

As is always the case, when the identified patient has been abused or traumatized, the process of treatment is often prolonged and requires great effort by the therapist, the patient, and the spouse. If the course of recovery from the eating disorder is prolonged, the couple is at risk of losing hope that things will ever settle down, and they will require ongoing support and encouragement. A very active approach by the therapist is often essential in treating such couples.

CASE REPORT

Angela, aged 39, and her husband Robert, aged 48, have been in treatment intermittently for the last five years, during which Angela has been struggling with severe anorexia nervosa and bulimia nervosa. They have been married ten years. This is the first marriage for Angela and the second for Robert, who has two children, a boy and a girl, both in their early 20s and both living away from home. The couple have no contact with Robert's family, who live in another country, and minimal contact with Angela's family, as discussed later.

The couple met while both were admitted to a psychiatric hospital, Angela for her eating disorder and Robert for his alcoholism and bipolar affective disorder. The initial attraction seemed to center on Angela's perception that Robert would be a nonthreatening caretaker for her, and Robert's perception that Angela would be a compliant, nondemanding spouse.

The first five years of the marriage were characterized by Robert's struggle to become abstinent from alcohol and to control his bipolar disorder. He was frequently suicidal and physically abusive while drunk, but Angela's stance was to do everything possible to maintain stability in the marriage in the face of her husband's difficulties. This effort involved working full-time as a health-care professional, tolerating the physical abuse, hiding her eating difficulties, and engaging in significant self-harm in response to the emotional overload her situation produced. Their sexual relationship, always difficult, became more troublesome as Robert developed impotence, partly psychological in nature and partly resulting from his alcoholism.

Once Robert's situation stabilized, Angela felt comfortable in engaging in treatment for her eating problems. During her first two admissions to our Day Hospital program, she shielded her husband from the treating team, allowing only a few marital sessions and blocking attempts to focus on any difficult issues. Her eating improved somewhat, with a return to a normal weight but with ongoing bingeing, vomiting, and laxative abuse.

Over the next two years, while Robert remained stable, Angela began to experience a gradual decline in her level of functioning. She became unable to work, was chronically suicidal, and engaged in hundreds of episodes of self-harm. In retrospect, this deterioration appears to have occurred within the context of her gradually recovering memories of having been sexually abused by a brother for a period of five years, and then having been brutally abused by a sexual predator for a year after she left home. During these two years, she continued to attempt to protect her husband by refusing to disclose to him any details about her situation, and she allowed only sporadic marital sessions. However, she became increasingly desperate about the state of her marriage, which she correctly viewed as becoming less stable.

Four years after initially coming to our clinic, she shifted individual therapists and made a decision to confront material related to her sexual abuse. This decision occurred after another futile attempt to complete the normalization of her eating had led to a spate of serious self-harm episodes and the recovery of some very clear material related to her traumatic experiences. She was able to contract with her therapist to allow concurrent marital sessions, in which she began to disclose to her husband the nature of her struggles and to negotiate with him strategies whereby she could define her struggle as belonging to her but also recruit his help as needed. This agreement included an initial total ban on physical contact, which was very distressing to her husband, who had substituted hugging and nonsexual physical contact for intercourse. Marital sessions began to occur regularly, every two to four weeks, running concurrently with her individual therapy.

Over the next nine months, Angela gradually became more comfortable with her husband's knowing about her situation and less anxious that this knowledge would cause him to relapse. The couple was better able to be physically comfortable together, and she no longer experienced flashbacks when he touched her, as long as he remembered to get her approval first. Her eating became marginally more stable, but was still quite disordered; her self-harm essentially stopped. The three occasions when she did harm herself generated mini-crises, in which the couple grappled with the extent to which Angela was able to care for herself. In the long run, Robert became more comfortable with her abilities in this regard and was able to adopt a position whereby he was available to her to help, but was not policing her behavior. However, he was unable to stop policing her vomiting, which has continued unabated.

Over the last three months, with most of Angela's memories recovered and both feeling more stable, the couple have begun to discuss what will happen when she is able to return to work. At the same time, Angela has become increasingly preoccupied with attempting to resolve some issues in her relationship with her mother, with whom she has had little contact for some years. She is fearful about the effect of this new focus on her marriage but continues to make progress in a climate of more openness with her husband and a greater sense of both personal competency and stability in the marriage. Her husband remains well in all areas.

Although the couple remain in treatment and the final outcome is not known, this case demonstrates many of the issues raised earlier. The initial period of treatment for the couple was prolonged, as the patient coped with her husband's gradual recovery by protecting him and shielding him from her own difficulties. Angela's early attempts to recover without involving her husband in her troubles proved to be a failure; the exclusion placed him at too great a distance to be of help to her, and she desperately needed his help.

When she eventually agreed to involve him, the initial phase of treatment included the delivery of significant psychoeducational material on the nature of her eating problem, sexual abuse, self-harm, and the connections between the three. Inclusion and boundaries were clearly defined—Robert had no access to the therapist outside the marital sessions, but either member of the couple could call a marital session at will. Autonomy for the patient was reinforced by identification of the areas in which Robert could be helpful to his wife—and it was most important that she be the one who was able to make these decisions, as opposed to having the therapist make them for the couple.

As the couple began to adapt well to the behavioral changes in their relationship, increased self-disclosure began to facilitate a sense of increased safety for both, allowing for a sense of stability to develop in the marriage and for the couple to gradually become more physically intimate. The ongoing, but gradual, improvement in Angela's level of functioning has forced the couple to begin to think about how they want to structure their marriage in the longer term, and the emergence of family-of-origin issues for Angela has allowed the therapist to reinforce appropriate boundaries, as well as Angela's competence to seek out appropriate therapeutic help and take care of the situation.

Angela's eating behavior remains unstable, but at a level low enough to permit her to do useful therapeutic work. Her therapist expects that the couple will again need to negotiate appropriate boundaries, concerning Robert's policing of her vomiting, at a time when she has the psychological strength to give up the last of her eating symptoms.

SUMMARY

This chapter has reviewed basic information about the nature of the eating disorders anorexia nervosa and bulimia nervosa and has provided a theoretical framework for understanding them. The effects of disordered eating on marriages has been reviewed and a model presented for the assessment and treatment of these marriages. Successful treatment of such illnesses requires a therapist who is knowledgeable about them, able to work collaboratively with others, and can employ an eclectic mix of therapeutic techniques. Many questions remain to be answered about the most effective methods of treatment, and numerous issues about the long-term outcomes of these marriages remain to be discovered.

REFERENCES

Alonel, M. J., McGuire, J., Daniles, S. R., & Speckler, B. (1989). Dieting behaviour and eating attitudes of children. *Pediatrics, 84,* 482–489.

American Psychiatric Association. (1994). *Diagnostic and statistical manual of mental disorders.* Washington, DC: Author.

American Psychiatric Association Practice Guidelines. (1993). Practice guideline for eating disorders. *American Journal of Psychiatry, 150,* 209–228.

Anderson, A. E. (1985). Family and Marital Therapy. In Anderson (Ed.), *Practical comprehensive treatment of anorexia nervosa and bulimia.* (pp. 135–148, 160–164). Baltimore: Johns Hopkins University Press.

Barrett, M. J., & Schwartz, R. (1987). Couple therapy for bulimia in college women. *International Journal of Eating Disorders, 9,* 487–492.

Brandes, J. (1991). Outpatient family therapy for bulimia nervosa. In D. B. Woodside & L. E. Shekter-Wolfson (Eds.), *Family approaches in treatment of eating disorders* (pp. 49–66). Washington, DC: American Psychiatric Press.

Brinch, M., Isager, T., & Tolstrup, K. (1988). Anorexia nervosa and motherhood: Reproductional pattern and mothering behavior of 50 women. *Acta Psychiatrica Scandinavica, 77,* 98–104.

Ciliska, D. (1990). *Beyond dieting. Psychoeducational interventions for chronically obese women: A non-dieting approach.* New York: Brunner/Mazel.

Crisp, A. H., Hsu, L., Harding, B., & Hartshorn, J. (1980). Clinical features of anorexia nervosa: A study of a consecutive series of 102 female patients. *Journal of Psychosomatic Research, 24,* 179–191.

Crisp, A. H., Kaluch, R. S., Lacey, J. H., & Harding, B. (1977). The long-term prognosis in anorexia nervosa: Some factors predictive of outcome. In R.A. Vigersky (Ed.), *Anorexia nervosa* (pp. 55–65). New York: Raven Press.

Dally, P. (1984). Anorexia tardive—late onset marital anorexia nervosa. *Journal of Psychosomatic Research, 28,* 423–428.

Evans, J., & le Grange, D. (1995). Body size and parenting in eating disorders: A comparative study of the attitudes of mothers towards their children. *International Journal of Eating Disorders, 18,* 39–48.

Fishman, H. C. (1979). Family considerations in liaison psychiatry: A structural approach to anorexia nervosa in adults. *Psychiatric Clinics of North America, 2,* 249–263.

Garfinkel, P. E., and Garner, D. M. (1982). *Anorexia nervosa: A multidimensional perspective.* New York: Brunner/Mazel.

Garfinkel, P. E., Lin, B., Goering, P., Goldbloom, D. S., Kennedy, S., Kaplan, A., & Woodside, D. B. (1995). Bulimia nervosa in a Canadian community sample: Prevalence, co-morbidity, early experiences and psychosocial functioning. *American Journal of Psychiatry, 152,* 1052–1058.

Garfinkel, P. E., Lin, E., Goering, P., Spegg, C., Goldbloom, D., Kennedy, S., Kaplan, A. S., & Woodside, D. B. (1996). Is amenorrhea necessary for the diagnosis of anorexia nervosa? *British Journal of Psychiatry, 168,* 500–506.

Heavey, A., Parker, Y., Bhat, A. V., Crisp, A. H., & Growers, S. G. (1989). Anorexia nervosa and marriage. *International Journal of Eating Disorders, 8,* 275–284.

Kwee, M. G. T., & Duivenvoorden, H. L. (1985). Multimodal residential therapy in two cases of anorexia nervosa (adult body weight phobia). In A. A. Lazarus (Ed.), *Casebook of multimodal therapy* (pp. 116–138). New York: Guilford Press.

Lacey, H., & Smith, G. (1987). Bulimia nervosa: The impact of pregnancy on mother and baby. *British Journal of Psychiatry, 150,* 777–781.

Levine, P. (1988). "Bulimic" couples: Dynamics and treatment. *The Family Therapy Collections, 25,* 89–104.

Lewis, L., & le Grange, D. (1994). The experience and impact of pregnancy in bulimia nervosa: A series of case studies. *European Eating Disorders Review, 2*, 93–104.

Madanes, C. (1981). *Strategic family therapy*. San Francisco: Jossey-Bass.

Maloney, M. J., McGuire, J., Daniles, S. R., & Speckler, B. (1989). Dieting behaviour and eating attitudes in children. *Pediatrics, 84*, 482–489.

The McCreary Centre Society. (1993). Adolescent health survey: Province of British Columbia. Vancouver: Author.

Pope, H. G., Hudson, J. L. (1992). Is childhood sexual abuse a risk factor for bulimia nervosa? *American Journal of Psychiatry, 149*, 455–463.

Root, M. P. P., Fallon, P., & Friedrich, W. N. (1986). *Bulimia: A systems approach to treatment*. New York: W. W. Norton.

Schwartz, R. C., Barrett, M. J., & Saba, G. (1984). Family therapy for bulimia. In D. M. Garner & P. E. Garfinkel (Eds.), *Handbook of psychotherapy for anorexia nervosa and bulimia* (pp. 280–310). New York: Guilford Press.

Stewart, D. E., Raskin, J., Garfinkel, P. E., MacDonald, O. L., & Robinson, G. E. (1987). Anorexia nervosa, bulimia and pregnancy. *American Journal of Obstetrics and Gynecology, 157*, 1194–1198.

Van Buren, D. J., & Williamson, D. A. (1988). Marital relationships and conflict resolution skills of bulimics. *International Journal of Eating Disorders, 7*, 735–741.

Van den Broucke, S., & Vandereycken, W. (1989a). The marital relationship of patients with eating disorder: A questionnaire study. *International Journal of Eating Disorders, 8*, 541–556.

Van den Broucke, S., & Vandereyckyen, W. (1989b). Eating disorders in married patients: Theory and therapy. In W. Vandereycken, E. Kog, and J. Vanderlinden (Eds.), *The family approach to eating disorders* (pp. 333–345. New York: P.M.A. Publishing.

Van den Broucke, S., Vandereycken, W., & Vertommen, H. (1995a). Conflict management in married eating disorder patients: A controlled observational study. *Journal of Social and Personal Relationships, 12*, 27–48.

Van den Broucke, S., Vandereycken, W., & Vertommen, H. (1995b). Marital communication in eating disorder patients: A controlled observational study. *International Journal of Eating Disorders, 17*, 1–21.

Van den Broucke, S., Vandereycken, W., & Vertommen H. (1995c). Marital intimacy in patients with an eating disorder: A controlled self-report study. *British Journal of Clinical Psychology, 34*, 67–78.

Wolf, N. (1992). *The beauty myth: How images of beauty are used against women*. First Anchor Books Edition. New York: Doubleday.

Woodside, D. B., & Shekter-Wolfson, L. F. (1990). Parenting by patients with anorexia nervosa and bulimia nervosa. *International Journal of Eating Disorders, 9*, 303–309.

CHAPTER 9

Physical Illness and Married Couples

Ross E. Carter
Charlene A. Carter

Sickness of the head, of the teeth, of the heart, heartache,
Sickness of the eye, fever, poison,
Evil Spirit, evil Demon, evil Ghost, evil Devil, evil God, evil Fiend,
Hag-demon, Ghoul, Robber-sprite,
Phantom of night, Night wraith Handmaiden of the Phantom,
Evil pestilence, noisome fever, baneful sickness,
Pain, sorcery or any evil,
Headache, shivering;
Roaming the streets, dispersed through dwellings, penetrating bolts,
Evil man, he whose face is evil, he whose mouth is evil,
He whose tongue is evil,
Evil spell, witchcraft, sorcery,
Enchantment and all evil,
From the house go forth!
Unto the man, the son of his god come not nigh,
Get thee hence!

Babylonian Incantation
From *Magic and Healing*
by C. J. S. Thompson (1989)

As reviewed by Thompson in *Magic and Healing* (1989), early attempts to treat physical illness were based in the belief that spirits of evil, thought to cause illness, could be overcome by the power of natural substances or special places inhabited by good spirits, through the physical touch of kings, or by chants and incantations. Given the primitive state of medicine at the time, it seems irrelevant as to whether Sir Kenneth Digby's Sympathetic Powder and Ointment of 1658 (p. 36) or Dr. James Grahm's Grand Celestial Bed of 1745 (p. 158) was fraudulent. Ointments and beds, along with herbs, stones, rings, horns, and saints, held out hope to the ill while calming their fear of death or loss of function in a way not otherwise available. In so doing, they may well have functioned as an important psychological support with indirect positive effects on the outcome of the illness treated.

The same fears are aroused by illness today and render the patient vulnerable. And just as fear caused the ill of other times to place hope in magical healing, so too may the patient of today believe in medical technology and in the words of mental health professionals who describe and define the psychological aspects of illness with the same certainty as ancient healers did when speaking of their own rituals. The difference between the two is that, technically, current practice is based in empiricism, which removes it from the arena of magic. Nonetheless, the risk of superstitious belief remains high, particularly as the psychology of illness shifts from the patient as individual to the patient as part of an interpersonal system. Incomplete understanding of these systems, especially of causality, makes emotionally based attribution, or transference-influenced conclusion, a temptation that carries serious risk to the welfare of the patient and others.

In writing this chapter on physical illness and married couples, we attempted to be mindful of our own warning and have tried to base our conclusions within the context of research. That has been possible in areas having extant literature. However, in areas lacking research, we may have strayed from the course. In so saying, we hope for reader understanding while still holding to the avowed need for empiricism.

Before we move to the topic of married couples and illness, it is important to present a review of the conceptual antecedents that evolved and established a logical foundation for the study of the psychology of illness in married couples. For this aspect of illness to be recognized as medically legitimate and admitted as a topic for medical research, it was first necessary to broaden the theories of disease to include psychosocial etiologies. That was partially accomplished through the work of social epidemiologists who defined stress or other social factors as important contributors to illness (Cannon, 1932; Engel, 1968; Henry, 1982; Mechanic, 1963; Selye, 1946).

Another area that contributed to the expansion was classical psychosomatics. An interaction between personality and disease, particularly in cancer and depression, was suspected as early as the eighteenth century (Kowal, 1955; Wittkower, 1977). However, formulation of the underlying mechanisms was not accomplished until the early part of the twentieth century when Dunbar (1954) presented her meticulous theory and Alexander and French (1948) published their research, which attempted to blend psychology and the biology of their time. Subsequently, a cascade of research was carried out, attempting to make sweeping links between broad categories of personality and diseases, particularly in breast cancer (Bahnson, 1970; Greer & Morris, 1975; Priestman, Priestman, & Bradshaw, 1985) and myocardial infarct (Friedman & Rosenman, 1959, 1971; Jenkins, 1971a, b).

The expansion of etiology to include biomedical as well as psychosocial factors occurred over such a short period that integration into a well-developed biopsychosocial model remains to be done. Nonetheless, a definitive step was signaled by the publication of several studies on families and illness. These included research that related streptococcal infection to irritable fathers (Schottstaedt et al., 1958), introduced the concept of circularity of effect (Haggerty & Alpert, 1963), identified factors resulting in a positive outcome to myocardial infarct in farm families (Jacobson & Eichhorn, 1964), and reported on specific maternal interactions associated with stunted growth in children (MacCarthy & Booth, 1970). These initial efforts were bolstered by Jackson's (1965) paper on homeostasis and Weakland's (1977) use of the term "family somatics," along with a cascade of studies of the effects on families of specific illnesses, or the "impact literature" (Ransom, 1981).

It is beyond the scope of this chapter to review the literature on illness and families. However, Coyne and Anderson's (1988, 1989) critique of the work on "psychosomatic" children (Minuchin et al., 1975; Minuchin, Rosman, & Baker, 1978) points out serious design flaws and conceptual misstatements in a body of work that is considered to be the intellectual flagship in family illness research. Our own work with either psychologically disturbed or physically ill families and married couples has led us to conclude that it is more important to study physical illness through the couple, rather than the family. Several factors have led to this conclusion.

First, of particular relevance are Meehl's (1995) comments regarding the legitimacy of inferred theoretical or latent entities and the lack of sharp boundaries in categories. To insist on sharp boundaries risks mixing indicators with latent taxons (or categories). It is often not known whether one is dealing with dimensions or categories. Confounding categories with underlying taxonomic entities is dangerous, yet such confounding is rampant in family theory/therapy. For example, constructs of cohesion and adaptability are both categories and dimensions, as is the concept of enmeshment. Family theory/therapy contain few ladders of inference and remain flat, without linear interrelatedness. Given a lack of emphasis on construct validity, there are few statements about family illness, family theory, or family therapy that can withstand rigorous scrutiny.

Second, variability among families risks unreliability when they are studied in relation to illness. Age of the family, access to health care, number and ages of children, presence or absence of prior marriages, time in life illness occurs, and the position of the ill person in relation to the family interact and covary to result in exceptionally confounded data.

Third, illness variables interact with family characteristics so that different psychological and emotional configurations result from differences in course of illness, changes in the illness from time to time, medication effects, and the more general parameters of degree of disability, predicted outcome, and psychological concomitants such as depression or disorientation.

Fourth, with the exception the findings of McDaniel, Hepworth, and Doherty (1992) and Rolland (1994), family interactions remain causally linked to illness. Any such link, however, risks negative attributions and requires neutralization because of a potential adverse effect. A bind exists, however, inasmuch as without such a link, current and future work on family illness belongs in family sociology and not in psychology, psychiatry, or medicine.

Fifth, much of the existing data on family illness are internally invalid owing to the confounding of family roles from study to study. Some studies focus on fathers without delineating their role as husband, whereas other research studies husbands who are not fathers but stepfathers.

Sixth, as suggested by Rowe (1994), the impact of genetic studies on socialization cannot be ignored, particularly as they suggest an alternate influence that may outweigh either the environment or the family. Genetics may simply be decisive. For example, coping with illness is influenced by spouse similarity, but both spouse selection and similarity appear to be genetically determined (Horgan, 1995). As yet, the role of genetics has not been addressed.

We have previously had a close association with family theory/therapy. However, we now regard it as less important and have decided to switch to a smaller unit, the couple. The relation between marital and family theory/therapy is obscure. Once they were defined as separate but parallel (Olson, 1970), but later as related (Olson, Russell, & Sprenkle, 1980). A more imperialistic position is taken by Broderick and Schrader (1991) who wrote:

> The marriage counseling [*sic*] movement has become so merged
> with the more dynamic family-therapy movement that it has all
> but lost its separate sense of identity (p. 15).

We take exception, in that marital therapy is critically different from marriage counseling because of the complexity of theoretical assumptions, the need to diagnose Axis I disorders, the need for intrapsychic formulations, and the techniques of treatment. Neither is family therapy more "dynamic." To the contrary. With some disorders such as oppositional disorders and school phobias, it becomes static and mechanistic. Further, we understand "movements" to be social or political phenomena. Nothing resembling a "movement" has occurred in marital theory/therapy.

Still further, we take strong exception to the definition of marriage as a subsystem of a family and, thus, subordinate to a superordinate organization. To the contrary, the family occurs within the context of the marriage, not vice versa. The relationship of the spouses to their children and other kin are a set of emotional and psychological entities that define the "family" as a set of enactments in which both spouses have temporally limited involvement.

Further, spouse relations differ from familial relations in several critical ways. First, the core of marriage is a projection system that may continue unchanged for the duration of the marriage and so provides constancy. In contrast, as described by Benedek (1959), the relation between the parent and the child is a mix of direct and remote experience, may be modified with maturation of the child, and may differ from child to child. Second, the profound effect of the sexual relationship of the spouses, the merging of personal boundaries, the consequent capacity for empathy and life-sustaining nurturance, as well as the distribution of power within the marriage, also make it qualitatively and quantitatively different from parent–child relationships or those with other kin.

At the same time, we are aware of the definition of dyads as remnants of altered triads that continue symbolically in the shared fantasy of the pair (Whitaker, 1969; Zuk, 1969). Becker and Useem (1942), however, have described interactions as rarely taking on a reality apart from the dyad, thus giving the dyad psychological legitimacy and reality. Although we may risk confounding, which may arise through Jungian shadows in the projective unconscious of spousal systems, we feel that we have avoided Meehl's (1995) dilemma of mixing categories and underlying entities.

It is important, however, to recall the skepticism of Cassileth and colleagues (1984), who reported no differences in the psychological factors associated with different diseases. Diagnosis-specific emotional responses were not supported, and no evidence was found for a relationship between illness and psychosocial factors. The same attitude is reflected by Angell (1985), who describes beliefs about a relation between disease and mental states as *folklore* (p. 1572). Such skepticism commands attention, because it may reflect a generalized attitude within the medical profession. Before a primary care physician may, in good conscience, call for a marital consultation, he or she needs sound empirical data that good medicine is being practiced. Existing literature on marriage and physical illness promises such data, together with better-designed studies. In this chapter, we review those data in a survey of bereavement, social support, coping, and caregiving. We have included data on the individual so that sources of variance may be identified as either individual or marital. Finally, attention will be given to data on immune system functioning and the psychotherapy of the physically ill couple.

BEREAVEMENT

Studies of bereavement have focused on the question of whether the death of a spouse may result in the untimely death of the surviving spouse. The question has implications for the development of psychotherapy for the surviving spouse, as well as implications for attachment theory and the consequences of broken relationships. The data suggest the following conclusions:

1. The probability that a surviving spouse will die within 6 to 12 months after the death of a spouse is higher than expected. After 12 months, the probability decreases significantly. The probability is higher for surviving males between 55 and 75 years of age, than for females. Women under 65 show a higher death rate in the second year following bereavement (Helsing & Szklo, 1981; Parkes, Benjamin, & Fitzgerald, 1969).
2. Unexpected death may be due to poor management of prior illness, "survivor shock," decline in health owing to lack of care, depression arising from loss, and lack of social support. Compromised immune systems following loss may result in greater susceptibility to disease among surviving spouses (Bowling, 1987; Schleifer, 1989).
3. Biological dysfunction resulting in death may be independent of bereavement. Yet such independence does not explain why death did not occur before the first spouse died or why it occurs within a year of the first death. Thus, it appears that there is a subset of marriages in which attachment is so strong that the loss of a spouse has profound physiological effects that may result in the death of the surviving male spouse in the first year following bereavement, and in the second year for some surviving females.

SOCIAL SUPPORT

The importance of attachment is shown in studies on social support that originated in early epidemiology. For example, Berkman and Syme (1979) found significantly higher death rates for socially isolated men and women, whereas House, Robbins, and Metzner (1982) reported social support derived from social ties distinguished between high and low survival rates for males but not for females.

The concept that social support facilitates physical health resulted in numerous studies that revealed the complexity of the topic. Questions emerged fast. What is the nature of support, when might it help health, and who benefits from it? Are men as likely to respond as women, and are there different kinds of support? Are all marriages supportive or just some types? Tentative conclusions regarding some of these questions include the following:

1. Social support may influence behavior patterns to enhance health and/or decrease risk (main effects model); it may also protect against illness-causing stress (buffering model) (Cohen, 1988).
2. It is unclear as to whether quality or quantity of social support is more important, whether support from kin is more effective than support from others, and whether support interacts with stress to moderate it or is mobilized by stress and suppresses it (Cohen & Wills, 1985; Thoits, 1982).
3. There are a variety of ways of providing social support, including giving information, improving self-esteem, and assisting in utilizing resources. One important way is to increase perceived efficacy and control over the effects of illness (Antonucci & Jackson, 1987; Kelman, 1958).
4. It is equivocal as to whether marriage is an enhancer of health or a buffer against illness. One major variable is the quality of the marriage. However, measures of quality rarely define pre-illness marital conditions, so it is unknown as to whether poor quality affects illness or if illness results in a deterioration effect (Burman & Margolin, 1992; Coyne & Bolger, 1990; Coyne & DeLongis, 1986).
5. It is also equivocal as to whether men derive more benefit (support) from marriage than do women (Gove, 1984; Verbrugge, 1989).
6. Simply living with another person may provide protective support but recovery from illness is better for patient–spouse pairs than for patient–significant and other pairs (Anson, 1989; Ell et al., 1988).

Our own experience in working with seriously ill women indicates that sexual stereotyping regarding males is rampant. The potential harm to a woman's support system is obvious, nonetheless, attitudes regarding males are conveyed by those who verbally or nonverbally communicate cynicism about her husband's interest and his ability to emotionally withstand the illness or to express his emotions. We take particular exception to those who formally espouse such a view, including Spiegel, a noted breast cancer researcher, who contends that being involved with a woman is good for one's health, whereas "a relationship with a man does not do your health much good, regardless of your gender" (1990, p. 364). In our own research (Carter & Carter, 1993), husbands of breast cancer patients exceeded the norm for the amount of expressed affection and clearly functioned as an exceptional support to wives for whom they emotionally and physically cared. In still another study (Carter & Carter, 1994), marital adjustment and support were found among spouse pairs when both spouses were ill but not when one spouse was well. That finding was true for men and women and suggests that complementarity of functioning may be more important than gender in evaluating the benefits of marriage.

COPING

If social support is the frame, then coping is the picture. Neither could have gained status in medical research without recognition of the legitimacy of psychosocial variables. Sutherland (1952) provided just that, with a clarion call to other physicians to regard the emotional reactions of women with breast cancer as normal and not as a sign of weak character. Following that lead, effort was made to study how people coped with illness. At this time, several mechanisms have been identified.

1. Coping consists of efforts to manage illness-related demands and conflicts. Problem solving, or effort to eliminate threat, differs from effort to regulate emotional distress related to threat. Coping may include obtaining information, direct action (including escape), avoidance of action, intrapsychic processes (including emotional and cognitive restructuring), and turning to others for support (Cohen & Lazarus, 1979).
2. Efficacy of coping is difficult to evaluate because the use of multiple strategies confounds outcomes. Some intrapsychic defenses are better than others; in women, use of displacement and projection predict poor adjustment, as does stoicism-fatalism. Denial may occur across all illnesses and in different degrees, including repudiation of diagnosis, dissociation of diagnosis, or renunciation of deterioration (Katz et al., 1970; Weisman, 1979).
3. A distinction has been made between coping style and coping strategy. Style includes focus on problems versus emotion, rationalization, denial, distraction, fatalism and inflexibility, locus of attribution, repressive effort, and emotional expression. Strategy includes harm-reduction behavior such as self-reliant action, mobilization of support systems, downward social comparisons,

search for meaning, use of humor, seeking information, and anticipatory desensitization. Emphasis has also been given to exploration of cognitive adaptation, which is helpful in the use of
cognitive-emotive therapy to promote adaptation (Ell, 1986;
Taylor, 1983).

4. Lack of methodological clarity has hampered research on the coping of couples. Couples may be divided into two subsets according
to gender or health, and then comparisons may be drawn between
the subsets. This approach suggests interdependence of adaptation and reciprocal influence. Another approach is to assume dual
triangulation consisting of spouse-spouse and a separate external
system for each. A third approach has been to compare different
groups of couples, varied as to diagnosis, length of marriage, and
age of spouses, with controls (Badger, 1992; Revenson, 1994).

Recovery from illness has so frequently been reported to be affected by
spousal support that it can only follow that how each spouse copes affects
adjustment and recovery. Consequently, further attention must be given
to the issue of couple coping, a complex and probably interdependent
process affected by a number of variables different from those affecting
the individual patient. Our data (Carter & Carter, 1994) call into question
Rolland's (1984) contention that diseases should be lumped together and
studied according to the biological systems involved. As a starting point,
our findings indicate a need to study different diseases separately because
of differences in medication, the variation in degree of illness for the individual patient, the different psychological consequences of different diseases, and the differences in degree of illness and impairment among
patients with the same diagnosis. As these factors vary, they establish a set
of conditions that require different coping mechanisms and exert different
pressures on the relationship of the couple.

Several studies tend to support the need for this methodological
approach. Terry (1992) reports both problem-focused coping and marital
quality unrelated to adaptation to illness, thus contradicting Coyne and
Bolger's (1990) contention regarding marital quality and induced stress.
Gotay (1984) reports action to be the most commonly used coping mechanism among cancer patients and spouses. In another study, spouse coping
was the best predictor of psychological distress among breast cancer
patients (Hannum, et al., 1991). Worby and Babineau (1974) found husbands of wives with breast cancer acted to buffer them against the
demands of children. Husbands of breast cancer patients consistently
report an absence of external support for them in coping with their wives'
illness, and particularly with their fear that the wife will die (Sabo, Brown,
& Smith, 1986).

CAREGIVERS

Research on caregivers is a study of the caregivers obligatory attachment without control of the relationship. It differs from studies of social support and coping in that it has typically focused on the detrimental effects of caregiving. As a result, caution is prudent, because an emphasis on the negative may have undesirable consequences for the ill spouse who is dependent on the well, caregiving spouse.

A survey of the data suggests the following: The caregiver's immune system functioning may be suppressed; the morale of the caregiver is contagious to the care receiver, and greater dependence on the receiver results in greater impairment of the caregiver's morale; male caregivers tend to be less aware of their feelings and, hence, underreport stress; females show more strain and burden; and social support relieves loneliness in the care receiver but not in the caregiver (Lutzky & Knight, 1994; Purk & Richardson, 1994). A subset of the data has focused on the increasing incidence of Alzheimer's disease and the particular demands it makes on caregivers, who have been shown to have more psychiatric symptoms than a control group with a history of psychiatric disorder. Optimism plays only a small part in the adaptation of caregivers of Alzheimer's patients. Caregivers show poor health and fall into two classes: one mourns the loss of the patient, and the other shows difficulty with the responsibility of coping with the disease (McNaughton et al., 1995; Morgan & Laing, 1991).

Data on the elderly run parallel to data on Alzheimer's patients, inasmuch as both reflect the same age group. High levels of support and satisfaction have been reported in elderly marriages with one spouse ill. Gender of caregiver and level of disability appear to have little impact on marital quality. Husbands tend to regard difficulties of their wives as the result of characterological factors and do not respond with caregiving until the problem becomes serious, when they then overcompensate. Older patients have been reported to adjust better to breast cancer than younger patients; elderly men were found to be excellent caregivers for ill wives but to be permanently affected by the death of their wives. Rural elderly couples have been found to be psychologically and physically healthier and to use fewer funded services than those in a comparison sample (Carter, 1995; Johnson, 1985; Vinokur & Vinokur-Kaplan, 1990).

PAIN, POTPOURRI, AND POSSIBILITIES

Because of space limitations, we do not discuss chronic pain in detail here. However, what emerges from the areas we reviewed is a complicated tapestry of interactions. Gender is important, because male and female differences have different effects on social support. Men view women differently than women view men, which results in different actions. Some men regard wives as unpredictable and, in times of frustration, may accuse them of having basic characterological faults that cause them to complain about their health. Men do not respond immediately with observable emotion to their own illness nor to the illness of a spouse. Nonetheless, they are seriously affected by the illness of their wives and, in the case of life-threatening illness, may go through anticipatory grief and mourning.

Women become tired of the burdens of caregiving and may not be as supportive as the culture supposes. As coping styles differ from coping strategies, the reward–gain paradigm seems inadequate to explain the intensity of reaction that illness causes in people. And as if that were not enough, the elderly, because of their age and experience, may function entirely differently from everyone else—as when a spouse is lost in the timelessness of a plaque-riddled brain, which causes outbursts of rage and then quickly recedes into the softness of pleasant, remote memories of olden times.

Sociology reigns in the area of social support theory and is good at it, whereas psychology captures several pieces in the area of coping, which entails definitions of functions at which psychologists are good. Psychiatrists do not fare well in the whole picture, as they appear to have little interest or much to contribute—even though they control in the areas of consultation liaison and geriatric psychiatry. Social workers write a little and take care of everyone, while nurses contribute silently and with a quality of research that commands respect and attention because they have secret, hidden knowledge that they are willing to share if only someone will listen to what it is like to work day-in and day-out with the physically ill. Surely all of this goes far beyond what Emily Mudd intended when she established the Marriage Council of Philadelphia. And while all that has been, and is still yet to be, written about social support, coping, and caregiving is important, it fails to address the critical issue of whether or not people make other people physically ill. Even though the implications are present in social support, coping, and caregiving data, the theoretical limitations of each make it necessary to look elsewhere. Hard core empirical data are required, at least by the ethical implications that arise when disease-causing interpersonal interactions are considered. Without such data, harm is risked, and the area that holds promise of such data is psychoimmunology and marital interactions.

IMMUNE SYSTEMS AND MARITAL INTERACTIONS

Historically, the immune system was downgraded in research. The publication of a number of animal studies, however, as well as the development of technologically refined biological measures, resulted in greater research possibilities so that the human immune system is now open for study.

Riley (1975) was among the first animal researchers to report decreases in immune system functioning as a result of induced stress and with consequent development of neoplastic tumors. Other studies with varied stressors and specificity of function have supported the finding that stress decreases immune system functioning (Ben-Eliyahu et al., 1991; Keller et al., 1981). In an attempt to study psychosocial factors more directly, Weinberg and Emerman (1989) found increased tumor growth in mice as a result of their being reared in isolation, or with siblings and then isolated. Conversely, their being reared in isolation and then moved to a large social group reduced tumor growth. Although technical information is rapidly outdated, basic information remains reliable and can be reviewed in publications by Ader (1980) and Fox (1981).

The implication of animal data for humans is that stressful life events may have a detrimental effect on immunity and make a person susceptible to disease. The findings of LeShan and Worthington (1955, 1956), who reported breast cancer concurrently with depression resulting from loss of a relationship, are among the earliest formulations of this idea. However, a significant amount of subsequent research was equivocal and the life events hypothesis was absorbed by social support theory.

More recent studies have explored social support as a mediator of stress and as interacting with immune system functioning. In this vein, spouses of cancer patients were found to have effective immune system functioning via measures of natural killer (NK) cell activity when they had high levels of social support (Baron et al., 1990). Other studies reporting compromised immune system functioning and life events in humans include those of Schulz, Visintainer, and Williamson (1990), who report on caregivers, and Schleifer (1989), who reports on bereavement.

A different series of studies are relevant inasmuch as they combine physiological and psychological measures. The series was initiated by Levy and colleagues (1987), who reported a high relation between NK activity, recurrence of breast cancer, and lack of social support. In another study, Levy and colleagues (1990a) found NK activity related to estrogen receptor status and social factors. At three months postsurgery, the seeking of social support and the perceived quality of support accounted for a significant amount of NK activity, with social support related to longer survival. In another study, NK activity was related to disease-free survival. However, rather than NK activity, psychosocial factors were more strongly predictive of the rate of disease progression in cases of recurrence (Levy et al., 1991).

In terms of interpersonal interaction, perceived social support was found to act as a buffer through NK activity when perceived emotional support from a spouse was of high quality, when the patient's physician was perceived as providing support, and when the patient actively sought social support (Levy et al., 1990a). The importance of these data rests in the relationship between rigorous physiological measures and the measures of psychological coping in patients with well-defined disease and treatment. The data show a strong relationship between interpersonal interactions, psychological variables, and immune system functioning, particularly as it may be compromised (or enhanced) and increase (or decrease) the risk of recurrence. O'Leary (1990) has reviewed other data on human immune system functioning and the variables of stress and emotion, including studies on personality style and type.

Other data published by Kiecolt-Glaser may be regarded as complementary to the work of Levy in that it focuses on the interaction of the immune system and both positive and negative psychological factors. In two separate studies, stress arising from examination was found to reduce immunocompetence (Kiecolt-Glaser et al., 1984), whereas relaxation training was found to increase NK levels (Kiecolt-Glaser et al., 1985).

Marital status was investigated in two parallel studies. The first (Kiecolt-Glaser et al., 1987) focused on separated/divorced women in comparison to married women and indicated that more recent separation and greater attachment to the ex-husband predicted psychological symptoms and immune functioning. Those separated within one year showed poorer proliferation in response to two mitogens, significantly lower percentages of NK cells, and significantly higher antibody titers. The second study (Kiecolt-Glaser et al., 1988), compared separated/divorced and married men. Those in the separated/divorced group reported more recent illness and had significantly higher antibody titers and herpes simplex viruses, which indicated poor cellular immune system control. Poorer marital quality in the married control group was also noted to be related to lower antibody titers and lower counts of suppressor cells.

Without physiological measures, claims about connections of psychological variables and physical systems might occupy a place next to the magical powers of herbs, stones, beds, and powders. With these data, however, excitement emerges regarding the possibility of an observable connection between illness and psychosocial variables, and particularly those studied in the early work done on breast cancer. These data do not generalize, however, to other areas of major concern, such as marital systems and myocardial infarct, because the relation, if any, between myocardial infarct and immune system functioning is unknown.

In relation to immune system functioning, psychosocial support, and breast cancer, we have attempted to define some possible contributory factors. Our data sample is small but may be suggestive of possible leads to follow in further research that attempts to extend the connection between breast cancer and immune functioning to marital interactions. Specifically, in a sample of married pairs with the wife diagnosed with Stage I breast cancer treated with mastectomy, we found personality types among husbands and wives that, if mixed, would result in a consolidation of interactions leading to emotional suppression, depression, and continual strife (Carter, Carter, & Prosen, 1992). With the use of the Millon Behavioral Health Inventory (MBHI) (Millon, Green, & Measher, 1982), A dominant type of wife was found to conform to rules, exert strong self-control, assume responsibility, and derive satisfaction from cooperative rather than antagonistic relationships. Further, these wives showed a tendency to deny physical symptoms, to regard illness as a personal weakness, and to attribute illness to an inability to overcome adversity.

In parallel, a number of husbands were found of the type who assume control of the environment and of others and who dominate others in interpersonal relations according to a set of principles, without regard for personal needs. This type also suppresses feelings and regards illness as a personal weakness. We hypothesize that if these two types of personalities are mixed within a marriage, a set of interactions will emerge that function to lower immune functioning of the wife, thereby making her more susceptible to illness, particularly to breast cancer. Efforts are now under way to develop research data to test this hypothesis.

PSYCHOTHERAPY OF THE WIFE, THE HUSBAND, AND THE COUPLE

The benefits of social support and improved coping for the physically ill patient are implied in the literature. Those implications have been extended in the form of formalized programs of support or information sharing either through hospital-based organizations or private structures that are dedicated to a particular illness, such as the American Cancer Society or the American Heart Association. Group support has been given a great deal of attention, particularly for cancer patients. Spiegel and colleagues (1989) reported on a long series of studies and noted that group support extended longevity for cancer patients. In contradiction, and perhaps more accurately, Morgenstern and colleagues (1984) identified sampling error in their previous report on increased longevity resulting from social support and then, in a later paper, reaffirmed the finding that social support does *not* extend longevity in cancer patients (Gellert, Maxwell, & Siegel, 1993).

A review of the research on psychotherapy with physically ill persons is difficult to carry out without risk of conveying erroneous information. Therapy research has increased in quality in the last decade so that preferences are now known for study designs, therapist variables, patient variables, type of therapy provided, and outcome measures needed. To organize reports on therapy with physically ill persons according to those variables is beyond the scope of this chapter. Further, matters are complicated by the confounding among studies of the variables of types of patients treated, time of treatment in the course of illness, and definitions of therapy. Some treatments have tended to provide support, some have consisted of providing information, and others have functioned to alleviate personality adjustment thought to be maladaptive to illness.

Still other therapies have focused on specific issues, such as marital discord (Rust & Golombok, 1990), caregiver distress (Toseland, Blanchard, & McCallion, 1995), or specific diseases such as back pain (Saarijarvi, Lahti, & Lahti, 1989) and cancer (Meyer & Mark, 1995). A meta-analysis of randomized experiments involving cancer patients has been published by Meyer and Mark (1995), who conclude that the evidence across studies indicates that it would be wasteful to continue to study the benefits of therapy with physically ill persons inasmuch as existing data consistently indicate improvement in adjustment.

Our own work in this area of psychotherapy with physically ill persons has been with breast cancer patients and spouses (Carter & Carter, 1994). We have been reluctant to adopt an existing model of psychopathological interaction in our work because we did not wish to imply through referral sources that patients were poorly adjusted or that some intrapsychic factor had resulted in cancer. To have done otherwise would, in our opinion, have risked irresponsibility, inasmuch as we were not offering general support usable to most, but intensive psychotherapy designed to alter personality functioning and structure of the husband and/or wife and of the interaction of both within the marriage. Over time, however, we have moved away from descriptive statements of interactions to the use of constructs drawn from object relations theory. Although that approach is typically associated with psychopathology, it is also a theory of normal functioning as determined by interpersonal interactions that are replicated in later life.

We think that the effects of physical illness may be best understood in marriage via attention to the alteration of defense mechanisms, ego-based coping skill, self-constancy, capacity to deal with tension, tolerance for delay, and the ability to express and maintain empathic concern for others. As these occur in one spouse, reciprocal patterns are established in the other but are undercut by the effects of illness so that internalized introjects are confounded, particularly for the well spouse. These conditions may become so severe as to interfere with recovery and require short-term psychotherapy.

In order to construct a criterion for decision regarding the need for therapy, we utilized a time line developed from literature-based reports on recovery. Specifically, we decided that if a patient was experiencing emotional or psychological difficulty two years subsequent to mastectomy or lumpectomy, then she was in need of psychotherapy. Prior to then, the need might be only for supportive interventions via individual or group work.

We have been able to describe cases that seem to benefit from individual therapy as well as from marital therapy. Wives may report difficulty with interpersonal relations, intrapsychic conflicts existing before the diagnosis of cancer, loss of functioning after a time when functioning should have returned, and the return of overwhelming emotionality. Husbands have tended to show one of two patterns: withdrawal with depression and anxiety, or overprotectiveness; others become so distraught with the marriage and the disease that they divorce and, in so doing, make themselves unavailable for treatment. We have noted that conjoint sessions with the husband and wife may be carried out by either a female or a male therapist, whereas individual sessions with the wife have to be done by a female therapist. We regard it important not to overgeneralize and assume that psychopathological processes are tied to all breast cancers or that all patients will benefit from or need psychotherapy.

What has been of interest to us is a predominate reaction of both the husband and wife that allows them to redefine the cancer experience as "growthful" to them as a couple and to each as individuals. Some have reported reorganization of their lives in such a way that they have developed a new sense of priority for life. Husbands, in particular, note their own increased sensitivity, not just to the emotional condition of their wives but also to their own pain and capacity for empathy.

As psychologists with general practices, however, we have noted in other nonmedical cases a trend toward the redefinition of marital roles so that the predominant form of marriage is now becoming that of the dual-career pair. Although this type of marriage may be dictated by economic necessity, for others it appears to represent an attempt at avoidance of intimacy, while one or both spouses enact the mode but not the substance. In this type of psychological relation, spouses typically tend to be highly functional and not demanding of emotional involvement from the other. They suppress overt displays of functional or emotional dependency, forge a symmetrical relationship, and maintain strong controls of interpersonal stress so that the balance necessary to function in the work world is maintained.

We worry that this type of marriage indicates a change in the psychology of spouses that may limit the emotional capacity of marriage. With the deemphasis of conscious emotional involvement or enactment of dependency, this form of marriage does not appear emotionally viable or resilient, particularly in times of externally caused stress. It has been our experience, with some but not all marriages of this type, that one or both spouses lack the staying power or commitment that allows him or her, or them, to personally tolerate the frustration arising from dysfunction in the other and to become egregiously intolerant of such problems as myocardial infarct or cancer, which they appear to unconsciously interpret as a narcissistic insult. As (and if) this type of marriage becomes more prevalent, basic research will be required to reevaluate the function of marriage in physical illness as a causally related entity to either wellness or illness.

APPENDIX

The references cited in this chapter were drawn from the authors' library and from a search of four data bases: Medline, 1976 to 1995; PsychInfo, 1984–1995; CancerLit, 1991–1995; and CINAHL (Nursing and Allied Health), 1982–1995.

We first identified between 10 and 15 diseases for each of 10 physical systems described in *Harrison's Principles of Internal Medicine* (1991). It became obvious that many would not have an appreciable effect on marriages or families. Accordingly, we elected to search on the basis of disorders found in our own work; these included asthma, arthritis, cerebrovascular disorders, chronic pain, diabetes mellitus, lupus erythematosus, multiple sclerosis, myocardial infarct, neoplasms, and Parkinson's disease. These topics were entered into databases and crossed against 12 marital and family identifiers, which resulted in 172,000 references on nondisease topics and 269,000 references on the 10 diseases selected.

Disease and nondisease topics were crossed, resulting in a drastic reduction in numbers. Further crossing failed to produce new references, so that 7,200 references were obtained by matching the 10 diseases with marriage, marital therapy, family, and family therapy derivatives. We scanned these by title and were able to retrieve approximately 1,000 abstracts; these were reduced to approximately 300 articles, which were then reviewed.

It is interesting to note that marital and family studies bunch in the categories of neoplasms and myocardial infarction. A few studies had been published on pain, asthma, diabetes, and cerebrovascular disorders. Almost none were found for lupus, Parkinson's disease, or multiple sclerosis. Over the last 11 years, just about one article a day has been published in PsychInfo on families, and about one and one-half articles have been published on family therapy; an article on marriage was published about every four days, and an article on marital therapy has appeared about every two and one-half days. These rates may be compared with an estimated number of 31 articles published per day in Medline. In further contrast, four articles on psychological topics appeared per day in MedLine whereas, over 11 years, 129 articles on general psychological topics were published per day in the PsychInfo data base.

Given differences in the numbers of journals covered by different data bases as well as differences in the numbers of authors with different interests, rates of publication may not fairly compare for more than general interest and information. In that vein, it is noteworthy that the number of marital therapy and theory articles has remained relatively constant year to year, as has the number for family therapy and theory. This consistency suggests a fairly flat level of growth and, between the two, far less work in the area of marital theory and therapy than in the area of family theory and therapy.

It was also interesting to scan the wide variety of topics published in the general areas of marriage and family theory and therapy. Over all data bases, these included an almost inexhaustible series of psychosocial topics such as supervision, cultural influences, attachment theory, health care, eating disorders, depression, child-focused issues, communication, fees, sexual dysfunction, relapse of schizophrenia, addictions, the elderly, feminism, cotherapists, alcohol abuse with and without violence, social policy, adoption, infertility, divorce, foster care, and anxiety. We concluded from this array that either those interested in marital and family systems do not have ready access to medical patients or, if they do, they are not publishing on their experiences.

REFERENCES

Ader, R. (1980). Psychosomatic and psychoimmunologic research. *Psychosomatic Medicine, 42*(3), 307–321.

Alexander, F., & French, T. M. (1948). *Studies in psychosomatic medicine: An approach to the cause and treatment of vegetative disturbances.* New York: Ronald Press.

Angell, M. (1985). Disease as a reflection of the psyche. *The New England Journal of Medicine, 312,* 1570–1572.

Anson, O. (1989). Marital status and women's health revisited: The importance of a proximate adult. *Journal of Marriage and the Family, 51,* 185–194.

Antonucci, T. C., & Jackson, J. S. (1987). Social support, interpersonal efficacy, and health: A life course perspective. In L. L. Carstensen & B. A. Edelstein (Eds.), *Handbook of clinical gerontology* (pp. 291–311). New York: Pergamon Press.

Badger, T. A. (1992). Coping, life-style changes, health perceptions, and marital adjustment in middle-aged women and men with cardiovascular disease and their spouses. *Health Care for Women International, 13,* 43–55.

Bahnson, C. B. (1970). Basic epistemological considerations regarding psychosomatic processes and their application to current psychophysiological cancer research. *International Journal of Psychobiology, 1,* 57–67.

Baron, R. S., Cutrona, C. E., Hicklin, D., Russell, D. W., & Lubaroff, D. M. (1990). Social support and immune function among spouses of cancer patients. *Journal of Personality and Social Psychology, 59*(2), 344–352.

Becker, H., & Useem, R. H. (1942). Sociological analysis of the dyad. *American Sociological Review, 7*, 13–26.

Benedek, T. (1959). Parenthood as a developmental phase: A contribution to the libido theory. *Journal of the American Psychoanalytic Association, 7*, 389–417.

Ben-Eliyahu, S., Yirmiya, R., Liebeskind, J. C., Taylor, A. N., & Gale, R. P. (1991). Stress increases metastatic spread of a mammary tumor in rats: Evidence for mediation by the immune system. *Brain, Behavior, and Immunity, 5*, 193–205.

Berkman, L. F., & Syme, S. L. (1979). Social networks, host resistance, and mortality: A nine-year follow-up study of Alameda County residents. *American Journal of Epidemiology, 109*(2), 186–204.

Bowling, A. (1987). Mortality after bereavement: A review of the literature on survival periods and factors affecting survival. *Social Science and Medicine, 24*(2), 117–124.

Broderick, C. B., & Schrader, S. S. (1991). The history of professional marriage and family therapy. In A. S. Gurman & D. P. Kniskern (Eds.), *Handbook of family therapy*, Vol. 2 (pp. 3–40). New York: Brunner/Mazel.

Burman, B., & Margolin, G. (1992). Analysis of the association between marital relationships and health problems: An interactional perspective. *Psychological Bulletin, 112*(1), 39–63.

Cannon, W. B. (1932). *The wisdom of the body*. New York: Norton.

Carter, L. (1995). *Physical and psychological health of rural elderly and their use of social services*. Unpublished manuscript.

Carter, R. E., & Carter, C. A. (1993). Marital adaptation and interaction of couples after a mastectomy. *Journal of Psychosocial Oncology, 11*(2), 69–82.

Carter, R. E., & Carter, C. A. (1994). Marital adjustment and effects of illness in married pairs with one or both spouses chronically ill. *American Journal of Family Therapy, 22*, 315–326.

Carter, R. E., & Carter, C. A. (1994). Some observations on individual and marital therapy with breast cancer patients and spouses. *Journal of Psychosocial Oncology, 12*(1/2), 65–81.

Carter, R. E., Carter, C. A., & Prosen, H. A. (1992). Emotional and personality types of breast cancer patients and spouses. *American Journal of Family Therapy, 20*, 300–309.

Cassileth, B. R., Lusk, E. J., Strouse, T. B., Miller, D. S., Brown, L. L., Cross, P. A., & Tenaglia, A. N. (1984). Psychosocial status in chronic illness: A comparative analysis of six diagnostic groups. *The New England Journal of Medicine, 311*, 506–511.

Cohen, F., & Lazarus, R. S. (1979). Coping with the stresses of illness. In G. E. Stone, F. Cohen, N. Adler, & Associates (Eds.), *Health psychology: A handbook* (pp. 217–254). San Francisco: Jossey-Bass.

Cohen, S. (1988). Psychosocial models of the role of social support in the etiology of physical disease. *Health Psychology, 7*(3), 269–297.

Cohen, S., & Wills, T. A. (1985). Stress, social support, and the buffering hypothesis. *Psychological Bulletin, 98*(2), 310–357.

Coyne, J. C., & Anderson, B. J. (1988). The "psychosomatic family" reconsidered: Diabetes in context. *Journal of Marital and Family Therapy, 14*(2), 113–123.

Coyne, J. C., & Anderson, B. J. (1989). The "psychosomatic family" reconsidered II: Recalling a defective model and looking ahead. *Journal of Marital and Family Therapy, 15*(2), 139–148.

Coyne, J. C., & Bolger, N. (1990). Doing without social support as an explanatory concept. *Journal of Social and Clinical Psychology, 9,* 148–158.

Coyne, J. C., & DeLongis, A. (1986). Going beyond social support: The role of social relationships in adaptation. *Journal of Consulting and Clinical Psychology, 54*(4), 454–460.

Dunbar, F. (1954). *Emotions and bodily changes: A survey of literature on psychosomatic interrelationships 1910–1953* (4th ed.). New York: Columbia University Press.

Ell, K. O. (1986). Coping with serious illness: On integrating constructs to enhance clinical research, assessment and intervention. *International Journal of Psychiatry in Medicine, 15*(4), 335–356.

Ell, K. O., Nishimoto, R. H., Mantell, J. E., & Hamovitch, M. B. (1988). Psychological adaptation to cancer: A comparison among patients, spouses, and nonspouses. *Family Systems Medicine, 6*(3), 335–348.

Engel, G. L. (1968). A life setting conducive to illness: The giving-up–given-up complex. *Bulletin of the Menninger Clinic, 32*(6), 355–365.

Fox, B. H. (1981). Psychosocial factors and the immune system in human cancer. In R. Ader (Ed.), *Psychoneuroimmunology* (pp. 103–157). New York: Academic Press.

Friedman, M., & Rosenman, R. H. (1959). Association of specific overt behavior pattern with blood and cardiovascular findings. *Journal of the American Medical Association, 169*(12), 1286–1296.

Friedman, M., & Rosenman, R. H. (1971). Type A behavior pattern: Its association with coronary heart disease. *Annals of Clinical Research, 3,* 300–312.

Gellert, G. A., Maxwell, R. M., & Siegel, B. S. (1993). Survival of breast cancer patients receiving adjunctive psychosocial support therapy: A 10-year follow-up study. *Journal of Clinical Oncology, 11,* 66–69.

Gotay, C. C. (1984). The experience of cancer during early and advanced stages: The views of patients and their mates. *Social Science and Medicine, 18*(7), 605–613.

Gove, W. R. (1984). Gender differences in mental and physical illness: The effects of fixed roles and nurturant roles. *Social Science and Medicine, 19*(2), 77–91.

Greer, S., & Morris, T. (1975). Psychological attributes of women who develop breast cancer: A controlled study. *Journal of Psychosomatic Research, 19,* 147–153.

Haggerty, R. J., & Alpert, J. J. (1963). The child, his family and illness. *Postgraduate Medicine, 34*(3), 228–233.

Hannum, J. W., Giese-Davis, J., Harding, K., & Hatfield, A. K. (1991). Effects of individual and marital variables on coping with cancer. *Journal of Psychosocial Oncology, 9*(2), 1–20.

Helsing, K. J., & Szklo, M. (1981). Mortality after bereavement. *American Journal of Epidemiology, 114*(1), 41–52.

Henry, J. P. (1982). The relation of social to biological processes in disease. *Social Science and Medicine, 16,* 369–380.

Horgan, J. (1995). The new social Darwinists. *Scientific American, 273,* 174–181.

House, J. S., Robbins, C., & Metzner, H. L. (1982). The association of social relationships and activities with mortality: Prospective evidence from the Tecumseh Community Health Study: *American Journal of Epidemiology, 116*(1), 123–140.

Jackson, D. D. (1965). Family homeostasis and the physician. *California Medicine, 4*(103), 239–242.

Jacobson, M. M., & Eichhorn, R. L. (1964). How farm families cope with heart disease: A study of problems and resources. *Journal of Marriage and the Family, 26*, 166–173.

Jenkins, C. D. (1971a). Psychologic and social precursors of coronary disease: First of two parts. *The New England Journal of Medicine, 284*(5), 244–255.

Jenkins, C. D. (1971b). Psychologic and social precursors of coronary disease: Second of two parts. *The New England Journal of Medicine, 284*(6), 307–317.

Johnson, C. L. (1985). The impact of illness on late-life marriages. *Journal of Marriage and the Family, 47*, 165–172.

Katz, J. L., Weiner, H., Gallagher, T. F., & Hellman, L. (1970). Stress, distress, and ego defenses. *Archives of General Psychiatry, 23*, 131–142.

Keller, S. E., Weiss, J. M., Schleifer, S. J., Miller, N. E., & Stein, M. (1981). Suppression of immunity by stress: Effect of a graded series of stressors on lymphocyte stimulation in the rat. *Science, 213*, 1397–1400.

Kelman, H. C. (1958). Compliance, identification, and internalization: Three processes of attitude change. *Journal of Conflict Resolution, 2*, 51–60.

Kiecolt-Glaser, J. K., Fisher, L. D., Ogrocki, P., Stout, J. C., Speicher, C. E., & Glaser, R. (1987). Marital quality, marital disruption, and immune function. *Psychosomatic Medicine, 49*(1), 13–34.

Kiecolt-Glaser, J. K., Garner, W., Speicher, C., Penn, G. M., Holliday, J., & Glaser, R. (1984). Psychosocial modifiers of immunocompetence in medical students. *Psychosomatic Medicine, 46*(1), 7–14.

Kiecolt-Glaser, J. K., Kennedy, S., Malkoff, S., Fisher, L., Speicher, C. E., & Glaser, R. (1988). Marital discord and immunity in males. *Psychosomatic Medicine, 50*, 213–229.

Kiecolt-Glaser, J. K., Glaser, R., Williger, D., Stout, J., Messick, G., Sheppard, S., Ricker, D., Romisher, S. C., Briner, W., Bonnell, G., & Donnerberg, R. (1985). Psychosocial enhancement of immunocompetence in a geriatric population. *Health Psychology, 4*(1), 25–41.

Kowal, S. J. (1995). Emotions as a cause of cancer: 18th and 19th century contributions. *The Psychoanalytic Review, 42*(3), 217–227.

LeShan, L., & Worthington, R. E. (1955). Some psychological correlates of neoplastic disease: A preliminary report. *Journal of Clinical and Experimental Psychopathology, 16*, 281–288.

LeShan, L., & Worthington, R. E. (1956). Loss of cathexes as a common psychodynamic characteristic of cancer patients: An attempt at statistical validation of a clinical hypothesis. *Psychological Reports, 2*, 183–193.

Levy, S., Herberman, R., Lippman, M., & d'Angelo, T. (1987). Correlation of stress factors with sustained depression of natural killer cell activity and predicted prognosis in patients with breast cancer. *Journal of Clinical Oncology, 5*(3), 348–353.

Levy, S. M., Herberman, R. B., Lippman, M., d'Angelo, T., & Lee, J. (1991). Immunological and psychosocial predictors of disease recurrence in patients with early-stage breast cancer. *Behavioral Medicine, 17*(2), 67–75.

Levy, S. M., Herberman, R. B., Lee, J., Whiteside, T., Kirkwood, J., & McFeeley, S. (1990a). Estrogen receptor concentration and social factors as predictors of natural killer cell activity in early-stage breast cancer patients. *Natural Immunity and Cell Growth Regulation, 9*, 313–324.

Levy, S. M., Herberman, R. B., Whiteside, T., Sanzo, K., Lee, J., & Kirkwood, J. (1990b). Perceived social support and tumor estrogen/progesterone receptor status as predictors of natural killer cell activity in breast cancer patients. *Psychosomatic Medicine, 52*, 73–85.

Lutzky, S. M., & Knight, B. G. (1994). Explaining gender differences in caregiver distress: The roles of emotional attentiveness and coping styles. *Psychology and Aging, 9*(4), 513–519.

MacCarthy, D., & Booth, E. M. (1970). Parental rejection and stunting of growth. *Journal of Psychosomatic Research, 14*, 259–265.

McDaniel, S., Hepworth, J., & Doherty, W. (1992). *Medical family therapy.* New York: Basic Books.

McNaughton, M. E., Patterson, T. L., Smith, T. L., & Grant, I. (1995). The relationship among stress, depression, locus of control, irrational beliefs, social support, and health in Alzheimer's disease caregivers. *Journal of Nervous and Mental Disease, 183*(2), 78–85.

Mechanic, D. (1963). Some implications of illness behavior for medical sampling. *The New England Journal of Medicine, 269*, 244–247.

Meehl, P. E. (1995). Bootstraps taxometrics: Solving the classification problem in psychopathology. *American Psychologist, 50*(4), 266–275.

Meyer, T. J., & Mark, M. M. (1995). Effects of psychosocial interventions with adult cancer patients: A meta-analysis of randomized experiments. *Health Psychology, 14*(2), 101–108.

Millon, T., Green, L. J., & Measher, R. B., Jr. (1982). *Millon behavioral health inventory manual* (3d ed.). Minneapolis: National Computer Service.

Minuchin, S., Rosman, B. L., & Baker, L. (1978). *Psychosomatic families: Anorexia nervosa in context.* Cambridge, MA: Harvard University Press.

Minuchin, S., Baker, L., Rosman, B. L., Liebman, R., Milman, L., & Todd, T. C. (1975). A conceptual model of psychosomatic illness in children: Family organization and family therapy. *Archives of General Psychiatry, 32*, 1031–1038.

Morgan, D. G., & Laing, G. P. (1991). The diagnosis of Alzheimer's disease: Spouse's perspectives. *Qualitative Health Research, 1*(3), 370–387.

Morgenstern, H., Gellert, G. A., Walter, S. D., Ostfeld, A. M., & Siegel, B. S. (1984). The impact of a psychosocial support program on survival with breast cancer: The importance of selection bias in program evaluation. *Journal of Chronic Diseases, 37*(4), 273–282.

O'Leary, A. (1990). Stress, emotion, and human immune function. *Psychological Bulletin, 108*(3), 363–382.

Olson, D. H. (1970). Marital and family therapy: Integrative review and critique. *Journal of Marriage and the Family, 32*, 501–538.

Olson, D. H., Russell, C. S., & Sprenkle, D. H. (1980). Marital and family therapy: A decade review. *Journal of Marriage and the Family, 42*(4), 973–993.

Parkes, C. M., Benjamin, B., & Fitzgerald, R. G. (1969). Broken heart: A statistical study of increased mortality among widowers. *British Medical Journal, 1,* 740–743.

Priestman, T. J., Priestman, S. G., & Bradshaw, C. (1985). Stress and breast cancer. *British Journal of Cancer, 51,* 493–498.

Purk, J. K., & Richardson, R. A. (1994). Older adult stroke patients and their spousal caregivers. *Families in Society, 75*(10), 608–615.

Ransom, D. C. (1981). The rise of family medicine: New roles for behavioral science. *Marriage and Family Review, 4*(1/2), 31–72.

Revenson, T. A. (1994). Social support and marital coping with chronic illness. *Annals of Behavioral Medicine, 16*(2), 122–130.

Riley, V. (1975). Mouse mammary tumors: Alteration of incidence as apparent function of stress. *Science, 189,* 465–467.

Rolland, J. S. (1984). Toward a psychosocial typology of chronic and life-threatening illness. *Family Systems Medicine, 2,* 245–263.

Rolland, J. S. (1994). *Families, illness, and disability: An integrative treatment model.* New York: Basic Books.

Rowe, D. C. (1994). *The limits of family influence.* New York: Guilford.

Rust, J., & Golombok, S. (1990). Stress and marital discord: Some sex differences. *Stress Medicine, 6*(1), 25–27.

Saarijarvi, S., Lahti, T., & Lahti, I. (1989). Time-limited structural couple therapy with chronic low back pain patients. *Family Systems Medicine, 7*(3), 328–338.

Sabo, D., Brown, J., & Smith, C. (1986). The male role in mastectomy: Support groups and men's adjustment. *Journal of Psychosocial Oncology, 4*(1/2), 19–31.

Schleifer, S. J. (1989). Bereavement, depression, and immunity: The role of age. In L. L. Carstensen & J. M. Neale (Eds.), *Mechanisms of psychological influence on physical health* (pp. 61–79). New York: Plenum Press.

Schottstaedt, W. W., Krause, J. H., Foerster, D. W., Dooley, R. T., & Kelly, F. C. (1958). Host factors affecting growth of B-hemolytic streptococci in the human pharynx: A pilot study. *The American Journal of the Medical Sciences, 235*(1), 23–32.

Schulz, R., Visintainer, R., & Williamson, G. M. (1990). Psychiatric and physical morbidity effects of caregiving. *Journal of Gerontology, 45,* 181–191.

Selye, H. (1946). The general adaptation syndrome and the diseases of adaptation. *Journal of Clinical Endocrinology, 6,* 117–230.

Spiegel, D. (1990). Can psychotherapy prolong cancer survival? *Psychosomatics, 31,* 361–366.

Spiegel, D., Bloom, J. R., Kraemer, H. C., & Gottheil, E. (1989, October 14). Effects of psychosocial treatment on survival of patients with metastatic breast cancer. *The Lancet, 8668,* 888–891.

Sutherland, A. M. (1952). Psychological impact of cancer surgery. *Public Health Reports, 67,* 1139–1143.

Taylor, S. E. (1983). Adjustment to threatening events: A theory of cognitive adaptation. *American Psychologist, 38,* 1161–1173.

Terry, D. J. (1992). Stress, coping and coping resources as correlates of adaptation in myocardial infarction patients. *British Journal of Clinical Psychology, 31*, 215–225.

Thoits, P. A. (1982). Conceptual, methodological, and theoretical problems in studying social support as a buffer against life stress. *Journal of Health and Social Behavior, 23*, 145–159.

Thompson, C. J. S. (1989). *Magic and Healing*. New York: Bell Publishing.

Toseland, R. W., Blanchard, C. G., & McCallion, P. (1995). A problem-solving intervention for caregivers of cancer patients. *Social Science and Medicine, 40*(4), 517–528.

Verbrugge, L. M. (1989). The twain meet: Empirical explanations of sex differences in health and mortality. *Journal of Health and Social Behavior, 30*, 282–304.

Vinokur, A. D., & Vinokur-Kaplan, D. (1990). In sickness and in health: Patterns of social support and undermining in older married couples. *Journal of Aging and Health, 2*(2), 215–241.

Weakland, J. H. (1977). Family somatics—a neglected edge. *Family Process, 16*, 263–272.

Weinberg, J., & Emerman, J. T. (1989). Effects of psychosocial stressors on mouse mammary tumor growth. *Brain, Behavior, and Immunity, 3*, 234–246.

Weisman, A. D. (1979). *Coping with cancer*, (pp. 27–43). New York: McGraw-Hill.

Whitaker, C. (1969). Dyads and triads: A critical evaluation of "Triadic-based family therapy". *International Journal of Psychiatry, 8*, 566–567.

Wilson, J. D., Braunwald, E., Isselbacher, K. J., Petersdorf, R. G., Martin, J. B., Fauci, A. S., & Root, R. K. (Eds.). (1991). *Harrison's principles of internal medicine* (12th ed.). New York: McGraw-Hill.

Wittkower, E. D. (1977). Historical perspective of contemporary psychosomatic medicine. In Z. J. Lipowski, D. R. Lipsitt, & P. C. Whybrow (Eds.), *Psychomatic medicine: Current trends and clinical applications* (pp. 3–13). New York: Oxford University Press.

Worby, C. N., & Babineau, R. (1974). The family interview: Helping patient and family cope with metastatic disease. *Geriatrics, 29*(6), 83–94.

Zuk, G. H. (1969). Critical evaluation of triadic-based family therapy. *International Journal of Psychiatry, 8*, 539–548.

CHAPTER 10

The Histrionic-Obsessive Couple

Len Sperry
Michael P. Maniacci

There was a time when relational conflict between an obsessional husband and a histrionic wife was the most common presentation in couples therapy (Martin & Bird, 1959). Although today the borderline-narcissistic couple—or the "narcissistic/borderline" couple, to use Lachkar's (1992) designation—may be overrepresented in couples therapy, the histrionic-obsessive couple is nevertheless still seen with regularity in clinical practice. Martin's research (1976, 1981) showed a preponderance of obsessive husbands and histrionic wives—represented by a couple he dubbed the "love sick wife and cold sick husband"—yet his data also showed a sizeable number of marriages with histrionic husbands and obsessive wives, which he called "in-search-of-a mother" marriages. In other words, either partner can manifest the obsessive or histrionic style. Nevertheless, the central conflicts are the same: intimacy (Barnett, 1971; Glick, Clarkin, & Kessler, 1987), power, and boundaries.

Early descriptions of the histrionic-obsessive couple emphasized personality structure and dynamics rather than systemic factors (Binder, 1966; Shapiro, 1965). Thus, the histrionic—then called "hysterical"—partner was typically profiled as the only girl, only child, or youngest child in a family constellation in which her mother was cold, masochistic, and resentful of being a mother and woman, so much so that she overindulged her daughter as compensation for not being able to love and nurture her. Her father was described as charming, indulgent, and seductive at times, while controlling and rejecting at other times. The end result was that the

187

histrionic girl-in-training came to believe that her father loved her more than he loved his wife. Thus, she learned to get her own way by playing each parent against the other by being coy, seductive, pretending she was ill, or having temper tantrums. Adulthood for the histrionic female became a search for a strong, idealized father-husband who would take care of her (Goldberg, 1975; Martin & Bird, 1959)

Later descriptions tend to emphasize both psychodynamics and systemic factors (Barnett, 1971; Bergner, 1977; Glick, Clarkin, & Kessler, 1987). From an integrative dynamic-systemic perspective, relational conflict is viewed as a function of both personality structure and interactional patterns. This chapter describes a dynamic-systemic view of the histrionic-obsessive couple that emphasizes personality and relational dynamics involved in conflict and its resolution in couples therapy. First, it is useful to consider diagnostic criteria and the process of mate selection.

DSM-IV AND THE HISTRIONIC-OBSESSIVE COUPLE

Couples with a histrionic-obsessive pattern may engage in couples therapy, wherein one or both meet the criteria for a DSM-IV personality disorder or exhibit histrionic or obsessive traits or style. In either circumstance, awareness of DSM-IV criteria is essential in establishing not only a prognosis, but also the type and duration of treatment. When both partners are diagnosed with personality disorders, treatment usually requires both couples therapy and individual psychotherapy (Perry, Frances, & Clarkin, 1990). Perry and colleagues present a detailed case study of the treatment of a couple in which the wife met the criteria for histrionic personality disorder and the husband for obsessive-compulsive personality disorder. Combined individual and couples therapy was utilized over a two-year period. In our experience, such extended and intensive combined treatment is the rule rather than the exception. On the other hand, couples who have histrionic and obsessive personality styles tend to be more amenable to a single treatment modality: couples therapy, usually of a shorter duration.

Exhibits 10.1 and 10.2 list the DSM-IV criteria for histrionic personality disorder and obsessive-compulsive personality disorder, respectively (American Psychiatric Association, 1994).

Surprisingly, relatively little research has been reported on couples with histrionic and obsessive styles and disorders, although many clinicians and theorists are convinced that their relational pattern is common. Gigy (1980) reported the results of a study of 37 married and 66 never-married women showing that never-married women endorsed items more suggestive of obsessive-compulsive personality style than married women. Martin (1981) found that in 300 couples studied, the majority of

Exhibit 10.1
DSM-IV DESCRIPTION AND CRITERIA FOR
HISTRIONIC PERSONALITY DISORDER
(American Psychiatric Association, 1994)

A pervasive pattern of excessive emotionality and attention seeking [in the patient], beginning by early adulthood and present in a variety of contexts, as indicated by at least five of the following:

1. Is uncomfortable in situations in which he or she is not the center of attention.

2. Interaction with others is often characterized by inappropriate sexually seductive or provocative behavior.

3. Displays rapidly shifting and shallow expression of emotions.

4. Consistently uses physical appearance to draw attention to oneself.

5. Style of speech that is excessively impressionistic and lacking in detail.

6. Self-dramatization, theatricality, and exaggerated expression of emotion.

7. Suggestibility, i.e., easily influenced by others or circumstances.

8. Considers relationships to be more intimate than they actually are.

male partners exhibited the obsessive-compulsive style, whereas the female partners exhibited the histrionic style. He also reports data on 200 other marriage relationships in which the male partners exhibited a histrionic style and the female partners showed the obsessive style. Goldberg (1975) reported on 200 physicians and their wives treated in couples therapy. He found that the majority of physicians exhibited the obsessive-compulsive style and their wives exhibited the histrionic style.

Exhibit 10.2
DSM-IV DESCRIPTION AND CRITERIA FOR
OBSESSIVE-COMPULSIVE PERSONALITY DISORDER
(American Psychiatric Association, 1994)

Obsessive-Compulsive Personality Disorder: A pervasive pattern of preoccupation with orderliness, perfectionism, and mental and interpersonal control, at the expense of flexibility, openness, and efficiency [in the patient], beginning by early adulthood and present in a variety of contexts, as indicated by at least four of the following:

1. Preoccupation with details, rules, lists, order, organization, or schedules to the extent that the major point of the activity is lost.

2. Perfectionism that interferes with task completion (e.g., inability to complete a project because one's own overstrict standards are not met).

3. Excessive devotion to work and productivity to the exclusion of leisure activities and friendships (not accounted for by obvious economic necessity).

4. Overconscientiousness, scrupulousness, and inflexibility about matters of morality, ethics, or values (not accounted for by cultural or religious identification).

5. Inability to discard worn-out or worthless objects even when they have no sentimental value.

6. Reluctance to delegate tasks or to work with others unless they submit to exactly his or her way of doing things.

7. Adoption of a miserly spending style toward both self and others; money is viewed as something to be hoarded for future catastrophes.

8. Rigidity and stubbornness.

Our view is that the personality styles of histrionic and obsessive partners are best understood as persistent, characteristic patterns of behavior that originate within the individual's family of origin. As such, these personality styles are the result of both temperamental and characterological influences, including genetics, family constellation, modeling, reinforcement, and the creative adoption of basic life-style convictions or schemas (Sperry, 1995). The next section describes the manner in which the histrionic-obsessive couple establish a relationship—mate selection—and how this relationship becomes maladaptive and symptomatic. Although we have noted that either sex can be histrionic or obsessive, for convenience we will follow the convention of indicating the histrionic partner as "she" and the obsessive partner as "he" in the rest of this chapter.

THE PROCESS OF MATE SELECTION

At the outset of a marriage between a histrionic person and her partner, neither feels like a whole, competent individual. Instead, each believes himself or herself to be unable to participate in life in significant ways. Thus, in the process of mate selection, each partner engages in what might be termed a search for his or her own missing "puzzle pieces" in the person of the other (Sperry, 1978). In other words, whereas healthier individuals base their selection of a life partner heavily on such factors as mutual liking and shared interests, goals, and world outlook, the histrionic person and her prospective partner characteristically underemphasize such factors and place a disproportionate emphasis on finding a mate who seems able to function in life in ways in which they personally feel incomplete and inadequate. It is as if each had a "private pact" (Sperry, 1978; Sperry & Carlson, 1991) that says, in effect, "Alone I can't make it in life, but if I can find someone who makes up for my deficiencies, perhaps together we can function as one whole, competent individual."

The histrionic partner conducts a search for the ideal mate with a number of expectations. Perceiving herself to be fundamentally weak, helpless, and incapable of adequately conducting her own affairs, she searches for an ideal caretaker who can help her navigate the stressful vicissitudes of life. More precisely, the histrionic person experiences herself as someone with a tendency to be swept away by the emotional currents of reality at the expense of clear, logical thinking and coping behavior. Not surprisingly, she places a premium on finding an individual who can maintain a considerable degree of calm and objectivity, appraise situations clearly and logically, and determine a reasonable course of action (Bergner, 1977). However, this search is doomed from the start. Besides her perceived weakness, she lives in fear of being overwhelmed by a truly assertive and competent male. Accordingly, she selects a male who will neither pressure her nor threaten her tentative sense of personal autonomy, but who will pamper and protect her (Dreikurs, 1946). The histrionic person's requirements for a partner then assume a contradictory quality of wanting him to be strong and help her deal with life, but not to exhibit those qualities when dealing with her. In her ultimate selection of a partner, it initially appears that she has succeeded in her quest.

The obsessive partner, for his part, also engages in a search for his missing "puzzle pieces." Logical, avoidant, and detached in his everyday demeanor, he experiences life as drab and colorless and so finds that the heightened emotionality and vivaciousness of the histrionic person adds needed spice to his life. Because he tends to be out of touch with his feelings and desires and locked into a stultifying daily routine, he finds the histrionic person's flair for life and spiritedness refreshing. Before meeting her, he never believed he measured up to the cultural stereotype of the real man. But in his relationship with her, he suddenly and unequivocally feels like a real man. In the face of her apparent weakness and helplessness, he takes on the role of the strong, steady guardian who finds the rational solution. In their relationship, he finds this role enormously rewarding (Bergner, 1977).

Marital and family theorists have long sought to explain how it is that two individuals who are so strongly attracted to each other come to a point when they can no longer tolerate each other. Dreikurs (1946) was one of the first to observe that the qualities that initially attract two people to each other are basically the same factors that cause discord and divorce. He noted that any human quality or trait can be perceived in a positive or a negative way. A person can be considered either kind or weak, or strong or domineering, depending on one's point of view. Dreikurs suggested that one person does not like another for his or her virtues, nor dislike that person for his or her faults. Rather, an emphasis on a person's positive qualities grows out of affection for that person, just as an emphasis on weaknesses grows out of rejection. This emphasis on the individual's weakness or negative trait provides an excuse for having to communicate, to negotiate, and to resolve conflicts. In other words, talking about problems is just about the only time they do talk.

When asked what attracted her to her partner, what made him different from others, the histrionic person often mentions physical attraction. But upon further probing she may admit, "I like his gentleness and stability . . . the way he could get things done, how he could plan things out . . . how well he used money." Looking at her background, we might discover that she experienced much instability in her upbringing, that she had difficulty making plans and commitments, that she had trouble budgeting and using money and time wisely. These traits reflect her histrionic style and some of the specific need fulfillment she seeks.

In responding to the same question, the obsessive person often gives the culturally expected response, "Physical attractiveness." Then he may add, "I like her free spirit; she really knows how to have a good time. . . . She's the kind of individual who doesn't get bogged down in things. . . . She can be the life of the party . . . and she's a very generous and giving person." An investigation into his background and personality style may suggest how his unfulfilled needs could be complemented in relationship with such a person. Each of these persons actually has qualities that the other craves and values, and thus they are attracted to each other.

Everything goes along smoothly until one or both are threatened, at which point courage begins to wane. When cooperation and courage decrease, defensiveness increases and the attracting qualities come to be perceived in a much more negative way. Whereas she previously viewed her partner as gentle and stable, now she describes him as weak and cowering. Whereas previously she perceived him as being able to plan and structure things, now she sees him as domineering and inflexible. Initially, he saw her as free-spirited, but now he views her as flighty, coquettish, and scatterbrained. Rather than generous and giving, she is now deemed a careless spendthrift. As courage wanes, so does trust. The more two partners become defensive, the more they are likely to disown any responsibility for a problem and blame each other. This is the basis of most couples' conflicts (Sperry, 1978). The next section describes relational conflicts from the perspectives of the histrionic and the obsessive partners.

RELATIONAL CONFLICTS IN HISTRIONIC-OBSESSIVE COUPLES

The histrionic person soon comes to recognize some of the costs of her partner's refusal to take authentic personal stands. She does things that she realizes he finds provocative and objectionable. Yet, seldom does he protest or react emotionally. Rather than voicing any strong personal wants or desires, he insists that "anything is fine" with him. In time, this predictable response leads the histrionic person to draw a number of conclusions. She comes to view her partner as indecisive, ineffectual, and emasculated. She thinks that he must be angry or have some objections to her behavior, but because he says nothing she concludes that he must be dishonest and untrustworthy in his dealings with her. And she wonders whether his failure to show anger means he no longer cares for her. She feels increasingly unloved, emotionally abandoned, and unable to make intimate contact with her husband. Furthermore, she experiences an increasing sense of rage.

The realization that her obsessive partner can respond to her need only superficially is devastating for her. Although her partner displays an endless willingness to listen to her troubles, to provide reassurance, and to present logical solutions to her difficulties, he offers little else. Consequently, she feels overburdened and overwhelmed. This state of affairs provides even more reason for the histrionic partner to experience an increasing sense of abandonment and rage as the months and years go by. In her anger and her desire to gain revenge, she resorts to predictable behaviors. Initially, she verbally attacks her partner. Rather than being informative and, thus, potentially constructive, these attacks are often marked by scathing, global indictments of her husband's character. She assaults him simultaneously on numerous fronts. Next, she becomes provocative: she overspends, has affairs with other men, or resorts to hypochondriacal preoccupations. And when her partner seems substantially unmoved by all of these behaviors, she may pull out her ultimate weapon, the suicidal gesture. All too frequently she is left with the painful notion that her husband is really a "nice guy" who deserves better, that she is the helpless victim of overpowering and irrational emotions and actions, and that she is doomed by external forces to be a "crazy bitch" (Bergner, 1977).

Like his partner, the obsessive person at first believes he has made the ideal mate choice. He has chosen a woman who makes him feel like a man without requiring him to be authentic and assertive—both of which he finds so difficult. Nevertheless, the enormous emotional consequences of this choice soon become increasingly evident. He begins to realize that he is being exploited, that their relationship is a one-way street in which his partner does all the taking and he all the giving. Her wants and desires always seem to take priority in the relationship. Furthermore, he has great difficulty in expressing the growing anger he feels toward his partner or taking a stand against her behavior. On those rare occasions when he is forthright, his assertiveness is met with dire consequences. Predictably, she becomes rageful.

Ultimately, the husband concludes that it is not worth fighting or taking a stand. Instead, he settles into other ways of expressing his anger and preserving his sense of autonomy. Typically, he employs passive-aggressive tactics learned in his family of origin. He withdraws more and more from his partner, often into his job, citing as his justification the requirements of the job and the increasing expenses of the family. He makes ever greater use of the tactic of "stonewalling" (Gottman, 1994) or emotional detachment. Finally, he gets even by abdicating his relational responsibilities outside those of breadwinner, resulting in his partner's becoming overburdened with responsibilities and enormously harried in her attempts to fulfill them. As the relationship progressively deteriorates and his partner engages in ever more extreme behavior, the obsessive person becomes ever angrier. He becomes furious at her seemingly unprovoked verbal attacks, her overspending, her affairs, her hypochondriasis, and her suicidal threats and gestures. At the height of the relational crisis, he feels thoroughly exploited. Even more devastating is the mounting conviction that he is neither loved nor respected and is kept around only because of his paycheck and because she is afraid to leave (Bergner, 1977).

THE TREATMENT PROCESS

There are three treatment phases, with specific treatment goals, for effectively treating the histrionic-obsessive couple in couples therapy: (1) establishing a working therapeutic alliance, (2) rebalancing the couple relationship, and (3) modifying individual dynamics in the partners. Sometimes an additional phase of skill training may be necessary. If so, skill training interventions are utilized concurrently with or following the second phase.

Establishing a Therapeutic Alliance

The first phase of treatment involves establishing and maintaining a therapeutic alliance. A couple's initial contact with the therapist frequently occurs during a period of extreme emotionality and behavior and of severe marital maladjustment. Such couples can be helped to a state of greater calm, order, and optimism about their relationship. It is particularly valuable for the couple and the therapist to share certain assumptions. The first is that neither partner is "crazy" or "mentally ill," but rather that each is an individual whose behavior makes sense and who is responsible for this behavior. The second is that neither partner is "the problem," but rather that each is in therapy in the role of client, because the behavior of each contributes to the shared marital difficulties (Bergner, 1977). The third is that each partner's family-of-origin pattern can powerfully influence the couple's relationship.

These assumptions short-circuit some destructive and distressing conceptions typically held by the histrionic-obsessive couple at the outset of the treatment. Initially, the couple believe that the histrionic partner is insane, because of this person's extreme behavior and emotionality in the apparent absence of any adequate reasons. The therapist's treatment of the histrionic partner as an individual whose behavior has rational antecedents, who is responsible for her behavior, and who is sane has a multiple impact. First, it reduces the distressing fear that the other partner will abandon her.

Second, it deprives her of an excuse for being irresponsible. Third, it deprives him of an excuse for not confronting her about her behavior.

Similarly, each partner believes that he or she alone is completely at fault for the relationship's problems. This phenomenon, most easily observed in the histrionic partner, accounts for vacillations, in each of the couple, between rage at the partner and severe self-condemnation. A consistent stance on the part of the therapist, in which he or she repeatedly insists, demonstrates, and acts in accord with the view that each partner is contributing to the marital difficulties, provides each with a more livable, realistic general view and, in the bargain, a better basis for responsible self-scrutiny and action. The achievement of such a therapeutic alliance usually results in a rapid and dramatic diminution of intense emotionality and extreme behavior. The end result is that the couple become amenable to viewing themselves and their relationship in a calmer and more orderly fashion.

Furthermore, discussion of how family-of-origin patterns develop and impact the relationship can be quite useful in calming the couple by helping them to understand the specific learned patterns they have acquired. Understanding such factors, which are often beyond each partner's conscious awareness, helps them to realize how much their relational problem is not of their own making, although they can still take responsibility for it.

Restoring Balance to the Couple Relationship

After a working relationship between the couple and therapist is achieved, the second phase of treatment consists of establishing or restoring *balance* in the couple's relationship. Rebalancing is typically needed in the areas of boundaries, power, and intimacy (Doherty, Colangelo, Green, & Hoffman, 1985) and represents the main systemic focus of change in couples therapy with histrionic-obsessive partners. Structural family techniques (Minuchin, 1974) as well as strategic family therapy methods and techniques (Haley, 1976) have been quite effective in accomplishing this rebalancing of boundaries and power. Issues of rebalancing the relationship of intimacy can be effectively addressed with communication (Satir, 1983) or family-of-origin (Framo, 1992) approaches.

Modifying Individual Partner Dynamics

The third phase of treatment involves modification of personality features in the individual partners. This phase often occasions psychodynamic change in couples therapy.

The primary individual goals for both the histrionic person and her partner are relatively similar, though their starting points differ. There are two goals: first, that each of them comes to adopt more direct, honest, and fair modes of influence and assertion; and, second, that each comes to both cooperate and communicate honestly in the face of the other partner's efforts to control.

As previously noted, both the histrionic and the obsessive partners are often dishonest in their attempts to control each other. She misrepresents facts, dishonestly seduces, and exaggerates her feelings, while he pretends he has no personal needs or desires, or that he is not bothered by her behavior. In addition, she pretends utter helplessness, feigns illness, threatens suicide, and finds other unfair means of exerting enormous pressure on him. He, for his part, resorts to passive-aggressive tactics such as physical and emotional withdrawal, avoidance of feelings, procrastination, and indecisiveness. Through all of this, both partners remain remarkably uninfluenced by the rather extreme means taken by the other. By their actions, each is saying to the other that he or she will not be controlled.

The goal of getting each partner to abandon such tactics and to employ more honest, forthright, and fair measures in relating to each other is central in the treatment of this relationship. This goal may be pursued therapeutically in any number of different ways. An Adlerian (Sperry, 1995) or cognitive therapy (Beck et al., 1990) treatment strategy that deals with these problems simultaneously and modifies the mistaken life-style conviction or maladaptive schemes is particularly valuable.

The maladaptive worldview of the histrionic person is that life is unpredictable, controlling, and demanding, but that she, nevertheless, is entitled to love and special care and consideration. Her self-view is that she is deserving of love and attention, and she needs others to love and admire her in order to be happy (Sperry, 1995). Furthermore, she views others favorably only as long as she can elicit their attention and affection. She uses deception, charm, flirtation, and manipulation to achieve and then reduce the unpredictability of life, especially regarding loss of love and attention. Finally, she believes that despite her incessant craving for love, real love is never possible. Despite her notorious craving for love, the histrionic person believes that her behavior is the result of coercion and thus cannot believe that real love is possible.

The worldview of the obsessive person is that life is demanding and unpredictable, and thus it is important to be in control, right, and proper. His view of self is that he must be reliable, competent, and righteous to cover for his deficits and shortcomings. Deep down, he believes he is flawed and unlovable. Furthermore, he believes he must take responsibility for others, as well as for things that go wrong (Sperry, 1995). These convictions lead him to work untiringly to achieve and be perfect. Accordingly, he fears failure, acts tentatively and indirectly, and takes few, if any, risks, especially interpersonal risks. Because of his fear of being overrun and losing control, he uses passive-aggressive behavior in an effort to prevent this from happening. The upshot is that he does not attempt appropriate, direct, and fair assertive measures and, further, remains markedly unmoved by his partner's attempts at controlling him. Again, a change in this conception of self in a more constructive direction is fundamental to a change in his assertive behavior and his willingness to be influenced by his partner.

CASE STUDY

Frank and Karen had been married for close to 20 years when couples therapy began. Karen, a high school teacher, had been in long-term treatment with a therapist for chronic, recurrent bouts of depression from which she seemed to achieve only temporary relief. Psychotropic medications proved relatively ineffective. She still reported intense periods of dysphoria, fleeting thoughts of suicide, and chronic dissatisfaction with her life. Her individual therapist provided supportive psychotherapy for her and claimed that "adjustment" to her "condition" was the best she could attain.

Well into her third year of supportive therapy, she began reporting that her husband's health had become an issue. After he had seen numerous physicians, the consensus of opinion was that he was experiencing "stress-related" disorders and should consider some form of counseling himself. Karen's psychotherapist referred him to one of the authors.

Frank was in his late 40s when he arrived at the office. He and Karen had one son in his mid-20s, who had recently been graduated from a well-known university with an advanced degree and had moved back home with his parents. The son's educational career had been paid for by his parents. Frank was a large man, mildly overweight and balding, with a noticeable skin rash about his forehead. He had a bachelor's degree from a local college, worked as a consultant for a large firm, and reported that in his duties as a logistics consultant he flew more than 80,000 miles per year.

He came in claiming that he was not sure he needed any counseling. His physicians had "sent" him because of two problems that they seemed unable to "fix." The skin rash, although considerably better than in past years, was still "bad," and caused him some irritation. More pressing was his insomnia. When he traveled and stayed in hotels, he had trouble sleeping, barely getting more than two or three hours of sleep per night. Because he was often on the road more than four nights a week, this was becoming a serious issue for him. Despite having trouble sleeping, he never missed a meeting or failed to report to work. He thought that if he kept this up, he would be "in a lot of trouble," and that sooner or later such a pace would catch up to him and more seriously affect his health.

In addition, he reported a third, "unrelated" problem. He had a fear of heights. Flying was a nightmare for him. He could not cross bridges, take escalators, or ride in glass elevators without a sense of panic. Given his considerable travel schedule, this could be problematic, but he felt confident he could manage it himself. He had some "tranquilizers" the physician had given him, and although he rarely used them, he knew he had them in his pocket should he need them.

Frank was reluctant to talk much about himself. He was an excellent, methodical reporter of the various details of his life, but he seemed to lack any sense of himself as the person to whom the assorted irritations and frustrations of life had happened. In other words, he talked about what happened to him, but rarely did he seemed to be present in any of his discussions. He was polite, even cordial, but not friendly in the usual manner; instead, he gave the impression of a man discussing with his mechanic the latest glitches in his car. "It" simply was not functioning up to speed. Could it be fixed?

A two-pronged approach was recommended. First, individual therapy was suggested in order to help Frank understand the nature of his problems. Second, couples therapy was recommended. Frank had reported numerous stresses and strains in his marriage. His wife was "moody, unpredictable" and given to outbursts that frustrated him. At one time during the initial interview, he hesitatingly admitted that he secretly looked forward to his trips away from home in order to get some peace. If he could not sleep on the road and he found no peace at home, he feared he might lose his mind. His coming to this admission was the most nearly emotional moment in the entire interview. Frank was told that by working on the relationship, he could perhaps get some "relief" at home *and* on the road. Such an approach, he was told, would be the most "efficient" way of working. He liked that concept and agreed to it. He would be seen twice a month individually and, with Karen, as a couple twice a month.

Modeling the Therapeutic Approach

According to the therapeutic practice as noted earlier in this chapter, it was explained to the couple that neither of them was "sick" and that each was simply expressing in his or her characteristic style what neither had "permission" or "ability" to say with his or her mouth. Both were interested in such an approach. Frank was fascinated by the concept that communication could occur beyond a person's control. He knew it happened, he had seen it at work many times, but he had never thought any such process would be going on in him without his knowing. Karen was amused by his comment and pointed out that if he "knew" he was doing such things, he would not be able to do them. She beamed at the therapist, as if waiting for a reward or praise. Karen was an attractive woman who seemed constantly tense and strained. She wore too much makeup, forced smiles that frequently seemed mildly insincere, gesticulated with her hands, and made facial expressions that seemed exaggerated within the context of whatever was being discussed. She gave the impression of a little girl playing the part of a grown-up, as if she had gotten into her mother's clothes and makeup and was playing dress up for an admiring but unseen audience.

The concept was offered that neither was "crazy," but each was attempting to communicate with the other. Not only did the receiving partner not understand the communication, but the sending partner was not completely aware of the message. Our job was to first accept responsibility for sending the message—that is, acknowledge that a message was being sent—and then to clarify, in clearly consensual terms, what the message was. Once we had gotten that far, we would see whether either would be willing to act in such a way as to respond favorably to the message being sent.

Rebalancing the Couple Relationship

Rebalancing the relationship was challenging. Power was fairly well distributed: Frank was "distant," didactic, in charge, until Karen became upset, emotional, "hysterical," and had a "fit." She typically got her way at that point. Frank would calm the situation by arranging things the way she wanted, and in the process he would take charge, organize, and structure the necessary changes and, therefore, be in power again. Karen would allow this until she felt he cared more about his "damn schedule" than he did about her; than she would grow impatient, become upset, and the cycle would be repeated. In a strangely satisfying way, such a cycle worked for them.

This very cycle, which in session became known as their "map," was pointed out to them. Frank readily grasped it and examined it in all its ramifications. Karen had a harder time comprehending the pattern. The therapist realized that two processes were at work: first, although the verbal-analytic presentation suited Frank's style well, it did not meet Karen's more global-imagistic processing; and, second, the very cycle that the couple engaged in at home was repeating in session. Frank, in best parental mode, began teaching and lecturing Karen, and she, in childlike manner, "tried" to follow but "couldn't." Graph paper was taken out, and the map was drawn up with colored pens, detailing the very transactions that were taking place, including those occurring in session. Karen readily grasped the relational transaction pattern once it was graphically represented by the map, and she wanted to post copies of it all over their house.

Boundaries and intimacy were not as easily addressed. A triangle existed, with their son vacillating between being a husband-surrogate for his mother when Frank was on the road and acting like a "buddy" and loyal student-child to his father when Frank was home. His presence both kept the marriage going in its current style and perpetuated the very problems that, without his presence, might lead to some kind of resolution.

The next several weeks of couples treatment struggled with these issues. On the one hand, although it was tempting to involve their son in the sessions and switch to family therapy, this became problematic for the clinician. To bring him into a couples therapy format would perpetuate the very issue he was helping to maintain, that is, his intruding on the couple's relationship. It was decided not to include him, and work began to strengthen the couple's bonds without their son in the sessions. A ritual was established: after every session, the couple was to go out on a date. This helped. In addition, the map was expanded (both verbally and pictorially) to show how their son fit within the pattern and how he could be removed.

To Frank, it was presented that his son needed to "stand on his own" and that Frank needed to expand his own social network. For Karen, the suggestion was framed in such a way to show that by encouraging her son to "separate," she would be strengthening not only her marriage, but her son's future as well. She agreed, but the weaning process was difficult for all of them. Eventually, their son was removed from the map.

Therapeutic Goals for Each Partner

Frank was being seen individually twice a month by the couple therapist, and Karen was being seen weekly by her individual therapist. Communication between the therapists became crucial. Although skeptical at first, Karen's therapist agreed to engage her in more exploratory treatment. The following dynamics slowly emerged for each of them.

Karen was the youngest born of four siblings, the prized little girl of the family. She was especially cute and received considerable attention for her brightness and vivaciousness. Shortly after her third birthday, her mother became ill with what was called—Karen believed—"some kind of involutional melancholia." Mother's illness was very difficult for the family. Father picked up much of the slack, worked two jobs, and withdrew much of his attention from Karen. While she was still the favorite grandchild of her grandparents, she secretly envied her mother's new, privileged position. Her mother gained considerable sympathy and seemed to be excused from much of the burdens of the household. Everyone regularly worked around her, and a common family motto was, "Don't upset your mother!" Karen's bouts of depression appeared during adolescence, after the failure of a "love" with an older, college-bound boy. He "left" her to go away to a major university, and she felt devastated, and she claimed to have never fully gotten over the "blow." She eventually decided to go into teaching, where she specialized in drama.

Her earliest memory was of her third birthday. She was sitting at the table with everyone looking at her. She felt special, loved, and amazed by all the gifts and the huge cake placed before her. Her next memory was of her first day of school, at age five. She remembers walking into class, feeling pretty in her new dress. The teacher, a woman, told her to take a seat near the back of the room—her name was at the "back" of the alphabet—and Karen felt offended. She believed the teacher did not like her. Her first reaction was to look at the teacher—and then at herself, for maybe she was not dressed "nice enough" to be up front. She felt sad.

Frank was the oldest of two and the only boy. His father was a violent alcoholic with unpredictable mood swings. His mother was a long-suffering woman, who used Frank as her sole support. His sister was born blind, and Frank remembers the frequent threats to send her "away" to an orphanage should she be too much of a bother. He took on as his mission to keep her out of the orphanage and became her surrogate parent, teacher, and friend. He kept her from such a fate almost single-handedly.

Frank worked from the time he was 14. His first job was on a loading dock, allowing him to see much of life's seamier side at too young an age. He vowed to make life better for himself, to never lose his temper or drink or become a "drunk" like his father. He eventually got his GED, went to college—which he paid for himself—and worked his way up through various jobs, eventually into management and then consulting with others about how to run their businesses.

His earliest memory is the following. He is five years old, and he walks out onto the fire escape of the family apartment. As he is looking around, admiring the view, he hears a scream. His mother comes rushing out, grabs him, and sweeps him back into the apartment. She yells at him and tells him how dangerous it is to be on the fire escape, warns him to be more careful, and scolds him. He feels confused, but vows to be more careful and not upset her.

The following interlocking dynamics were explained to the couple. Karen grew up feeling special but cheated. Although she was aware that she could get attention for her specialness, she was also aware of how fleeting it could be. Getting attention was wonderful, but being able to hold onto it was another matter. She measured life and others as to how they could take care of her, notice her, and she became a master at playing roles to attract their attention. As she grew older, she felt her "specialness,"—her beauty, youth and energy—fading. When her son (a planned only child, so that he would always feel special) left home, the empty-nest syndrome hit her hard. She felt abandoned by her husband, who worked too many hours, soon to be abandoned by her son (he too had left her for college some five years earlier, as her first love had, and might eventually move out and go on his own), and lonely and pessimistic. The onset of her current, chronic depression roughly coincided with her son's leaving for college. She was using depression as a coping device to deal with life, to draw others to her as she had seen modeled by her mother. She was probably genetically loaded for depression, and she learned to use it in such a way as to rally support for herself.

Frank grew up believing it was "all on him." In many ways he was right—his conscientiousness helped keep his family intact. Gradually, the line between conscientiousness and control began to blur; unless he controlled his own life and that of others, he sensed a somewhat uneasy, impending doom. His solution was to do more, to work harder, to control more, and to be busier. His only break from such a rigid, tense style was to be "ill." By being afraid of heights and unable to sleep, he could ask for a break or perhaps seek to take some time for himself without having to admit that he was shirking responsibility. His rash was his way of saying, "This is irritating me. It's getting under my skin."

The interlocking dynamics gradually became clear to the couple. Karen's depression was reframed as a way of asking to be cared for and her "moodiness" as her trying to keep the relationship together. She valued love and the marriage, and she wanted her family to be happy. She was trying to keep them together and to look out for her husband and his health. Frank was trying to keep his family together too, and the motive for his working so hard was reframed as being the same motive Karen had. In effect, they were told that their symptoms were serving the same purpose, just in different ways. Could they now communicate such desires in more prosocial, constructive ways?

Frank's controlling and Karen's emotionality were complementary. She was encouraged to "teach" him to be more passionate, and he was urged to be her consultant on matters of organization. They grasped this way of working, and though they still had characteristic "rough spots," they found that they grew more affectionate with each other. Karen's depression lifted and she found more satisfaction with Frank, even though she could still be somewhat "blue." He was encouraged to go into business for himself and, after some hesitancy, he did. He began to work out of his home, and his consulting business flourished. He gained greater control over his schedule, worked fewer hours more efficiently, and found more pleasure at home. A brief course of cognitive-behavior therapy for his phobic issues—with his wife as "coach" and "cotherapist"—worked very well. Within a short time, he found himself crossing bridges, riding escalators, and flying with virtually no anxiety.

These dynamics were worked on in individual and couple therapy. The road was rocky at times, but after a year and a half, the couple progressed to the point of monthly maintenance sessions. Karen still sees her individual therapist for supportive work. Frank occasionally "checks in" for an individual session, mostly to make sure he does not "overdo it." Each reports considerably more satisfaction with the marriage and little, if any, conflict. Frank has learned to be less rigidly controlling, and Karen, although still somewhat "dramatic," feels more connected and valued. Having her husband work out of the home and spend more time with her, she reports, has helped her tremendously.

REFERENCES

American Psychiatric Association. (1994). *Diagnostic and statistical manual of mental disorders* (4th ed.). Washington, DC: Author.

Barnett, J. (1971). Narcissism and dependency in the obsessional-hysteric marriage, *Family Process, 10,* 75–83.

Beck, A., Freeman, A., & Associates. (1990). *Cognitive therapy of personality disorders.* New York: Guilford.

Bergner, R. (1977). The marital system of the hysterical individual. *Family Process, 16,* 85–95.

Binder, M. (1966). The hysterical personality. *Psychiatry, 29,* 227–235.

Doherty, W., Colangelo, N., Green, A., & Hoffman, G. (1985). Emphasis of the major family therapy models: A family FIRO analysis. *Journal of Marital and Family Therapy, 11,* 299–303.

Dreikurs, R. (1946). *The challenge of marriage.* New York: Hawthorn.

Framo, J. (1992). *Family-of-origin therapy: An intergenerational approach.* New York: Brunner/Mazel.

Gigy, L. (1980). Self-concept of single women. *Psychology of Women Quarterly, 5,* 321–340.

Glick, I., Clarkin, J., & Kessler, D. (1987). *Marital and family therapy* (3d ed). New York: Grune & Stratton.

Goldberg, M. (1975). Conjoint therapy of male physicians and their wives. *Psychiatric Opinion 12*(4), 19–23.

Gottman, J. (1994). *Why marriages succeed or fail.* New York: Simon & Shuster.

Haley, J. (1976). *Problem-solving therapy.* New York: Harper & Row.

Halleck, S. (1967). Hysterical personality traits, psychological, social, and iatrogenic determinants, *Archives of General Psychiatry, 16,* 750–757.

Lachkar, J. (1992). *The narcissistic/borderline couple: A psychoanalytic perspective on marital treatment.* New York: Brunner/Mazel.

Martin, P. (1976). *A marital therapy manual.* New York: Brunner/Mazel.

Martin, P. (1981). Defining normal values in marriage. *International Journal of Family Psychiatry, 2,* 105–114.

Martin, P., & Bird, H. (1959). The "love-sick" wife and the "cold-sick" husband. *Psychiatry, 22,* 242–246.

Minuchin, S. (1974). *Families and family therapy.* Cambridge, MA: Harvard University Press.

Perry, S., Frances, A., & Clarkin, A. (1990). *A DSM-III-R casebook and treatment selection.* New York: Brunner/Mazel.

Satir, V. (1983). *Conjoint family therapy* (3d ed.). Palo Alto, CA: Science and Behavior Books.

Shapiro, D. (1965). *Neurotic styles.* New York: Basic Books.

Sperry, L. (1978). *The together experience: Getting, growing and staying together in marriage.* San Diego: Beta Books.

Sperry, L. (1995). *Handbook of diagnosis and treatment of DSM-IV personality disorders.* New York: Brunner/Mazel.

Sperry, L., & Carlson, J. (1991). *Marital therapy: Integrating theory and technique.* Denver: Love Publishing.

CHAPTER 11

The Narcissistic Couple

Ikar J. Kalogjera
George R. Jacobson
Gerald K. Hoffman
Patricia Hoffman
Irving H. Raffe
Herbert C. White
Ardis Leonard-White

She loved me for the dangers I had past;
And I loved her that she did pity them.

Othello (Act I, Scene 3)
William Shakespeare

All of the authors are members of the Milwaukee Group for the Advancement of Self-Psychology, of which Dr. Kalogjera is the director and founder. The group is accredited by the Medical College of Wisconsin and is hosted by Milwaukee Psychiatric Hospital.

The authors wish to express their gratitude to Anna Ornstein, M.D., and William M. Pinsof, Ph.D., for their generosity in providing independent reviews of the initial draft of this chapter.

We are particularly grateful to Lili Kalogjera for her unending hospitality, generosity, and patience at all hours of the many days and nights it took to complete this chapter.

As Heinz Kohut has explained, "A good marriage is one in which one or the other partner rises to the challenge of providing the selfobject functions that the other's temporarily impaired self needs at a particular moment. And who can potentially respond with more accurate and empathic resonance to a person's needs than his or her marital partner?

"And, conversely . . . who can traumatize a person more than wife or husband who, like the traumatizing parental selfobject of childhood, responds with flawed understanding or, feeling overburdened, refuses to respond at all? This is indeed the stuff of which the breakup of marriages, accompanied by the undying hatred of the marital partners for each other . . . is made" (Kohut, 1984, p. 220).

It is toward a fuller amplification and comprehension of Kohut's observation that this chapter is directed, within the context of identifying, understanding, and treating a couple in which narcissistic personality disorders play a significant role in the development and functioning of their marital relationship.

Kohut first described the narcissistic personality disorder in 1966, and in 1968 published a new treatment approach that has been recognized in the realm of psychoanalysis and individual psychoanalytically oriented psychotherapy. He further developed this treatment approach in his subsequent work (Kohut, 1971, 1972, 1977, 1978, 1984).

The self psychology of Kohut provides an optimal system and framework for the treatment of a narcissistically disordered couple in which their conflicts and current problems can be understood as re-creations and re-presentations of individual developmental sequences that led to less-than-optimal outcomes for the individuals. In the same way that self psychology enables us to understand early individual development within the context of the relationships in which it occurs, so does it provide us a similar framework for understanding and treating the disordered relationship that we now find in adulthood.

A self psychological approach, or its modifications, has been utilized in the treatment of narcissistically disordered couples by several authors (Lansky, 1981, 1983; Berkowitz, 1985; Solomon, 1985, 1988, 1992, 1994; Schwartzman, 1984; Lachkar, 1984, 1985, 1992). In our own clinical work we have found this theoretical model very useful.

Early Greek mythology provides us a picture of Narcissus as a handsome and unduly self-involved and self-indulgent young man who became so enamored of his own image in a quiet pool that the gods, angered by his behavior, transformed him into a flower, perpetually nodding at its own reflection at the pool's edge. From this myth, people often infer that narcissism is an unhealthy or exaggerated or unbalanced state of self-interest. One must recognize, however, the existence and value of normal or healthy narcissism, a state of being that is postulated on the acquisition of structural integrity of the self and the acquisition of self and object constancy, a state of balance between libidinal and aggressive drives, a harmonious stabilization of self and superego structures, the capacity for ego-syntonic expression of impulses, a vital capacity to receive gratification from external objects, and a state of physical well-being. Normal narcissism leads to sustained and realistic self-regard, mature aspirations and ideals, and the ability or capacity for developing and maintaining deep, intimate, enduring object relations (Moore & Fine, 1990).

Only recently has the term *narcissism* begun to lose its pejorative connotations, as Nicholson (in Jackson, 1994) points out that "the newer theories of self psychology expanded the concept of narcissism to include healthy forms of narcissism as prerequisites for developing and maintaining self-esteem and self-cohesiveness. From self psychological perspectives, narcissism exists on a continuum from healthy to more pathological forms. In healthy narcissism, self-confidence and self-esteem develop in conjunction with stable and growth-producing relationships. An individual with healthy narcissism experiences [not more than] a manageable degree of self-doubt when faced with the minor disappointments and frustrations of every day life" (pp. 27–28). Although all individuals are subject to narcissistic injuries or to regression in their feelings of self-esteem, "these feeling states usually pass; the regression is temporary and the [healthy] individual recompensates when the crisis is averted" (Nicholson, 1994, p. 28).

Other observations (Ornstein & Kay, 1990) suggest that the development of normal or healthy narcissism results in the appearance of normal assertiveness and ambition, including self-esteem regulation, enjoyment of physical and mental activities, and the pursuit of goals and purposes. Furthermore, this healthy or normal direction of growth and development allows an individual to acquire methods of self-soothing and self-calming, regulation of feelings of drivenness, the capacity for enthusiasm, and devotion to ideals. Highly evolved aspects of normal or healthy narcissism encompass the capacity for empathy, creativity, humor, wisdom, and the acceptance of one's transience in life.

DESCRIPTION OF NARCISSISTIC PERSONALITY DISORDER USING DSM-IV TERMINOLOGY

Narcissistic Personality Disorder, as elaborated in clinical terms, can be seen and understood as an exaggeration of normal developmental outcomes, or the lack of optimal development in skills, functions, attributes, and processes. Chief among these traits is a heightened or exaggerated sense of self-importance, along with grandiose feelings of being unique, special, and therefore deserving of extraordinary treatment. Individuals manifesting this particular impairment have extreme difficulty in managing criticism of any sort and may readily become enraged by any comment that is perceived as critical; on the other hand, it is not unusual for such persons to appear to be totally indifferent to criticism, regardless of how valid or appropriate it may be. One frequently sees also an exaggerated ambitiousness, a strong need or desire for fame, perhaps notoriety, and such persons are easily offended if they do not receive the attention or adulation they feel is due them. A pronounced sense of entitlement is often evident. Relationships with other people are often fragile or tenuous, owing to difficulty in experiencing and expressing any significant degree of empathic understanding of others.

People with narcissistic personality disorders may be capable of presenting a façade of sympathy toward others, but it is often manipulative or exploitive. The inadequately developed ability for self-regulation and the deficiency in self-soothing or self-calming functioning may often lead to anxiety, depression, addictions, and related pathological patterns (see Exhibits 11.1 and 11.2). Experiences of loss or rejection are intolerable, and such experiences may lead to further regression or sense of disintegration. Crises and exacerbations are most likely to be provoked by significant developmental transitions (e.g., adolescence, marriage, retirement).

According to DSM-IV (American Psychiatric Association, 1994, p. 660), narcissistic personality disorder is relatively infrequent in the general population (<1 percent), but more common (2 to 6 percent) in clinical populations, and the number of individuals exhibiting significant narcissistic traits is very large indeed (Stone, 1993), of which 75 percent are male (American Psychiatric Association, 1994, p. 660).

To illustrate the symptom pattern often typical of narcissistic personality disorder, we first present a description of a young married couple, Bob and Kathy, who entered for treatment of their marital problems: lack of intimacy, Bob's recent extramarital affair, episodic amphetamine and marijuana abuse, frequent arguments, physical abuse, marital separation, and doubts about the continuing viability of the marriage. In addition, each reported feeling depressed and oppressed by perceived simmering anger in the other partner.

Bob is a 42-year-old attorney and Kathy is a 37-year-old teacher with a 9-year-old daughter from a previous marriage. The couple had been married seven years at the time of their entry into treatment and were feeling hopeless, helpless, and despondent about resolving their problems. Both were striving for an ideal loving relationship in which they could feel completely understood and accepted without reservation, but they were unable to communicate this need to each other because of the fear of exposing their vulnerability.

Exhibit 11.1
DSM-IV DIAGNOSTIC CRITERIA FOR
NARCISSISTIC PERSONALITY DISORDER
(American Psychiatric Association, 1994)

A pervasive pattern of grandiosity (in fantasy or behavior), need for admiration, and lack of empathy, beginning by early adulthood and present in a variety of contexts, as indicated by five (or more) of the following:

(1) Has a grandiose sense of self-importance (e.g., exaggerates achievements and talents, expects to be recognized as superior without commensurate achievements)

(2) Is preoccupied with fantasies of unlimited success, power, brilliance, beauty, or ideal love

(3) Believes that he or she is "special" and unique and can only be understood by, or should associate with, other special or high-status people (or institutions)

(4) Requires excessive admiration

(5) Has a sense of entitlement, i.e., unreasonable expectations of especially favorable treatment or automatic compliance with his or her expectations

(6) Is interpersonally exploitative, i.e., takes advantage of others to achieve his or her own ends

(7) Lacks empathy; is unwilling to recognize or identify with the feelings and needs of others

(8) Is often envious of others or believes that others are envious of him or her

(9) Shows arrogant, haughty behaviors or attitudes

Exhibit 11.2
DSM-IV DIAGNOSTIC CRITERIA FOR
NARCISSISTIC PERSONALITY DISORDER:
ASSOCIATED FEATURES AND DISORDERS
(American Psychiatric Association, 1994)

Vulnerability in self-esteem makes individuals with Narcissistic Personality Disorder very sensitive to "injury" from criticism or defeat. Although they may not show it outwardly, criticism may haunt these individuals and may leave them feeling humiliated, degraded, hollow, and empty. They may react with disdain, rage, or defiant counterattack. Such experiences often lead to social withdrawal or an appearance of humility that may mask and protect the grandiosity. Interpersonal relations are typically impaired due to problems derived from this entitlement, the need for admiration, and the relative disregard for the sensitivities of others. Though overwhelming ambition and confidence may lead to high achievement, performance may be disrupted due to intolerance of criticism or defeat. Sometimes vocational functioning can be disrupted due to intolerance of criticism or defeat. Sometimes vocational functioning can be very low, reflecting an unwillingness to take a risk in competitive or other situations in which defeat is possible. Sustained feelings of shame or humiliation and the attendant self-criticism may be associated with social withdrawal, depressed mood, and Dysthymic or Major Depressive Disorder. In contrast, sustained periods of grandiosity may be associated with a hypomanic mood. Narcissistic Personality Disorder is also associated with Anorexia Nervosa, and Substance-Related Disorders (especially related to cocaine). Histrionic, Borderline, Antisocial, and Paranoid Personality Disorders may be associated with Narcissistic Personality Disorder.

Bob and Kathy were diagnosed with Narcissistic Personality Disorder, as defined by DSM-IV criteria. This pattern of symptoms, beginning around late adolescence, pervaded numerous spheres of their lives. Their initial symptoms included grandiosity and preoccupation with fantasies of success, beauty, and ideal love; they believed they were special and could be understood only by other special or high-status people. Both required excessive admiration and had a sense of entitlement (reflected primarily in their expectations of automatic compliance with their wishes). At times arrogant, they had difficulties recognizing or identifying with the feelings and needs of others.

Bob was outwardly boastful and at times pretentious. Kathy had similar problems but a more subtle manner. Her great need for admiration created her excessive preoccupation with being well received and regarded by others. It caused her to be unusually careful about her interactions at work, monitoring her every step in order to leave a favorable impression. Kathy's sense of entitlement was frequently manifested in her relationship with Bob. Without checking with him first, she expected him to comply with her plans regarding contacts with her family. Bob's sense of entitlement was more likely to be expressed at work, where he expected people to cooperate in his projects without first securing their agreement to do so. In fact, the notion of even needing such agreement was foreign to him.

Associated features of Narcissistic Personality Disorder (see Exhibit 11.2) as manifested in this couple included their exquisite sensitivity to criticism, more so within the context of their families and their marriage than in other circumstances. Bob and Kathy both experienced feelings of humiliation, rage, and emptiness in response to being criticized, slighted, or ignored, especially by their families. Their overt responses did not reflect these inner feelings. Instead, Bob reacted with a mixed pattern of anger and withdrawal. It was more typical of Kathy to avoid any potential conflict or confrontation with her family, and she was, therefore, overcompliant and humble in their presence. The vulnerability of this couple's self-esteem, sensitivity to criticism, and sustained feelings of humiliation and shame was seldom evident to others.

As is common among individuals with Narcissistic Personality Disorder, other associated disorders were noted. In Bob's case, there was a history of episodic marijuana and amphetamine abuse. In differential diagnosis, Obsessive-Compulsive Personality Disorder was considered and ruled out. Although Bob and Kathy both professed a commitment to perfection, it seldom impaired their ability to successfully complete their tasks, nor were they excessively self-critical, overscrupulous, or unusually conscientious. In the context of their respective jobs, they both felt as if they had achieved near-perfection, while believing that others were less competent than they. In differential diagnosis, Dysthymic Disorder and Major Depressive Disorder were considered, but were ruled out because Kathy's and Bob's depressed mood and social withdrawal were not pervasive or sustained (to fulfill DSM-IV criteria for these disorders) but were limited to the direct result of their narcissistic vulnerabilities. Bipolar Disorder was similarly ruled out. Although Bob and Kathy experienced periods of grandiosity with accompanying elevated mood, these periods were not sufficiently sustained for fulfillment of diagnostic criteria for Bipolar Disorder.

PSYCHODYNAMICS

As a means to understand the narcissistically disordered couple, Kohut's contributions are especially relevant in the development of the self within the context of interpersonal relationships. His emphasis on the continuity of needs to sustain the self throughout the life span is of particular importance: he cited people's "need to experience mirroring and acceptance; . . . to experience merger with greatness, strength and calmness; and . . . to experience the presence of essential alikeness from the moment of birth to the moment of death" (Kohut, 1984, p. 194). Kohut's concepts are equally applicable for comprehension of both normal development and pathological variations as seen in Narcissistic Personality Disorder. His theories have permitted us to gain a deeper understanding of phenomena that previously had been considered mostly pathological.

Self and Selfobjects

The key concept of self psychology is the notion of self, viewed as the core of personality. Self emerges into a coherent and enduring configuration through the interaction of inherited factors and environmental influences. Central among those environmental influences are parents and/or other primary caregivers appearing in the course of one's lifetime. Such significant individuals (or groups, institutions, or agencies) are conceptualized in a manner that, at least superficially, bears resemblance to the earlier Freudian concept of object. In Kohut's construction, however, one instead encounters "selfobjects," described as one's subjective experience of another person who provides a sustaining function to the self within a relationship, evoking and maintaining the self and the experience of selfhood by his or her presence and activity.

Though the term is loosely applied to the participating persons (objects), it is primarily useful in describing the intrapsychic experience of various types of relationships between the self and others. Both normal and pathological development of the self is related to the internalization of interactions between the self and selfobjects. The effects of such interactions are processed within the individual in the course of those early experiences, and the ultimate unity of the self develops in a gradual and predictable manner. The self, then, is the center of initiative, the recipient of all impressions, and the depository of the individual's ambitions, ideals, talents, skills, values, and related attributes and functions (Moore & Fine, 1990).

Central to the understanding of Kohut's concept of the self and the applications of self psychology are three fundamental human needs and experiences, which are referred to as *twinship* (alter ego), *idealization*, and *mirroring*.

The structure and functions of the self are outlined in Exhibit 11.3 (Ornstein & Kay, 1990), depicting normal development of the self from archaic to mature forms. It also describes the functions of the mature self. These functions include self-esteem regulation, enjoyment of physical and mental activities, pursuit of goals and purposes, empathy, creativeness, humor, wisdom, acceptance of one's transience, self-soothing, self-calming, regulation of feelings of drivenness, capacity for enthusiasm, and devotion to ideals. The process by which these self-functions are internalized is defined by Kohut as a *transmuting internalization* and is differentiated from the more traditional construct of identification inasmuch as only important selfobject functions are internalized, rather than the entire individual. "What results from . . . transmuting internalization is the acquisition of psychological functions and structures that provide a sense of self-cohesion" (Palombo, personal communication, 1995). In the process of transmuting internalization, the new self-structure is formed so that internalization of selfobject functions leads to development of autonomous self-functions. Such development is facilitated through intentional or unintentional *optimal frustrations* by the selfobjects, rather than through perfect and constant gratification of all needs, thereby modifying and transforming archaic and unrealistic grandiosity into mature and reasonable self-concept, self-esteem, and intrapsychic and interpersonal functioning in ongoing self-selfobject relationships over one's lifetime. For the grandiose self to mature, it is necessary for parents (caregivers) to mirror the child's grandiosity and exhibitionism. Optimal development leads to healthy self-esteem and its regulation, the child's prideful enjoyment of physical and mental activities, and the capacity to pursue his or her own goals and purposes.

Kohut has also outlined the importance of the child's needs to idealize and at the same time be attached to an idealized parent. The parent's (caregiver's) ability to be a reliable, idealizable selfobject enables the child to internalize parental values and ideals. This leads to development of an idealized parent imago, which provides the basis for self-soothing and self-calming, regulation of feelings of drivenness, capacity for enthusiasm, and devotion to ideals. The child's archaic alter ego or twinship can develop only in the context of an alter ego or twinship selfobject matrix when a parent (caregiver) provides the selfobject experience of likeness or sameness. This line of development is facilitated by concomitant transformation of the grandiose self and the idealized parent imago. It results in acquisition of empathy, creativeness, humor, wisdom, and acceptance of one's transience. It forms an essential ingredient for the pursuit of learning in acquiring necessary skills based on available talents.

Exhibit 11.3
STRUCTURE AND FUNCTIONS OF THE SUPRAORDINATE BIPOLAR SELF (NORMAL DEVELOPMENT) (Ornstein & Kay, 1990)

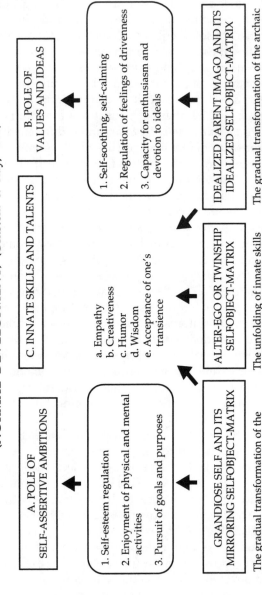

A. POLE OF SELF-ASSERTIVE AMBITIONS

1. Self-esteem regulation
2. Enjoyment of physical and mental activities
3. Pursuit of goals and purposes

GRANDIOSE SELF AND ITS MIRRORING SELFOBJECT-MATRIX

The gradual transformation of the archaic grandiose self within the mirroring selfobject matrix into self-assertive ambitions will create one pole of the bipolar self, with the functions 1 through 3 reliably available.

C. INNATE SKILLS AND TALENTS

a. Empathy
b. Creativeness
c. Humor
d. Wisdom
e. Acceptance of one's transience

ALTER-EGO OR TWINSHIP SELFOBJECT-MATRIX

The unfolding of innate skills and talents takes place within the alter-ego or twinship selfobject matrix. The higher mental functions from (a) through (e) emerge with the transformation of the grandiose self and the idealized parent imago.

B. POLE OF VALUES AND IDEAS

1. Self-soothing, self-calming
2. Regulation of feelings of drivenness
3. Capacity for enthusiasm and devotion to ideals

IDEALIZED PARENT IMAGO AND ITS IDEALIZED SELFOBJECT-MATRIX

The gradual transformation of the archaic idealized parent imago within the idealized selfobject-matrix will create the other pole of the bipolar self, with the functions 1 through 3 reliably available.

Source: P.H. Ornstein & J. Kay. Development of psychoanalytic self psychology: A historical-conceptual overview. *American Psychiatric Press Review of Psychiatry*, Vol. 9. A. Tasman, S.M. Goldfinger, & C.A. Kaufman, eds. Washington, D.C.: American Psychiatric Press. Reprinted with permission.

Empathy and Selfobject Failures

Stern (1985) emphasizes that the infant's need for affect attunement begins at the stage of subjective self (7 to 9 months) and remains a lifelong need. Basch (1991) suggests that failure by the parent to provide affective validation (which for Basch is synonymous with Stern's concept of affective attunement) during the stage of subjective self may result in the later development of Narcissistic Personality Disorder. It is our position that affective validation and affective attunement are both subsumed within the concept of *empathy*, which is as crucial to the conduct of successful therapy as it is to normal development. For Kohut, empathy is "vicarious introspection" (1984, p. 82), an imaginative act in which one imagines oneself to be that particular other person (the developing child, one's spouse, a patient) and then constructs how that individual would feel under a given set of circumstances. Or, in other words, "Empathy involves gaining access to another's psychological state by feeling oneself into the other's experience" (Moore & Fine, 1990, p. 176).

These conceptualizations of empathy provide a very natural transition between our brief examination of the various processes associated with normal development, and our examination of ways in which derailed development or inadequate developmental experiences may lead to the evolution of psychopathology in general and Narcissistic Personality Disorder or traits in particular.

One significant component of such deficient or derailed development is parental failure in empathy, lack of understanding of the child's specific phase-appropriate needs, or inappropriate or unattuned responsiveness to them. Although empathic failures are discussed in the context of parent (caregiver)-child relationships, it is important to understand that they do occur in other relationships (e.g., marriage, psychotherapy, mentoring, friendship) throughout the life span. The empathic process used by parents and therapists is fundamentally the same, although technical elaborations are expected of the clinician for diagnostic and therapeutic purposes.

Parental (caregiver's) failure of empathy may occur in three categories:

1. *Mirroring selfobject failure* indicates parental (caregiver's) inability to consistently reflect pride in the child's accomplishments on a developmentally phase-appropriate basis, leading to a deficient pole of self-assertive ambitions with resultant feelings of inadequacy and constant need for reassurance, feelings of emptiness and despair, and feelings of meaninglessness and purposelessness in life (see Exhibit 11.4) (e.g., Bob's mother's unwillingness to recognize and acknowledge her son's role in taking care of his sick

younger brother during his adolescence when she was unavailable because of her illnesses).

2. *Idealizing selfobject failure* encompasses parental (caregiver's) characteristics or behaviors that interfere with the capacity to be a consistent, idealizable selfobject (e.g., a parent who is a drug addict and declines to seek treatment), as well as those parents who discourage their children from idealizing them because they feel undeserving of such admiration. This failure leads to deficiency in self-soothing or self-calming, self-regulation, and inability to experience enthusiasm or pursue ideals with commitment (see Exhibit 11.2) (e.g., Kathy's mother's discouragement of her daughter's attempts to use her as a role model, in that she felt inadequate and repeatedly depreciated her own accomplishments as wife and mother).

3. *Twinship–alter ego selfobject failure* encompasses parental (caregiver's) inability to consistently provide experiences of likeness and belonging, as well as inability to join the child in activities without intrusion or control. This failure results in deficiencies in empathy, creativeness, humor, wisdom, and acceptance of one's transience (see Exhibit 11.4). Such parents (caregivers) are unable to teach skills needed for developing competence within educational, vocational, and social environments, in spite of their respective talents (e.g., Bob's father was unable to teach him how to play baseball even though Dad was an excellent player and Bob was a good athlete).

Narcissistic Vulnerability, Narcissistic Injury, Narcissistic Rage, and Blaming Couples

It is important to emphasize that deficiencies in the structure of the self are more likely to develop as a result of multiple, chronic selfobject failures. These defects in the structure of the self will predispose a person to the development of a *narcissistic vulnerability*: increased sensitivity to disappointments and extreme difficulty in dealing with real or imagined rejections, slights, and failures. *Narcissistic injury* follows such experiences and culminates in *narcissistic rage*—"reaction to narcissistic injury that suffuses the individual with unforgiving hatred, cruelty, and the need to hurt, in contrast to ordinary aggression, which is mobilized to eliminate an obstacle to a goal" (Moore & Fine, 1990, p. 175). Narcissistic injury is often externalized as blame, so that narcissistically disordered couples are often seen as blaming couples. *Narcissistic injury could thus be conceptualized in a broader sense as any change in the selfobject matrix that jeopardizes cohesiveness of the self.*

Exhibit 11.4

STRUCTURE AND FUNCTIONS OF THE SUPRAORDINATE BIPOLAR SELF (DEFICIENT OR DERAILED DEVELOPMENT) (Ornstein & Kay, 1990)

A. POLE OF SELF-ASSERTIVE AMBITIONS

1. Lack of self-esteem, and deficient self-esteem regulation—feelings of inadequacy and constant need for reassurance
2. Inability to enjoy physical and mental activities—feelings of emptiness and despair
3. Inability for sustained pursuit of goals and purposes—feelings of meaninglessness and purposelessness in life

Unavailability or deficient mirroring of the grandiose self within the mirroring selfobject-matrix—hence deficient transformations resulting in deficiencies or defects in this pole of the bipolar self

(In the treatment process these deficiencies lead to the development of a *mirror* transference for the belated acquisition of these missing psychic structures in the bipolar self.)

B. POLE OF VALUES AND IDEALS

1. Deficiency or inability for self-soothing or self-calming, eg., proneness to diffuse anxiety, insomnia, eating disturbances, etc.
2. Deficiency or inability for self-regulation, expressed through uncontrolled drivenness in addictions, perversions, acts of criminality, etc.
3. Inability to be excited about anything, invest interest in or pursue ideals with commitment to them, etc.

Unavailability of idealized selfobjects, or early and massive traumatic disappointment in them—leads to deficient transformation of archaic idealizations into internalized values and stable ideals

(In the treatment process such deficiencies lead to the development of an *idealizing* transference for the belated acquisition of these missing psychic structures and functions in the bipolar self.)

C. INNATE SKILLS AND TALENTS

A lack of, or deficiency in:

a. Empathy
b. Creativeness
c. Humor
d. Wisdom
e. Acceptance of one's transience

Unavailability of, or deficiency of, support in the alter-ego or twinship selfobject matrix

(In the treatment process these deficiencies lead to the development of an *alter-ego* or *twinship* transference—for the belated unfolding of innate skills and talents.)

Source: P.H. Ornstein & J. Kay. Development of psychoanalytic self psychology: A historical-conceptual overview. *American Psychiatric Review of Psychiatry,* Vol. 9. A. Tasman, S.M. Goldfinger, & C.A. Kaufman, eds. Washington, D.C.; American Psychiatric Press. Used with permission.

The essential homeostatic function of the self is to preserve its own cohesion. Narcissistically vulnerable people use defensive reactions such as blaming, distancing, or initiating marital conflict rather than experience the devastating sense of imminent fragmentation (loss of self-cohesion reported by patients as experiencing feelings of "falling apart," "coming unglued," "losing it," "having a nervous breakdown," feelings of "impending doom," and "going crazy"). These defense reactions serve the purpose of decreasing narcissistic vulnerability, preventing further fragmentation and restoring (increasing) self-cohesiveness. From a self-psychological point of view, these defenses are seen as a compensatory mechanism to protect the defective self from feelings of shame or humiliation and subsequent impending loss of self-cohesion. *In assessing narcissistically disordered couples, it is especially important to go beyond the symptoms and overt behaviors to identify and understand the underlying threat to the integrity of self and how it is perceived by the patient.*

The concepts of narcissistic vulnerability and narcissistic injury can be clarified by returning to the couple we presented earlier. In conjoint marital sessions, Bob expressed his feelings of disappointment and hurt that his father did not accept his advice regarding a legal matter. This was particularly painful to Bob, in light of the fact that he is an expert in this field. This is one of the few instances in which Bob was able to be open regarding his feelings about his family. He was expecting an empathic and validating response from Kathy. Instead, she looked at him in an icy manner and, in a cold tone, stated, "I don't think that should be affecting you anymore." At that point, Bob became visibly angry; he turned toward the therapist and, in an agitated voice, shouted, "Would you want to be married to a woman like this?"

Bob's current narcissistic vulnerability is the product of multiple chronic selfobject failures in his relationship with his parents and of frustrations of his selfobject needs in his marriage. He was hurt not only by his father's recent rejection, but also by his wife's current critical condemnation. This frequently observed type of interaction illustrates an important concept in marital therapy, particularly with narcissistically disordered couples: *Often, both marital partners are narcissistically injured at the same time*, both inside and outside of therapy. Bob was hurt by his wife's lack of empathic attunement to his painful interactions with his father, and Kathy's narcissistic injury arose from her perception that Bob's father was more important to him than she was (see Exhibit 11.5). Therapeutic techniques used at this point, including the therapist's empathic attunement, clarifications, and interpretations (to address both of the partners' narcissistic injuries and their perceptions of the ongoing process), are clarified in the later section entitled "treatment").

Exhibit 11.5
NARCISSISTIC VULNERABILITY, NARCISSISTIC INJURY, AND NARCISSISTIC RAGE

Multiple Chronic Selfobject Failures (Parents/Primary Caregivers and Family of Origin)

↓

Precipitants: Deficiencies in the Structure of the Self
Selfobject failures in the
marital/dyadic relationship   ↓
brought on by disappointments,
rejections, slights, failures   Narcissistic Vulnerability
and/or imperfections and
flaws revealed   ↓

                              Narcissistic Injury

                              ←————————→   Narcissistic Rage

     Fragmentation   ↓
     (Loss of Cohesion)
                                                    Externalization of rage
   Individual   Marriage/   in the marriage/
                 Dyadic Relationship   dyadic relationship of
                                                    blaming couples
                                                    defensive maneuvers
                                                    (e.g., blaming, distancing,
                                                    counterattack)

Traumatic De-idealization and Fragmentation of the Marriage/Relationship

Couples in the process of establishing relationships use idealization as a predominant precursor to the attachment and development of mature love. The process of idealization is based on expectations that a partner will fulfill selfobject needs: twinship, idealizing, and mirroring. The partners' fulfillment of these needs increases self-cohesion in each other and strengthens the idealization process. The bidirectional process of idealization is an essential prerequisite for establishment and maintenance of individual self-cohesion and mutual cohesiveness within the marital bond. The expectations that the partner will fulfill selfobject needs is an essential corollary to this process, but is seldom recognized and/or communicated by the partners.

In the preceding exchange between Bob and Kathy, both failed to recognize or verbalize their own individual need to be valued (idealized) by each other.

Our clinical experience indicates that weakening or destruction of the idealization process leads to deterioration or impairment of the marital bond, manifested by individual and relational dysfunction. Repeated chronic selfobject failures are experienced by the partners as being very traumatic and result in the activation of defensive reactions, such as distancing, blaming, withholding, mistreatment, attacking, counterattacking, substance abuse, violence, and extramarital affairs. Parallel to this traumatization process is the development of de-idealization, beginning with early selfobject failures in the marriage and eventually culminating in development of full-blown traumatic de-idealization. Our definition of traumatic de-idealization is similar to the concept described by Kay (1990) in the context of medical school education: "Unjust criticism and abuse on the part of faculty and house officers is indeed destructive, and clearly undercuts a student's sense of self-worth. These insults and assaults also contribute to lowering of student's ideals about their teachers and medicine itself" (p. 572). The process in a marriage resembles that described by Kay, but with important modifications.

In the marriage (1) there is a complex interaction of self-regulating feedback processes between one partner and the other, (2) the de-idealization is bidirectional, bidirectional, and (3) there is a more equitable and dynamic distribution of power. As the result of traumatic de-idealization there is also an increase of narcissistic vulnerability, a decrease in individual and marital cohesion, feelings of hopelessness and helplessness about the future of the marriage, and progressive deterioration of the relationship. Kay (1990) stated, "If they [medical students] can look up to their teachers, find them enthusiastic, dedicated and caring about their patients and students, the students experience an exhilarating idealism and a capacity for enthusiasm in themselves, which sustains them during the hardships of their professionalization and may endure for the rest of their professional lives" (p. 572). Just as Kay emphasizes the importance of idealization in the education of medical students, so are we emphasizing the importance of ongoing idealization in a marriage. In a healthy marriage, idealization is maintained throughout the life span in evolving and maturing forms.

Curative Fantasy and Hope in the Marriage/Relationship

A closely related concept, the *curative fantasy*, enables us to understand the impact of traumatic de-idealization and the dynamics of the narcissistically disordered couple. The concept of curative fantasy was introduced by Ornstein and Ornstein (1977): "The affective matrix of the doctor-patient relationship is primarily provided by what we will now describe as the 'curative fantasy.' Its universal nature can be most readily seen in disturbed marital relationships. Infantile expectations 'to be made up to,' to have past hurts undone and old, frustrated wishes fulfilled, are readily activated in marital relationships. Since these infantile expectations are always compounded by guilt and shame, marital transactions frequently have the appearance of a neurotic interaction between a demanding, guilty child and a frustrating, punitive, or acquiescing parent" (pp. 341–342). Relatedly, inasmuch as it has been noted that curative fantasies "are readily activated in any intimate relationship" (p.342), it should come as no surprise to our readers that they are further defined as "organized sets of hopes and expectations for recovery that have to be recognized by a psychotherapist as an essential aspect of the treatment process" (Ornstein, 1992, p. 21).

We conceptualize traumatic de-idealization within the marriage as an ongoing, gradual, abrasive process rather than a sudden cataclysmic destruction of hopes, beliefs, and desires. Although there are frequent instances of overpowering events that seem to trigger a sudden de-idealization, these occur within the context of multiple selfobject failures. Without the cumulative narcissistic vulnerability from previous self-object failures, these apparently devastating events would not have the same destructive power.

It is necessary to emphasize the *destructive effect of traumatic de-idealization on the curative fantasy* and subsequent development of feelings of hope-lessness and helplessness about the outcome of the marriage (relationship).

Turning for a moment for clarification to the popular literature (Seeley, 1993), one sees an increasingly sophisticated viewpoint regarding rela-tionships and a rudimentary understanding of significant aspects of our current discussion regarding idealization, de-idealization, narcissistic injury, narcissistic rage, and curative fantasy. For example, we find that "when a man treats you like the woman of his dreams from the start, of course it's wonderful . . . it's the stuff romantic poetry is made of [curative fantasy]. But, before you buy into his adoration, you need to ask yourself what his motivation is. Is he putting you on a pedestal out of love and admiration or out of some need to possess you in order to elevate himself?" (p. 81). Relatedly, "his attempt to idealize her and see her as perfect is really a subverted attempt to make himself feel wonderful, to bolster his own self-esteem [idealization] by telling himself, 'Hey, I was able to get this woman, now she's mine.' What he really wants is to feel important, to be on a pedestal himself [mirroring]. But the first flaw the woman demon-strates reminds him of his own imperfection, so he gets angry with her for ruining his fantasy" (p.82) [de-idealization, narcissistic injury, and narcis-sistic rage]. Another example of the process of de-idealization is expressed in this passage: "It's like I have all of this emotion, these intense feelings, but normal day to day relationships can't match my expectations." Furthermore: "A man like this needs to be continually caught up in romantic passion [idealization, curative fantasy] because he is so desperate to be adored and have self-esteem. The woman a man like this fixates on is just a player in his drama" (p. 84). And, finally: "Are you looking for a healthy relationship, or do you want someone to treat you like a princess to bolster your self-esteem, by catering to your every whim?" [mirroring] (p. 84). The process of de-idealization in narcissistically disordered couples is particularly devastating because their idealizations are excessive (see pages 229–230 for an explanation of Bob's and Kathy's traumatic de-idealizations).

SYSTEMIC AND INTERACTIONAL DYNAMICS

To fully understand the interactional dynamics in the marital/dyadic relational system, we feel that it is imperative to clarify some important systemic concepts. Although we use the terms *marriage* and *marital relationship* to refer to the couples, the legal convention of matrimony is not essential. We are generally referring to any two-person or "dyadic relational unit" (American Psychiatric Association, 1994, p. 758) or dyadic relational system with close emotional ties, intimate relationships, and a degree of affective commitment by the two people to each other that is expected to remain stable over a reasonable period of time.

The marital/dyadic relational system is seen as a unit, an *integrated whole* with its overall form and structure determined by the patterns of mutually causal relationship between the partners. According to the principle of *nonsummativity*, the whole is more than the sum of its parts. A marital/dyadic relational system consists of the individual spouses plus their relationship with each other (modified after Feldman & Pinsof, 1982).

We consider these principles particularly important in narcissistically disordered couples because of their vulnerability and propensity for narcissistic injuries and fragmentation. Their difficulties in achieving intimacy may cause them to experience themselves as separate and disconnected rather than as part of a dyadic relational system, (e.g., it is difficult for Bob and Kathy to use the pronoun *we* when describing their marriage).

According to the principle of *mutual causality*, the thoughts, feelings, and behaviors of a partner have important effects on the thoughts, feelings, and behaviors of the other partner, directly or indirectly. These effects, in turn, influence the subsequent thoughts, feelings, and behaviors of the originally acting partner (modified after Feldman & Pinsof, 1982).

A closely related concept is that of *marital/dyadic relational system homeostasis* (morphostasis). This is the process whereby a marital/dyadic relational system maintains its internal stability by keeping particular behaviors, thoughts, and feelings within prescribed (homeostatic) limits.

Some degree of homeostasis (morphostasis) is essential for maintenance of marital/relational stability. But when there is excessive homeostasis (morphostasis), the marriage/dyadic relationship is rigid and cannot make adaptive changes. A process by which marital/dyadic relational systems change is called marital/dyadic relational system *morphogenesis*, which can be *constructive (growth-producing) or destructive (problem-escalation)* (modified after Feldman & Pinsof, 1982).

Narcissistically disordered couples are especially prone to using defensive reactions such as blaming, attacking, counterattacking, and distancing in response to narcissistic injuries. However, such reactions are also *restorative* attempts to elicit an *empathic response* from the selfobject, which often is an *enactment of the initial curative fantasy*. Because most narcissistically disordered couples come from dysfunctional family systems, their curative fantasies incorporate hopes that they will not be retraumatized but, rather, will be able to establish a marriage or a family that will be an improvement over their childhood experiences. According to Ornstein (1992), "the hope and expectation that this time and in this relationship the rage, hurt and vulnerability will not be met with criticism and will not be dismissed as unreasonable and inappropriate" (p. 23) is one of the foundations of the marriage/dyadic relationship.

A central *homeostatic function* of the narcissistic marriage/dyadic relationship system is prevention of experiencing narcissistic injuries and traumatic de-idealization. A central *constructive (growth-promoting) morphogenic function* of the narcissistic marriage/dyadic relationship system is fulfillment of selfobject needs and support for appropriate curative fantasies. A *central destructive (problem-escalation) morphogenic function* of the narcissistic marriage/dyadic relationship system is dissolution of any remaining mutual cohesiveness under the impact of narcissistic rage. Partners would rather risk escalation of marital/relational problems and/or loss of the marriage/relationship than experience fragmentation of the self as the result of narcissistic injuries. To avoid such a possibility, there may develop an excessively homeostatic state, in which all likelihood of change of any sort is highly limited. Dread of change is motivated by a need to avoid further traumatization, thereby ensuring a certain degree of personal safety but at the same time equally ensuring the blocking of morphogenic growth-promoting changes. Excessive homeostasis (morphostasis) promotes the continuation of the pathologic circular, repetitive interactional dynamics of the couple (e.g., withdrawal, reduced communication, simmering rage, etc.), who are no longer able to fulfill each other's selfobject needs and are unable to extricate themselves from that vicious circle of mutual victimization.

Another significant concept is that of marriage contracts, which are generally of three different types (Sager, 1976): verbalized, secret, and beyond awareness. The weighting of the three contracts is unique in the narcissistically disordered couple, in that the verbalized contract (openly discussed between the partners) is constricted by the existing narcissistic vulnerabilities and fear of retraumatization. The secret contract (conscious and known to the individual but not shared or discussed because of fear of the consequences of disclosure to the partner) and the beyond awareness contract (based on preconscious and unconscious needs) are disproportionately expanded. To compensate for the fears of narcissistic injury and ongoing narcissistic vulnerability arising from unsatisfied archaic selfobject needs generated by experiences in the family of origin, the latter two types of contracts become more important in regulating the dynamics of the relationship. This results in the unspoken agendas determining and controlling the interactions of the couple, with ensuing confusion and disorganization and the experiencing of unsatisfied selfobject needs.

An example of a verbalized contract between Bob and Kathy prior to getting married was a successful agreement on how to manage their finances jointly. An example of a secret contract was Kathy's unexpressed expectation that she and Bob would provide financial assistance to her family of origin should such a need ever arise. Bob's beyond-awareness contract was his expectation that he would never experience from Kathy what he had experienced from his mother, and that the relationship with Kathy would make up for the repeated traumatizations by his mother. Kathy's beyond-awareness contract was that Bob would take care of her as her father never had; in fact, she chose to marry a man who was very skillful and responsible with money matters, in contrast to her father. An unknowingly shared beyond-awareness contract was their expectation that each would rescue the other from the grips of their respective families of origin. Both had sacrificed their own earlier development to maintain cohesion in their families of origin, and that process was being continued. They needed to discover for themselves that it was permissible to have a mature relationship with their parents, in which their needs as individuals and as a couple were primary, thus allowing Bob and Kathy to function on an adult, reciprocal level rather than on the level of a child's automatic compliance with parental wishes based on archaic selfobject needs.

The narcissistically disordered couple's communication pattern includes their own characteristic multilevel messages. What may seem like a surface here-and-now issue may, in actuality, reflect a core selfobject need. Multilevel messages fulfill three essential functions: *restorative, defensive,* and *expressive.* The aim of the restorative (healing) function is reestablishment of selfobject bonds in the hope of fulfillment of selfobject needs and recreation of curative fantasies. The defensive function of multilevel messages is protection of the self from experiencing the hurt of current narcissistic injuries and traumatic de-idealization. The expressive function serves the purpose of communicating the pain of narcissistic injuries, traumatic de-idealizations, the need for the hope derived from curative fantasies, and additional feelings, thoughts, and selfobject needs. Because of narcissistic vulnerability, there is an overreliance on the defensive function of communication, by the listener as well as by the speaker, at the expense of the restorative and expressive functions.

TREATMENT

To begin this section on treatment, we refer back to Kohut's explanation at the beginning of the chapter as a reminder that although repeated self-object failures are unavoidable in marital interactions, they are particularly devastating to the narcissistic couple, with their vulnerabilities and exquisite sensitivities in regulating self-cohesion. The therapeutic process provides an opportunity for understanding and repairing the effects of traumatic selfobject failures from the past and their manifestation within the marital context. Presenting symptoms of the narcissistically disordered couple can be conceptualized on a continuum ranging from relatively mild to extreme forms. Such symptoms often include failure of intimacy, sexual dysfunction, failure of empathy, mutual blame, inability to accept responsibility for one's own contributions to marital problems, subtle and overt contempt and disdain for the partner, chronic anger (ranging from frequent irritability to explosive rage), feelings of entitlement, expectation of the partner's automatic compliance with one's own wishes, anticipation of the partner's fulfilling unexpressed needs, preoccupation with self to the exclusion of recognizing the partner's needs, exploitation of the partner to fulfill one's own needs, proneness to shame, unresolved enmeshment with family of origin, physical abuse, and substance abuse.

According to the DSM-IV (American Psychiatric Association, 1994) Global Assessment of Relational Functioning Scale (GARF, p. 758–759), marital functioning was markedly impaired for Bob and Kathy at the time of their entering treatment. Their score was assessed to be 45–50. They experienced occasional times of satisfying and competent functioning together, but it was clear that, dysfunctional and unsatisfying relationships tended to predominate. Communication was frequently inhibited by unresolved conflicts, and there were significant difficulties in adapting to family stress and any transitional changes. Kathy and Bob's decision making was only intermittently competent and effective within the marriage. A much better level of functioning was observed at their workplaces. Bob and Kathy's responsiveness to each other's needs, as well as common needs within the marriage, was overpowered by their self-absorption in their own archaic selfobject needs. They exhibited pain and ineffective anger, culminating in abusive behaviors and emotional deadness within the context of the marriage. There was little warmth, support, or respect for each other, and there was a lack of sexual interaction. All three areas of functioning were impaired within the marriage: problem solving, organization, and emotional climate (American Psychiatric Association, 1994, p. 758–759).

In determining the most effective or the most appropriate approach to treatment of a couple in which each partner has a narcissistic personality disorder, it is necessary to make a sufficient clinical evaluation to allow an understanding of other concurrent individual pathology that is likely to affect the outcome of the conjoint treatment (simultaneous treatment of both spouses in joint sessions). While it is not possible to anticipate all contingencies, we recognize that in many cases both members of the couple may need *individual* therapy; for example, Bob and Kathy had each been in individual psychotherapy preceding conjoint marital therapy for approximately one year. Another contingency may require *concurrent* therapy, that is, simultaneous individual treatment of both spouses by the same therapist, but in separate sessions. Another treatment modality utilizes a *combined* treatment (mixing conjoint and concurrent sessions), or *collaborative* therapies conducted by two therapists, each of whom sees one spouse and who regularly meet to discuss and plan the treatment. Complications may require additional interventions, such as pharmacotherapy, individual or group counseling for alcohol and other drug problems, family therapy if children of the narcissistic couple are affected, and other possibilities.

Curative Fantasy Marital/Relational Questionnaire

At the initial session, therefore, it is appropriate to attempt to determine the historical origins of the current problems, as well as to determine the real or potential threat to individual self-cohesion and cohesiveness of the marriage. A method we have developed to approach these processes is the utilization of the Curative Fantasy Marital/Relational Questionnaire, a copy of which is found in the appendix to this chapter. We find very consistent and unusually similar responses (between and within couples) to questions designed to elicit the curative fantasy and selfobject needs, all of which tend to validate and support the underlying foundations of self psychology regarding the importance and universality of selfobject needs throughout the life span. Thus, the need for "empathy" is most frequently mentioned as part of the curative fantasy, along with "supportive and nonjudgmental attention," "patience," and "attentive listening" from the partner, all indicative of *mirroring selfobject needs*. Other responses certainly indicate the importance of *twinship selfobject* needs: "physical contact," "Hug me when I need it," soothing and comforting through "nonsexual touching and holding," "sharing," and "having more in common." Relatedly, in response to other items in the questionnaire, a very commonly expressed need, "respect," is inferred to be an expression of the idealizing selfobject needs. Thus, we have no doubt about the importance of self psychology as a means of understanding normal and pathological development, as well as presenting the key to successful treatment of the narcissistically personality disordered couple.

These same selfobject needs were expressed by Bob and Kathy in their respective questionnaires. Kathy's experience of repeated selfobject failures in the marriage (i.e., Bob's inability to provide adequate mirroring, twinship, and idealization because of his absorption in his own hurt) resulted in reactions of blame, counterattack, withdrawal, avoidance of sexual intimacy, and, ultimately, her de-idealization of Bob from initially competent spouse to an inadequate marital partner. Kathy felt progressively more alone and abandoned. Her blaming comment, "I don't think that should be affecting you anymore," was a multilevel message. One level implied her desire for Bob to change and value her, reinvest in the relationship, and make their marriage a priority. Thus, her sudden attacking outburst was a reaction to the perceived threat that her curative fantasy (the marriage would bring about a fulfillment of her unmet childhood needs) was not going to materialize. Her blaming Bob served multiple functions. In its defensive function, it protected Kathy from reexperiencing narcissistic injuries accumulated earlier in life, when she perceived her father as being too busy, otherwise involved in interests outside of the family, to provide her the fulfillment of archaic selfobject needs. Simultaneously, she was able to fend off the development of emotional intimacy, which would have been reminiscent of similar affect from childhood. Kathy made it evident that she was feeling as though she, herself, was being de-idealized, because the marriage was of less importance to Bob than his relationship with his own family of origin. Thus, we saw the destruction of Kathy's curative fantasy that the marriage would be the principal relationship in Bob's life, that Bob would place the marriage ahead of all other interests in a way that her father was never able to do.

Concomitantly, Kathy's statement was a de-idealization of Bob, reminiscent of ways in which Bob's parents withheld recognition and acknowledgment of his role in maintaining the family when his parents were not able to do so. They invalidated his attempts to be the reliable and dependable child. Bob's curative fantasy regarding the marriage was equally damaged, as he was being denied fulfillment of his need to be seen as an intelligent and caring person, something he had also been deprived of during his developmental years. For both of them, their curative fantasies regarding the marriage had been seriously threatened. The unexpressed wish, desire, or need was a hope that the marriage would be the vehicle by which they could each escape from the imprisoning influences of their respective families of origin and find achievement of their needs for sanctuary. Release from the powerful pull of their respective families of origin could not be attained. The anticipated salvation, which they had expected to find in each other and in the marriage, was denied them. The curative fantasy of the therapy became even more important for Bob and Kathy as a way to help them find fulfillment of these expectations, which they had both previously felt very helpless and hopeless to accomplish on their own.

Bob's initial message to Kathy was an indirect request for empathy and acknowledgment (mirroring) of his painful interaction with his father, inasmuch as "severely abused or frequently disappointed people will be hesitant to reveal their most fervent hopes and expectations; they have to protect themselves from renewed disappointments and the possibility of retraumatization" (Ornstein, 1992, p. 21–22). No wonder, then, he experienced her response as a narcissistic injury. His reply, "Would you want to be married to a woman like this?" carried multilevel messages, the first of which was a defensive reaction to narcissistic injury, which he externalized as rejection of Kathy and distancing from her. A second message was an attempt to elicit the needed empathic mirroring from the therapist, since "in the therapeutic relationship, patients hope that the maintenance of contact with the therapist will not require the same compromises to the self that were required in the original relationship" (Ornstein, 1992, p. 22). Thus, this may be Bob and Kathy's opportunity "to shed the defenses that have been protecting the self from retraumatization and to get in touch with those aspects of his [her] self that had to be repressed or disavowed in the past. The appearance of the curative fantasy in psychotherapy indicates the reactivation of long abandoned and, by now, highly intensified childhood needs and aspirations" (Ornstein, 1992, p. 22). It is necessary to recognize that resultant dysfunctional marital interactions serve not only defensive, but also expressive and restorative functions, and it is of high priority for the therapist to identify all three and to use them in treatment. Ornstein (1992) also emphasized the importance of emergence of rage: "To summarize, once a selfobject transference has been established and the curative fantasy has been mobilized, as can be expected to occur in an empathic environment, the patient feels free to experience—and to express—the rage that in his [her] childhood would have destroyed the tenuous emotional contact with the most important people in his [her] life" (p. 24).

Such rage, when it is expressed, can be accepted by the therapist and decoded in the context of multilevel messages and the underlying motivation based on unfulfilled selfobject needs. Other therapeutic techniques at this point include the therapist's emphathic attunement, clarifications, and interpretations for Bob and Kathy, both individually and as a couple, to address their *simultaneous* narcissistic injuries. Examples of these techniques follow, also utilizing the modified "three/step sequence" process explicated by Kohut, (1984, p. 103–104).

> **Therapist (T):** Bob, you felt very hurt . . . you very much wanted Kathy to know how you felt about your painful interactions [rejections] with your father. You hoped Kathy would understand your pain and help you deal with it. (*The therapist empathically expresses the identification of narcissistic injury, unfulfilled selfobject needs for mirroring and twinship, and recognition of curative fantasy.*)
>
> **Bob:** Uh huh (*visible diminution of signs of anger*).
>
> **T:** Kathy, for you Bob seemed preoccupied with his relationship with his father . . . it felt as if his father was more important to him than you and your marriage. (*Again, the therapist empathically identifies narcissistic injury and unfulfilled selfobject needs for mirroring and twinship. The simultaneity of addressing both members of the couple is essential, to maintain alliances with both and avoid creating new narcissistic injuries by appearing to take sides with one or the other.*)
>
> **Kathy:** Yeh (*she nods her agreement*).
>
> **T:** Bob and Kathy (*addressing both together, to provide mirroring for them as a couple and twinship by joining them, thereby enhancing cohesion of the marital bond*), due to feeling deeply hurt, you have not been able to understand and meet each other's needs (*emphatic attunement and identification of selfobject failure*). You did not feel safe, and you both withdrew from each other (*identification of defensive reaction to fear of narcissistic injury*). Since you perceived each other as uncaring and blaming, a lot of resentment has built up in both of you (*identification of a source of de-idealization and subsequent development of narcissistic rage*). The risk for both of you was being hurt and yet not being heard again (*repetition of traumatization from childhood mirroring selfobject failures*). As a consequence it became very difficult to invest emotionally in your partner and your future (*identification of destruction of curative fantasy*). Your marriage became less important, and you started having doubts about your commitment to it. . . . You both withdrew from each other (*identification of idealizing selfobject failure and further weakening of the curative fantasy, and defensive withdrawal from the relationship*).

Repetition of such therapeutic interchanges are necessary for integration of learning experiences and progress in treatment. In the course of these interpretive explanations, painful childhood and adolescent memories are evoked, leading to "reactivation of thwarted developmental needs in the transference" (Kohut, 1984, p. 104). An example of this process follows.

> **T:** For you, Bob, it (Kathy's earlier statement) brought back into focus your mother's lack of understanding and appreciation at a time when you were single-handedly taking care of your siblings because of mother's illness" (*therapist identifies genetic precursors for current narcissistic vulnerabilities and provides a restorative experience of the previously thwarted developmental needs through selfobject transference*). You needed your mother's recognition of how difficult it was for you, and you needed some appreciation and approval for your efforts (*mirroring selfobject needs*).
>
> **Bob:** That's what I needed from her (*and he elaborates on how he felt at that time*).
>
> **T:** Kathy, for you, Bob's apparent loss of interest in the marriage and his withdrawal brought back your feelings from the past . . . your father's difficulties in understanding that you needed his attention and support, his participation in your life . . . he withdrew . . . your needs did not seem to count (*failure of mirroring and twinship selfobject needs, both genetic and current*).

Kathy's verbalizations and nonverbal behaviors indicated the therapeutic benefit of these empathic interpretations of her feelings. In subsequent sessions with Bob and Kathy there was a marked improvement in the directness and openness of their communications with each other, as well as a less guarded expression of affect and improved empathic attunement to each other's needs.

In addition to the selfobject functions provided by the therapist in the preceding passages, it is also the therapist's responsibility to express appreciation and respect for the couple's needs, feelings, hopes, expectations, and aspirations. In this manner, therapy is greatly enhanced, and the therapist conveys his or her understanding of their curative fantasies about the therapy itself. Moreover, the therapist's respect also serves to provide fulfillment of idealizing selfobject needs for the individuals and for their marriage. By so doing, the therapist enhances and promotes the essential therapeutic alliance and reduces resistance to treatment.

This process can be further enhanced by the therapist's responding to the patient's archaic grandiosity empathically, within a mirroring selfobject matrix, understanding its origins and purposes rather than responding at a more personal level and expressing negative countertransference.

The therapist's or spouse's failure to provide selfobject functions may activate or exacerbate the patient's narcissistic rage. Such failures are inevitable and may lead to premature termination of treatment or to divorce. On the other hand, they can also provide opportunities for restorative experiences, thereby actually enhancing the patient's therapeutic outcome. It is essential for the therapist, therefore, to respond empathically to narcissistic rage, identifying the expressive and restorative elements (in addition to defensive ones) and communicating his or her understanding to the couple. Failure to do so is the most frequent error in the treatment of narcissistic couples and may result in blaming, disillusionment, fragmentation, depression, or shame. The rage must be acknowledged and validated within the context of chronic multiple selfobject failures; only then can the restorative function be experienced by the patient.

If the couple can remain feeling safe and protected during their expressions of rage in an empathic and secure therapeutic environment, the archaic fears of abandonment/rejection/engulfment are unrealized, enabling them to establish a continuity between archaic and current experiences, permitting significant therapeutic advances toward the development of new curative fantasies encompassing "dormant hopes and expectations" (Ornstein, 1992, p. 24). Identification of new, mutually shared curative fantasies about the marriage obviates the need for secret contracts and brings to consciousness the beyond-awareness contracts. This then allows for clarification of previous confusions within the marriage and promotes the formation of verbalized contracts, on the basis of which the marriage can develop in a more adaptive manner. Neither member of the couple then feels victimized, controlled, or manipulated, and both can come closer to enactment of their mutual curative fantasies. As part of this same therapeutic process, there are significant reductions of narcissistic vulnerabilities in both spouses.

Because recurrences of narcissistic rage are part of the recovery process, they can be recognized and used by the couple as opportunities to apply their new understandings of the meaning of that behavior. Such experiences, which had previously been destructive and led to maladaptive defenses, are now part of the restorative healing process in which mutual selfobject needs are fulfilled and increased self-cohesion and cohesiveness of the marriage are created, as the marriage itself becomes a selfobject.

The resulting increased self-cohesion promotes introspection and positive understanding that can be applied outside the marital relationship as well as within the marriage.

Successful therapy neutralizes and reverses the destructive effects of traumatic de-idealization and can free the individual and the couple to formulate a mature and developmentally appropriate idealization. The interference of the archaic needs and their inherent rigidity is significantly reduced, and a more creative and vibrant marriage emerges (see Exhibit 11.6).

Exhibit 11.6
TREATMENT

Mutiple Chronic Selfobject Failures in the Marriage/Dyadic Relationship

Preexisting
Narcissistic Vulnerabilities ⟶ ↓

Mutiple Narcissistic Injuries and Chronic Narcissistic Rage
in the Marriage/Dyadic Relationship
↓
Traumatic De-idealizations and Fragmentation of the Marriage/
Dyadic Relationship
↓
Destruction of Curative Fantasies
↓
Couples Therapy Begins

Identification of selfobject failures, ⟶ ⟵ Decoding of multilevel messages
narcissistic injuries, chronic (defensive, expressive, and restorative
narcissistic rage, traumatic functions) in communications between
de-idealizations, curative partners throughout couples therapy
fantasies, marriage/dyadic
relationship contracts and
catastrophic fears of retraumatizations

↓

Inevitable Selfobject Failures, Narcissistic Injuries, and Narcissistic Rage
in Couples Therapy and in Marriage/Dyadic Relationship
↓
Optimal Frustration in Couples Therapy and Marriage/Dyadic Relationship
↓
Selfobject Transferences—Therapist as Selfobject for Partners and for Marriage/
Dyadic Relationship
↓
Marital/Dyadic Relationship as Selfobject for Partners
↓
Fulfillment of Selfobject Needs and Increase of Empathy in Couples Therapy
and Marriage/Dyadic Relationship
↓
Further Therapeutic Goals, Processes and Outcomes:

1. Working through and decrease of traumatic de-idealizations and catastrophic fears of retraumatizations in couples therapy and marriage/dyadic relationship
2. Emergence and utilization of curative fantasies in couples therapy and marital/dyadic relationship
3. Working through and decrease of defensive maneuvers in couples therapy and marital/dyadic relationship (e.g., blaming, distancing, counterattack)
4. Maturation of selfobject needs in relationship to parents/primary caregivers and family of origin—primacy of marriage/dyadic relationship
5. Decrease in partners' narcissistic vulnerabilities and increase in their self-cohesion
6. Increased marital/dyadic relationship system cohesion (its wholeness and nonsummativity)
7. Increase in verbalized marriage/dyadic relationship contracts and decrease in secret and beyond-awareness contracts
8. Improved communications between partners; increase in expressive and restorative functions and decrease in defensive functions
9. Stabilization of dysfunctional marital/dyadic relationship system homeostasis
10. Mature idealization of partner and marriage/dyadic relationship

In Bob and Kathy's case, many favorable changes have taken place during their 18 months of conjoint treatment. Selfobject needs are more fully met in a variety of ways: Kathy now calls Bob "my buddy" (twin-ship needs); Bob is more affectionate and attentive toward Kathy (mirroring needs); they have come to value each other and their marriage (idealization needs). The enhancement of their mutual respect is reflected in their increased capacity to empathically listen to each other and respond appropriately. Bob has not been abusing marijuana or cocaine, nor have there been any episodes of physical abuse or extramarital affairs. They are able to laugh and joke with each other, freely expressing their humor. Their Global Assessment of Relational Functioning (GARF) score (American Psychiatric Association, 1994, pp. 758–759) at the conclusion of their active treatment (after which they have been seen on an as-needed basis) was in the range of 81–85. Agreed-on patterns or routines are in place that help meet the usual needs of Bob, Kathy, and the family. Conflicts and stressful transitions are resolved through problem-solving communication and negotiation. A wide range of feelings are freely expressed and managed within the marriage and the family. There is a general atmosphere of warmth and caring, and there is an enhancement of intimacy and satisfying sexual relations. Problem solving, organization, and emotional climate are markedly improved (American Psychiatric Association, 1994, pp. 758–759). It must be acknowledged that the synergistic effects of conjoint marital ther-apy and Bob and Kathy's individual therapies combined to produce these favorable outcomes. Narcissistic Personality Disorder is an enduring state prone to fragmentation in times of crises, so that additional, usually briefer, treatment may be required at those times. However, the frequency and intensity of crises typically subside as the key issues have been addressed and worked through in treatment.

It is important to emphasize that brief interventions in times of crisis, through short-term focused therapy can provide some relief and tempo-rary stabilization; for enduring changes to take place, however, a longer-term conjoint treatment is necessary.

Bob and Kathy are also working toward improving the relationships with their respective families of origin. We agree that "the developments that characterize normal psychological life must . . . be seen in the changing nature of the relationship between the self and its selfobjects, but not in the self's relinquishment of selfobjects" (Kohut, 1984, p. 47). Hence, another focus of their treatment was an emphasis on maturation and individual development, as well as on more appropriate relationships between Bob and Kathy and their families of origin.

With improvement, there is a shift in marital homeostasis, owing to decreased narcissistic vulnerability and stabilization of traumatic de-idealization. Because Bob and Kathy are no longer so fearful of retraumatization and fragmentation of the self, they do not rely on excessive homeostasis to prevent experiencing narcissistic injuries and traumatic de-idealization. They are not afraid to reach out, to move beyond their previous limits. There is an enhancement of central constructive (growth-promoting) morphogenic function within the marriage, fulfillment of selfobject needs, and support for curative fantasies. Bob and Kathy had been fearful of even verbalizing such a hope. The shift in homeostasis also resulted in stabilization of a central destructive (problem-escalation) morphogenic function (dissolutions of mutual cohesiveness under the impact of narcissistic rage). In Bob and Kathy's case, they are not afraid of escalation of conflicts resulting in attack, counterattack, distancing, withdrawal, and unresolved rage because they are able to experience mutual fulfillment of selfobject needs. Because of the decrease in narcissistic vulnerability and the increase in marital cohesion, Bob and Kathy are able to tolerate periodic selfobject failures without fragmentation, thus greatly enhancing their individual and marital functioning and overall well-being.

APPENDIX: CURATIVE FANTASY MARITAL/RELATIONAL QUESTIONNAIRE

Instructions: Please complete the following questions before the initial interview with your therapist. Do not consult your spouse (partner) in responding to the questions. Each spouse (partner) is requested to complete the questionnaire separately.

1. What do you feel is missing in your marriage?
2. What three things can your spouse (partner) do to make this a better marriage?
3. What would you like your spouse (partner) to understand about you?
4. What do you feel your spouse (partner) needs to believe about you?
5. What are the most meaningful ways your spouse (partner) can participate in the marriage to improve it?
6. List your three most important priorities in the marriage at the present time.
7. List your three most cherished fantasies.
8. List your three most important talents or skills.
9. List three ways in which you want your partner to help you when you are in despair or feeling distressed.
10. What are your three most important wishes?

11. What are your three most important wishes for your marriage?
12. What are three things your spouse (partner) can do to make you feel loved, valued, or cherished.
13. What are the three most important things you would like to gain from marital therapy?
14. What can you do to make your marriage a better one?
15. Name the person you most admire, and describe his (her) three most important qualities.
16. List three ways in which you would describe yourself.

© 1994. Bedi, Hoffman, Hoffman, Jacobson, Kalogjera, & Raffe.

REFERENCES

American Psychiatric Association. (1994). *Diagnostic and statistical manual of mental disorders* (4th ed.). Washington, DC: Author.

Basch, M. F. (1991). Are selfobjects the only objects? Implications for psychoanalytic technique. In A. Goldberg (Ed.), *The evolution of self psychology* (pp. 3–15). Hillsdale, NJ: The Analytic Press.

Berkowitz, D. (1985). Selfobject needs and marital disharmony. *Psychoanalytic Review, 72*, 229–273.

Feldman, L.B., & Pinsof, W.M. (1982). Problem maintenance in family systems: An integrative model. *Journal of Marital and Family Therapy, 8*, 295–308.

Jackson, H. (Ed.). (1994). *Using self psychology in psychotherapy*. Northvale, NJ: Jason Aronson.

Kay, J. (1990). Traumatic deidealization and the future of medicine. *Journal of the American Medical Association, 263*(4), 572–573.

Kohut, H. (1966). Forms and transformations of narcissism. *Journal of American Psychoanalytic Association, 14*, 243–272.

Kohut, H. (1968). The psychoanalytic treatment of narcissistic personality disorders. *Psychoanalytic study of the child*, XXIII (pp. 86–113). New York: International Universities Press.

Kohut, H. (1971). *The analysis of the self*. New York: International Universities Press.

Kohut, H. (1972). Thoughts on narcissism and narcissistic rage. *Psychoanalytic Study of the Child, 27*, 360–400.

Kohut, H. (1977). *The restoration of the self*. New York: International Universities Press.

Kohut, H. (1978). The disorders of the self and their treatment: An outline. *International Journal of Psychoanalysis, 59*, 413–425.

Kohut, H. (1984). *How does analysis cure?* Chicago: University of Chicago Press.

Lachkar, J. (1984). Narcissistic/borderline couples: A psychoanalytic perspective to family therapy. *International Journal of Family Psychiatry, 5*, 169–189.

Lachkar, J. (1985). Narcissistic/borderline couples: Theoretical implications for treatment. *Dynamic Psychotherapy, 3*, (Fall/Winter), 109–127.

Lachkar, J. (1992). *The Narcissistic/borderline couple*. New York: Brunner/Mazel.

Lansky, M. R. (1981). Treatment of the narcissistically vulnerable marriage. In M. R. Lansky (Ed.), *Family therapy and major psychopathology*. 163–182 New York: Grune & Stratton.

Lansky, M. R. (1983) Masks of the narcissistically vulnerable marriage. *International Journal of Family Psychiatry, 3*, 439–449.

Moore, B. E., & Fine, B. D. (1990). *Psychoanalytic terms and concepts*. New Haven: The American Psychoanalytic Association and Yale University Press.

Nicholson, B. L. (1994). Narcissism. In H. Jackson (Ed.), *Using self psychology in psychotherapy* (pp. 27–50). Northvale, NJ: Jason Aronson.

Ornstein, A. (1992). The curative fantasy and psychic recovery. Contribution to the theory of psychoanalytic psychotherapy. *The Journal of Psychotherapy Practice and Research, 1* (1), 16–28.

Ornstein, P. H., & Kay, J. (1990). Development of psychoanalytic self psychology: A historical conceptual overview. In A. Tasman, S. M. Goldfinger, & C. A. Kaufmann (Eds.), *Review of Psychiatry*, Vol. 9 (pp. 303–322). Washington, DC: American Psychiatric Press.

Ornstein, P. H., & Ornstein, A. (1977). On the continuing evolution of psychoanalytic psychotherapy: Reflections and predictions. In Chicago Institute for Psychoanalysis (Ed.), *The Annual of Psychoanalysis* (pp. 329–370). New York: International Universities Press.

Palombo, J. personal communication with author, 15 December 1995.

Sager, C. J. (1976). *Marriage contracts and couple therapy*. New York: Brunner/Mazel.

Schwartzman, G. (1984). Narcissistic transferences: Implications for the treatment of couples. *Dynamic Psychotherapy*, Vol. 2, No. 1, Spring/Summer (pp. 5–14). Brunner/Mazel.

Seely, D. (1993). He loves me too much. *New Woman*, April, 80–84.

Solomon, M. F. (1985). Treatment of narcissistic and borderline disorders in marital therapy: Suggestions toward an enhanced therapeutic approach. *Clinical Social Work Journal*, July, 141–156.

Solomon, M. F. (1988). Treatment of narcissistic vulnerability in marital therapy. In A. Goldberg (Ed.), *Learning from Kohut. Progress in self psychology*, Vol. 4 (pp. 215–230). Hillsdale, NJ: Analytic Press.

Solomon, M. F. (1992). *Narcissism and intimacy: Love and marriage in an age of confusion*. New York: W. W. Norton.

Solomon, M. F. (1994). Adults. In H. Jackson (Ed.), *Using self psychology in psychotherapy* (pp. 117–133). New York: Jason Aronson.

Stern, D. (1985). *The interpersonal world of the infant*. New York: Basic Books.

Stone, M. (1993). *Abnormalities of personality: Within and beyond the realm of treatment*. New York: W. W. Norton.

CHAPTER 12

Treating Narcissistic and Borderline Couples

Marion F. Solomon

The bonds of marriage are in many ways adult re-creations of the bonds between baby and caretaker. All marriages bring out infantile feelings. In troubled marriages, both the need to express repressed infantile feelings and the awareness that such expression is likely to result in harmful interactions cause regression and defensive reactions. In marriages hampered by narcissistic and borderline defenses, disagreements serve as opportunities to vent repressed infantile rage and vengefulness in the form of blame. The manifest issues serve as justification for primitive defensive operations that bring to the forefront fear of abandonment, of disappointment, and of not being cared for. Demands and a sense of entitlement pervade vulnerable marriages because expectations can never be fulfilled.

When both partners have histories of early emotional injury and primitive defenses, their relationship becomes a collusive means for protecting themselves and each other. A collusion is an unspoken agreement to maintain the consistency of each partner's perceptions. Because of this covert agreement, neither partner is forced to deal with overwhelming negative feelings or extreme conflict. Hiding emotional problems from themselves and each other, the partners create a joyless pretense of safety and security, not a true haven of comfort and love. In this way, one or both partners may temporarily avoid dealing with a serious problem. Instead of helping each other to grow and mature, each may use the other to reinforce a distorted view of reality. The collusive contract is maintained because each partner needs to keep destructive forces at bay. Instead of changing and adapting, the relationship relies on static or regressive defensive strategies (Lansky, 1981).

THE NARCISSISTICALLY VULNERABLE SELF

Many people suffer from deep wounds at the foundation of a damaged self. Early in life they developed certain defenses that were used to protect themselves from shame, humiliation, fear of disintegration, aversions to need, or vulnerability. These people are subject to severe relational difficulties, and are deemed to have poor prognosis in treatment. Nevertheless they are in a wide range of relationships. They are husbands, wives, parents, children, and they live with partners in short- and long-term relationships. They are involved in intimate friendships, and yet they fall into diagnostic categories such as borderline and narcissistic personality disorders and behavior disorders, indicating extremely volatile or disconnected relationships. The more severely disturbed individuals may be unable to function in relationships. But many people function adequately in a wide range of situations, moving into narcissistic or borderline states when they experience disappointment or stress in their expectations (often these are unrealistic demands based upon idealization of what needs will be met).

Roger, attempting a reconciliation after a one-year separation, invited his wife, Sue, to a Superbowl party that he was giving. She accepted. Three weeks prior to the football game, the 1994 Los Angeles earthquake occurred and Sue learned that her sister's child had been severely injured. Wanting to be with her sister at the hospital, Sue declined to go to the party. Her husband interpreted her change of plans to mean that she did not really want the reconciliation, since she was more concerned with her sister than with wanting to please him. He responded with a verbal attack of indignation.

This inflated sense of entitlement—the unreasonable expectation that his desires would be her total focus—no matter what, is a sign of the underlying narcissism. The intense anger and uncontrollable release of emotion is part of his disorder. Two days later, he was ready to put aside his outburst and once again try to get together. He did not understand why she insisted on talking further about his reaction. He saw her insistence as, once again, proof that she did not want to work out their relationship. In fact, he was treating her as an object to bolster his self-image, not as a person who might have needs and feelings of her own. Roger devoted his life to achieving material success—antique cars, several homes—and expected the people around him to bombard him with accolades and admiration for his accomplishments. He could not fathom why she failed to appreciate him.

Another patient, John, complained that he was constantly doing things for others and was always frustrated by what he perceived to be a lack of appreciation. He had been married four times. He could not stand being alone and was tormented by his wife's unavailability. No matter what he did for her, she kept pulling away from him. "I don't understand what she wants from me and why she doesn't take care of my needs," he said. What his needs were seemed simple to him—"a meal once in a while, sex on occasion . . what any husband expects."

What John did not realize is that he did for others what he wanted done for him. He had absolutely no awareness of what others wanted and little awareness of his own deep need for constant emotional nurturing. In fact, as he delved deeper into all of his relationships, it became apparent that John lived in a world of shadows. Others barely existed for him, although he appeared to be quite focused on them. They served only as a reflection of him. They had to think, feel, and act according to his script or he became angry and frustrated. What he "gave" was intended to guarantee the outcome of his script rather than to actually meet the genuine needs of others. And there was no chance for him to get what he sought in relationships— affirmation, acknowledgment, understanding, attention—things that the vulnerable parts of him needed in order to shore up a diminished sense of self-esteem.

The self-image of people like John, who have exquisite sensitivity to slights and intense emotional reactions when disappointed, is typically very fragile. When there are narcissistic vulnerabilities, shame and protective defenses, there is likely to be constant preoccupation in two areas: (1) performance evaluation by others, and (2) maintaining the needed supplies of "psychic feeding." There is often confusion and conflict between the need to be close to the source of narcissistically enhancing supplies and the fear of being overwhelmed by the needs of others. Thus, many who are in partnership with such individuals complain about the constant demands along with elaborate distancing devices.

Jason and Angela describe how it works in their marriage. She often complains that he never seems there for her. He disconnects at the exact time that she needs something from him. "I feel like it's hopeless," she says. "In fact, it's always hopeless when I ask for what I want." Pressed to explain, she describes growing up a child of Holocaust survivors. She knew she had to be the grown-up. No one was there emotionally to take care of her, hold her when she cried, or reassure her when she was scared. Now, married to Jason, the same thing happens. If she cries or is hurting, he gets angry and pulls away. When she feels it is hopeless, she thinks of escape, just as she did when she was a child. Then she thought of how she would someday grow up and leave. Now she thinks, "I will get a divorce and leave."

Jason knows Angela's moods. When she is sad or upset with him, he anticipates her leaving. To avoid being left, he preempts by initiating the withdrawal. "Who needs you anyway. I have lots of women who would want me. I can go to a massage parlor for sex. I can't talk to you when you look at me with those sad, hurt eyes." Of course, anticipating hurt, they protect themselves in ways that perpetuate and re-create their earlier, failed relationships.

Through constant striving toward ever more difficult achievements and preoccupation with the means of meeting their goals, people like Jason and Angela can temporarily avoid underlying feelings such as rage, envy, or despair of emptiness and chaos. Often they feel an urgency to fill up with and use substitutes: alcohol and drugs, cars, computers, or a variety of people and things to ameliorate the pain of their inner world.

PRIMITIVE DEFENSES IN ADULT RELATIONSHIPS

The core issues that determine borderline and narcissistic defenses relate to the ability to experience oneness and twoness, self and other, self with other, each with separate boundaries. This awareness of self in relation to others is a task that babies deal with the first months and years of life (Mahler, Pine, & Bergman, 1975). Successful achievement of awareness of self in relation to others is a prerequisite to other developmental tasks such as gender differentiation, size difference, and loss of the omnipotent fantasy of being the center of the world, to awareness of unchangeable reality and recognition of the need to come to terms with society's expectations (i.e., sitting quietly when wishing to move, toilet training, acceptable manners and behaviors) (McDougall, 1986).

Defenses that develop early to protect the young child from being emotionally overwhelmed can interfere with later development. When the ability to experience emotions is restricted, children may withdraw from any interactions that bring up painful needs unfilled. In adult life, the continued reliance on defensive patterns molds peculiar or idiosyncratic behavior, often overemphasizing the need for solitude and privacy and downplaying the basic need for human connection.

The question is, how do people develop such defenses? Current developmental research (Stern, 1985) and the work of attachment theorists (Bowlby, 1982; Ainsworth, 1984; Main & Hesse, 1990) indicates that it is based on failures in early attachment to the caretaker.

There are two types of painful situations that may influence personality development and defense patterns. The first includes various traumas that are caused by unmet needs. These may include internal experiences that are unpleasant: hunger, painful body sensations, or respiratory distress. The second category of events may be single events or chronic failures that frustrate or traumatize: struggles that impinge on a child who lacks adequate defenses. Defenses initially used as a protection against trauma are programmed into the psyche and reemerge intermittently in an effort to take charge of the traumatic experience in ways that maintain self-cohesion and esteem.

The more primitive defenses are often wordless, but are experienced as, "I don't feel the rage, Mom feels it. I hope she doesn't get angry at me, it would hurt me" or even more primitive, "I don't experience mother, only I can exist. I must withdraw into myself when I get upset." The patterns that begin in the first year of life continue even as the child develops and matures in other ways.

As children become increasingly able to use language as a mode of interaction, they become more adept at identifying basic affects and complex emotions. But recognizing the various emotional states in symbolic terms does not necessarily define them in a systematic way. A child might be able to define one type of feeling, then use it to defend against another that is less well defined.

For example, a child wishing to please "mother" and to gain her love and devotion, may simultaneously feel a need to assert an independent action, which stimulates a fear of the power of "mother's" disapproval. If the fear of disapproval is the strongest reaction, it may provoke so much anxiety that the child's thought processes fail to recognize the sequence of events. Only the earlier dread of danger or destruction is experienced at that moment, thus inhibiting any further desires for independence.

As another example, the child who grows up in an abusive family is likely to experience many conflicting emotions and feelings. Watching an alcoholic father beating a crying, cringing mother, a child might assume burden of guilt and shame, and make a conscious decision to always be "good" to avoid further unpleasant experiences. A lifetime of "goodness" hides awareness of frightening internal emotions whenever problems arise or when there are reminders of the painful experience that created the need.

Another child in the same situation, might experience the mother as weak and vulnerable, while the father's abuse might be interpreted as strength. The child would develop defenses to protect against anything perceived as weakening. The "strong" adult, determined never to be vulnerable, may avoid experiencing any emotions at all by being oblivious to real problems, or may be unable to maintain a close relationship. Maintaining strength at all times means never allowing anyone to know what is inside.

It is when early developmental experiences are thwarted, that what are generally called narcissistic or borderline defenses emerge. They are designed to protect the vulnerable self from unnamed dread, terror of fragmentation, or destruction. If the baby has not developed words or symbols with which to conceptualize the trauma, the internal experience, often a nameless dread, is imprinted in the psyche through bodily reactions. The tension felt as the body tenses and reacts to the trauma is part of a template or blueprint that has no words—an emotion that cannot be named feels out of control and must be avoided.

DSM-IV ON NARCISSISTIC DISORDERS

Patterns of narcissistic and borderline defense share many similar features. They both originate in early preverbal object relations and are often based on the use of whatever internal or external resources are available to maintain self-cohesion and self-esteem. Defenses develop as they are needed in the limited repertoire of infancy and continue to be used in adulthood. Regression to infantile defenses occur in times when strong emotions emerge.

DSM-IV notes that among the essential patterns of narcissistic personality is a grandiose sense of self-importance, a hypersensitivity to the slightest negativity in the evaluation of others, and lack of empathy for others. In response to criticism, he or she may react with rage, shame, or humiliation, but mask these feelings with an aura of cool indifference.

There is a tendency to exaggerate accomplishments and talents, and an expectation to be seen as "special." The person may be preoccupied with how well he or she is doing and how well he or she is regarded by others. This often takes the form of an almost exhibitionistic need for constant attention and admiration. The person may constantly fish for compliments, doing so with great charm.

Individuals with narcissistic personality often assume that because of their "specialness," their problems are unique and they have the right to do things not allowed to others—they thwart laws, break rules, and ignore social courtesies. Frequently this sense of self-importance alternates with feelings of special unworthiness. These people are preoccupied with fantasies of unlimited success, power, brilliance, beauty, or ideal love, and with chronic feelings of envy for those whom they perceive as being more successful than they are. Although these fantasies frequently substitute for realistic activity, when such goals are actually pursued, it is with a driven, pleasureless quality and an ambition that cannot be satisfied.

Nurturing interpersonal relationships are invariably disturbed. Often the narcissistic person is painfully self-conscious and preoccupied with grooming and remaining youthful. Personal deficits, defeats, or irresponsible behavior may be justified by rationalization or lying. Feelings may be faked in order to impress others. Interpersonal exploitativeness, in which others are taken advantage of in order to achieve one's ends, or for self-aggrandizement, is common. Friendships are often made only after the person considers how he or she can profit from them. In romantic relationships, the partner is often treated as an object to be used to bolster the person's self-esteem. Depressed mood is extremely common. Frequently, many of the features of Histrionic, Borderline, and Antisocial Personality Disorders are present.

DSM-IV ON BORDERLINE DISORDERS

The defining factors in borderline personality according to DSM-IV, is a pervasive pattern of instability of self-image, interpersonal relationships, and mood, beginning by early adulthood and present in a variety of contexts. DSM-IV goes on to say of the borderline diagnosis that emotional instability is common, with marked mood shifts from baseline mood to depression, irritability, or anxiety, that can last for minutes, hours, or even days. Individuals with borderline personality disorder often display inappropriately intense anger or lack of control of their anger; they have frequent bouts of temper, resulting sometimes in physical fights. The problems are marked by impulsive behavior that may be self-damaging, such as shopping sprees, substance abuse, reckless driving, casual sex, shoplifting, and binge eating.

There may also be a marked and persistent identity disturbance, manifested by uncertainty about several life issues, such as self-image, sexual orientation, long-term goals or career choice, types of friends or lovers to have, or which values to adopt. In addition, persons with borderline disorders experience an instability of self-image and chronic feelings of emptiness or boredom.

These persons have a high degree of need for others but generally have interpersonal relationships with fluctuating patterns of closeness and upset with others, characterized by extremes of overidealization and devaluation. They have difficulty tolerating being alone, demand the other's presence, and feel chaotic and sometimes violent when the other withdraws. They often make frantic efforts, including suicidal gestures, to avoid real or imagined abandonment.

People who are prone to borderline defenses may also manifest many narcissistic features. In fact, there is considerable diagnostic overlap in the DSM-IV (American Psychiatric Association, 1994); associated features of borderline personality disorders include histrionic, narcissistic, and antisocial personality disorders, and in many cases, more than one diagnosis is warranted. A narcissistic subcategory of the borderline disorder can be identified by a grandiose sense of self-importance with an underlying sense of worthlessness (Kernberg, 1993; Stone, 1980). There is a hypersensitivity to the judgments of others, a lack of empathy that is present in a variety of interpersonal contexts, and a pervasive pattern of grandiosity in fantasy or actual behavior that sometimes leads to extraordinary feats of heroism and, occasionally, risky but surprisingly successful endeavors.

MANIFESTATIONS IN ADULT LIFE

Various forms of borderline and narcissistic pathology are engendered by an accumulation of early experiences that were too painful or too fearful to allow into consciousness. The result of these intolerable experiences is typically two-fold: Internally, there is a defense against feelings, perceptions, and fantasies; externally, there is a distancing from whatever caused the painful exposure to needs. Often there is an extensive identity disturbance manifested by uncertainty in regard to major life areas such as long-term goal, career choice, types of friends or lovers, values and principles, sexual orientation, work and school experiences, and many difficulties in familial and social relationships.

The tragedy of these individuals is that while they need so much from others, they are unable to internalize what they receive. Their mistrust of others causes a replay of early deprivation that is chronically reinforced by their feelings of emptiness. Because they have never achieved satisfactory experiences of drawing emotional sustenance from others, they are like atoms floating alone in space, constantly trying to connect with someone or something in order to feel grounded and whole. They may try using computers, cars, or houses to fill their emptiness. They experience little of the support they seek, and that support is temporary at best. Like a car with a hole in the gas tank, they never can retain the feeling of being full.

In response to criticism or intrusiveness by partners, people with such underlying fragility may react with humiliation followed by rage and acting out. Often they can mask these feelings with an aura of cool indifference until something jars their emotional stability. They then defend themselves through verbal or physical aggression, and afterwards behave as if the emotional outburst had never occurred. They generally refuse to discuss the incident, expecting the relationship to continue as it was. Partners, friends, and coworkers may find this pattern unnerving. Left with intense reactions, they must withhold expressing their feelings for fear of recreating the emotional outburst or being punished in some way. Thus, relationships in which borderline defensive patterns are pervasive tend to be shallow, distant, and self-protective, with general feelings of depression and worthlessness prevailing on both sides.

While a DSM-IV diagnosis helps therapists to better understand various forms of psychological problems, there are certain difficulties inherent in making a differential diagnoses when treating relational problems. Diagnostic categories of DSM provide standards that enable a therapist to recognize specific psychological disorders. In couples therapy, DSM criteria for narcissistic and borderline diagnoses tends to focus on specific individual pathology of one or both partners. The model presented here looks at interpersonal psychodynamics and the effect of each partner's defensive system on the other. It is the dynamic interaction of mutual defensive structures that creates havoc in many relationships.

Both narcissistic and borderline disorders fall into the category of primitive mental disorders. (Solomon, 1989) These disorders develop in interactions with significant others during the first two years of life. The defenses develop before conscious thoughts or verbal narratives enable the child to explain to him- or herself what is wrong. Primitive defenses such as splitting and projective identification, narcissistic encapsulation, or explosive volatility develop in response to early failures. They remain unconscious but interfere with relationships throughout life. Often what is presented in couples therapy is the emergence of primitive defensive patterns in response to the stresses of family living.

Many people with borderline qualities according to DSM-IV also manifest narcissistic features. Similarly, those who meet the criteria of narcissistic personality disorder according to DSM-IV also have associated borderline features. To resolve the underlying problems, it is necessary to understand the person in the context of a relationship. Thus, conjoint therapy is the treatment of choice for people whose presenting problem is a distressed relationship in which the same pattern is repeatedly enacted.

DESTRUCTIVE COLLUSIONS

When partners have histories of early injury and narcissistic or borderline defenses, their relationship becomes a collusive means of protecting themselves and each other. A collusion is an unspoken agreement to maintain the consistency of each partner's perceptions. Neither partner is forced to deal with overwhelming negative feelings or extreme conflict.

But by hiding emotional problems from themselves and each other, the partners create a joyless pretense of safety and security, not a true haven of comfort and love. By hiding their doubts and fears, one or both partners may temporarily avoid dealing with a serious problem. Instead of helping each other to grow and mature, each may use the other to reinforce a distorted view of reality. The collusive contract is maintained because each partner needs to keep destructive forces at bay (Lanksy, 1981, 1993). Instead of changing and adapting, the relationship relies on defensive strategies.

Some relationships are created to contain unrecognized fears developed in infancy, such as terror of abandonment, or terror created by destructive fantasies. Partners develop a pattern of interacting, based on projecting their doubts and fears into each other. When difficulties arise, each partner sees the problem coming from the other. Should their defensive arrangement falter, the vulnerable partner may become irrational, demanding attention or justice with a rage that goes beyond the immediate issues.

In such relationships, communication is not viewed as a way to improve a problematic situation, but as a danger that might expose underlying fears of falling apart and being humiliated (Lansky, 1981). Both partners may think of their relationship as a disaster. They may not be able to explain even to themselves why they remain attached to someone who is so despicable. Yet through years, even decades, of unremitting misery, these attacking relationships endure.

There seems significant indication that people with complementary patterns often marry (Bowen, 1978; Solomon, 1989) After a period of time together, an unconscious fusion can form, with each fitting into the others' patterns of expectation. In this situation, the internal representations of each partner, although separate, become so interlinked that any aspect of one implies a reciprocal aspect in the other. Within this context, marital therapy serves to help the couple break the fusion that underlies the frozen complementarity. Breaking this fusion requires a profound understanding of its intrapsychic and relational aspects.

ISSUES IN ONGOING TREATMENT

All marriages include infantile feelings between the partners. Happy marriages allow freedom for deeply repressed feelings without loss of dignity or security (Nadelson & Paolini, 1978). In troubled marriages, the need to express repressed infantile feelings and the awareness that such expression is likely to result in harmful interactions, cause regression and defensive reactions. In marriages hampered by narcissistic vulnerabilities and defenses, disagreements serve as opportunities to vent repressed infantile rage and vengefulness in the form of blame.

Therapists generally enter the picture at the point where discharge of overwhelming emotions takes the form of mutual blaming or acting out. Treating relationship disturbances requires an understanding of the core issues and internal representations of each partner, as well as a grasp of the multilevel communications that underlie interactions and intense affect at work when a couple is in a high-stress situation. By having the couple come together from the first session, it is possible to begin to untangle the joint self of the relationship and to clarify the contribution of each partner to the marital collusion. "Cross-complaining" couples defend themselves by attacking each other. Both come into therapy hoping that the therapist will perceive the situation and "straighten out" the partner. Underneath this facade of rationality is often a frightened child expecting to be blamed and attacked.

Many people with narcissistic disorders appear to function as highly successful, accomplished, creative, and attractive individuals. They cultivate and collect "interesting" friends and have learned ways to attract and use others for their own purposes. Sometimes a person with severe narcissistic features appears to be the healthier partner when the couple first enters therapy. Observing the process of the couple's interaction and the transference process with the therapist provides the information necessary to determine the degree of narcissistic and/or borderline pathology and therapeutic treatment plan. By becoming aware through the emergence of dysfunctional patterns in treatment, and learning to recognize the inner reality of the other, each comes to understand how blame or destructive behavior is being used as a protection against humiliation or fear of abandonment. Connecting the triangle of transference in the session, at home interactions and early relationships in family of origin, members of the couple begin to understand their current behavior as learned ways of protecting a damaged, fragile self. Although the origins of the problem can be traced back to early life experiences, change takes place in a corrective experience in the here-and-now of the relationship. The therapist must function as decoder of messages by empathically responding to the underlying affects and emotions of each partner, reframing the partner's perceptions along the way. As the treatment progresses, it is possible to slowly uncover the underlying wounds and vulnerabilities.

In the treatment of partners who had failures in early childhood, it is crucial not to underestimate the threat of abandonment. Many people have repeatedly experienced abandonment. This occurs not only when parents physically leave the child through death or divorce, but also when a postnatal mother is very depressed and detached, when there are family problems and the parent is unavailable to provide caretaking, when there are more children or greater needs than the mother can cope with, or when the child has many needs because of genetic or biological deficits. This experience of felt abandonment is a part of memory that emerges in later relationships. Independence cannot be risked by spouses in a blaming marriage; the fear of separateness and loss of the object is too great. This is the impasse. Change and growth are necessary, but the fear of dangerous repercussions to the relationship is often neglected by therapists who value change at all costs without full consideration of the role of other factors in emotional growth. Sometimes it is not growth and maturity that is required, but meeting the emotional needs of childhood. It is the child who needs affirmation, understanding, and the security of love that must be taken care of in order to grow independently.

CONJOINT THERAPY
WITH JASON AND ANGELA

Jason and Angela made a commitment when they entered couples therapy not to use their escape defenses. When her hopelessness lead to thoughts of divorce or his angry cutting off patterns lead to emotional disconnection, they learned to stop the action and think about what they were feeling.

In the early sessions of couples therapy, Jason reacted to Angela's moods by expressing how upset he was. Angela then looked more dejected and said their relationship felt hopeless. As they progressed, peeling the layers of pain and vulnerability, Jason described his feelings of loss and abandonment when Angela looked sad and dour. He could feel her pulling away and he could not allow himself to be powerless in the face of her turning away. So he took charge by showing her that he had no need for an upset, overly emotional partner.

Angela described the experience from her view. When she needs him, and he makes himself unavailable, she feels he has no interest in what she needs. She knows that he is busy when he is in his office at home, and she does not intrude, but sometimes there is something important and she needs his attention for a moment. "I walk in and he doesn't even look up. I feel dismissed. I can't get his attention and I have this hopeless feeling," Angela said in a session. "But you know I am working and its important that I not be distracted," Jason replied.

"That's where we have problems," Angela said. "when I feel completely transparent—when you look right through me."

"Do you recall feeling like that as a child?" I asked.

"I never let myself be transparent. I had ways of making myself noticed." Angela went on to describe parents who were survivors of concentration camps during World War II. Her mother and father had deadened themselves emotionally and had little vitality to keep up with the bright, active child they had adopted when they were in their forties. Angela felt the burden of keeping them alive. She learned to sing, dance, and entertain. She found ways to clean the house, and daydreamed constantly of escaping the burden that she carried. " 'I've got to grow up before I can leave,' I thought. So I grew up as fast as I could. I never felt like a child."

"And the child who is you wants to be seen and cherished," I said. "And what about the child in you?" I asked, turning to Jason.

"I have no recollection of being a child," he replied.

"The sense of loss and abandonment that you carry comes from earlier in your life," I said.

Jason began telling the story of his father's death at a time when Jason was achieving the greatest success in his career. "I still think about my father. I miss him. We have unfinished business."

"We'll have to look at it, and also look at where you are with your mother," I remarked.

"Oh, I still see her," he said. "She's ninety and still a formidable woman. I guess all of the women in my life have been pretty powerful women. Both of my wives and all of my girlfriends before and between my marriages."

"I guess you were looking for something from the women in your life," I suggested. "Is there something that you know about that you needed from your mother but didn't get?"

"It's a funny thing," he began. "My mother was ill as a child and was paralyzed on one side of her face. My first wife told me that my mother had this facial paralysis. I had never noticed. My wife couldn't believe that I was unaware of it. All I could remember is that she never smiled. I guess it was because of her facial paralysis."

"Do you recall her being warm and comforting in other ways?" I asked.

Angela interrupted and said, "Jason's mother does not come across as a warm and comforting type. Even at ninety she is clear and focused on what she wants to do."

Jason said, "I don't remember my childhood. But I know everyone said that I was my father's favorite. My brother was my mother's favorite. My brother had some special health problems and I guess he got her attention."

I thought for a moment and then explained, "So you got the emotionally disconnected mother who could not or would not smile at you, who didn't respond to your accomplishments. What you recall was your father dying before you could show him what you accomplished. But children need to know that they are seen and approved of by both parents. It sounds as though that was missing for you and you are still looking for it. You want Angela to give you the responses that you need. When she doesn't, or feels it is a burden, or gets upset that you don't notice her, then you do what you did as a child. You act as if you don't need it. The result is neither of you get your child needs met."

Angela said, "Jason tells me not to be a child. He thinks we all have to be mature."

"Mature," I said, "is what you always were. But we all have child needs. They last throughout life. Those are the things you have been talking about. You both want to feel secure, to know that you are loved, seen for who you are, accepted, that someone understands you and responds to your special needs. It is when you don't get these things that you each think of escaping the relationship, you by divorcing, Angela, and Jason, by emotionally denying any needs of your own."

The following session began by Jason talking about what had happened between them a day after our session. Angela woke up feeling hopeless. Jason got out of bed and told her he was leaving. She began crying. "My first inclination was to scream at her to stop it," Jason recounted. "Then I stopped myself. It was as if I got out of *my* chair and sat in *hers*. I knew since we had just awakened, that I hadn't caused her feelings. It's a burden she carries all the time. I went over to her and put my arms around her and held her. She cried and then she stopped."

"I suddenly didn't feel hopeless anymore," Angela added.

"Jason was attuned to you. You were seen—no longer invisible," I said.

Jason and Angela did not resolve their problems so simply. There were many regressions, they had issues around money and sexuality. But they were willing to take themselves out of their own selves, each recognizing their narcissistic tendencies and knowing that they are using this relationship as they did in the past to try to heal old wounds and vulnerabilities.

The therapist treating a couple must resist being drawn into their collusive pattern and, at the same time, not shame them for their behavior. Instead, both the behavior and the underlying need must be identified and reframed as a normal reaction to the way they learned to relate in their family of origin.

ONGOING TREATMENT OF THE NARCISSISTIC, VULNERABLE PATIENT

Couples therapy with narcissistic patients who relate in blaming, shaming patterns is not a short-term treatment. Therapists must be prepared to stay with the treatment through what invariably will be a turbulent period and see it through with the couple. The goal is to examine the relationship between the intrapsychic and the interpersonal and to provide avenues for modification. This requires a focus on the process rather than on the surface or content of the encounter. Only by taking the time during the session to stop the process and consciously focus with the partners on the minute details of feelings as they emerge—anger or withdrawal, attack or defense—can the cycle of injury and fear be broken.

The "working through" phase begins when the spouses feel safe enough with the therapist that they no longer act "on their best behavior" and instead begin to show their pathology. Some of the at-home arguments now are played out in the sessions. Reframing their behavior as an effort to show the therapist what they live with allows the opportunity to examine the behavior together, to see what pain, what shame, what fears bring out the defenses of each partner. With the help of the therapist they can look at how the relationship protects them.

Acceptance over time enables spouses to shed their outer defenses and reveal their basic conflicts, which provide the material for depth interpretations. The dysfunctional patterns of attack and counterattack, blame and refutation, hurt and defense, increasingly emerge for examination in the therapy session. The couple is so used to their patterns and processes that they will engage in their usual destructive interaction quite naturally in the therapeutic sessions, provided nothing is done to stop the process. A couple's willingness to fight in front of the therapist may be accepted positively as a sign of a willingness to present their true interactional pattern in order to find ways to change it.

Allowing partners to engage freely in problem behaviors and examining the related processes—the needs and defenses—with each other in detail, while developing alternative responses, is the essence of long-term treatment of marital partners. As the work expands beyond the reality, problem solving, or behavioral change aspects of shorter-term treatment of the marriage, it reaches the *level of disturbed object relations* (Slipp, 1984; Scharff & Scharff, 1987). Therapy may remain at this level for a long time, in a slow process of uncovering and treating narcissistic vulnerability, emotional injury, and related defense patterns.

Together, the couple and therapist go through aspects of each partner's sense of being hurt and the recurring regressive sequences that result from repeated disappointments. The spouses are helped to understand their vulnerable reactions and the connections between regressive behavior, perception of narcissistic loss, and subsequent revenge reactions. The therapy repeatedly works through disappointment in one partner, which causes angry reactions, withdrawal, falling apart, and even regression into acting out behavior. They may be helped to deal with terror of abandonment, and its reverse, expressed in emotional distancing.

It is during this phase of therapy that spouses can learn to utilize their observing egos for themselves and for each other. For example, each construes the other's projective defenses against anxiety and rejection as indifference. A couple in such a bind is doomed to endless frustration and unhappiness because, armed with an ironclad expectation of disappointment, each is afraid to relinquish a defensive posture. By pointing out ways each partner regulates self-esteem and self-cohesion for the other, a therapist can model not only an observing ego but an empathic ear. In time, the critical attacks and the belligerent complaints about the partner's defects begin to fall by the wayside as each individual acknowledges a sense of inadequacy and insecurity.

By this point, there may be a greater capacity for supportive empathy. Parallel to this development, partners react less to every lapse of positive responsiveness in each other as if it were an intentional rebuff. Marital therapy supports this process by letting each spouse see the other in a realistic perspective, complete with their more vulnerable parts. Once they have learned how to communicate better and how to understand defenses and anxiety, couples can proceed to work on their discrepant views of each other.

In treatment, the issue is presented by saying, "I am getting two different pictures from what each of you is saying. People are used to seeing each other in a certain way and sometimes it is hard to get used to having mates behave differently. If we can understand why you each get a mixed view of the other, and make sure that what gets communicated is received accurately, we might be able to figure out together things you can do that will make it better for you both."

The goal at this point is not only to raise the question of how each partner distorts his or her perception of the other but to do so in a way that will help the couple assimilate the information without raising their anxiety levels. Thus, it is important to show both partners how logical it is that certain behaviors and interchanges between them naturally cause an increase in anxiety and, therefore, distort how they view one another. As treatment proceeds through the midphase, spouses sometimes regress to behaviors that resemble those that first brought them to therapy. There are many opportunities for old transference patterns to reemerge because the partners spend more time together outside treatment than they do in therapy. Until changes become well ingrained, there is the tendency for couples to revert to their old behavior patterns and old complaints.

It is important to listen to the process as the couple share what is troubling them rather than hearing only the content of their complaints. By moving away from specific issues that have become charged with blame and resentment and examining instead how certain defenses have gotten mobilized to protect a vulnerable or injured self, it is possible to help partners understand behavior that otherwise seems inexplicable, withdrawing, or attacking. When this kind of demonstration occurs in an atmosphere of safety, it need not be experienced as an attack, and can teach each partner to more fully understand the other.

The therapist must allow the couple's communications, verbal and nonverbal, conscious and unconscious, to flow into a holding place within the therapist. This allows the free play of the therapist's stream of associations at different levels of consciousness to be triggered by nondefensive immersion in the material the couple presents. This does not imply that self (therapist) and other (couple) have become fused or confused, but may be likened to a symbiosis in which the fantasy of merger, far from being based upon a desperate neediness, is characterized by open boundaries that are voluntary and temporary. By its nature, this form of immersion is never imposed, but rather offered, and it requires that the therapist not be defensively rigid about protecting his or her boundaries. The result is an empathic access to the deeper regions of the couple's affective experience, allowing the therapist to receive and process both partners' feelings, defenses, and pathologies.

During the course of treatment, many therapists experience memories of sights, sounds, and even smells that do not seem to correspond to what is occurring in the treatment session. These are drawn from subliminal representations of the therapist's personal experiences with literature, art, poetry, or other elements of the therapist's personal history. Upon reflection therapists may recognize the deeper levels of communication that take place at an unconscious level, and may use this understanding to give feedback about the dynamic interaction that is taking place between the partners (Solomon, 1989).

Reinforcing the Transformation

As the need to mobilize defenses against old wounds decreases, the opportunity emerges for true change in each of the partners. Demandingness and entitlement may be replaced by normal assertiveness. Timidity and withdrawal as a way to protect against embarrassingly childlike grandiose fantasies may be replaced by a willingness to expose high aspirations and devotion to ideals, as well as by a joyful acceptance of a healthy grandiosity. Chaos and instability between partners diminish as the couple expand their ability to contain explosive reactions. There are opportunities to examine with the therapist a range of emotions such as shame, guilt, fear, and disgust that are covered by surface outbursts.

At-home arguments are reframed as opportunities for the couple to try thinking for themselves about feelings as they emerge. Sessions following at-home arguments are another chance to examine which aspects of the couple's individual psyches are still very vulnerable and reactive to narcissistic injury. Thus, the problems themselves become part of the treatment plan, always with the goal of tolerating emotions—to hold them rather than act them out or defend against them, and to think as well as feel.

Kohut noted in his last book that an ill-disposed critic accused him of showing his true colors—accusing him of believing in the curative effect of the "corrective emotional experience" (Kohut, 1984, p. 78). But he did indeed believe in the corrective experience as an agent of change. Kohut explained that the concept of a "corrective emotional experience" was tainted by its use as a form of brief analysis in which the therapist play-acted being the opposite of what the patient experienced with parents in childhood.

Perhaps we need a new term such as a "reparative interpersonal experience." This is what occurs in successful therapy, in a healing religious
experience, as well as in an ongoing, loving intimate relationship such as
marriage. Providing a sustaining echo of empathic resonance to someone
who has lacked it in earlier relationships is a reparative experience that
unlocks the gates and releases the interrupted maturational push
thwarted in childhood, enabling the developmental process to begin to
reassert itself.

Wounds heal slowly. They take a long time to develop and a long time
to repair. Nevertheless, I have seen the change that takes place in the sense
of excitement, vitality, and use of inner resources when crises force people
to reexamine old patterns and discover new paths to follow. Where there
is giving as well as getting, the cycle of narcissistic injury and entitlement
fantasies can be broken.

Ultimately the goal of marital therapy is not only to promote a greater
degree of empathy in the relationship, but to rebuild slowly the damaged
or enfeebled structures of the self. Each partner comes to trust the marital
relationship and the therapist as a safe environment where intense affect
may be experienced in relative safety. Both learn to tolerate painful affect that emerges in the courses of interpersonal experience, and each develops capacities that enable one partner to serve temporarily as a selfobject for the other in times of stress. Each is able to grow through the
healing relationship. The therapist provides the container in which the reparative work can take place.

REFERENCES

Ainsworth, M. D. S. (1984) Attachment. In N. S. Endler & J. McV. Hunt (Eds.),
    Personality and the behavioral disorders (Vol. 1, pp. 559–602). New York: Wiley.
American Psychiatric Association. (1994). *Diagnostic and statistical manual of mental
    disorders* (4th ed.). Washington, DC: Author.
Bowlby, J. (1982). *Attachment and loss. Vol 1: Attachment* (rev. ed.) New York: Basic
    Books.
Bowen, M. (1978). *Family therapy in clinical practice.* New York: Jason Aronson.
Kernberg, O. (1993). Narcissism and love relations. Presented at the American
    Psychoanalytic Association, New York, December 17.
Kohut, H. (1977). *Restoration of the self.* New York: International Universities Press.
Kohut, H. (1984). *How does analysis cure?* A. Goldberg & P. E. Stepansky (Eds).
    Chicago: The University of Chicago Press.
Lansky, M. (1981). Treatment of the narcissistically vulnerable marriage. *Family
    therapy and major psychopathology.* M. Lansky (Ed.), pp. 163–183. New York:
    Grune & Stratton.
Lansky, M. (1993). Family genesis of aggression. *Psychiatric Annals.* 23:9,
    September, 1993.

Mahler, M. S., Pine, F., & Bergman, A. (1975). *The psychological birth of the human infant: Symbiosis and individuation.* New York: Basic Books.

Main, M., & Hesse, E. (1990). Parents' unresolved traumatic experiences are related to infant disorganized attachment status: Is frightened and/or frightening parental behavior the linking mechanism? In M. Greenberg, D. Cicchetti, & E. M. Cummings (Eds.), *Attachment in the preschool years.* Chicago: The University of Chicago Press.

McDougall, J. (1986). *Theaters of the mind: Illusion and truth on the psychoanalytic stage.* New York: Basic Books.

Nadelson, C. C., & Paolini, T. J. (1978). Marital therapy from a psychoanalytic perspective. In T. J. Paolini & B. S. McCrady (Eds.), *Marriage and marital therapy: Psychoanalytic, behavioral and systems perspectives* (pp. 89–165). New York: Brunner/Mazel.

Scharff D. & Scharff, J. (1987). *Object relations family therapy.* Northvale, NJ: Jason Aronson.

Scharff D. & Scharff, J. (1991). *Object relations couple therapy.* Northvale, NJ: Jason Aronson.

Slipp, S. (1984). *Object Relations: A dynamic bridge between individual and family treatment.* New York: Jason Aronson.

Solomon, M. (1989). *Narcissism and intimacy: Love and marriage in an age of confusion.* New York: W. W. Norton.

Solomon, M. (1994). *Lean on me: The power of positive dependency in intimate relationships.* New York: Simon & Schuster.

Stern, D. (1985). *The interpersonal world of the infant.* New York: Basic Books.

CHAPTER 13

Narcissistic/Borderline Couples: A Psychodynamic Approach to Conjoint Treatment

Joan Lachkar

There is a common aphorism that when people marry they become one. But no one ever explains what kind of a "one" they become: a healthy "one," a symbiotic "one," a fused "one," or a parasitic "one."

J. L.

Although a voluminous amount of material has been written on narcissistic and borderline disorders and many authors have increased our understanding of narcissistic vulnerabilities, few have explored what happens when a narcissist and a borderline personality join together in a marital bond or "bind." In fact, an individual with a borderline character is inclined to *attract* as an object choice a narcissistic personality, and vice versa. In *The Narcissistic/Borderline Couple: A Psychoanalytic Perspective on Marital Treatment* and earlier contributions (Lachkar, 1984, 1986, 1992), I have described the particular kind of couple I have clinically observed and called the narcissistic/borderline couple.

What is it that attracts, bonds, and keeps these individuals together? This is the pivotal question a clinician must ask when dealing with the narcissistic/borderline relationship. When paired, these oppositional types appear to maintain a bond in which their repetitive behaviors appear as the enactments of many unresolved wishes and childhood dreams. These two personality types enter into a psychological "dance" in which each fulfills the other's unconscious needs. The revelation is that each partner needs the other to play out his or her own internal object rela- ♡ tions drama, as each stirs up some unresolved conflict in the other. For example, when the borderline person is in the presence of his or her object choice, the narcissist, the borderline person experiences that partner as the source of all psychic pain. The borderline person holds to the fantasy that if only he or she were better, the other would meet his or her needs. ♡

DSM-IV AND THE NARCISSISTIC/BORDERLINE COUPLE

Narcissistic/borderline couples present specific vulnerabilities whereby either one or both partners may meet the criteria for a DSM-IV personality disorder. The DSM-IV (American Psychiatric Association, 1994) is designed to categorize individuals and does not offer a classification for couples or for a "couple diagnosis." This chapter, therefore, attempts to fill the gap by providing clinicians a treatment procedure for couples insofar as narcissistic personality disorders and borderline personality disorders are concerned.

Although narcissistic and borderline characteristics, traits, and states tend to shift back and forth between individuals or even within an individual over time, discussion would be impossible without making certain delineations from which to view these conflictual and complex relationships. The therapeutic challenge is to differentiate a "collective couple diagnosis," to determine whether individuals within the couple (dyad) suffer from more severe pathology stemming from infancy or whether their momentary relational conflicts are less chronic and relate only to neurotic aspects of personality functioning. The goal is not only to understand the dynamics of what occurs when a narcissistic and a borderline person join together, but also to diagnose and organize a suitable treatment program. Some couples will benefit from short-term treatment, whereas others may require long-term conjoint therapy concomitant with individual psychotherapy.

Exhibits 13.1 and 13.2 provide DSM-IV criteria for Narcissistic Personality Disorder and Borderline Personality Disorder (American Psychiatric Association, 1994).

Exhibit 13.1
DMS-IV DIAGNOSTIC CRITERIA FOR
NARCISSISTIC PERSONALITY DISORDER
(American Psychiatric Association, 1994)

A pervasive pattern of grandiosity (in fantasy or behavior), need for admiration, and lack of empathy [in the patient], beginning by early adulthood and present in a variety of contexts, as indicated by five (or more) of the following:

(1) Has a grandiose sense of self-importance (e.g., exaggerates achievements and talents, expects to be recognized as superior without commensurate achievements)

(2) Is preoccupied with fantasies of unlimited success, power, brilliance, beauty, or ideal love

(3) Believes that he or she is "special" and unique and can only be understood by, or should associate with, other special or high-status people (or institutions)

(4) Requires excessive admiration

(5) Has a sense of entitlement, i.e., unreasonable expectations of especially favorable treatment or automatic compliance with his or her expectations

(6) Is interpersonally exploitative, i.e., takes advantage of others to achieve his or her own ends

(7) Lacks empathy; is unwilling to recognize or identify with the feelings and needs of others

(8) Is often envious of others or believes that others are envious of him or her

(9) Shows arrogant, haughty behaviors or attitudes

Exhibit 13.2
BORDERLINE PERSONALITY DISORDER
(American Psychiatric Association, 1994)

A pervasive pattern of instability of interpersonal relationships, self-image, and affects, and marked impulsivity [in the patient], beginning by early adulthood and present in a variety of contexts, as indicated by five (or more) of the following:

1. Frantic efforts to avoid real or imagined abandonment. **Note:** Do not include suicidal or self-mutilating behavior covered in Criterion 5.

2. A pattern of unstable and intense interpersonal relationships characterized by alternating between extremes of idealization and devaluation

3. Identity disturbance: markedly and persistently unstable self-image or sense of self

4. Impulsivity in at least two areas that are potentially self-damaging (e.g., spending, sex, substance abuse, reckless driving, binge eating). **Note:** Do not include suicidal or self-mutilating behavior covered in Criterion 5.

5. Recurrent suicidal behavior, gestures, or threats, or self-mutilating behavior.

6. Affective instability due to a marked reactivity of mood (e.g., intense episodic dysphoria, irritability, or anxiety usually lasting a few hours and only rarely more than a few days)

7. Chronic feelings of emptiness

8. Inappropriate, intense anger or difficulty controlling anger (e.g., frequent displays of temper, constant anger, recurrent physical fights)

9. Transient, stress-related paranoid ideation or severe dissociative symptoms

The Narcissist

To meet the criteria of Narcissistic Personality Disorder, the following characteristics are described (American Psychiatric Association, 1994). The narcissist is overpreoccupied with self, has an exaggerated sense of achievement and talents, is engaged in fantasies of unlimited success, power, brilliance, beauty, or ideal love. To an unusual degree, these patients exhibit a need to be loved and admired by others. The narcissist has an exaggerated sense of entitlement and unreasonable expectations of others and may take advantage of others to achieve or attain his or her own self-serving interests. The narcissist is lacking in empathy and is unwilling to recognize the needs of others.

At an interpersonal level (Lachkar, 1992), the narcissistic lover is the "entitlement lover," in love with self, one who cannot imagine that the needs of the other exist. When not properly mirrored or when their personal sense of pride has been threatened, narcissists respond with rage or withdrawal. One can imagine what this withdrawal does to a borderline partner, who already has a thwarted sense of self. On a deeper level, narcissists are unable to form healthy dependency bonds and confuse normal states of vulnerability with imperfection. Narcissists have more integrated superegos and better impulse control, responding more to interpretation than to confrontation. Narcissists are quick to become bored and restless when their accomplishments wear thin and, very often, are considered to be dependent because they need so much attention from others.

It is not uncommon that the narcissist was once mother's special child until the birth of a sibling. Suddenly, this child's position is usurped and he or she grows up perceiving the parents as cruel and rejecting. To find refuge, such persons turn to valued parts of themselves: "I'll show them. I'll become famous, and they'll be sorry." Mothers lacking in attunement will minister to the infant's physical needs, but are unable to attend to the emotional needs. The following case illustrates this injury.

> A couple in their mid-50s, each with grown children from their first marriages, are having dinner with the wife's adult children. The husband accuses the wife: "Susan, you gave everyone at the dinner table something to eat first, and you totally ignored me. You gave your son a chicken breast, and what did you give me? You gave me the backs!"

In this scenario, the borderline wife has unconsciously communicated to her narcissistic husband that he is not entitled to "the breast," this enactment playing into his original narcissistic injury that he was not entitled to his mother's breast after his baby brother was born.

In couples treatment, the narcissist cannot allow the kind of dependency the borderline partner yearns for because the exposure would make him or her feel fragmented and too vulnerable. Narcissists become libidinally connected to those who mirror their beauty, success, or achievement or will offer them any semblance of power, fortune, or fame.

To maintain their ties with their archaic objects, narcissists form idealized relations and attachments. Their emotional life is shallow, as they obtain very little satisfaction in life other than from the adulation they receive from others. Unlike the borderline person, the narcissist believes the world owes him or her something; thus, many narcissists are unable to achieve their lifelong goals and dreams. They are dominated by such defenses as projection and withdrawal in response to their feelings of shame, guilt, omnipotence, and grandiosity. Because they must struggle against the impact of their harsh and punitive superegos, they become obsessed with perfectionism. Narcissists are markedly different from their borderline counterparts in that borderline partners fuse with the object, while narcissists critically withhold or withdraw from the object.

The Borderline Personality

To meet the criteria of Borderline Personality Disorder, the following characteristics are described (American Psychiatric Association, 1994). Borderline persons have a pervasive pattern of instability of interpersonal relationships, self-image, and affects, and marked impulsivity beginning by early adulthood and present in a variety of contexts, as indicated by at least some of the following: (1) they are frantically invested in avoiding real or imagined abandonment, (2) they exhibit an array of unstable interpersonal relationships characterized by alternation between extremes of idealization and devaluation, (3) they have marked identity confusion and low self-image, and they are impulsive and self-damaging (in the areas of spending money, sex, substance abuse, binge eating, etc.), (4) some exhibit recurrent suicidal behaviors, gestures, or threats, or self-mutilating behavior, (5) they suffer from chronic feelings of emptiness and display inappropriate anger or difficulty in controlling their temper, often with recurrent physical fights.

In interpersonal terms (Lachkar, 1992), the borderline person is one who does not have much of a sense of self, does not feel entitled, and will do anything to feel a semblance of bonding or relatedness. Borderline persons defend against intolerable shame and abandonment by splitting or projection, fearing that if their real needs are expressed they will be ridiculed, ignored, betrayed, or rejected. Typically, borderline persons have been abandoned by absent parents, alcoholic parents, abusive parents, psychotic parents, or emotionally unavailable parents. As a result, they remain forever faithful to an allegorical world of lost mothers, fathers, and abandoned babies.

As a consequence, they exhibit poor reality testing and impaired judgment, have poor impulse control, and tend to fuse with their objects. They frequently perpetuate the cycle by getting themselves into abusive, controlling, addictive, or other malaptive relations. They have difficulty with setting boundaries, as they lack the self-regulatory mechanisms to self-soothe, self-regulate, and self-affirm (Manfield, 1992). In severely disturbed relationships, the borderline person's love feelings intersect with aggression, unconsciously converting love into a malignant experience instead of one of intimacy and bonding.

Unlike narcissists, who withdraw when injured, borderline persona fuse or merge when injured and respond with splitting or projective defenses. Some may spend the rest of their lives getting back or getting even, using their hurt to spur attacks of shame and blame on their partners (Lachkar, 1984, 1986, 1992, 1997, 1998). One such patient remarked: "He's always working, and when he's off, he's always with his friends. He never has time for me, and when I ask him to spend more time with me, he claims I'm too needy or too demanding. This is where I lose it and go crazy. I start to eat, binge, and stuff myself to pieces. At other times, I scream, yell, or else I just go along and pretend that everything is fine."

Just as the narcissist is trying to prove a special sense of existence, the borderline person is trying to prove his or her existence as a thing in itself. The borderline person, like a chameleon, develops a persona, a false self, to shield the true self from real desires, needs, feelings, and yearnings, which he or she has learned will not be met.

THEORETICAL CONSIDERATIONS

Drawing from various theoretical frameworks, mainly concepts from classical psychoanalysis, including Freud (1914), self psychology (Kohut, 1971, 1977), object relations (Klein, 1935, 1936, 1937, 1940, 1946, 1957a, 1957b), Fairbairn (1952), Winnicott (1953, 1965), Bion (1959, 1962, 1967), group psychology (Bion, 1961), and psychohistory (Lachkar, 1993), and more contemporary theorists such as Grotstein (1981, 1987) and Kernberg (1990, 1991, 1992), I have attempted to integrate the complements of these theories into a viable treatment process applicable for narcissistic/borderline couples. Object relations is extremely effective in helping couples face their internal deficits and conflicts and can offer invaluable contributions to marital treatment. Self psychology has been found to be valuable in working with narcissists, whose exaggerated entitlement fantasies and search for approval make them more responsive to empathy, introspection, and interpretation.

Conversely, object relations proves beneficial in working with the abandonment anxieties of borderline persons and in meeting their containing, holding, soothing, and bonding needs. Self psychology techniques may be misperceived by a borderline person as the therapist's weakness, with the therapist being seen as a "pushover," not a "hard enough object" to deal with the aggressive forces the borderline partner may act out within the dyad. As clinicians, we must be empathic with the borderline person's vulnerability, but not to the aggression. To empathize with the borderline person's pathology is a collusion, a grave clinical error that can lead only to further destructiveness: the tendency to find fault/blame for all the shortcomings in the relationship.

There are distinct differences, however, in the way each one of these theoretical perspectives arrives at truth or psychic "reality." The methodology for the self psychologist is via intrasubjectivity and introspection, whereas for the object relationist it is via the patient's projections, splitting mechanisms, and other primitive defenses emanating from infantile fantasies. In self psychology, one strives to understand the interpersonal experience of patient and therapist, whereas in object relations, the patient's distortions, projections, and misperceptions are considered to shed light on important intrapsychic processes. Unwittingly, many self psychologists gratify the patient's distorted needs in order to allow a selfobject transference to emerge. So as not to lose sight of these distortions and delusions, the therapist must have a good grasp of normal development, keeping a clear image of how a healthy couple would respond. In healthy relationships, both spouses are mutually invested in the same goals. Aggression and other conflicts do not destroy or overcome the desire for love and intimacy. But in unhealthy relationships, love, hate, envy, control, and other aggressive forces divert the relationship away from love (Kernberg, 1990, 1991, 1992; Lachkar, forthcoming); conflict overcomes the relationship.

What is most helpful in terms of marital treatment? The therapist should not take the position of deciding who is right or who is wrong; doing so will only foster further delusions of grandiosity in the narcissist and further feelings of shame in the borderline partner. Instead, the therapist must create a holding environment in which each partner's issues can emerge safely. Such a therapeutic space will allow each partner the opportunity to experience an abundance of his or her own subjective experiences, leading to an understanding not only of those affectual experiences, but also of those of the partner.

THE DANCE

In narcissistic-borderline relations (Lachkar, 1992), the metaphor of "the dance" is used to explain why couples stay in painful conflictual relations, a choreographic web of entanglements, behaviors, and interactions that are circular—like a rondo—destructive, and never ending. Each borderline person needs a narcissist, and each narcissist needs a borderline partner to play out their dramas, to "do the dance."

In this psychological dance, the borderline partner attacks, the narcissist withdraws. If the narcissist feels guilty for abandoning the borderline partner, he or she cannot tolerate the guilt and returns. To woo the narcissist back, the borderline partner promises, "I'll do anything, I'll be anything you want me to be, just don't leave! For a short while the borderline person can playact at being the perfect mirroring object for the narcissist, but because of the lack of impulse control, inability to contain, hold, or sustain, or because of recurring and uncontrollable rages (Lachkar, 1984, forthcoming), the borderline partner cannot maintain the fulfillment of the promise. Feeling seduced by the partner's "promises" (the false self), the narcissist finds that such pledges are meaningless. The cycle repeats, the narcissist demanding to have perfection mirrored, the borderline partner feeling persecuted by the repeated need to comply with the narcissist's demands. Their interactions culminate in repeated object failures and disappointments.

WHY DO COUPLES STAY IN PAINFUL CONFLICTUAL RELATIONSHIPS?

Why is it that partners involved in primitive bonds find it so difficult to heed the clinician's advice? Why is it that even after a divorce or a separation these individuals maintain a bond, albeit a destructive one? Are they crazy, perverted, sadomasochistic? Any attachment is better than no attachment at all. There are those individuals who cannot feel a semblance of aliveness unless they are fused in a maladaptive attachment. Although this situation may be enraging to such patients, at least they feel a sense of aliveness instead of deadness (Kernberg, 1991).

Fairbairn (1952) more than anyone helps us to understand painful relationships, why people stay attached to a "bad" rejecting object (a tantalizing, tormenting, or unavailable object) over a prolonged period of time. It is the parent who promises, disappoints, and frustrates the child over a prolonged period of time. The parent who is loving and kind is also the same parent who can be cruel and sadistic. Although Fairbairn did not talk about narcissistic and borderline relationships, his conception of how the

ego splits and subdivides into several parts crystallized the notion of traumatic bonding. The borderline person will remain forever attached to an
unavailable, abusive, or an aloof object, such as a narcissist, who stirs up
hope for a connection to his or her earliest craving (the deprived or lost
self). Grotstein (1989) maintains the borderline person will stay because the
pain is still preferable to the emptiness, the black hole, the meaninglessness, or the dread. It is therefore the "meaninglessness that epitomizes states
of terror more than the deprivation itself." (p. 4) Borderline patients often
develop a preoccupation with pain as expressed through psychosomatic
illness, additions, suicidal ideation, or form sadomasochistic attachments
as a means of parasitic bonding with their objects. "When I burn myself
with a cigarette, then I know I'm alive. I exist! Now, he'll be sorry."
Anything is better than facing real needs—drugs, alcohol, or even this relationship!" Many narcissistic/borderline relationships border the fringes of
perversity dominated by the need for excitement and eroticism as the surrogate for a real loving and intimate bond (perversion is the confusion
between what is good and what is bad). It is primarily part object thinking,
shielding one from getting too close to the "good thing." Eroticism then
becomes the replacement for love, an emotional insurance policy against
vulnerability of the "real relationship."

In narcissistic/borderline relationships, pain stirs up an amalgam of
unresolved developmental issues as both partners need each other to play
out their internal drama. Ultimately, this is done in the effort to get in contact with some split-off undeveloped part of themselves. Paradoxically,
within these primitive unions the very same elements that bonds/binds
such individuals may also be the very elements that perpetuate the conflict between them. It is not unusual when in this state, couples often panic
and have great difficulty tolerating the confusion and chaos. "Should we
stay? Should we leave? What must be conveyed is that while in this
mental state of disarray, it is virtually impossible to make decisions and to
know what "to do," let alone to get a sense of what is real and what is not
real. The nature of primitive defenses and level of their defensive structures
makes it infeasible to get a sense of the "real relationship"*. As Goethe
once said, "It's difficult to know what to do at this point, especially when
there is so much blaming and attacking going on!"

---

* The "real relationship" refers to the task-oriented couple, those who can learn
from experience, see the relationship as it is (not as it should be, could be, or ought
to be). This is in contrast to the "fantasized relationship," those who cannot learn
from experience or cannot tolerate pain or frustration. The regressive couple are
those who form collusive bonds, display a diminution of reality testing, have
impaired judgment, and bond parasitically rather than through the maintenance
of healthy dependency bonds (Lachkar, 1992).

Couple Transference

The couple transference does for the couple what transference does for the individual, but is slightly more complex. Couple transference interpretations are derived from the analyst's experience and insights designed to produce a transformation within the dyadic relationship (Lachkar, 1997). To understand its complexity, I have integrated the notion of intersubjectivity, a well-known construct elaborated by many contemporary psychoanalysts (Brandchaft & Stolorow, 1984). The couple transference refers to mutual delusions, distortions, or shared couple fantasies, which are projected onto the therapist. Frequently, a couple will "invite" the therapist in by trying to draw the therapist into the "dance," that is, projecting into the therapist feelings of confusion and inadequacy. For example, two spouses may share a mutual fantasy, that if they begin to depend on the therapist, he or she will "abuse" or take advantage of them. Couples need to learn that dependency needs enhance the relationship, do not destroy, are normal, and when negated or denied, stir up fierce anxieties. (*Maybe you worry that if you both become dependent on me or begin to form a close attachment, I will take advantage or mistreat you as others have done in the past.*)

The notion of the "couple/therapist" transference within the matrix of a couple transference opens up an entirely new therapeutic or transitional space in which to work. It is within this space that "real" issues come to life.

PSYCHODYNAMICS AND PRIMITIVE DEFENSES

Not only is there a "dance" between the couple, there is also a dance between their psychodynamics, between guilt and shame, between envy and jealousy, between rejection and withdrawal. Both narcissists and borderline persons have a fragmented sense of self, both have been traumatized in early life (known as archaic injury), both suffer from feelings of displacement, annihilation anxieties, and preoedipal strivings. Even though there is some overlap, there are distinct qualitative differences in the way each experiences anxiety related to these archaic injuries and dynamics and the way each idiosyncratically identifies with the negative projections of the other (Lachkar, 1984, 1985, 1986, 1992, forthcoming). Becoming aware of these qualitative differences is invaluable to the clinician treating such couples.

Primitive defenses consist of a predominance of splitting and projection. Extensions of these primary defenses are projective identification, loss of identity, boundary confusion, lack of differentiation between self and other, shame/blame/attacking, omnipotent denial, idealization, and magical thinking. The primitive mind cannot hold onto both the good and bad parts of self, and so must shift back and forth between these unmentalized states. The very nature of primitive defenses obscures thinking, along with establishing a propensity for intense exaggeration and the distortion of reality. These states, in turn, lead to further denial and devaluation of the self (the tendency to turn against the self and/or feel responsible for all the shortcomings in the relationship). It is for this reason that we not only need to address with these narcissistic/borderline couples their conflicts, pain, and sufferings, but also to acknowledge and make use of their virtues, strengths, and sensibilities.

Projective Identification

Projective identification is a concept devised by Melanie Klein (1957a) as identifying a primitive form of communication. It is an unconscious psychic process whereby one disclaims some unwanted or disowned aspect of the self, and translocates it to the other. It is the nature of projective identification that weakens the self, not strengthens it. Put another way, it makes one feel internally helpless. Under the influence of projective identification, the one receiving the projection becomes vulnerable to the coercion, manipulation, or control of the person doing the projecting (Bion, 1962, 1967; Grotstein, 1981).

Dual Projective Indentification.   Dual projective identification is a term I originated to understand the projective/introjective process as it occurs in conjoint therapy. It is designed to zero in on what happens when both partners project back and forth as they identify with each other's negative projections. As projective identification is a one-way process, it does not explain the mutuality of shared projections. Dual projective identification is a two-way process whereby the partners project back and forth as each identifies with the negative projections of the other (Lachkar, 1992, 1997, forthcoming). It is a state of fusion, where both partners lose all sense of boundaries between self and other. In marital treatment, one partner (the narcissist) may sit impatiently silent, unconsciously compelling the other (the borderline) into taking on a caretaking role. "Whenever he acts like this, I always feel it is up to me to be responsible for everything!" Given such vigorous psycho-aerobics, this concept is particularly useful in sorting out very complex mental states, especially when there is a preponderance of primitive defenses. These projections are felt to be so intense that even reality testing does not relieve them. Instead, reality is replaced by infantile enactments of the primary loss of self. In normal bonds, it is the reverse, as reality testing does offer relief (Vaquer, 1991). Later in this chapter, the case of Mr. and Mrs. D. illustrates the power of dual projective identification.

THERAPEUTIC FUNCTIONS

Containment

Bion's conception of the container and the contained is perhaps one of the most useful and all-inclusive concepts of the function provided by the therapist for the patient. The importance of the therapist as both the mirror and the container becomes even more vital in the conjoint setting, because the central issues revolve around confusion, ambivalence, dependency, and aggression. The mother/therapist not only teaches the baby/patient to learn to tolerate and process frustration, but the mother/therapist serves as a filter, transforming affect back to the baby/patient important meaning, detoxifying the bad into something good or meaningful. A child needs an object who can contain destructivenss. If baby feels that his rage destroys his objects, he then becomes addicted to the fantasy that he can control the object (the spouse, the therapist). The mother/therapist, who is able to withstand the child's/patient's anger, frustrations, and intolerable feelings becomes the containing mother. This will be a new experience for the narcissist or the borderline partner.

Empathy/Mirroring Versus Containment

Alongside containment, there must be empathy and mirroring responses. As clinicians, we need to know when and how to offer containing functions, when to offer empathic interpretations versus offering mirroring responses. When do we contain and when do we mirror? When do we confront? Narcissists are more in need of mirroring. Borderline patients are more in need of containment or a hard object to stand up against. Many borderline patients become confused with empathic responses, misperceiving them as collusion or lack of clear boundaries. These patients need distinct boundaries. They need clarity. The therapist must be able to speak directly to the heart of the issue and stand up to this patient's distortions, delusion, and aggression.

Selfobject Functions

Some therapists believe it is the task of the therapist to "teach" selfobject functions. I believe, instead, that providing selfobject functioning for the patient is one of the primary tasks of the therapist, especially in treating narcissistic and borderline couples. While partners are in primitive bonds, they do not have the capacity to perform selfobject functions for each other. To "teach" prematurely can recreate an old scenario, reinforcing compliant, "false self" enactments or instigating a rapprochement crisis.

Selfobject is a term devised by Kohut referring to an interpersonal process between the therapist and the patient. These are basic functions designed to make up for psychological disturbances caused by failures from early caretakers (those who were lacking in mirroring, empathic attunement, and had faulty responses with their children). *"You'll never amount to anything!"* The purpose of the selfobject is to repair defects in the structure of the self. In the service of development, the function is of a revival nature, with the intent to reconstitute an arrested or thwarted self. There is ongoing discussion among therapists as to whether it is up to the couple to provide selfobject functions for one another. Although Kohut reminds us that some individuals may need selfobjects the rest of their lives, my view is that while couples are in the early phase of treatment, it is impossible for them to provide selfobject functions. This is the task of the therapist! To enforce this may reenact the false self, a self which belies the true self, one forced to grow up much too quickly and much too soon.

Psychoanalytic technique and theory are meaningless unless they are artistically, emotionally, and creatively executed. Every psychological movement, like every step of a dance, must be sensitively expressed with meaning, purpose, and conviction. The therapeutic task is to link what occurs externally with the internal life of the patient(s). The following case of a narcissistic/borderline couple shows in-depth the creation of a therapeutic space and the treatment that was offered within that space.

THE CASE OF MR. AND MRS. D

The case of Mr. and Mrs. D not only portrays what transpires in these beleaguered narcissistic/borderline relationships and how the "dance" is played out, but also serves as an example of how the therapist works within the "couple transference."

> Mr. D, 50 years old, attractive and well-dressed, is an engineer, a borderline personality who initiated treatment complaining of marital difficulties. He presented the problem of a sexually unavailable wife who withholds time, attention, and affection. Mrs. D, the narcissistic wife, is a 40-year-old, pretty, slim, and impeccably dressed schoolteacher. The couple have been married for 10 years and have two children. Mr. D was seen individually until Mrs. D was "invited" into treatment, which is when conjoint

treatment began. In borderline/narcissistic relations, it is the borderline partner who typically seeks help, as narcissists rarely offer themselves willingly to marital treatment. The couple therapy of Mr. and Mrs. D continued over a period of a year and a half, along with concomitant individual psychotherapy sessions for each.

Mr. D, the borderline husband, showed a marked degree of destructive behaviors and primitive defenses, as compared with Mrs. D, the narcissistic wife, who operated at a more developed level of superego functioning, which critically withheld from the object (the "withholding self").

Mr. D was an only child whose father died when the boy was 10 years old. His mother was an alcoholic. She remarried but divorced shortly thereafter. Although Mr. D did have some male connection in his formative years, he unconsciously blamed his mother for his father's death and his subsequent poor male bonding experiences. He felt very insecure about his role as husband and father, identifying with his helpless mother. At first, he was thought to be an obsessive-compulsive personality, but upon further exploration he revealed a typical borderline personality structure.

In the months before treatment began, Mr. D became unable to maintain a full erection, although he claimed he was never impotent prior to that time. This failure was felt as a severe blow to his self-esteem and produced intense anxiety within him. In addition, he expressed growing resentment toward his wife, had difficulty taking a stand with her, and saw any expression of desire or need for her as a losing proposition.

Simultaneously, he complained about his wife's withholding of sex, blaming her for his impotence and fearing that she would, one day, banish him. He believed that they had a good marriage in the early days before his wife began to reject him. Now, "all she expects is for me to pay the bills," he confided.

In the early sessions of the therapy, Mr. D wanted to blame his wife. Any attempts by the therapist at addressing the issues of his own internal world were to no avail. His response to the therapy induced in the therapist powerful countertransference reactions, causing her to offer quick remedies to provide immediate relief for his overwhelming anxiety. When these quick-fix solutions proved ineffective, Mr. D would have intense and sudden outbursts. He began to demand that his wife participate in the therapy, an apparent replication of his demands for her to have sex. He worried that his attempt to have his wife join him in therapy would end up as fruitless as asking her for sex. On an unconscious level, Mr. D was enacting the helpless, impotent mother role, projecting onto his spouse his "bad" dependency needs, which met with rebuffs. This cycle threw him into a whiny, desperate-baby position as an impotent husband. The therapist, failing in her efforts to encourage Mr. D in dealing with his internal issues, succumbed to his wishes and invited his wife to join the therapy.

Mrs. D did agree to come to some sessions on the basis that the problems in the marriage had nothing to do with her and in the hope that her attendance would facilitate her husband's improvement (the narcissist's need to hold on to the "perfect self"). According to Mrs. D, the problems began soon after the wedding when Mr. D's desire for intimacy diminished gradually (the diminishment of idealization). She felt he did the opposite of what she requested: "If I asked him to rub my back, he would pinch or pull at me. He hurt me, so, of course, I withdrew." She revealed that she no longer wanted to have sex with him because he was insensitive when they had sex, almost as if he hurt her "on purpose."

Mrs. D described her mother as a very domineering, religious, and rejecting mother, and her father as passive, cold, and detached. She recalled being the special child until her baby brother was born; then, at his birth, she felt that she had been dethroned and replaced by her new sibling. Mrs. D was left with deep feelings of never being special enough: "I spent the rest of my life trying to prove to my parents how perfect I was, and would do anything for their attention." This loss became an unforgettable, narcissistic injury, from which she had no opportunity to recover. She recounted how her mother never supported her burgeoning femininity, but favored her brother. So, she became "a tomboy," eschewing playing with dolls. "Eventually, I learned I didn't need anyone. Even when I got my period, my mother ignored me and never offered any help, advice, or concern."

Mr. D's poor male identification made him feel uncertain about his role as a husband and father, and Mrs. D suffered the contrariety of gender and identification (Benjamin, 1988). Ultimately, she disidentified with her mother and fused with her father, either by becoming competitive with him or by taking on his cold and detached ways. Both of these states became intolerable for her needy and insecure husband (the "rejected self").

Discussion

In their "dance," Mrs. D became the "dead" parent whom Mr. D tried desperately to revive. Similarly, Mrs. D took on the role of an unavailable mother, intoxicated with her own self-involvement. Mr. D's needs became the "disgusting" split-off part of his wife's original dependency, the feminine part of her that yearned for a special place with a parent, of which she had been deprived. In this scenario, Mr. D's "normal" requests for sex were felt to be rebukes of Mrs. D's sense of self and how she viewed herself as a woman. Because of her guilt and anxieties about her own sexuality, Mrs. D projected her guilt onto Mr. D, which in turn ignited his shame (the delusion that dependency needs are dangerous or "bad for one's health"). Conversely, Mr. D projected his envy and shame back onto Mrs. Γ, along with feelings of guilt, of being less than perfect, and of normal femininity being a sign of imperfection, the disfigurement of a woman.

As their psychological dance unfolded, we could see Mr. D fusing with his mother's/wife's body, living psychically within her. His need became insatiable and his sexualization often became linked to perversion (the pinching and the hurting). In this early stage of treatment, Mrs. D continued to rebuff Mr. D's sexual advances, inducing in him increased desperation and neediness: "If she loves me, she will have sex with me. If she doesn't, she won't. She makes me feel as if I don't exist."

As the therapy advanced, there was an opening of the therapeutic space as bonding developed with the therapist. Both partners began to tolerate states of confusion, "not-knowing," and healthy dependency on the therapist. The therapist took on a more active role, using interpretation, confrontation, and management techniques. The major shift for Mrs. D was in the gradual diminishment of her omnipotence, her all-knowing attitude that conveyed, "I just know what he's going to do and say." Once she could grasp the idea that her "absolute knowingness" of her husband as forever being a nothing, and that "nothing will ever change," Mrs. D was quite relieved to find how her omnipotence actually worked against her. During the next few months, Mrs. D began to feel some assurance in her newly acquired sense of being a feminine woman, the result of her preliminary identification with the therapist's qualities of sensitivity and vulnerability. Her developing capacities to tolerate her own "imperfections" and those of her husband, her feeling that she could get mad at him instead of projecting onto him and then rejecting him, contributed greatly to her feeling of increased security and the knowledge that the marriage was of paramount importance to her.

As his wife became more receptive to him and committed to their relationship, it came as quite a shock to Mr. D that he was not so much interested in intimacy and making love as he was in using sex as an act of aggression (a perverse use of love) against his passive, self-involved mother/wife. His striving for bonding transcended sex, as sex had served as the substitute for emotional contact and responsiveness. As he began to comprehend his own true dependency needs, he not only began to appreciate his wife's vulnerabilities, but displayed an increased capacity for abstract thinking, ("thinking about" feelings and needs instead of "acting them out"). Mr. D became intrigued with his new thinking tools, was astonished to learn how his bonding needs became intertwined with aggression and persecutory anxieties. Even more notable was his newly gained tolerance for ambiguity, the notion of many forces operating simultaneously within him and around him. He didn't have to "abuse," "seduce," or demand; he could simply ask.

In the final phase of treatment both partners expressed a desire for reparation. Mrs. D observed how her underlying fears of deficiency not only related to the difficulties in her marriage but impacted every area of her life, including her career and her children. Her defenses of withdrawal, isolation, and the demands for perfection, for "flawlessness," had given her a false sense of power, but ultimately kept her unprotected in a hostile internal world. Within the couple transference, the working through of Mrs. D's desire for special treatment manifested itself in several ways, such as insistence on fee reduction, changing hours to suit her schedule, or "perfect understanding." Mrs. D came to understand that just as her husband substituted sex for intimacy, she substituted omnipotence and control for dependency. She also noticed how anxious she felt whenever she had to take in nourishment from the therapist. She defended against this by being the one who had to know it all or being the one with all the answers. This need for perfect mirroring is exemplified by the following exchange:

> **Mrs. D:** You don't understand. I was not mad, I was infuriated.
> **Therapist:** So, you were angry.
> **Mrs. D:** No, I was not angry, I was frustrated.

When the therapist brought up important issues, Mrs. D accused her of an "agenda" mother; when she was more silent and reflective, she was accused of being the passive, impotent father. When the therapist tried to point out specific issues that Mr. D needed to deal with, he accused her of "ganging up on him."

Still, it was very affirming for Mr. D when the therapist could see positive aspects of his impulsive outbursts, that they really were representative of his wish to feel alive, to exist, and to feel loved, rather than to destroy or mutilate his mother/wife. Mr. D came to understand and appreciate how another part of him had a genuine need to depend on his wife and to love her. As he began to feel more contained, his ability to encompass ambiguous states and tolerate and consider ideas increased. Mrs. D was also moved and impressed by the notion that needing was not disdainful/sinful and would not necessarily result in abandonment. Gradually, both realized their true needs could actually enhance their relationship rather than diminish it. The conjoint sessions ended with Mrs. D requesting to see the therapist in individual sessions, and Mr. D requesting a referral to a male therapist for analytic work.

Summary

In the case of Mr. and Mrs. D, issues clearly centered around dependency needs. Working within the milieu of the couple transference and the dual projective identifications, the therapist gradually diminished the defenses against dependency by moving the couple away from shame/blame/ attacking defenses to that of healthy dependency needs (bonding with the therapist). For Mr. D, to need represented an anguished tormented part of himself, subject to disapproval and rejection, and linked with aggression and persecutory anxieties. For Mrs. D, dependency represented disgust and disdain against a rebuffed feminine side of herself she equated with impotence and rejection. As treatment continued, the work consisted of showing how each projected and identified with each other's negative projections (dual projective identification). Mr. D, the borderline husband, felt he existed solely through his wife's affection and affirmation (living inside the object), and that it was his insatiable needs that actually drove her away. Mrs. D projected her shameful feminine side onto her husband to ward off her own inadequacies, compelling him to become even more needy, attacking, and sadistic. Mr. D. identified with Mrs. D's projection that it was bad to be vulnerable, equating femininity with an early narcissistic injury (birth of a brother). Eventually Mrs. D was able to relinquish some of the guilt and shame surrounding her dependency needs as she began to bond and identify with the therapist's "femininity." As the therapist was able to provide important selfobject and containing functions, they both began to feel more alive. Mrs. D. was reassured that giving her husband attention was also a way of giving her attention, and was not denigrating her, rebuffing her, but, in fact, supportive of her. As Mr. D became more observant of his earlier aggressive assaults, he became aware of how they had stripped him of his inner resources, making him feel emotionally impotent. He felt more contained and that there was someone to listen to him, to understand his pain (did not have to "act out" to get the attention he needed). Finally, both partners comprehended how they had disidentified with the parent of the same gender and identified with the parent of the opposite gender: Mrs. D had disidentified (Benjamin, 1988) with her mother, eschewing her feminine nature, and identified with her detached father, enacting that role within her marriage; Mr. D had disidentified with his father, who had abandoned him through death, and identified with his passive mother, becoming a demanding, insatiable infant with his wife. As Mrs. D embraced the feminine aspects of her nature and Mr. D reclaimed his masculine nature, their love life became a mutual experience of discovery, tenderness, and satisfaction.

THREE PHASES OF TREATMENT

Phase One: A State of Oneness—The Borderline Person Lives Within the Mental Space of the Narcissist (Fusion/Collusion)

During the initial phase of treatment, the borderline person often lives "inside" the emotional space of the narcissist, as in the case just introduced. It is a state of "oneness," of fusion/collusion (paranoid-schizoid position), which exhibits a propensity for living within the psychic space of the other (Lachkar, 1992, 1997, in press). Because of the predominance of primitive defenses, the major therapeutic task is to assist each partner in relinquishing blame, finding fault, omnipotent control, deciding who is right, who is wrong (the one responsible for all the shortcomings in the relationship). This is accomplished by gradually "weaning" the couple away from their destructive, painful, and aggressive behaviors by bonding through their vulnerabilities. In this phase, there is much name calling, stonewalling, scapegoating, envy, jealousy, and guilt. There is not space for another person's ideas or feelings: "My needs are your needs!" The formation of parasitic ties are enacted repeatedly as each acts out unresolved unconscious infantile fantasies. "I'll show him what it feels like to make demands on me!" Both partners show little awareness of the inner forces that pervade and invade the psyche via their splitting mechanisms, mutual and dual projective identifications.

Mr. D's defenses caused him to operate at the level of a primitive superego (persecutory and attacking), while Mrs. D's defenses of withholding and withdrawal operated at the level of a more advanced superego (critical, harsh, relentless). In this phase the therapist is often used as a "toilet breast" (Klein, 1940). The borderline partners typically cannot make use of the mother as a container, will display intense ruthlessness toward their objects (the therapist) in the effort to rid the psyche of the bad parts of the self.

Phase Two: A State of Twoness (Transitional Phase)

In the second stage of treatment, there is an emergence of twoness, a tentative awareness of two separate emotional states, even a feeling that treatment can be helpful. Couples begin to feel better without knowing why. The reason is because they feel contained. There is greater tolerance for ambiguity, greater capacity to live within the space of "not knowing," and more awareness of conscious, unconscious, and other compelling forces. It is the beginning of their bonding with the therapist, of separation from living emotionally "inside" the object, and moving toward mutual interdependence. As the therapist emerges as both container and new self-object, there is a broader range of experience, an opening of a new therapeutic space, or what Winnicott (1953) has referred to as the transitional space or holding environment.

This is the hopeful stage, there is a burst of new energy and feeling of excitement. There is a profound shift, a movement away from the act of doing toward acts of feeling, being, and thinking. Each partner begins to get a glimmer of the part each plays in "the dance." This is the transitional stage, and the beginning or the movement into the depressive position.

Phase Three: Awareness of Two Emerging Separate Mental States (Dependent and Interdependent)

The third phase of treatment marks the beginnings of the depressive position, where reparation occurs, a wish to "repair" the damage, to embrace guilt and pain, and to express remorse and sadness. It is a time where each partner comes to terms with uncertainty, ambivalence, and dependency needs, a time to heal, repair, and listen nondefensively to each other's hurts. There is new depth and richness to the work and an awakening to the depressive position, where true reparation can take place. The couple begins to psychically live "outside" the mental space of the other, as two separate, yet connected, emerging mental states. For the first time, mutuality and movements between dependence and interdependence take place. Healthy dependency needs are recognized as each partner begins to respect the needs of both self and other. We see the gradual diminishment of repetitive negative projections along with a window of opportunity for further treatment in individual psychodynamic psychotherapy. This is the "thinking" and healing phase where expression of true feelings begin to replace the act of "doing" or "acting out" (as we saw in the case of Mr. D). There is less need to "spill over," evacuate, or "tell all" and greater capacity to contain. This is the weaning stage, away from the preoccupation with "the relationship" to concentration on self-development. Both partners begin to see that they have their own inner conflicts, and growing awareness of how they impact their relational bond (the "real relationship").

Having moved through the phases of treatment in the case of Mr. and Mrs. D, we can now apply some specific procedures to the treatment of narcissistic/borderline relationships.

GENERAL GUIDELINES

- The therapist must see the couple together before transition into individual therapy to form a safe bond. *Cautionary note:* Do not move into individual work until the couple is ready (separation too early can induce a "rapprochement crisis").
- Be aware that couple interaction can diminish individuality. Avoid such phrases such as, "You *both* suffer from feelings of abandonment."
- Be aware that each partner experiences anxiety differently, and these differences must be respected (qualitative differences).
- A therapeutic alliance must first be with the narcissist (the tendency to flight/flee/withdraw can pose a serious threat to treatment). The borderline patient will be able to tolerate waiting as long as he or she knows therapeutic bonding is taking place. A further challenge is how do we provide empathic responses to the narcissist without betraying or abandoning the borderline patient?
- Be aware that development of the therapeutic alliance is slow and the creation of a secure framework (structure, boundaries, commitment) takes time. The more primitive the couple, the more we need to emphasize the need for commitment. As resistances unfold in the relationship, use these opportunities to wean them into the "couple transference."
- When individual treatment occurs in conjunction with conjoint treatment, the same basic guidelines apply. Privilege and confidentiality is still under the umbrella of conjoint treatment (Lachkar, 1986, 1992).

TREATMENT POINTS AND TECHNIQUES

Finally, we must consider some vital guidelines to technique.

- Do not be afraid to confront the patient's aggression. Speak directly to the aggression with technical neutrality by making clear, definitive statements. Be empathic toward the pain and the patient's vulnerabilities, but avoid getting drawn into the couple's battle.
- Continually set goals, reevaluating and reminding patients of treatment goals of why they came in the first place.
- Avoid asking too many questions and obtaining lengthy histories. Do not waste time. Start right in. The history and background information will automatically unfold within the context of the therapeutic experience and the transference.
- Avoid self-disclosure, touching or consoling the patient, and making unyielding concessions.
- Listen and be attentive. Maintain good eye contact, speak with meaning and conviction. Talk directly to the issues.
- Use short, clear sentences; keep responses direct; mirror and reflect sentiments with simple responses and few questions.
- Keep in mind a "normal couple" or "ideal couple." This image will sharpen your focus and safeguard you from getting lost within the couple's psychological "dance."
- Explain how one may project a negative feeling onto another person, but still understand why the other identifies with what is being projected (focus on the *dual projective identification*).
- Listen for themes. Be aware of repetitive themes. The subject and feelings may change, but the theme is pervasive (betrayal, abandonment, rejection fantasies).
- Help the couple to recognize "normal" and healthy dependency needs.

CONCLUSION

Narcissistic/borderline couples express their pain by repeating blindly their dysfunctional behaviors without learning or profiting from their experiences. The uncertainties of diagnosis have been acknowledged, as well as the difficulties in differentiating between borderline and narcissist states. I have discussed why partners in these beleaguered relationships are in complicity with one another through their psychological "dance."

Couples therapy is an experience that occurs among three persons: the two partners and the therapist. This is a deep emotional experience of intense communication and feelings that begins with the profound challenges of a primitive relationship and matures into the awareness of healthy dependency needs and mutual respect. With each session, the curtain opens, and the opportunity for a new experience begins.

REFERENCES

American Psychiatric Association. (1994). *Diagnostic and statistical manual of mental disorders*. (4th ed.). Washington, DC: Author.

Benjamin, J. (1988). *The bonds of love*. New York: Pantheon.

Bion, W. R. (1959). Attacks on linking. *International Journal of Psycho-analysis*, 39, 266.

Bion, W. R. (1961). *Experiences in groups*. New York: Basic Books.

Bion, W. R. (1962). *Learning from experience*, London: Heinemann.

Bion, W. R. (1967). *Second thoughts. Selected papers on psychoanalysis*. New York: Jason Aronson.

Brandchaft, B., & Stolorow, R. (1984). The borderline concept: Pathological character and iatrogenic myth. In J. Lichtenberg et al (Eds.), *Empathy II*. Hilldade, NJ: Analytic Press.

Fairbairn, W. R. D. (1952). *Endopsychic structure considered in terms of object relationships: An object relations theory of the personality* (pp. 82–136). New York: Basic Books.

Freud, S. (1914). *Freud's On Narcissism: An introduction*. New Haven: Yale University Press, 1991.

Grotstein, J. (1980). A proposed revision of the psychoanalytic concept of primitive mental states. *Contemporary Psychoanalysis, 16*, 479–546.

Grotstein, J. (1981). *Splitting and projective identification*. New York: Jason Aronson.

Grotstein, J. (1983). A proposed revision of the psychoanalytic concept of primitive mental states, II. The borderline syndrome. Section I. *Contemporary Psychoanalysis, 19*, 570–604.

Grotstein, J. (1984a). A proposed revision of the psychoanalytic concept of primitive mental states, II. The borderline syndrome. Section 2. *Contemporary Psychoanalysis, 20*, 77–118.

Grotstein, J. (1984b). A proposed revision of the psychoanalytic concept of primitive mental states, II. The borderline syndrome. Section 3. *Contemporary Psychoanalysis, 20*, 266–343.

Grotstein, J. (1987). Meaning, meaninglessness, and the "black hole": Self and interactional regulation as a new paradigm for psychoanalytic and neuroscience. An introduction. Unpublished manuscript.

Kernberg, O. (1975). *Borderline conditions and pathological narcissism*. New York: Jason Aronson.

Kernberg, O. (1990). Between conventionality and aggression: The boundaries of passion. Paper presented at the cutting edge 1990. The Heart of the matter:

Helping Improve Vital Relationships. University of California, San Diego, Department of Psychiatry, School of Medicine, San Diego, California, April 28–29.

Kernberg, O. (1991) Sadomasochism, sexual excitement, and perversion. *Journal of the American Psychoanalytic Association, 39*, 333–362.

Kernberg, O. (1992). *Aggression in personality disorders and perversions.* New Haven: Yale University Press.

Klein, M. (1935). A contribution to the psychogenesis of manic-depressive states. In R.E. Money-Kyrle (Ed.) *The writings of Melanie Klein, Volume I—Love, guilt and reparation and other works 1921–1945*, pp 262–289. New York: The Free Press, 1975.

Klein, M. (1936). Weaning. In R.E. Money-Kyrle (Ed.), *The writings of Melanie Klein, Volume 1—Love, guilt, and reparation and other works 1921–1945*, pp. 200–305. New York: The Free Press, 1975.

Klein, M. (1937). Love, guilt and reparation. In R. E. Money-Kyrle (Ed.), *The writings of Melanie Klein, Volume I—Love, guilt and reparation and other works 1921–1945*, pp. 306–343. New York: The Free Press, 1975.

Klein, M. (1940). Mourning and its relation to manic states. In *Contribution to psychoanalysis 1921–1925* (pp. 311–338). London: Hogarth Press, 1948, (pp. 311–325).

Klein, M. (1946). Notes on some schizoid mechanisms, In J. Riviere (Ed.) *Developments in psychoanalysis*, (pp. 198–236). London: Hogarth Press, 1952.

Klein, M. (1957a). *Envy and gratitude.* New York: Basic Books.

Klein, M. (1957b). On identification. In M. Klein, D. Heinmann, & R. Money-Kyrle (Eds.), *New direction in psychoanalysis* (pp. 309–345). New York: Basic Books.

Kohut, H. (1971). *The analysis of the self.* New York: International Universities Press.

Kohut, H. (1977). *The restoration of the self.* New York: International Universities Press.

Lachkar, J. (1984). Narcissistic/borderline couples: A psychoanalytic perspective to family therapy. *International Journal of Family Psychiatry, 5* (2), 169–189.

Lachkar, J. (1985). Narcissistic/borderline couples: Theoretical implications for treatment. *Dynamic Psychotherapy, 3* (2), 109–127.

Lachkar, J. (1986). Narcissistic/borderline couples: Implications for mediation. *Conciliation Courts Review, 24*(1), 31–43.

Lachkar, J. (1992). *The narcissistic/borderline couple: A psychoanalytic perspective to marital conflict.* New York: Brunner/Mazel.

Lachkar, J. (1993). Parallels between marital and political conflict. *Journal of Psychohistory. 20*:275–287.

Lachkar, J. (forthcoming). *The many faces of abuse: Emotional abuse of high functioning women.* Northvale, NJ: Jason Aronson.

Lachkar, J. (1998). The many faces of abuse: Emotional abuse of high functioning women. *Journal of Emotional Abuse.*

Lansky, M. (in press). The Stepfather in Sophocles' Electra In S. Cath, L. Tessman, & M. Shopper (Eds.). *Stepfathers.* Hilldale, NJ: The Analytic Press.

Mahler, M. S., Pine, F., & Bergman, A. (1975). *The psychological birth of the human infant.* New York: Basic Books.

Manfield, P. (1992). *Split self split object.* New York: Jason Aronson.

Meltzer, D. (1967). *The psycho-analytic process*. London: William Heinemann Medical Books.

Vaquer, F. (1991). An object relation approach to conflict and compromise. In S. Dowling (Ed.), *Conflict and compromise: Therapeutic considerations.* Monograph 7 of the workshops series of the American Psychoanalytic Association (pp. 115–132). Madison, CT: *International Universities Press.*

Winnicott, D. W. (1953). Transitional objects and transitional phenomena in a study of the first not-me possession. *International Journal of Psycho-Analysis,* 34(2), 89–97.

Winnicott, D. W. (1965). *The maturational process and the facilitating environment.* New York: International Universities Press.

CHAPTER 14

Borderline Personality Disorder and Relationship Enhancement Marital Therapy

Michael Waldo
Marsha J. Harman

Persons with personality disorder are described in the *Diagnostic and Statistical Manual of Mental Disorders*, fourth edition (DSM-IV) (American Psychiatric Association, 1994), as exhibiting "an enduring pattern of inner experience and behavior that deviates markedly from the expectations of the individual's culture, is pervasive and inflexible, has an onset in adolescence or early adulthood, is stable over time, and leads to distress or impairment" (p. 629). It describes persons with Borderline Personality Disorder (BPD) as exhibiting "a pattern of instability in interpersonal relationships, self-image, and affects, and marked impulsivity" (p. 629). This chapter briefly describes BPD, then offers an explanation of Relationship Enhancement Marital and Family Therapy and a rationale for the use of Relationship Enhancement couples therapy as a part of the treatment of BPD. A case study provides an example of how Relationship

This chapter is a revision of the journal article "Relationship Enhancement Therapy with Borderline Personality" in *The Family Journal:Counseling and Therapy for Couples and Families*, 1, 25–30.

Enhancement (RE) therapy was used with a couple in which the woman was diagnosed with BPD.

DSM-IV AND
BORDERLINE PERSONALITY DISORDER

Individuals with BPD are described by the DSM-IV as alternating between dependency and self-assertion. For a diagnosis of BPD, five out of nine diagnostic criteria must be met: instability in interpersonal relationships, potentially self-damaging impulsivity, instability of mood, intense anger, recurrent suicidal behavior, identity disturbance, chronic feelings of emptiness, intense fear of abandonment, and stress-related paranoid ideation or dissociative symptoms.

The disorder often begins by early adulthood and manifests itself in a variety of contexts, including home, school, and work settings. There is a greater prevalence of the diagnosis among females. Although there has been some concern regarding the validity of the DSM diagnosis of BPD (Pope et al., 1983), Meyer (1989) suggested that the BPD characteristics resemble the previously common diagnosis "emotionally unstable personality disorder." Prevalence of the disorder in the general population is approximately 2 percent. Impairment and risk of suicide are greatest in the young adult years but subside as the individual ages. People with BPD appear to attain greater stability in various settings during their 30s and 40s American Psychiatric Association, 1994).

THEORETICAL PERSPECTIVES

Hypothetical explanations for BPD have recently shifted from drive theory, which suggests that repressed memories and feelings manifest themselves in alternate situations, to object relations theory and self psychology, which suggest that lack of differentiation from initial primary relationships results in a lack of differentiation in subsequent relationships (Kernberg, 1975; Silver, 1983). Although the DSM-IV (American Psychiatric Association, 1994) indicates a lack of information regarding predisposing factors and family patterns, sexual and/or physical abuse histories have frequently been reported in BPD research literature (Brown & Anderson, 1991; Herman, Perry, & Van der Kolk, 1989; Wonderlich & Swift, 1990). BPD is occasionally treated in inpatient settings, including hospital emergency rooms (Beresin & Gordon, 1981), short-term hospitalization (Koenigsberg, 1984), long-term hospitalization and residential treatment (Stern, Fromm, & Sacksteder, 1986), and day-hospital treatment (Simon, 1986). The ultimate

objective of most inpatient treatment is to stabilize the patient in preparation for outpatient care (Chessick, 1982).

Outpatient treatment of BPD has been described by a number of
authors. Reid (1989) described short-term therapy with BPD clients and
stressed that the therapist's expectation of the client's success was
imperative. Waldinger and Gunderson (1984) suggested that the longer
clients remained in therapy, the more they improved. Tryon, DeVito,
Halligan, Kane, and Shea (1988) suggested that setting consistent limits
for college students diagnosed with BPD provided structure and produced positive changes in their behavior. Conjoint marital therapy has
also been attempted with couples in which one spouse was diagnosed
with BPD, using psychodynamic therapy models (Koch & Ingram, 1985;
Solomon, 1985) and mediation (Lachkar, 1986).

Bowen's (1978) theory of differentiation of self offers a potentially useful
perspective on the dynamics of BPD. Bowen postulated an emotional
family system from which individuals, to varying degrees, differentiate
through maturation. Highly differentiated persons are capable of purposeful thought and choice when responding to emotional interaction with
significant others. They are able to process their reactions intellectually and
choose person-to-person relationships with significant others. Persons who
are less able to differentiate remain emotionally dependent on others, in
that their emotionality fluctuates automatically in response to emotional
exchanges in their relationships. Their opinions, self-evaluations, and sense
of self-worth are dependent on a positive emotional atmosphere in their
significant relationships. Highly undifferentiated individuals may feel
panic, terror, and rage when they experience negative emotions in their
relationships or threats to the continuation of a relationship.

IMPLICATIONS FOR COUPLES

Couples therapy for treatment of BPD has been attempted in the past
with varying rates of success. Lachkar (1984, 1985) has assisted narcissistic/
borderline couples, using a psychoanalytic perspective to view the
pathology of the relationship. However, Paul (1985) cautioned against
the use of pathological terms, noting that Lachkar's description of nar-
cissistic/borderline couples aptly described the interaction between
many other couples. Several therapists have described failure in working
with narcissistic or borderline disordered couples (Berkowitz, 1985;
Miller, 1985; Seeman & Edwardes-Evans, 1979).

Uncontrolled panic, terror, and rage typify the emotions underlying the
behaviors that are symptomatic of BPD (Kernberg, 1975). Persons suffering
from the disorder who are treated in counseling centers have often

threatened and/or acted in aggressive and self-destructive ways that suggest desperation. Invariably, these symptoms have emerged in response to some real or perceived break in the emotional harmony of their significant relationships. Persons suffering from BPD often become highly upset over minor criticisms or indications of indifference from their significant others. If their reaction generates a negative response from the other, they become increasingly threatened until eventually (often very quickly) BPD behaviors emerge, including verbal assault, physical violence, self-mutilation, and suicide attempts. Ironically, their dependence on emotionally positive relationships results in negativity and instability in their relationships.

RELATIONSHIP ENHANCEMENT THERAPY

If BPD characteristics result at least in part from lack of differentiation in significant relationships, Relationship Enhancement (RE) therapy (Guerney, 1977) may be an appropriate treatment approach. RE therapy integrates principles and methods of psychodynamic, humanistic, behavior-modification, and interpersonal therapies. It involves training clients to express their deepest emotions, facilitate such expression by the partner, and achieve insight into their own and their partner's previously unrecognized conflicts and motives. The nine specific skills taught to improve the depth and quality of the relationships are self-expression, empathic responding, discussion/negotiation, problem/conflict resolution, self-changing, helping others change, generalization, facilitation of appropriate communication, and maintenance (Guerney, 1987).

RE has been used to teach communication skills to college roommates (Waldo, 1989), wife abusers (Guerney, Waldo, & Firestone, 1987; Waldo, 1988), students and their teachers (Rocks, Baker, & Guerney, 1985), parents and adolescents (Guerney, Coufal, & Vogelsong, 1981), and single females (Overton & Avery, 1984). It has also been used with premarital couples (Ridley, Jorgensen, Morgan, & Avery, 1982), married couples (Brock & Joanning, 1983; Granvold, 1983; Jessee & Guerney, 1981), and couples undergoing treatment for alcoholism (Waldo & Guerney, 1983). In a recent study (Griffin & Apostal, 1993), RE was shown to directly affect increases in differentiation and adjustment in married couples.

Extensive research has demonstrated that RE improves the quality of relationships and the adjustment of the individuals in those relationships (Guerney, 1977; Levant, 1983). The use of RE skills by persons suffering from BPD could greatly improve their adjustment in their significant relationships, both by helping them resolve specific conflicts in a productive fashion and through the reduction of stress in the relationship. Furthermore, training in these skills may directly affect the problems with differentiation manifested by BPD symptoms. When clients are taught empathic skills (compassion), they are encouraged to understand their significant others' experiences, especially their emotions, as they are for those persons. This involves putting aside their own opinions and reactions for the moment and concentrating on what an experience is like for their partners. Putting aside their own reactions can be an important first step in differentiation. Understanding their partners as they are, separate human beings with separate emotions, can further the differentiation process.

The Expressive skill taught by RE encourages clients to express themselves fully and honestly, including their emotions, in subjective terms (using "I" statements). The emphasis on subjectivity results in clients' expressing their thoughts and emotions as their own, and only their own, thereby potentially increasing their differentiation. When in the Expresser role, clients are also encouraged to indicate the specific behaviors in which they would like their partners to engage, and to provide a rationale regarding what this would mean for the relationship. This activity furthers differentiation by demonstrating the Expressers' desires as distinct from their partners' behavior. It also serves as a mature approach to expressing their desires, in contrast to emotional outbursts and emotional behavior.

Discussion, the third skill, involves switching back and forth between being empathic and expressive during a dialogue with a significant other. Practicing this skill entails sequentially understanding the other person's experience and emotions (as that person's own), expressing one's own experience and emotions (as one's own), again understanding the other, and so forth, throughout the course of a dialogue. In this process, it is possible that clients are actively differentiating through interaction with a significant other.

When conducting Relationship Enhancement therapy, the therapist or cotherapists coach the couple in the use of RE skills. First, the couple are given a written explanation of the skills before sessions begin. During the first session the therapist(s) describe and demonstrate the Expressive and Empathic skills. When the spouses begin practicing, they alternate assuming the Expresser and Empathic Responder roles. The therapist(s) make suggestions when needed, praise when appropriate, and monitor times for switching roles. Additional skills are added as the couple are better able to negotiate their needs in their relationships.

Although session limits vary among clients, we prefer to work with couples for two-hour sessions when possible. Depending on the duration of the therapy, some couples have moved from initial two-hour sessions to one-hour sessions. We believe the initial extended sessions facilitate skill development. We prefer to work as cotherapists when possible; however, RE therapy may be successfully conducted with a single therapist.

CASE STUDY

The application of Relationship Enhancement therapy to a case of border-line personality disorder is offered in the following case study. A description of the clients is given, followed by a transcript demonstrating use of the skills.

John and Sara were living in a common-law marriage. Both were approaching 40 years of age when they entered therapy. Both had been in individual therapy for several months prior to begin-ning marital therapy. Sara was particularly apprehensive regard-ing couples counseling because of the anxiety produced in the relationship a year before, when the couple participated in an interpersonal skills workshop. She agreed to engage in RE therapy after hearing a description of the attitudes and skills she and John could expect to develop, and how this could benefit their relationship.

Sara met six of the DSM-IV criteria for BPD, including a pattern of unstable and intense interpersonal relationships, affective instability, and inappropriate anger. Also present were identity disturbance in self-image and long-term goals, feelings of empti-ness, and frantic efforts to avoid abandonment. These characteris-tics also met the time-period criterion of the DSM-IV. Sara had reported sexual abuse at the age of 5 by an 11-year-old-brother. She described the experience as both frightening and comforting. She also reported that she had attempted suicide at age 18. She had previously been diagnosed with Bipolar Disorder, Panic Disorder, Depression, and, finally, Borderline Personality Disorder. She had been prescribed several medications, including Wellbutrin, desipramine, lithium, Prozac, and Xanax. The med-ications did not appear to alleviate symptoms for Sara. John described incidents in which Sara had become irrational, thrown a heater at him, and beaten him with her purse while he was driv-ing an automobile. John responded to Sara's outbursts with a depressed mood, and would withdraw and become nonreactive. John had been previously diagnosed with Major Depression. He had responded favorably to Prozac and desipramine. John's withdrawal appeared to motivate Sara to escalate her behavior in order to feel heard by John.

Therapy with this couple, as of this report, consisted of three two-hour sessions (a total of six hours). During that brief time, John and Sara progressed from relatively safe topics—telling each other of positive elements in the relationship, such as John enjoying Sara's singing older songs and Sara's enjoying hearing about John's fantasies and plans for the future—to working out an extremely intense and angry situation involving their respective children. Additional topics of discussion were marriage, finances, and current jobs.

When therapists are working with persons suffering from BPD, therapist coaching in the use of the RE skills is of critical importance. Because such patients seemingly have a great deal of difficulty differentiating themselves from their partners, they often fail to show understanding of the partner's experience when trying to be empathic, or fail to subjectively "own their own experience" when trying to be expressive. At these moments, they need the support and guidance of the therapist, who coaches them back to the use of empathy or expressive skills and shows them how use of the skills helps them to differentiate themselves from a partner. The following transcript illustrates the couple's use of RE skills during the third session:

John (*as Expresser*): I think that one of the most difficult issues that we deal with is that of you bringing in most of the support and my bringing in very little. I feel very strange being in that role of not being the primary supporter, and it scares me to be in that role. I'm very frightened, sometimes, when we argue and you say, "Get out," or whatever. I get afraid and think where am I going to go? I've committed myself to school. That's a real difficult issue for me to deal with. You've discussed with me the men in your past who have been in that same role, and I try hard not to fall into that, but I'm afraid I fall into the trap of "user." There's a lot of fear and discomfort inside of me, not having me be the breadwinner.

Sara: I feel very strongly about that issue.

Female Counselor (FC) (*to Sara*): You're just listening. You're repeating what he's saying.

Sara: You feel very strongly about that issue. I hear that you're talking about the fear that I may have put you in by talking about other men who have been in my life, that you're uncomfortable with the situation and that you may not have a lot of choices, and your feelings are stuck between scared and wanting to be in the relationship, and you're doing the best you can.

John: I think that's pretty accurate. Your past relationships don't bother me except that I'm afraid I'll fall into the same ranks. I guess there's some guilt associated with this role as well—that maybe I should be doing more here. I struggle a lot of times between "should I get a job, should I cut down on school?"—a zillion things. A lot of those feelings are intensified when we argue about it.

Sara: I hear you saying that you don't want to fall into the same roles that I've possibly put in front of you when I'm being angry with you, that you're pulled in a lot of different directions about what to do in the situation that you feel causes a strain in the relationship. And you'd like to have a little peace of mind that it was an issue that could be settled where you felt comfortable in the situation.

Male Counselor (MC) (*to John*): I think you're doing great, using "I" statements and expressing emotions. Now, I'd like to see you add how you'd like it to be and what that would say about your relationship.

John: I'd like there to be some peace between us and to settle on how we feel about it and that someday in the future I'll be through with this and get a real job and have a better life. So, I feel, in the long run, benefits are going to outweigh what's happening now. I don't want it to take any longer, and for us to work on it and to settle on that and keep it out of our relationship.

MC (*to John*): What would "settle" mean?

John: I wish we could come to understand that even though you're providing for the entire family right now, that the future will be better and we could just accept that.

Sara: I'm hearing that you would like for the turmoil to cease about money, and what's yours is mine and what's mine is yours, instead of being I, I, I. You'd like to see acceptance of where we are now and look toward the future when it will be better.

John: What's your view of this?

Sara (*as Expresser*): I felt a lot of fear in being the sole support of the family. I've always been a caretaker of sorts and sometimes I resent that, and it causes a lot of fear that if I withdraw then things will change, because they have in the past. I tend to project that. I project my fear and get so angry about money situations that I don't allow myself the chance to know that it's just for now. I feel just angry because I feel you have not put anything into the relationship. Those are the feelings that I have, and I feel as soon as we're all done with school, that I've put all this into the relationship—that you'll leave. I have a real fear of your leaving.

John: So, you're scared I'll leave.

Sara: I just don't have enough confidence in myself for being me that someone would stay in my life to love me who cared for me. I've always felt I had to do something really huge to keep love in my life and that I have those nagging tapes in back of my mind that say that you're going to leave. Sometimes, they're real overwhelming, and when it comes to the money issue I get a feeling of more control that I can manipulate, and I do, to the point that you become defensive and there's a part of me that feels a sense of winning, that I've made you feel small and I felt big, and it's the same feeling I had with my parents, and sometimes that's what role I'm playing out and I'm not the little girl anymore. I'm the daddy. I'm strong. I can do anything I want to by making others miserable . . .

Further in the dialogue, Sara is still the Expresser.

Sara: I guess I feel that when I fear that you're going to leave, then when you do something, then I do something drastic to make you leave and then I feel justified that I made you leave—you didn't leave on your own and I think that's money, sex, or anything. It's a feeling and it's a manipulator that I can use to protect myself. And I feel that I use that when I'm the most insecure . . .

The dialogue continued with John expressing and Sara listening. The following excerpt is the beginning of Sara's next expressive role.

Sara: I feel a lot of emotion right now about not listening to things that you've said. I feel an awareness of the feelings that you have. I'm not sure that I like it. It takes away a barrier of mine. I'm scared of honesty, too. It's easier for me to hide. I feel that what you've said really means something. It's just that I don't feel manipulated. I don't feel the things that you've been saying, or have said that you're saying just so I'll get off your back. . . . I feel that in the long run if you got a job that I'd probably be miserable thinking I'm not spending enough time with you either. I forget that we made a commitment that we would make this work. I feel right now that we have a chance to be "*we*" again. I feel scared, but I feel really good.

Finally, Sara expresses further insight regarding the use of RE skills.

Sara: When I see you in the speaker role and then me in the speaker role, I see so many times when I need to shut my mouth and listen.

CONCLUSION

RE therapy provided John and Sara with an arena in which to express emotions, thoughts, and desires, as well as to express understanding and acceptance. Using the RE skills allowed both individuals to share concerns, problem solve, and process what were usually volatile situations. Perhaps most important, Sara was able to express her individual self (separate from John) and understand John as he was. She also experienced being heard and understood for who she was. We believe this helped her differentiate herself in the relationship, while being more fully aware of John.

After a six-week break in therapy (because of the university schedule), this couple reported that they were still able to step back and talk to each other in a more respectful manner, even in times of increased stress. At a 12-month follow-up, Sara reported that she and John had maintained their skills and the quality of their communication. If they were too angry to use RE skills, she reported, they took some time to calm themselves and then returned to the issue and use of the skills. The couple has recently made plans to marry.

It has been shown that, once acquired, RE skills have been maintained by the people who learned them (Waldo, 1989). This is thought to be the result of the rewarding responses generated by the use of these skills. When a person is empathic, the partner typically is appreciative and more cooperative, which reinforces empathic behavior. When a person is expressive, full honesty can be revealed without provoking defensiveness, criticism, and rejection in the partner, which reinforces expressiveness. Used in combination in a discussion, the skills allow a dialogue that fosters mutual respect and understanding in the relationship, which is reinforcing to both participants. In the instance of a couple of whom one member suffers from BPD, use of RE therapy may reduce the painful volatility that often pervades their relationship. This reduction itself could be highly rewarding. Moreover, use of the skills can increase differentiation and lower maladaptive dependency by the person suffering borderline symptoms, which can be experienced as a positive change for both partners. With these many reinforcing attributes, it may be expected that use of RE skills will be self-perpetuating and will be sustained when the clients are not in treatment. This appeared to be true for Sara and John.

The results derived from examination of a single case study such as this may be useful, in that they provide direction for future research. The conceptual base for the use of RE therapy in treatment of BPD seems sound. Our recent experience, although limited to only a few couples, has been positive. Future controlled research with a larger number of couples, employing a variety of assessment techniques and comparing treatment and control groups, seems warranted.

REFERENCES

American Psychiatric Association. (1994). *Diagnostic and statistical manual of mental disorders* (4th ed.). Washington, DC: Author.
Beresin, E., & Gordon, C. (1981). Emergency ward management of the borderline patient. *General Hospital Psychiatry, 3,* 237–244.

Berkowitz, M. (1985). Failure experiences in couples therapy: An overview. 92nd Annual Convention of the American Psychological Association: Failure Experiences in Couples Therapy (1984, Toronto, Canada). *Psychotherapy in Private Practice, 3(3)*, 69–73.

Bowen, M. (1978). *Family therapy in clinical practice.* New York: Jason Aronson.

Brock, G. W., & Joanning, H. (1983). A comparison of the relationship enhancement program and the Minnesota couple communication program. *Journal of Marital and Family Therapy, 9*, 413–421.

Brown, G. R., & Anderson, B. (1991). Psychiatric morbidity in adult inpatients with childhood histories of sexual and physical abuse. *American Journal of Psychiatry, 148*, 55–61.

Chessick, R. D. (1982). Intensive psychotherapy of a borderline patient. *Archives of General Psychiatry, 39*, 413–419.

Granvold, D. K. (1983). Structured separation for marital treatment and decision-making. *Journal of Marital and Family Therapy, 9*, 402–412.

Griffin, J. M., & Apostal, R. A. (1993). The influence of relationship enhancement training on differentiation of self. *Journal of Marital and Family Therapy, 19*, 267–272.

Guerney, B. G., Jr. (1977). *Relationship enhancement: Skill-training programs for therapy, problem prevention, and enrichment.* San Francisco: Jossey-Bass.

Guerney, B. G., Jr. (1987). *Relationship Enhancement: Marital/Family Therapist's Manual.* State College, PA: Ideals.

Guerney, B. G., Jr., Coufal, J., & Vogelsong, E. (1981). Relationship enhancement versus a traditional approach to therapeutic/preventative/enrichment parent-adolescent programs. *Journal of Consulting and Clinical Psychology, 49*, 927–929.

Guerney, B. G., Jr., Waldo, M., & Firestone, L. (1987). Wife-battering: A theoretical construct and case report. *American Journal of Family Therapy, 15*, 34–43.

Herman, J. L., Perry, J. C., & Van der Kolk, B. A. (1989). Childhood trauma in borderline personality disorder. *American Journal of Psychiatry, 146*, 490–495.

Jessee, R. E., & Guerney, B. G., Jr. (1981). A comparison of gestalt and relationship enhancement treatments with married couples. *American Journal of Family Therapy, 9*, 31–41.

Kernberg, O. (1975). *Borderline conditions and pathological narcissism.* New York: Jason Aronson.

Koch, A., & Ingram, T. (1985). The treatment of borderline personality disorder within a distressed relationship. *Journal of Marital and Family Therapy, 11*, 373–380.

Koenigsberg, H. W. (1984). Indications for hospitalization in the treatment of borderline patients. *Psychiatric Quarterly, 56*, 247–258.

Lachkar, J. (1984). Narcissistic borderline couples: A psychoanalytic perspective to family therapy. *International Journal of Family Psychiatry, 5*, 169–189.

Lachkar, J. (1985). Narcissistic/borderline couples: Theoretical implications for treatment. *Dynamic Psychotherapy, 3*, 109–125.

Lachkar, J. (1986). Narcissistic borderline couples: Implications for mediation. *Conciliation Courts Review, 24*, 31–38.

Levant, R. F. (1983). Client centered skills training programs for the family: A review of the literature. *Counseling Psychologist, 11*, 29–47.

Meyer, R. G. (1989). *The clinician's handbook: The psychopathology of adulthood and adolescence* (2d ed.). Boston: Allyn & Bacon.

Miller, J. B. (1985). Is conjoint therapy a viable treatment modality for individuals with narcissistic or borderline disorders? 92nd Annual Convention of the American Psychological Association: Failure Experiences in Couples Therapy (1984, Toronto, Canada). *Psychotherapy in Private Practice, 3(3),* 105–108.

Overton, D. D., & Avery, A. W. (1984). Relationship enhancement for single females: Interpersonal network intervention. *Psychology of Women Quarterly, 8,* 376–388.

Paul, M. I. (1985). Discussion of "Narcissistic/borderline couples: Theoretical implications for treatment," by Joan Lachkar. *Dynamic Psychotherapy, 3,* 126–127.

Pope, H. G., Jonas, J. M., Hudson, J. I., Cohen, B. M., & Gunderson, J. G. (1983). The validity of DSM-III borderline personality disorder: A phenomenologic, family history, treatment response, and long-term follow-up study. *Archives of General Psychiatry, 40,* 23–30.

Reid, W. H. (1989). *The treatment of psychiatric disorders: Revised for the DSM-III-R.* New York: Brunner/Mazel.

Ridley, C. A., Jorgensen, S. R., Morgan, A. C., & Avery, A. W. (1982). Relationship enhancement with premarital couples: An enhancement of effects on relationship quality. *American Journal of Family Therapy, 10,* 41–48.

Rocks, T. G., Baker, S. B., & Guerney, B. G., Jr. (1985). Effects of counselor-directed relationship enhancement training on underachieving, poorly communicating students and their teachers. *The School Counselor, 32,* 231–238.

Seeman, M. V., & Edwardes-Evans, B. (1979). Marital therapy with borderline patients: Is it beneficial? *Journal of Clinical Psychiatry, 40(7),* 308–312.

Silver, D. (1983). Psychotherapy of the characterologically difficult patient. *Canadian Journal of Psychiatry, 28,* 513–521.

Simon, J. I. (1986). Day hospital treatment for borderline adolescents. *Adolescence, 21,* 513–521.

Solomon, M. F. (1985). Treatment of narcissistic and borderline disorders in marital therapy: Suggestions toward an enhanced therapeutic approach. *Clinical Social Work Journal, 13,* 141–156.

Stern, B. A., Fromm, M. G., & Sacksteder, J. L. (1986). From coercion to collaboration: Two weeks in the life of a therapeutic community. *Psychiatry, 49,* 18–32.

Tryon, G. S., DeVito, A. J., Halligan, F. R., Kane, A. S., & Shea, J. J. (1988). Borderline personality disorder and development: Counseling university students. *Journal of Counseling and Development, 67,* 178–181.

Waldinger, R. J., & Gunderson, J. G. (1984). Completed psychotherapies with borderline patients. *American Journal of Psychotherapy, 38,* 190–202.

Waldo, M. (1988). Relationship enhancement counseling groups for wife abusers. *Journal of Mental Health Counseling, 10,* 37–45.

Waldo, M. (1989). Primary prevention in university residence halls: Paraprofessional-led relationship enhancement groups for college roommates. *Journal of Counseling and Development, 10,* 37–45.

Waldo, M., & Guerney, B. G., Jr. (1983). Marital relationship enhancement therapy in the treatment of alcoholism. *Journal of Marital and Family Therapy, 9*, 321–323.

Wonderlich, S. S., & Swift, W. J. (1990). Borderline versus other personality disorders in the eating disorders: Clinical description. *International Journal of Eating Disorders, 9*, 629–638.

CHAPTER 15

The Passive-Aggressive Couple

Steven Slavik
Jon Carlson
Len Sperry

Marital therapy with couples in which one partner uses a passive-aggressive style or passive-aggressive methods has historically proven challenging. However, if therapists formulate a treatment plan based on consistent theory, effective intervention is possible. This chapter describes the passive-aggressive personality, its Adlerian formulation and impact on a marital system, and strategies for treatment.

THE PASSIVE-AGGRESSIVE PERSONALITY

The diagnosis of Passive Aggressive Personality Disorder (American Psychiatric Association, 1987) is currently considered of doubtful validity and reliability (Fine, Overholser, & Berkoff, 1992; Millon, 1993) and has not been brought forward into DSM-IV (American Psychiatric Association, 1994). Nonetheless, there is reason to discuss treatment of an oppositional or negativistic personality (Millon, 1993). In this discussion, it is assumed that some individuals use a passive-aggressive style or methods that can be characterized as passive-aggressive (PA) and that individuals may display various degrees of PA qualities (Fine, Overholser, & Berkoff, 1992; Magnavita, 1993a).

A PA style is characterized by a hostile attitude that is expressed *indirectly and nonviolently* in resistance to demands for adequate performance in both social and occupational functioning. Typical hostile behavior includes irritability, procrastination, stubbornness, or intentional "forgetting." In various degrees ineffective in both social and occupational settings, individuals using PA methods enter therapy with anxiety or depression, with pessimism regarding the future, and generally do not see that their behavior is related to their difficulties.

Persons using this style tend to perceive other persons, themselves, the world, and life in general through a negative lens (Millon, 1993). They search for faults, flaws, mistakes, and injustices in almost any situation or environment in which they find themselves (Millon, 1981; Fine, Overholser, & Berkoff, 1992). They are indecisive and torn between hope and hopelessness, compliance and noncompliance, and action and inaction. Their ambivalence, in turn, leads to irritable moodiness, discontent, dissatisfaction, and further contrariness, frequently expressed by an individual's doing a task slowly or poorly and being unwilling to take useful suggestions.

The verbal behavior of such an individual reflects pessimism, indecisiveness, and ambivalence. Often, these individuals display negativism through incessant complaining, grumbling, and faultfinding. The content of their verbalizations usually centers on themes of being unappreciated, unloved, overworked, overburdened, unfairly treated, misused, and abused (Millon, 1981). Their nonverbal behavior includes procrastination, delaying tactics, dawdling, inefficiency, obstructionism, and errors of omission.

This behavior may serve to vent hostile, envious, or jealous feelings and aggressive striving while simultaneously permitting an individual to appear ingratiating, friendly, and even submissive. Furthermore, these tactics manipulate, maneuver, or induce others, especially those on whom the individual depends and who may be viewed as superior, to behave in a manner that will increase feelings of safety or security. If passive methods fail and anxiety and frustration mount, the individual may switch to angry, emotional outbursts centering on issues of exploitation, unfair treatment, and unappreciation.

THE ADLERIAN FORMULATION

Adlerians view individuals who use PA methods as discouraged and pessimistic about their effectiveness in life. They are unwilling to correct injustices that happen to them because these injustices prove how mistreated and ineffective they are. In addition, they do not express feelings or make wants known in order to claim their powerlessness in response to others' alleged unfair actions. Methods of depreciation of tasks of life used by these persons are those Adler called "hesitation and back and forth" and "construction of obstacles" (Adler, 1929). In these patterns, a difficulty in life is created and an attempt is made to master it. Those who fail can hesitate ambivalently before it continuously, blaming it all the while with "I tried, but the difficulty is too great," or "I tried, but others didn't want me to do it." Thus, they do not lose self-esteem and, even while engaging others in a pampering relationship, maintain distance from others no matter what the circumstances.

When these methods become persistent character traits, they are "mental readinesses" or apperceptual schemata that serve consistently to justify a hesitating or depreciating attitude in the face of a decision (Adler, 1956). In sum, an individual who uses a PA style is the "yes, but" person, one who blames others, self, or the world for difficulties. This person creates his or her own ambivalence by creating obstacles and hesitation and, thereby, justifies and excuses loss of intimacy and success in work. At the same time, the individual preserves self-esteem.

These apperceptual schemata can be thought of as rules for behavior, or *life-style convictions* (Mosak & Shulman, 1988). The individual using passive-aggressiveness has certain life-style convictions that promote and maintain PA ambivalence. He or she views him- or herself with contradictory appraisals such as, "I am competent/I am incompetent." Life appears as a bind: "Life is unfair, unpredictable, and unappreciative." Other people "try to push you around," and "You can't win." A person may conclude that the best plan is to "vacillate, temporize, oppose and anticipate disappointment and betrayal." The best plan is to sit on the fence (Sperry, 1990).

Similar formulations are noted in the cognitive therapy and transactional analysis (TA) literature. Cognitive theory describes this style in terms of guilt-inducing, helplessness-inducing, and anxiety-inducing schemata (Burns & Epstein, 1983). The TA theorist understands the dynamics as the opposition between a driver, "Try hard, struggle," and injunctions like "Don't make it" (Ware, 1983).

THE PASSIVE-AGGRESSIVE MARITAL SYSTEM

Individuals who use a PA style retain an interest in relationships. They give and receive affection, despite frequent verbal battles and outbursts in which they try to influence and coerce their partners. Interactions are intense, variable, and manipulative in an enduring, long-term relationship. There is great interpersonal ambivalence in a relationship. Their unpredictable and vacillating behavior provokes edgy discomfort and exasperation in a partner. A partner may feel uncomfortable, consistently on edge—as if nothing one can do were right, as if it were inappropriate to make demands (Millon, 1981)—and sucked in (Ware, 1983). Those using a PA style typically push a spouse to the limits of endurance.

Such individuals are ambivalent about goals and preferences in life and hide their ambivalence primarily through covert hostility toward a partner. Not knowing what they would like, they resist a partner's demands for clarity, decision, and performance. Resistance appears in issues of finances, sexual behavior, parenting, "trust," "communication," the purpose of a relationship, and other issues, in which no decisions are made or are made by default by a partner. A partner who stays in such a relationship pampers the one using passive-aggressiveness and makes use of ambivalence and indecision for his or her own purposes. The systemic features of such a relationship are subservient to goals of both members (Slavik, 1994).

Resistance to increased performance is communicated indirectly to family members whom it is likely to disturb. A covert expression of resistance has the an effect of exerting pressure on another to become more demanding or to take over and complete the task in question, depending on that person's goal. A non-PA partner may feel undermined and resentful, wondering what happened to his or her romantic ideals of marriage. But because resistance is covert, a person using PA methods is able to be nice, soft-spoken, and perhaps even reasonable, whereas a demanding party gets louder, demanding, more shrewish, more justified, or more harshly independent (Kaslow, 1983).

PA behavior is more effective in a marriage arena than assertive actions would be; otherwise, it would not be used (Burns & Epstein, 1983). It works where more assertive behavior would be undermined, disregarded, and disqualified in some fashion. In addition, being oppositional can be effective attention-getting behavior. In a family system that does not recognize good or assertive behavior and that does not support positive interactions, any attention may be better than no attention (Kaslow, 1983). It can both maximize gains and minimize losses. In short, PA transactions, whether they are representative of rigid or diffuse boundaries, and whether they appear in symmetric or complementary relationships (Watzlawick, Bavelas, & Jackson, 1967), are self-reinforcing.

This idea can be cast in DSM-IV terminology (American Psychiatric Association, 1994). Partners who tolerate the ambivalence of living with one using a PA style may have interactional styles meeting some criteria for the Compulsive Personality Disorder and be eager to criticize PA ambivalence. They may have paranoid features and be quick to respond to emotional outbursts or sullenness in kind. They may have narcissistic features and be unwilling to extricate or differentiate themselves from the ambiguities of a relationship. Or, possibly, such partners may also use passive-aggression themselves. One or the other, or both partners, may experience anxiety or depression.

GOAL OF TREATMENT

The goal of treatment must address the goal of the client. In the Adlerian formulation, the goal of the individual using PA is to salve self-esteem by prevention of failure. Ambiguity and indecision prevent failure. A partner, in some fashion, depends on this and so cooperates, for better or worse, in the treatment of his or her partner (Dreikurs, 1973). A primary difficulty presented by this couple is a power struggle or indecision, which is evidenced through specific symptomatology or issues. Accordingly, rather than any type of characterological change, specific cognitive adjustments, or specific problem-solving goal, a primary goal for therapy with this couple is *effective decision making*. This is in accord with Perry and Flannery's (1982) goal of assertiveness training for a person using PA methods. Although this chance to focus on decision making prejudices treatment selection, it is plainly necessary to make some nonglobal assumptions regarding the goal of therapy.

For the goal under consideration, conjoint marital therapy is recommended so each can learn to accommodate the partner and each other's particular issues in decision making. Through a conjoint process, a person using passive-aggressiveness may develop an interest in and capacity for self-observation. However, work with this couple will be difficult. Gehrke and Moxom (1962) suggest that the pattern of a PA marriage is never discontinued. It is, perhaps, made more tolerable through therapy.

STRATEGIES OF TREATMENT

Although research does not support any one effective treatment strategy with a couple of whom one uses passive-aggressiveness, there are several strategies presented from various perspectives.

1. Never engage passive-aggressive defenses (Magnavita, 1993b).
2. Early in therapy, differentiate hostile from assertive behavior. Encourage assertive behavior within a relationship, along with a recognition of aspects of a relationship that require compromise (The Quality Assurance Project, 1991).
3. In a marital system, the style of passive-aggressive individuals is maintained by the behavior of a partner. A partner's lack of clarity and decision in his or her life, and the likely discouragement of direct expression and resolution of anger, support a PA style.
4. Individuals using passive-aggressiveness may decompensate into anxiety and depression in order to delay change and retain a noncooperative relationship.
5. Clear limit setting is an effective technique with such individuals.

6. Be aware that such couples love to play the game of power struggle, in which the individuals using passive-aggressiveness resist authority in a "You can't make me do it" fashion. In this game, they are dependent, passive, and reactive participants, unwilling to determine useful goals for themselves when they can involve others. This forces cooperating partners to look after or respond to the individuals using PA games.

AN ADLERIAN TREATMENT PLAN

Based on Adlerian theory, which is holistic, couples treatment involving an individual who uses PA methods often includes affective, behavioral, and cognitive interventions to effect a goal of cooperative decision making. Effective decision making increases social interest and cooperative ability. The treatment plan has two aspects: first, a description of goal alignment and therapist qualities; second, a description of the therapeutic strategy.

Goal Alignment and Therapist Qualities

Goal alignment is an essential first move in avoiding confrontation and a power struggle with the couple. This is done in two respects. A therapist accepts what spouses offer as their overt goal. It may be sexual, financial, parental, or relate to household roles or other issues. A therapist is careful not to upset their goal, or he or she becomes an obstacle. If the therapist cannot work with this goal, he or she declines and refers the clients elsewhere.

In aligning goals, a therapist may encourage a time-limited contract with a definite end point, or with a definite, clear-cut result that suits the clients' goal, *in order to encourage success*. But a therapist does not impose such a contract. It may be offered paradoxically by a statement like, "I have an idea of what might help here. It has helped others, but I don't know whether you want it yet." Goal alignment also includes a clear contract regarding the therapist's job, as well as it can be defined initially. Ongoing changes should be clearly agreed upon. One should also be clear about the model of therapy used, insofar as the clients care.

Goals are also aligned through the therapist's recognition of the difficulties he or she may have in working with a couple. Therapists who likely to become frustrated in working with passive-aggression (Magnavita, 1993b) may well decline and refer. Burns and Epstein (1983) offer an approach to how therapists can help themselves in this event. To avoid being stymied by a couple, therapists need certain personal qualities: they are clear, unambiguous, and use transparent activity in therapy; they engage with goodwill, warmth, friendliness, even playfulness and humor; and they are able to back down easily and lose a power struggle without rancor. A specific technique therapists master to their advantage is the Disarming Technique (Burns & Epstein, 1983), in which a client is always right. Therapists must be alert to sideshows (Adler, 1956), which are described by Burns and Epstein (1983) as "cognitive distortions" and in TA literature as "games" (Bonds-White, 1984). Therapists must also be alert to and able to use their own feelings of irritation and satisfaction therapeutically, that is, as cues that something needs to be done or has been done (Magnavita, 1993b).

In general, therapy should be managed so as to ensure that frustration and anxiety, which draw out the worst from both client and therapist, do not appear in a therapy session. Proper goal alignment, limit setting, goodwill, humor, and ease will help to ensure that clients return to therapy sessions. Limit setting, transparency, immediate clarification of therapist/client interactions when needed, as well as prompt clarification of frequently transgressed limits, serve to disperse covert client anger. Burns and Epstein (1983) discuss the issue of anger in detail and outline techniques to clarify PA anger. The focus here, however, is task effectiveness. Perry and Flannery (1982) and Adler (1946) assert that anger decreases as task effectiveness increases, and is not the focus in working with persons using PA methods.

Strategy

The general strategy of therapy addresses how partners discourage, rather than encourage, each other. Each calls out the worst in the other, and each helps to provide the circumstance that brings out the worst behavior of the other. The general alternative to aim for is how each can encourage the other, pulling encouragement from each in return. It is a therapy that slowly and carefully guides a person to use the partner as a mirror for evaluating his or her own behavior. This is a specification of Dreikurs's (1946) statement that in marriage one does what one likes best, but not what is not to the liking of one's partner.

Current thinking (Beutler & Clarkin, 1990) strongly favors initial behavioral therapy with this couple. Eventually, should clients continue, therapy will be cognitively and affectively oriented. It will, to some extent, be all of these at any given time, not only because of the Adlerian model, but because of the practical facts of therapy. Therapy will be psychoeducational about self, the other, and relationships.

Treatment strategy must be aimed at specific obstacles to treatment of the PA style. Passive-aggressive individuals typically view all problems in a relationship as the partner's. The world must adjust to them; they do not need to adjust to the world. They justify this stance with beliefs regarding their "integrity," their difficulty in changing habits, the obduracy of the world or of the partner, their fear of being overwhelmed, anger, blame, and an aggrieved attitude: "Why must it always be me who changes?" In due time, all this may be interpreted to them as pessimism regarding their efficacy in the world.

There are at least three ways of conducting behavioral therapy that will be useful with this couple. With a somewhat compliant couple, one might take a direct method. If they are somewhat noncompliant, an indirect method may be more fruitful.

Direct Method

A direct method emphasizes contracting. The therapist can find a contract that both members of the couple agree will bring about desirable change in the issue they present: If she does A, he will do B. This task should he emphasized until it is performed well enough for the couple to call it a success. The therapist should, lightheartedly and humorously, ignore diversions and resistance as much as possible (Perry & Flannery, 1982) and should avoid being stymied by a couple by staying "one down."

Other behavioral methods are also useful. Practice in carrying out a contract between the couple can be assigned. In-session role enactments can clarify a contract and subsequent responses. Contracts can include withdrawal of reinforcement: If she does not do A, but does B instead, he will do C. Direct instruction regarding the consequences of behavior, as well as plain advice, is possible. Self-monitoring by a person using PA methods, at least early in therapy, may be contraindicated but acceptable to a dependent partner. Shaping behavior may help,but it is best to keep a contract simple enough so as to know without ambiguity whether or not it has been met. Disclosing self-talk, fantasies, feelings, and covert agendas can be useful when one is discussing either success or failure in meeting a contract during practice. Cognitive distortions and life-style convictions will become apparent and can be either ignored or treated lightly as excuses. Good-humored discussion of how one or the other can, would, or might sabotage tasks and contracts, and how the other partner might respond, is useful in keeping on track. However, early in therapy, the goal is to keep the process clear, simple, and, above all, successful.

Difficulties to be expected with a direct method are failure to contract, inasmuch as that is the original issue, and failure to comply with assignments. These failures are mutually supported PA games (Bonds-White, 1984). Thus, to avoid PA resistance, it is important to contract for minimum changes that will be felt as useful. The therapist's reminding the couple of an agreed-upon contract and dealing with consequent anger in session can also help in dealing with these difficulties.

Indirect Method

An indirect method is paradoxical. It does not immediately address a given issue; rather, it attempts to develop a more cooperative attitude in a couple. It involves a strategy such as the following:

> At the end of a first session, with your hand on the doorknob, let drop to the individual using a PA style, "I know you're not ready for this yet, but I know a way for your partner to get his (her) act together easily." In the next session, reluctantly let the PA individual drag from you a prescription for performing one specific cold, hostile behavior (as defined on Kiesler's [1983] Interpersonal Circle) that is more intense than any he or she already performs. The usual "go slow" and paradoxical reasons must be given to the PA person to justify the prescription.

This is a specific strategy for putting a client in control of a symptom (Sherman & Fredman, 1986). If he or she performs the suggested behavior, the partner will respond in the usual way, and both may realize that this type of behavior is controllable. If the client does not do it, the couple may reduce the intensity of their usual behavior, or get closer to understanding, and they may get an idea that such behavior is controllable. No matter what the result, the therapist then has both members discuss the covert agendas that this process makes available.

As the therapist's knowledge of a non-PA partner increases, he or she might slowly change the prescription to provide something warm and friendly for the person using a PA style to do that would please the partner. These moves initiate partners' training in how to elicit from each other a minimal desired behavioral change regarding a specific issue. A possible difficulty is that these individuals may not effect changes if they think they must do so in order for the partner to behave in an encouraging manner. This would violate their premise that life must be demanding and one must be contrary. If so, "go slow" is a viable injunction to both therapist and clients.

Another paradoxical technique is to prescribe specific games clients play, or merely indecision. The exact technique can be modified from Sherman and Fredman's (1986) prescription regarding indecision. The timing of prescribing a game or indecision is important, however. Because of the inflexibility of a PA couple, a prescription given too early may not moderate the game playing or indecision (Lansky, 1986). It may simply produce justification for a PA position, rather than detachment or blocking.

Intermediate Method

An intermediate method is a structural family therapy method incorporating TA methods. It begins with *noticing*. The therapist and both clients begin by noticing the couple's actual behavior and transactional patterns. The therapist must notice his or her own behavior so as to avoid intervening precipitously; he or she must be able to sustain a certain amount of anxiety or frustration without responding to "fix" a couple. The therapist helps clients notice their transactional patterns without prejudice or blame and without arousing resistance. If the therapist maintains an attitude of warm, friendly *curiosity* about what is happening—with him- or herself and with clients—he or she can encourage the clients' own curiosity and ability to notice (Slavik, 1994).

A pertinent question that can be used in various ways is, "How do you respond (think, feel, behave) when he (she) does that?" The therapist points out patterns, at a pace at which both he or she and the clients can accept seeing them. The therapist helps clients to label such patterns with humor so that they can refer to them with ease, and helps clients to notice whether these are task-effective or task-avoiding patterns. This approach may include the use of anger by either partner. He or she also helps clients to discuss the intrapersonal consequences of each other's behavior, including covert agendas, maladaptive thinking, and cognitive distortions. The therapist elicits the partners' explanations for their own and each other's behavior. Any interpretations a therapist offers must be very concrete and based on what is accepted by and obvious to both clients. At this point, the therapist might use a distinction between hostile and assertive behavior, but may decide to refer only to task-effective and task-avoiding behavior.

Eventually the therapist and the couple approach alternatives to a given behavior. The therapist may encourage this by asking each, "How would you prefer to behave, and how would you prefer your partner to behave?" and "How can you encourage that behavior in your partner?" Specific, acceptable combinations of initiation and/or response can be elicited.

A number of exercises can be used effectively in this method; the therapist may be familiar with those described in Sherman and Fredman (1986). In the initial stages, having a couple role-play each other, and then themselves, may be helpful. Later, modeling and practicing their games and new behavior are vital. With the passive-agressive couple, however, exercises must be used to clarify specific issues or task-avoiding interactions within the relationship. They must be presented with specific aims so as not to arouse resistance.

A difficulty that may be expected in this therapy is that unless the therapist is alert to the couple's games, a therapy session can circle fruitlessly. Yet, if the therapist intervenes too quickly, clients do not notice their own games or find their own solutions. Hence, this method may be slower than behavioral contracting and clients may begin to feel discouraged. On the other hand, for them to find their own way out of such discouragement can itself be effective therapy.

Termination

Adlerians believe that cognitive and affective adjustments will be made if behavioral adjustments are secure. However, in order to gain further and generalized control over their behavior in a relationship, individuals must notice how they attempt to elicit complementary behavior (Kiesler, 1983) from each other in order to identify the other as an obstacle and to justify blame. They must then be able to understand to some degree, how they would prefer the partner to behave and to learn what it would take for them to encourage the behavior they want from each other. Only then can they teach each other to be encouraging rather than discouraging. However, they first need to have had some experience in noticing themselves in relationship and the difficulties they have in modifying their own behavior—that is, their difficulties must have become somewhat ego-dystonic, rather than ammunition or an excuse for that behavior.

A way to enter into a more insightful therapy is to focus on questions of the costs and benefits of the cycles of task-avoiding behavior that clients engage in and, further, why they refuse to change or have difficulty in changing their behavior even when their partners can tell them how to elicit the desired responses from them. The former clarifies the goal for each. The latter naturally leads to a discussion of "how I've always been." At this point, an Adlerian life-style (Mosak & Shulman, 1988), a Bowenian intergenerational genogram (Kerr & Bowen, 1988), a cognitive-behavioral approach (Burns & Epstein, 1983), or an Intensive Short-Term Dynamic Psychotherapy approach (Magnavita, 1993b, 1994) can be proposed to the clients to further their understanding of how each operates in the world.

CASE STUDY

Jim and Judy had been married for almost 20 years when couples therapy began. Judy, 39, was trained as a nurse; however, she had stopped her career 16 years ago to raise their two daughters, now ages 16 and 12. Recently, Judy has gone back to college for a one-year refresher course to regain her nursing certification. Jim, 40, also works in the medical field.

When the couple came for the first session of therapy, it was on an exploratory basis. They were looking for a new therapist. Previously, they had been working with a human potential specialist who also claimed to be a marital therapist. The couple had seen her for two months, when Jim informed Judy that he had been having an affair with a woman he had met at a human potential seminar eight months before. As treatment continued, it was explained, Jim had also been seeing the human potential therapist with his girlfriend to help him decide just what he should do in regard to whether to continue the marriage. Judy was furious; she thought that the therapist had a conflict of interests and refused to continue. She wanted to see whether she could find an ethical therapist.

The first session involved the new therapist's answering three pages of single-spaced questions that Judy had compiled. At the end of the session, Judy said that she would get back to the therapist after the couple had had a chance to go over the answers and discuss the situation. Four hours later she called, indicating that both she and her husband would like to continue treatment. For the next session, the couple came together and their marital issues were discussed. At this meeting it was decided that each would have weekly individual therapy and—when (and if) Jim ended his affair—couple therapy. Psychological assessment revealed that Judy had an obsessive-compulsive personality disorder and Jim had a passive-aggressive personality disorder.

Both Jim and Judy were raised in a father-absent home (both fathers died at a young age), and both were, therefore, raised in a family with a very strong mother figure. Judy was not sure what a father's role was, and being a father was not a role that Jim had experienced in his mother-governed house. Jim needed to learn how to express his anger directly. Although he often claimed not to understand, when pushed he was quickly able to come up with explanations of some of the things that happened that bothered him.

The presenting issues appeared to be that Judy was very angry at Jim's affair and the fact that she could no longer trust him. She was upset with his undependable nature. He often said one thing and did another, and she found it hard to pin him down whenever she asked him questions. Jim entered therapy with many health-related issues that he used as excuses. His major issue with Judy was that she overfunctioned at home. She did everything, including taking all responsibility for their two children. When Judy had free time, she spent it as a volunteer at the local Catholic church. She was greatly involved with all aspects of volunteer work. At one session, Jim reported that it was as if she were married to the church and not to him. He resented this greatly.

Early in therapy it became clear that boundaries were a major issue. Although Judy was very upset with Jim, she never followed through on her threats and he did not take her seriously. When it became apparent that Jim was not willing to stop his relationship with the other woman, Judy was confronted with having to make good on her threat that he would have to leave. Finally, after two sessions, Judy had the courage to establish a boundary and to follow through on what she said. Jim moved out but soon found that he spent most of his time at home, and within a short period of time he was living more at home than in his new apartment. However, he was continuing his relationship with the other woman. After two months of this behavior, Judy finally said that he must go, and this time she was unwilling to let him return to the home. He could visit the children whenever he wished, but visits must occur outside the home. After a three-week period, Jim indicated that he really wanted to try again, that he was willing to end the affair and begin marital therapy.

Couple therapy proceeded very slowly. At one point the couple decided to go away for a weekend. Judy, with her obsessive-compulsive nature, had the time planned out and Jim indicated that he agreed with her plans. Jim returned home from work two hours late with seven different excuses as to why he had not arrived at the agreed-upon time. This behavior bothered Judy immensely; however, she tried to be the perfect wife and act as though she understood and that it did not matter. That night the couple got to the motel and had a nice meal, but when love making occurred, he finished very quickly and indicated that he was just too tired to meet her needs. The next day the couple decided to surprise each other; each was to go to a bookstore to buy a book that he or she would really like the partner to read. Judy bought Jim a book about Ireland, his ancestors' native land, a place he had often wanted to visit. Jim bought Judy a book on being a nun in the Catholic church. Although this appeared to be a nice gift, he was just continuing to endorse her trend of being "holier than thou."

During the course of therapy it was possible to help the couple step back and look at what the real issues were: what it was that Judy did that made Jim want to hurt her, what it was that Jim did that hurt Judy in a manner she could not deal with. The subtleties of Judy's put-downs, her not allowing a place for Jim to be in the family, and the subtleties of his hurting her back soon became apparent. Jim stopped complaining about work, which was a common weapon that he used to upset Judy. Judy stopped being so involved in church. A solution was negotiated whereby Jim did not have to attend all church functions, but should go half the time. Jim became more of a father to his children. Judy decided to return to nursing school to prepare for going back to full-time work. This decision necessitated a role reversal; because Judy attended school on weekends, Jim would have to be actively involved with chauffeuring and monitoring the children's many activities: In addition, he had to take increasing responsibility for activities in the house during the week so that Judy could study. Although this arrangement was a burden for both of them,—for Judy, in letting Jim function this way and for Jim in taking on a new role—with time they both began to report a benefit. At last contact, Judy had finished her nursing program; however, she began to work, which made her still unavailable. Therefore, Jim had to continue having a real role in his family.

The dynamics of this case were worked on in both individual and couple therapy. It is very unlikely that Jim or Judy would have changed if either had been engaged in only one modality of treatment.

CONCLUSION

An Adlerian therapy is recommended for couples in which one partner uses a PA style, because it addresses directly the purpose of ambivalence and how both behavioral patterns and cognitive patterns are subservient to a goal of ambivalence. Without addressing purpose, symptom or method substitution is likely to occur without lasting change. First-order change may occur, but not second-order change (Kern & Wheeler, 1977).

In life-style work with such a couple, the emphasis is on how both the couple's difficulties and their good times with each other are a result of their life-styles (Slavik, 1994). They provoke each other because it suits their purposes. They let themselves feel good when the other behaves a certain way and let themselves feel bad when the other behaves differently. Then they can demand one way and reject the other, attributing both feelings to the partner's behavior. In a covertly aloof, harmful, and antagonistic rejection of the partner's undesired behavior and their covert demands for desired behavior, they elicit cold and hostile responses from the partner. It suits the purposes of those using PA methods to elicit cold and hostile responses from a partner in order to create obstacles, just as it suits the partner's goal to return those responses. In this way, a guideline of creating obstacles can be clarified, as well as the cognitive/affective/behavioral unity of the personality, and eventually the couple's ambivalence and the games they use to protect it can be addressed.

REFERENCES

Adler, A. (1929). *The practice and theory of individual psychology.* London: Kegan Paul.

Adler, A. (1946). *Understanding human nature.* New York: Greenberg.

Adler, A. (1956). *The individual psychology of Alfred Adler. A systematic presentation in selections from his writings.* H. L. Ansbacher & R. R. Ansbacher (Eds.). New York: Basic Books.

American Psychiatric Association. (1987). *Diagnostic and statistical manual of mental disorders* (3d ed., revised). Washington, DC: Author.

American Psychiatric Association. (1994). *Diagnostic and statistical manual of mental disorders* (4th ed.). Washington, DC: Author.

Beutler, L. E., & Clarkin, J. F. (1990). *Systematic treatment selection: Toward targeted therapeutic interventions*. New York: Brunner/Mazel.

Bonds-White, F. (1984). The special it: The passive-aggressive personality. Part I. *Transactional Analysis Journal, 14*(2), 124–130.

Burns, D. D., & Epstein, N. (1983). Passive-aggressiveness: A cognitive-behavioral approach. In R. D. Parsons & R. J. Wicks (Eds.), *Passive-aggressiveness: Theory and Practice* (pp. 72–97). New York: Brunner/Mazel.

Dreikurs, R. (1946). *The challenge of marriage*. New York: Hawthorn/Dutton.

Dreikurs, R. (1973). *Psychodynamics, psychotherapy, and counseling*. Chicago: Alfred Adler Institute.

Fine, M. A., Overholser, J. C., & Berkoff, K. (1992). Diagnostic validity of the passive-aggressive personality disorder: Suggestions for reform. *American Journal of Psychotherapy, 46*(3), 470–484.

Gehrke, S., & Moxom, J. (1962). Diagnostic classification and treatment techniques in marriage counseling. *Family Process, 1*, 253–264.

Kaslow, F. W. (1983). Passive-aggressiveness: An intrapsychic, interpersonal, and transactional dynamic in the family system. In R. D. Parsons & R. J. Wicks (Eds.), *Passive-aggressiveness: Theory and practice* (pp. 134–152). New York: Brunner/Mazel.

Kern, R. M., & Wheeler, M. S. (1977). Autocratic vs. democratic child rearing practices: An example of second-order change. *Journal of Individual Psychology, 33*(2), 223–232.

Kerr, M. E., & Bowen, M. (1988). *Family evaluation: An approach based on Bowen theory*. New York: W. W. Norton.

Kiesler, D. J. (1983). The 1982 interpersonal circle: A taxonomy for complementarity in human transactions. *Psychological Review, 90*(3), 185–213.

Lansky, M. R. (1986). Marital therapy for narcissistic disorders. In N. S. Jacobson & A. S. Gurman (Eds.), *Clinical handbook of marital therapy* (pp. 557–574). New York: Guilford.

Magnavita, J. J. (1993a). The treatment of passive-aggressive personality disorder: A review of current approaches. Part I. *International Journal of Short-Term Psychotherapy, 8*, 29–41.

Magnavita, J. J. (1993b). The treatment of passive-aggressive personality disorder: Intensive short-term dynamic psychotherapy. Part II. Trial therapy. *International Journal of Short-Term Psychotherapy, 8*, 93–106.

Magnavita, J. J. (1994). The process of working through and outcome: The treatment of passive-aggressive personality disorder with intensive short-term dynamic psychotherapy. Part III. *International Journal of Short-Term Psychotherapy, 9*, 1–17.

Millon, T. (1981). *Disorders of personality: DSM-III: Axis II*. New York: John Wiley & Sons.

Millon, T. (1993). Negativistic (passive-aggressive) personality disorder. *Journal of Personality Disorders, 7*,(1), 78–85.

Mosak, H. H., & Shulman, B. H. (1988). *Life style analysis*. Muncie, IN: Accelerated Development.

Perry, J. C., & Flannery, R. B. (1982). Passive-aggressive personality disorder: Treatment implications of a clinical typology. *Journal of Nervous and Mental Disease, 170*(3), 164–173.

Sherman, R., & Fredman, N. (1986). *Handbook of structured techniques in marriage and family therapy*. New York: Brunner/Mazel.

Slavik, S. (1994). Intimacy as a goal and tool in Adlerian couples therapy. *The Canadian Journal of Adlerian Psychology, 23*(2), 65–78.

Sperry, L. (1990). Personality disorders: Biopsychosocial descriptions and dynamics. *Individual Psychology, 46*(2), 193–202.

The Quality Assurance Project. (1991). Treatment outlines for avoidant, dependent and passive-aggressive personality disorders. *Australian and New Zealand Journal of Psychiatry, 25*, 401–411.

Ware, P. (1983). Personality adaptations (doors to therapy). *Transactional Analysis Journal, 13*(1), 11–19.

Watzlawick, P., Bavelas, J. B., & Jackson, D. D. (1967). *Pragmatics of human communication*. New York: W. W. Norton.

CHAPTER 16

The Dependent/Narcissistic Couple

A. Rodney Nurse

The dependent female and the narcissistic male are "made for each other." They constitute a fine couple if consistency with some traditional gender stereotyping is the standard. She focuses her nurturance, warmth, and attention on him, while leaning on him to gain her sense of self. She may be referred to as the "little woman," the "helpmate," needing the presence of a strong and noble hero. She is supportive of him and his efforts. He, in turn, can be independent, self-focused, seeking power and prestige (particularly as long as he can depend on her depending on him). Any dimming in the light of this star can be reversed by the adoration of his satellite spouse spinning around him. He can protect her, she can depend on him.

All of these characteristics in moderation are, or at least have been, applauded as appropriate for a female in many parts of our culture. A male's appearing supremely confident, having a firm faith in himself, making commitments, having goals, assuming natural leadership, going "where no man has gone before," tend to be viewed as male attributes and are rewarded in our culture for men in particular; old Western movies seem to be replete with such heros. Where these dependent and narcissistic styles of behaviors are reinforced by contemporary societal male/female stereotypes, they may prove to be adaptable to many of life's conditions, at least initially, before children are born to a couple and before much individualizing development of the couple as adults takes place. As definite disorders, such styles of course, often mean problems from the beginning.

THE DEPENDENT PERSONALITY DISORDER

The DSM-IV briefly describes Dependent Personality Disorder as "a pattern of submissive and clinging behavior related to an excessive need to be taken care of" (American Psychiatric Association, 1994, p. 629). The diagnostic criteria for Dependent Personality Disorder are shown in Exhibit 16.1.

The DSM-IV description of Dependent Personality Disorder contains numerous cautions against overdiagnosing this disorder. Judgment is needed to ascertain whether the degree of dependence is beyond what would be expected for others who are from similar cultural backgrounds, who have illnesses, or who are elderly, for example.

The actual prevalence of this frequently diagnosed disorder seems not to vary by sex, according to the DSM-IV (American Psychiatric Association, 1994, p. 667), even though one cultural stereotype for females emphasizes dependence. In this writer's experience, focusing now on couples who come for therapy in a suburban upper-middle-class setting, those diagnosed with Dependent Personality Disorder are more often women. These dependent women are frequently married to or living with men diagnosed as narcissistic; hence, these couples are the basis for this chapter.

Consistent with this writer's experience is the opinion of a leading personality theorist (whose theoretical framework is described subsequently):

> More women than men develop the dependent pattern. Some theorists attribute this fact to an inherent dependent predisposition on the part of the female sex. Equally plausible is the thesis that the cultural roles that are sanctioned in most societies reinforce the learning of the dependent behaviors among women (Millon, 1996, p. 349).

THE NARCISSISTIC PERSONALITY DISORDER

The DSM-IV briefly describes the Narcissistic Personality Disorder as "a pattern of grandiosity, need for admiration, and lack of empathy" (American Psychiatric Association, 1994, p. 629). The diagnostic criteria for Narcissistic Personality Disorder appear in Exhibit 16.2.

The DSM-IV states that 50 to 75 percent of those diagnosed with Narcissistic Personality Disorder are male (American Psychiatric Association, 1994, p. 660). In the upper-middle-class suburban area where the writer practices, this diagnosis appears relatively more frequently with males than with females. Of course, it is important to determine the extent to which indications of narcissism are aspects of the personality style, but with failure to reach the diagnostic threshold, or whether such

Exhibit 16.1
DEPENDENT PERSONALITY DISORDER
(American Psychiatric Association, 1994)

A pervasive and excessive need to be taken care of that leads to submissive and clinging behavior and fears of separation [in the patient], beginning by early adulthood and present in a variety of contexts, as indicated by five (or more) of the following:

1. Has difficulty making everyday decisions without an excessive amount of advice and reassurance from others

2. Needs others to assume responsibility for most major areas of his or her life

3. Has difficulty expressing disagreement with others because of fear of loss of support or approval (**Note:** Do not include realistic fears of retribution.)

4. Has difficulty initiating projects or doing things on his or her own (because of a lack of self-confidence in judgment or abilities rather than a lack of motivation or energy)

5. Goes to excessive lengths to obtain nurturance and support from others, to the point of volunteering to do things that are unpleasant

6. Feels uncomfortable or helpless when alone because of exaggerated fears of being unable to care for himself or herself

7. Urgently seeks another relationship as a source of care and support when a close relationship ends

8. Is unrealistically preoccupied with fears of being left to take care of himself or herself

categorization of the disorder may legitimately be made. Sometimes, when a person has achieved, going to the "right" school and university, joining the "right" fraternity or sorority, and establishing a clearly successful "career path" with an accompanying sense of superiority, entitlement, and snobbishness, it is difficult to separate style from disorder

Exhibit 16.2
NARCISSISTIC PERSONALITY DISORDER
(American Psychiatric Association, 1994)

A pervasive pattern of grandiosity (in fantasy or behavior), need for admiration, and lack of empathy [in the patient], beginning by early adulthood and present in a variety of contexts, as indicated by five (or more) of the following:

(1) Has a grandiose sense of self-importance (e.g., exaggerates achievements and talents, expects to be recognized as superior without commensurate achievements)

(2) Is preoccupied with fantasies of unlimited success, power, brilliance, beauty, or ideal love

(3) Believes that he or she is "special" and unique and can only be understood by, or should associate with, other special or high-status people (or institutions)

(4) Requires excessive admiration

(5) Has a sense of entitlement, i.e., unreasonable expectations of especially favorable treatment or automatic compliance with his or her expectations

(6) Is interpersonally exploitative, i.e., takes advantage of others to achieve his or her own ends

(7) Lacks empathy; is unwilling to recognize or identify with the feelings and needs of others

(8) Is often envious of others or believes that others are envious of him or her

(9) Shows arrogant, haughty behaviors or attitudes

in this subcultural context without looking closely at the quality and process of the marital relationship. The narcissistic pattern appears to be mainly typical of North America; it has not been deemed sufficiently prevalent internationally to be included in the International Classification of Diseases-10 (ICD-10).

One conjecture is that the prevalence of the narcissistic style or disorder may be attributed in part to a historical hangover in that narcissistic qualities, as in the Western movies noted earlier, were the very same qualities that were needed for survival and achievement when the North American West was "conquered" in the last century. Another hypothesis, perhaps equally plausible, is that what we call narcissism in egalitarian North America may in other parts of the world be associated with upper-class behavior, so that it is not considered psychopathological but is considered culturally syntonic.

THEORETICAL CONSIDERATIONS: A BASIS FOR COUPLES ANALYSIS

Following Kurt Lewin's (1936) dictum, written more than a half century ago, that "there is nothing so practical as a good theory," this chapter briefly reviews the theoretical underpinnings of the Dependent and Narcissistic Disorders with reference to the DSM-IV criteria (American Psychiatric Association, 1994). For this undertaking, *Disorders of Personality, DSM-IV and Beyond* (second edition), by Theodore Millon (1996), will serve as a guide (there is every reason to believe that the long-range professional acceptance of this book will rival, if not surpass, Millon's initial classic volume (1981) which went through 21 printings). After briefly considering the individual dependent and narcissistic personality cardinal types, their prime variants, and their qualities, the following sections of this chapter describe the dependent/narcissistic couple system and offer recommendations for treatment, with examples.

THE MILLON THEORY OF PERSONALITY DISORDERS

Whereas the DSM-IV provides an overview of the Dependent and Narcissistic Disorders, focusing on description and diagnostic criteria, Millon's recent writing in *Disorders of Personality, DSM-IV and Beyond*, second edition (1996) supplies a fuller theoretical and clinical view of these disorders. Furthermore, there is room within his theoretical approach for blends of these cardinal types, such as are often seen in the reality of the clinical consulting room. These blends include patterns such as those exemplified by the dependent person who is also avoidant, and the narcissistic person who is also histrionic. Millon's work informs us about etiology, along with analysis, resting on the standard of three major personality polarities:

Pleasure (enhancement)/pain (preservation)
Passive (accommodation)/active (modification)
Self (individuation)/other (nurturance)

Millon's book supplies a complex and in-depth clinical net for thinking about human personality and disorder. Although the book is focused on the individual, it does supply a useful basis, because of its breadth and depth, for designing treatment interventions with a couple.

DEPENDENT PERSONALITY: ELEMENTS PULLING TOWARD A NARCISSISTIC MATE

Following Millon (1996), clinical domains may be subdivided into four levels: behavioral, phenomenological, intrapsychic, and biophysical.

The dependent personality may be observed as *behaviorally expressively incompetent*, thus withdrawing from adult responsibilities, calling for another to take over. The dependent person is *behaviorally interpersonally submissive*; seeking advice and reassurance and subordinating self to another are characteristic. Thus, in a relationship, there is a powerful pull to have a seemingly strong "other" to fill the void of behavioral incompetence; the narcissist can well fit this need.

Phenomenologically, the dependent personality is *cognitively naive* in that the thinking process is characterized by seeking to avoid any thoughts of difference from the "other" that might lead to a recognition of independence and, hence, probable rejection. Thus it is important for the dependent person to retain *an inept self-image*. Just as the self-image remains inept and therefore immature, images of others remain *immature* in the dependent person's mind, with the images retaining a more childlike character. This immaturity calls for a strong-appearing person with special qualities—the narcissist is one appearing to be so.

According to Millon's theory, *intrapsychically* the dependent personality possesses an *intrapsychic mechanism* that "is firmly devoted to another to strengthen the belief that an inseparable bond exists between them" (Millon, 1996, p. 332). Correlatively, the dependent person's personality has *an inchoate organization* because of the underdeveloped potentials for independent functioning. The characteristics of the narcissist appear to be the reverse of these qualities.

Finally, the dependent personality may be seen at the *biophysical level* to be characterized by *a pacific mood*; qualities of warmth, tenderness, and noncompetitiveness may be anticipated, which can be matched by the surface tranquillity of the narcissist.

NARCISSISTIC PERSONALITY: ELEMENTS PULLING TOWARD A DEPENDENT MATE

As with the dependent personality, the complexity of the narcissistic personality may be subdivided into four levels: behavioral, phenomenological, intrapsychic, and biophysical (Millon, 1996, p. 405).

The narcissistic personality may be seen *behaviorally* as *expressively haughty*, acting in an arrogant, sometimes pompous, and frequently disdainful manner, "flouting the conventional rules of shared living" in spousal relationships (Millon, 1996, p. 405). He (more frequently male, as noted earlier) is *interpersonally exploitive*, behaving in a fashion to indicate that he is entitled to special considerations while not sharing reciprocal responsibilities with his mate; this spells a complementary but asymmetrical relationship (although one not characterized by malice). Maintaining these characteristics of haughtiness and interpersonal exploitiveness in an intimate relationship requires that the "other" look up to him from a position of helplessness. The dependent person's submissive attitude and allowance for some degree of self-denigration in order to keep the relationship make the dependent person an attractive mate for the narcissist.

At a *phenomenologic* level, the narcissistic personality is *cognitively expansive*, fed by self-glorifying fantasies of success, beauty, or love, minimally constrained by reality. These cognitions, in turn, serve to maintain and expand *an admirable self-image*, a sense of being special, but without commensurate achievement. Given this internal "house of cards," the narcissist's internalized representations—memories of past relationships—are contrived and reshaped to meet his needs of the moment. This expansive structure calls for external support, which can be naturally provided by a dependent partner's focus on the other's positive, if grandiose, expressions.

Intrapsychically, the narcissistic personality must rationalize to present himself consistently in a favorable light to himself and others. There is a *spurious* quality to his personality organization, wherein coping and defensive strategies are unsubstantial, easily overriding potential inner conflicts and failures and quickly covering over psychic wounds, providing an appearance of seeming solidity, which is attractive to the personally unsure dependent person.

Considered at a *biophysical* level, the narcissist ordinarily appears unflappable, cool, and unimpressionable—except for brief periods of rage, shame, or emptiness when wounded—labeled by Millon as an *insouciant* mood (1996, p. 405). This mood calls for someone who will smooth over any troubled waters and not challenge him, such as a dependent partner.

THE RELATIONAL SYSTEM IN THE DEPENDENT/NARCISSISTIC COUPLE

Exhibit 16.3 provides a schematic presentation of the relationships in a dependent/narcissistic couple, with reference to the four levels and various domains of personality for these cardinal types, as discussed earlier. The exhibit places the levels and domains next to each other so as to suggest patterns of how the personality patterns dovetail.

It is probably most useful in studying any couple relationship to first look at the Behavioral Level, summarized in Exhibit 16.3, for the dependent/narcissistic couple. Expressively, the dependent person's helplessness meshes with the seemingly extra-competent behavior of the narcissist. Interpersonally, the dependent spouse's submissiveness is a perfect fit with the exploitive, entitled behavior of the narcissist.

In treating some dependent/narcissistic couples it may be useful for the clinician to look next at the Phenomenological Level of personality organization, but it may pay greater dividends to move to the Intrapsychic Level. The dependent person's experience of having an inseparable bond with the spouse may well be felt by the narcissist as love focused on him, as he focuses so much on himself, lacking empathy with his dependent partner. The personality organization of the dependent person is underdeveloped, but so in actuality is the narcissist's, despite a solid appearance on the surface. It may be that an unconscious collusion provides that neither pushes the other, in the sense of in-depth personality exploration, so that their flawed development does not rise to distinct awareness and their flawed images of self and other may be maintained.

With the dependent person's calm mood and the feigned tranquillity of the narcissist evident at the Biophysical Level, a couple of this type appear to have a very nonconflictual, warm relationship. Others may even envy their apparently smooth relationship. When others know them more closely, they may recognize that such calmness covers a lack of depth in the relationship.

Phenomenologically, while the dependent person is having unduly agreeable thoughts aimed at the partner, the narcissistic partner is expansive

Exhibit 16.3
RELATIONSHIP SYSTEM OF THE
DEPENDENT/NARCISSISTIC COUPLE

	Dependent Spouse	Narcissistic Spouse
Behavioral Level		
Expressively:	Incompetent, helpless	Haughty, extra-competent
Interpersonally:	Submissive, needs strong other	Exploitive, entitled, unempathetic
Phenomenological Level		
Cognitively:	Naive, overagreeable thoughts	Expansive, self-glorifying thoughts
Self-Image:	Inept, inadequate	Admirable, special
Internalizations:	Immature images, easily overwhelmed	Contrived, readily refashioned
Intrapsychic Level		
Mechanism:	Inseparable bond with other	Rationalizations, Self-focused
Organization:	Inchoate, underdeveloped	Spurious, solid look yet flimsy actually
Biophysical Level		
Mood:	Pacific, warm, noncompetitive	Insouciant, feigned tranquillity

Note: The contents of this exhibit are adapted from *Disorders of Personality: DSM-IV and Beyond,* Chapters 9 and 11 (Millon, 1996).

and self-glorifying in his own thoughts. Also complementary are the dependent spouse's inept self-image and the narcissist's overrated self-image. This couple also fit in the sense that, aided by immature images, the dependent person can easily feel overwhelmed and, at the same time, overawed by how readily the narcissist can fashion a self-image to meet the moment. Thus, the dependent partner gains by focusing on the other in an admiring way, while the narcissist gains by quickly changing to meet a given situation, without having to struggle deeply to keep up with changing circumstances. Of course, in the long run, both lose by adopting this avoidance and rationalization rather than struggling to reshape their self-images at some depth.

A statement by Millon summarizes the essence of this couple's relationship, although it is given from the narcissist's viewpoint. Narcissists "frequently select a dependent mate who will be obeisant, solicitous, and subservient, without expecting anything in return except strength and assurances of fidelity" (Millon, 1996, p. 406). Dependent persons, states Millon, "have learned to play their 'inferior' role well. They are able, therefore, to provide their 'superior' partners with the feeling of being useful, sympathetic, stronger, and competent—precisely those behaviors that dependents seek in their mates." (Millon, 1996, p. 333). Who is more dependent, the dependent person or the narcissist?

AN APPROACH TO TREATMENT

In an initial appointment with a dependent/narcissistic couple, as with other couples, the therapist establishes a therapeutic contract. The focus of treatment is to be on the disturbed marital relationship. However, no sooner is this focus established than the therapist proposes that emphasis be placed on each individual's needs, requiring each partner to reflect on his or her psychological state and to operationalize this reflection by responding to the Millon Clinical Multiaxial Inventory-III (MCMI-III) (Millon, 1994). Thus, a primary goal is established to improve the couple's relationship, which both partners usually acknowledge is in trouble, while at the same time emphasizing the uniqueness of each through the use of this inventory. Results of the MCMI-III provide the therapist with a running start in understanding the couple: not only does it assess mood states and symptoms sometimes not identified or clarified in a first interview, but, more important, it supplies the therapist with some hypotheses about the partners' personality styles or disorders.

Individual sessions are recommended for the second contact with the couple, each with the therapist alone. The stated purpose of this individual interview is to feed back some inventory-derived information about each partner's style or "way of being in the world" and to obtain individual information to enable the therapist to work with the couple more quickly and effectively. The therapist is thus given an opportunity to ascertain each partner's private motivation for treatment and depth of desire to leave the relationship, and to see the degree to which personality styles or disorders hypothesized on the MCMI-III fit the brief history taken and the behavior demonstrated. The therapist is also given a way to establish an alliance with each individual so as to begin balancing the triangle consisting of the couple and the therapist; this can further the effectiveness of the therapist by increasing his or her power.

After the sessions spent in reviewing the inventory results, the next session begins with each person describing to the other the most important learnings they have obtained about themselves from the feedback sessions. By the time this step occurs, the therapist has had a chance to consider strategic interventions and specific tactics that can come into play as the couple shares with each other in this session. In this discussion, the couple often demonstrate their relationship and communication problems.

The hearing of complaints and wishes for change in the first interview, followed by the collection of inventory information that is incorporated into the therapy process as the therapist takes charge of the structure, helps greatly in establishing the overall therapeutic alliance with the dependent/narcissistic couple. The couple with these interlocking dynamics, as described earlier, are particularly "slippery"—colluding, when under moderate therapeutic pressure, to leave therapy precipitously, perhaps more easily than couples with other disordered dynamics. When the self-image of either the dependent person or the narcissist is threatened by the therapeutic process, the couple can, in their collusion, reinforce each other in the rightness of their relationship as it stands and then withdraw from therapy, often to the surprise of the therapist, who believes progress is being made. By retreating defensively, the therapist can allow for the narcissist to "care for" the dependent partner, a core dynamic of their relationship. Their symptoms may then recede (for the moment). They may thank the therapist for the excellent assistance, saying, in effect, "Don't call us, we'll call you."

As therapy gets under way, it is useful to review which of the three basic polarities that Millon proposes needs most attention. As mentioned earlier, these polarities are pleasure (enhancement)/pain (preservation); passive (accommodation)/active (modification); and self (individuation)/other (nurturance). With a dependent/narcissistic couple, two polarities call for priority attention: the active/passive and the self/other. In the case of the dependent/narcissistic couple, the self/other polarity needs rebalancing first.

The dependent person is strong in focusing on the "other." The narcissist is strong in focusing on self. Thus, an initial and continuing feature of therapy with this couple and their interaction, regardless of overt content, is the therapist's reinforcement of any acts by the dependent partner leading toward individuation, such as assertion, reflection on self, and consideration of her own needs (possibly more often a female, as noted earlier). It is equally important for the therapist to actively help the narcissist with problems of empathy; he (as noted earlier, more often a male) is terribly lacking in ability to empathize, but has the relational need so that it is possible for him to improve this quality. When she can be led to be more self-expressive and he can be led to be more empathetic in the same transactional segment, this can be a magic moment for the couple and should be pointed out, regardless of the content, because distortions in the self/other polarity are at the heart of their relational disorder.

The other polarity to consider is the active/passive. The partners are similar in that they settle into the passive polarity. The narcissist passively waits for what he believes he is entitled to. The dependent partner, on the other hand, waits passively, because of presumed incompetence, for support and nurturance from others. If each can be induced in the relationship to speak directly to the other about what is needed from the other, the personality balance can begin to shift toward active responsibility for themselves. The couple can be taught particular communication skills, and the therapist can monitor them in therapy, helping them to avoid "mind reading" to identify incorrect cognitions such as, "If he (she) loved me he (she) would . . . ," as opposed to saying what is needed and being empathetic and sensitive. They can be given "homework" to regularly work on communication between sessions, learning to support and be openly encouraging of the other's learning to be more active and assertive. That they both have this problem and actively help each other with it can reduce the negative interactions and increase the positive. Gottman (1994) has found that stable marriages have a ratio of no less than five to one in the incidence of positive feelings and interactions versus negative experiences. (p. 57).

For dependent/narcissistic couples, both homework and work within therapy sessions can usefully include instruction in identifying Gottman's four disastrous ways of sabotaging attempts at communication: criticism, contempt, defensiveness, and stonewalling (1994, Chapter 3). Both partners are typically oversensitive to criticism, she because it may confirm the negative self-view she is working to modify, and he because it threatens to damage his superior view of himself if it is presented too harshly. Contempt for the dependent person by the narcissist is a particularly damaging attitude, tending to maintain the problem of false superiority in the narcissist. Defensiveness, used by both partners in maintaining their positions with each other, does not lead to effective problem solving. Stonewalling, remaining impassive during an argument, is ordinarily a characteristic of the male that helps him avoid physiological arousal—the potential to be overwhelmed is particularly congruent with the narcissistic style. Stonewalling by her mate, however, escalates the female's physiological arousal.

These four characteristics—criticism, contempt, defensiveness and stonewalling—interfere with problem solving and the resolution of conflict in daily life. Gottman's research shows that, regardless of marital relationship style, longer-lasting marriages are those in which the partners are likely to find ways of resolving conflict (p. 28). A role of the therapist is to actively point out these four attitudes as they are expressed during the therapy hour in order to help reframe them through therapeutic discussion. Moreover, again according to Gottman, it is important for the therapist to point out when partners show interest, affection, caring, appreciation, empathy, acceptingness, joy, and humor, so that they may learn to more openly express these outside therapy (1994, p. 59–61).

Finally, when some couples have progressed reasonably well and the narcissist's superior attitude is modified, they may be placed in a couples group, such as is recommended by Framo (1982). Observing other couples' struggles can be particularly helpful in countering feelings of shame—in the narcissist, for having any problems, and in the dependent for sometimes reverting to a submissive position. Both can learn by negotiating, and watching others negotiate, that independence and dependence are not dichotomous but gradations of experience and behavior. Dependent persons and narcissists can easily think in black-and-white terms, assuming that one is either entirely independent or dependent, rather than realizing that there is a constant ebb and flow of these relational qualities. As in other areas of difficulty, identifying such cognitions and altering them can help a couple move toward change (McMullin, 1986; Shapiro, 1995).

JILL AND JACK:
A DEPENDENT/NARCISSISTIC COUPLE

Jill was raised in a privileged family. Her father was a high-ranking military officer whose profession demanded his absence or unavailability for significant periods of time during Jill's childhood. Her mother, a worrying woman whose excessive drinking gradually developed into alcoholism, focused on mothering Jill as her major family relationship and expressed anxiety when Jill ventured at all beyond expected behavior patterns. Jill was a beautiful child who focused on the "good" role in the family, whereas her brother behaved in a more out-of-control, delinquent fashion as the "bad" child.

Although Jill, to some extent, broke out of the good-girl role when she went to college and learned to achieve and explore, in relationships with males she always hoped for the attention, protection, and closeness she had experienced with her mother, but with the added feature of closeness that she had never experienced consistently with her father. So when she met Jack, who was a big man on campus, her beauty enabled her to play with satisfaction and warmth the "campus queen" to his "fraternity president king" role.

Jack had been, and continued to be, the apple of his parents' eyes. An only child, he arrived late in his parent's life after they had long wished for a child. His parents were affluent, and he had every material advantage plus the opportunity to advance socially. As he developed, his parents continued to indulge him, assuming that their perfect child was even more gifted than he actually was. His real intelligence and his social popularity assured his success in school.

The marriage of Jill and Jack appeared to others to be a calm and smooth relationship. They joined the right clubs and enjoyed extensive vacations, partly financed by Jack's parents. He soon made his own money as he went up the corporate ladder, while she was the good wife for the business leader, especially when their two children were young. As the children grew and Jill matured in doing the primary parenting, she became restless and ultimately went to graduate school. She found further freedom through individual therapy. In graduate school she achieved some development personally and intellectually, with recognition apart from Jack.

Although Jill remained emotionally dependent on Jack and continued to play the role of Jack's hostess and helpmate, an increasing portion of her waking hours reinforced her independence and she began moving out of her dependent mode. As a result, Jack became upset. According to him, she was not mothering their children enough (read *nor Jack*). Now adolescents, the children were developing their own lives. Jack felt he was not attended to sufficiently by any of them. He was jealous of Jill's close relationship with a mentor at the university. When the opportunity arose, Jack felt entitled to have an affair with an office secretary who appeared similar to Jill when she was younger. The marriage deteriorated. When Jill discovered the affair, Jack and Jill entered couple therapy at her insistence.

In therapy, Jack's complaint to Jill was that she "was no longer the girl he married." She had, indeed, begun to move beyond the original dependent style, and Jack felt abandoned, hurt, and as if she had broken the contract to be his helpmate—which, in a very real sense, she had. She, in turn, feeling rejected and hurt, wanted a deeper relationship such as she was glimpsing as possible in her peer and mentor relationships in graduate school. In her less secure moments she did continue to struggle with a need to give in to Jack and hold him up as ideal, presenting her original self-image as inept, incompetent, and expecting to be cared for. This struggle was counterbalanced by her open recognition that Jack seemed superficial, pompous, and too concerned about status.

Jill wounded Jack by pointing out that he had changed firms whenever more personal involvement and commitment were demanded by his employer; a "public relations sort of push" on his part was not sufficient to attain the upper levels of responsibility in a corporation. He rationalized by pointing to his increasing experience that was bound to set him up soon for the even bigger jobs to which he believed he was entitled. He thought it was just a matter of time until he could get to the right firm that would really recognize his talents, where he would not be bogged down with inferior peers.

Because the partners had a fundamental liking for each other and a strong bond, they were able to continue in couple therapy and make changes. Jack was able to look at the realism of Jill's observations. Using the MCMI-III findings that pointed to his marked self-focus, the therapist intervened to actively help him empathize with Jill. He learned cues to remind himself to pay more attention to the feelings of others as well. Partly because he was actually dependent on Jill emotionally and feared being alone, he was able to continue with couple therapy through difficult times. Had he instead been involved in individual therapy, he might well have discontinued.

As for Jill, the couple therapy allowed a forum where she could learn to express her negative, even angry, feelings. She discovered that with the therapist's help, she and Jack could still negotiate couple and family relationships even while she asserted her independence. With the availability of the therapist's gentle interventions, Jack began to change from the stonewalling that so infuriated Jill.

Jill and Jack renegotiated in regard to household tasks. Jack could experiment with engaging the children more—not just as reflections of himself, but as individuals to be understood and appreciated. Some family therapy sessions furthered this process. Jill obtained continued support from a therapy group for both her family involvement and her career development. Thus, by moving into a career focus after finishing her program and away from dependency on graduate school, and by becoming less conflicted in her family involvement, she was able to express the warm, loving aspects of herself for the benefit of her children and to emotionally invest in a reciprocal relationship with her husband. He, on the other hand, was able to become more grounded within himself and to modify his egocentrism sufficiently to do an excellent job in a top-flight public relations firm while being more empathetically involved with his family.

From a theoretical standpoint, the couple therapy focused particularly on modifying the self-other polarity for Jack and Jill, with Jack becoming more empathetically oriented toward the other and Jill becoming more competently self-focused and thus able to be assertive. They both gained in ability to directly ask for what they needed by working on the communications aspect of marriage in couple therapy; this served to move them toward the active side of the active/passive polarity, the second major overall goal of therapy for the dependent/narcissistic couple. So therapy helped Jack not to fall down and break his crown; he just removed it slowly. And Jill stopped leaning so much, did not retreat to her earlier ineptness, and so did not come tumbling after.

IDENTIFICATION OF COUPLES WITH MIXED DISORDERS

The focus in this chapter has been on the cardinal types of clear-cut dependent and narcissist marital partners. In clinical practice, however, combinations of disorders are frequently found. The MCMI-III can easily provide clues for identifying secondary areas that are important (Nurse, in press). For example, the dependent-histrionic type, identified by Millon as the *accommodating dependent* (Millon, 1996, p. 336) appears frequently in this writer's experience. When the emphasis is more strongly on the histrionic and secondarily on the dependent aspects, Millon labels these person the *appeasing histrionics*. The difference appears to be that the latter demonstrate more social gregariousness, self-dramatization, and attention-seeking behaviors. The accommodating dependent person is rather characterized by submissiveness, agreeableness, and leaning on others for nurturance. She (probably more often female) is more naive about interpersonal problems, tending to smooth over conflict and use repressive and suppressive mechanisms, while presenting an attitude of marked admiration for her mate.

The accommodating dependent person's attitude is particularly congenial with another type, the narcissistic-avoidant-negativistic, whom Millon calls the *compensatory narcissist*. This type is frequently described in the psychoanalytic community as having wounds received early in life that are covered over by illusions of superiority and specialness.

When the accommodating dependent person is married to the compensatory narcissist, there is an even more fragile, intensely driven link between the submissiveness and adoration expressed by the accommo-dating dependent partner and the search for satisfaction in the illusion of superiority of the compensatory narcissist. They fit each other's needs at the level of behavioral expression and have a need to maintain an appear-ance of tranquillity so as to paper over their inner emptiness as they pursue, sometimes seemingly successfully, false lives in a theater of their own making.

REFERENCES

American Psychiatric Association. (1994). *Diagnostic and statistical manual of mental disorders* (4th ed.). Washington, DC: Author.

Framo, J. (1982). Marriage therapy in a couples group. In *Explorations in Marital and Family Therapy*. New York: Springer.

Gottman, J. (1994). *Why marriages succeed or fail*. New York: Simon & Schuster.

Lewin, K. (1936). *Principles of topological psychology*. New York: McGraw-Hill.

McMullin, R. (1986). *Handbook of cognitive therapy techniques*. New York: W. W. Norton.

Millon, T. (1981). *Disorders of personality*. New York: John Wiley & Sons.

Millon, T. (1994). *Millon Clinical Multiaxial Inventory-III*. Minneapolis: National Computer Systems.

Millon, T. (1996). *Disorders of personality: DSM-IV and beyond*. New York: John Wiley & Sons.

Nurse, R. (in press). MCMI in treating couples. In T. Millon (Ed.), *The Millon Inventories*. New York: Guilford.

Nurse, R. (work in progress). *Psychological testing with families*. New York: John Wiley & Sons.

Shapiro, F. (1995). *Eye movement desensitization and reprocessing*. New York: Guilford.

Name Index

Subject Index